GOLF

SCOTLAND'S GAME

GOLF

SCOTLAND'S GAME

David Hamilton

THE PARTICK PRESS
1998

COVER ILLUSTRATION: Charles Lees' *Summer Evening on Musselburgh Links* (1860)
By courtesy of Tom Tew, Dornoch

© Copyright David Hamilton 1998

ISBN 0-9510009-3-4

Catalogue record available from British Library

THE PARTICK PRESS
'Dalliefour'
Barclaven Road
Kilmacolm PA13 4DQ
Scotland UK

Design by George Bowie

Set in Palatino 10.5 on 13pt, production by The House, with colour separations
by Reproscan, Glasgow and printed by Howie and Seath, Edinburgh.

Acknowledgements and Thanks

To Dr John McConachie of Lossiemouth, Fred Hawtree at Woodstock,
John Burnett in Edinburgh, John Adams and Peter Lewis at St Andrews, who
read and improved the text throughout, and prevented many errors, as did
David B. Smith of Troon.

To Archie Baird and David White who, early on, answered many questions
and pointed me in the right direction, and to Joseph Murdoch who from the
first organised and encouraged our group of embryonic golf historians.

To Tom Tew of Dornoch, who supplied the cover illustration.

To the Mitchell Library, Glasgow and the National Library of Scotland who hold
many golfing treasures and helped with many illustrations.

To George Bowie and Fiona Mackie, who guided the text through the electronic
jungle and designed the pages.

To Bill Mortland of California and the Edinburgh City Council, who provided
the features for the St Andrews Edition.

To my wife Jean, who coped, while I hid away to finish this work, but repeatedly
failed to finish it.

CONTENTS

Introduction

This book meets the need for a new history of the formative period of the game of golf. Recent interest and research into the development of the game have changed many of our old ideas. The resulting publications have produced remarkable bibliographies and specialist accounts of the development of golf clubs and balls, plus new descriptions of early stick-and-ball games in many countries. In addition, professional historians have also turned their attention to the history of leisure, and exciting academic work on the history of sport has emerged. Golf history, always interesting, has now come of age.

Golf is a precise game: the ball is either in the hole, or it is not. Golf history should be as precise. We can now dump all old fanciful notions about shepherds hitting stones with sticks, and other related nonsense, and take a critical look at the evolution of an important game, first in Scotland and now one with a remarkable world-wide following.

When I started collecting material for this book many years ago, it was then the received wisdom that all sources on early Scottish golf had been examined and were exhausted. To my surprise, new material was, after all, forthcoming, and further study showed that the familiar older material had not been fully analysed. A steady supply of further scraps also accumulated and helped illuminate previously mysterious areas of the history of the game, and it was clear that the usual histories were unsatisfactory. Together, these finding and data forced a new appraisal: this book resulted.

Some of the main new findings in this book may be mentioned here. It appears that early golf was a winter game, not a summer one. This odd finding, when accepted, explains much which is otherwise inexplicable, and may even be the main reason why the game evolved first in Scotland. A second finding is that the game of golf played by the poor differed from that of the rich. The earlier humble game in Scotland was a short, primitive, street and churchyard sport, popular enough to be mentioned in national and town legislation. It was probably similar to the early 'colf' game of the Low Countries. But I conclude that these churchyard and street games of both countries were not golf in the later sense of the word. The nobles and well-off players in Scotland played a different sport, a long game with sophisticated clubs and balls, and this game can be called the origin of golf. And I conclude that it was in Scotland alone that this game evolved.

Some other conclusions about the early game are also challenged here. It is often suggested that golf took a great step forward when the first organised golf clubs appeared in the early 1700s and that little significant golf existed prior to these clubs' appearance. Instead all the evidence suggests that golf was widely popular before the club foundations, and that the founders of the early golf societies were playing together regularly long before they formalised their relationship. It was the 'clubbiness' that was new, not the golf.

Another new finding in this book is that there was a serious crisis in golf, as in some sports in Scotland, starting about 1800. As a result of this decline, golf almost died out in the following decades. The game was rescued in mid-century by a new enthusiasm for healthy recreation in Britain, and for sport on holidays. This new interest in golf coincided with the appearance of a new, cheap golf ball made of gutta percha. New players appeared in large numbers, including those who flocked by train to Scotland on holiday. These Scottish holidays also enabled women, now with new leisure and freedom, to experiment with golf for the first time.

I have taken this detailed account of early golf only up to the beginning of the twentieth century, when the game spread rapidly to much of the rest of the world. There was a natural historical break about this time. The dominant Scottish influence was over, and the game took on diverse national characteristics in the countries to which it reached so quickly and successfully. However, Scotland continued to exert a remarkable influence on golfers worldwide, out of proportion to the shrinking Scottish presence in tournament play or ball and club manufacture or in golf course design. Scotland and her players no longer dominated the game, but in spite of this, Scotland continued to have a powerful hold on the imagination of golfers elsewhere. This mystique draws huge numbers of visiting golfers each year to tour and play in Scotland, travelling and playing without difficulty or formality. This is the same spirit of the original game of golf in Scotland - a democratic sport played on common land - and has never been transplanted elsewhere. And much of the world is also content to allow a golf society in St Andrews - the Royal and Ancient Golf Club - to govern the game and to run the world's greatest tournament - the Open Championship. It is played on traditional links land and is open to all players of skill, without exclusion or prejudice.

Accordingly, in the last chapter of this book, this continuing influence of Scotland in golf is analysed, and the modern game looked at from a Scottish perspective. This book is about golf rather than golfers, and particularly about the game as viewed from Scotland, past and present.

DAVID HAMILTON
Kilmacolm 1998

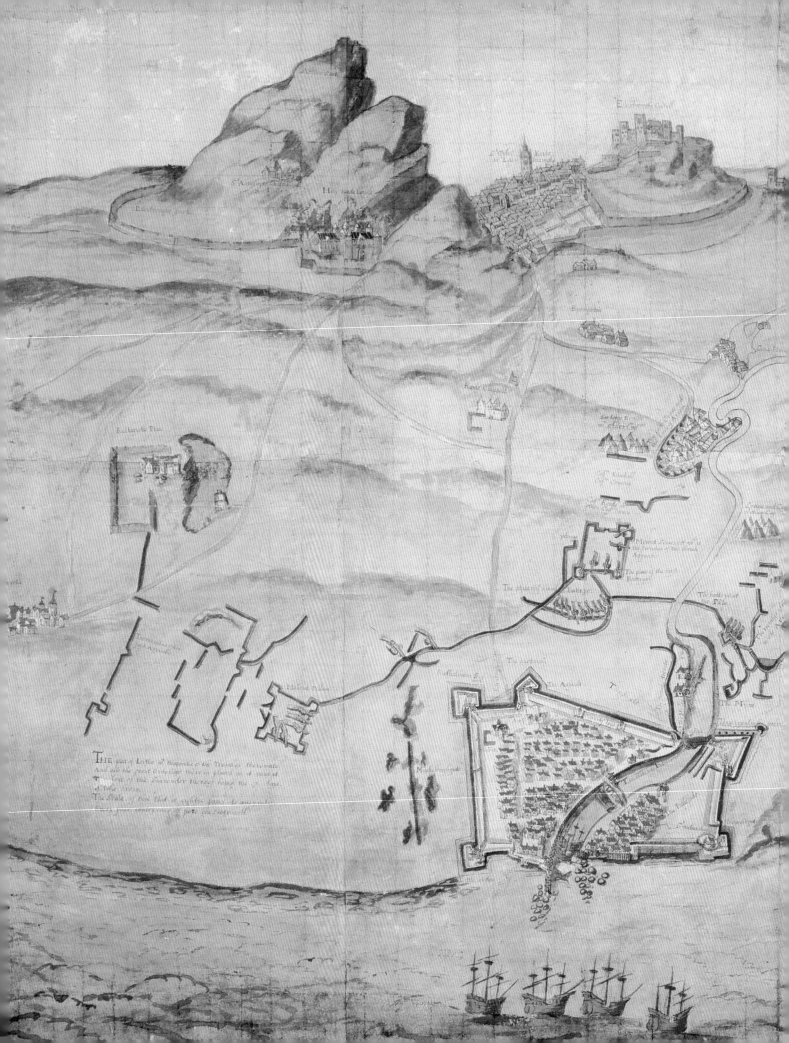

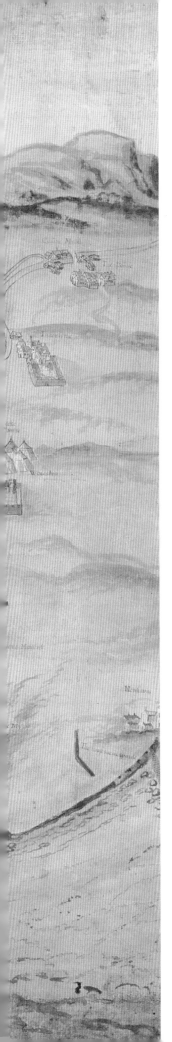

CHAPTER ONE

THE LINKS

The Scottish links are the undulating sandy land close to the Scottish shoreline beside the coastal towns and villages. Often close to the lowest point of rivers before they reach the sea, the glacial alluvium deposited by the rivers joined the sand of the bay to form broad fertile deposits. The prevailing off-shore wind and storms constantly blew sand inland, creating the uneven grassy land immediately behind the beach, known as the links.

More abrupt in effect are the winds which from time to time raise sandstorms, resurfacing parts of the links. These rejuvenating incidents are but part of the ancient natural ecosystem. Such Scottish links often have a local name - such as Barry Links, Gullane Links, Pilmour Links - but they are part of the usual coastal terrain throughout much of the east and west coasts of Scotland. Huge un-named and little-used stretches of natural links still exist along the Scottish coast: they would be immediately available for golf in the simple manner of early Scotland. Such a coastline is rarely found elsewhere and seldom close to major towns, or in areas with mild winters. The Scottish links are unique.

The Soil

The links have a thin layer of soil which is moderately fertile and the sandy sub-soil drains well. The soil was enriched in former days by the presence of sheep, rabbits and other animals. On and beside the links grow heather and gorse, and wild flowers give a pleasing ambience - wild roses, forget-me-nots, Scottish lovage, dove's foot cranesbill, thyme, ragwort and daisies. Tall tough marram grass with its complex root structure anchors the dunes and frames the fairways, the grass changing from green to silver in spring and autumn.

OPPOSITE: An early military scene from 1560 showing Edinburgh in the distance and the fortified town of Leith on the coast, and under siege at the time. The Leith golfing links which served the early Edinburgh golfers were, and are, to the south-east of the port, on the left of the painting.
By courtesy of LORD EGREMONT.

The grasses of the Scottish links from earliest times were fescue and bents (*Agrostis* species). These grasses have deep roots and are remarkably hardy: their tightly rolled leaves survive heat, drought and frost, and the grass revives when apparently dead. Salt spray is also tolerated, and there is no lasting damage to these grasses from an occasional inundation by the sea. It is a fine turf for sport, particularly in winter when though grass does not grow it remains firm and playable. In the twentieth century, man took a hand by watering and fertilising the links, removing the sheep and other animals, and encouraging instead green, tender meadow grass. The nemesis came in the 1970s. The soft, fragile green grass, prone to thatching, died in heat or drought. A return to the ancient basics of greenkeeping and the restoration of the traditional grasses followed.[1]

The Dunes

Many Scottish links have another feature - a ridge of dunes between the links and the beach. These sand hills were caused and maintained by sand blown from the beach and are fixed there by the deep-rooted marram grass. These dunes gave comfortable enclosure and protection to many golf courses. To this day at Montrose, Lossiemouth, Turnberry, Fraserburgh and elsewhere, golfers nestle under the full force of winter winds. Summer golfers are puzzled that they are denied a view of the beach, failing to understand the needs of winter: to please these players, new scenic tees have been built.

The early rules from the clubs of the coastal links had no 'out-of-bounds' rule. There were no boundaries on the links, and enclosures were to come. The spaciousness of the links had another benefit later in the world of commercial twentieth-century golf. Huge audiences can be admitted to the links golf courses for championships, and the dunes give vantage points for spectators, giving a capacity not possible at private inland clubs.

Adding to the sense of space, there is, in parts of Scotland, a sharp rise in the ground on the landward side of some links. In the Ice Age millions of years ago, Scotland was covered in permafrost and glaciers. Relieved of the weight of ice after the thaw, the land rose again, and some parts of the coastline lifted out of the ocean. The original beach was left elevated and dry, and a new beach and its links were formed at a lower level, overlooked by the original 'raised' beach. This gives an additional quality to some golf courses. At Dornoch in particular, this spectacular raised beach gives a natural amphitheatre for the game on the links below. At Turnberry, the hotel on the raised beach overlooks its links, formerly beneath the sea.[2]

The Coastline

The links were formed from the changes of glaciation, de-glaciation, wind and weather. But slow changes continued thereafter. This continuing movement is imperceptible, except at times of crisis. At Barry Links near Carnoustie the coastline has changed slowly and the earliest lighthouse built for mariners at Buddon Ness has now been steadily submerged. New warning lights on this important navigation point were erected further inland.[3] The water level may be rising again at present, and the links at Troon, Nairn, Dornoch, St Andrews and Turnberry are being reached at high tides

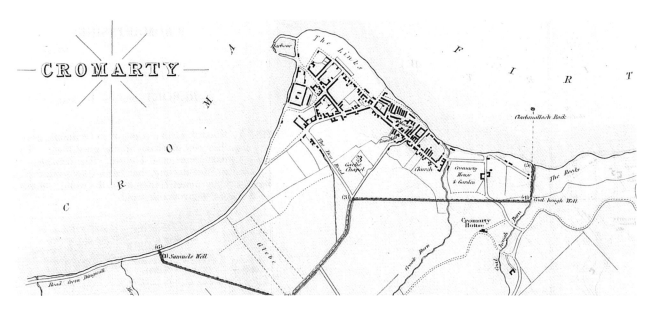

and steadily eroded. In 1959 the sea swept away part of the coast at Peterhead and erosion reached the golf clubhouse by 1969. Sudden movements of the sea are rare, but can make permanent changes. Ancient golf links at Pittenweem may have been washed away, and in a storm at Carnoustie in 1904, high winds aided by a strong spring tide, flooded and altered the links. At Golspie in 1901, a sandstorm buried the 4th hole. The Brodick links and golf course on the Island of Arran are regularly inundated by the year's highest tides, as were the Aberdeen golf links in earlier times. Elsewhere the reverse is happening and sand is building up. At Leith the ancient beach is widening, and the high-water mark is in retreat.[4]

Cromarty was one of many east coast towns with an area called 'The Links' for general use by the people of the town.
From BOUNDARY COMMISSION REPORT 1832.

Other Linksland

As well as the links on the east and west coast of Scotland, there were other areas well away from the coast which were suitable for sport and the early game of golf. Some of these inland expanses were the alluvial banks of rivers in their lower reaches - the 'Inches', 'Haughs' or 'Greens.' The rivers dumped their fertile silt at these sites, and as the build-up continued, the rivers slowly or suddenly moved course and broadened the area of deposit. Early royal golf was played at Perth (St Johnstone) on such an area - the North and South Inches, beside the Tay, and these are still used for golf today. At Glasgow the common land beside the tidal river Clyde was called the 'Green', and at Irvine, in Ayrshire, old maps show the 'Golf Fields' beside the tidal part of the river estuary. At inland Haddington there was golf on the haugh beside the river, and at Dumfries, golf was later found on the flat sandy 'Kingholm' beside the river.

Some inland parks were also suitable for sport and might even be called 'links' by the citizens. One such area, Bruntsfield Links in Edinburgh, was important in early Edinburgh golf. The park at Stirling, a town far from the sea, was also used for golf. These ancient inland eighteenth-century golfing grounds, though not typical seaside links, were used because the grass was short and suitable for the winter sport.

Facies Ciuitatis ABERDONIÆ Veteris. The Prospect of Old ABERDIEN.

A view of Old Aberdeen with its coastal links to the right, an ancient site of Scottish golf. From Slezer's *Theatrum Scotiae* 1693.
By courtesy of the NATIONAL LIBRARY OF SCOTLAND.

But in summer the grass could grow. It was high-quality grass and a valuable crop for the town, and was auctioned off to the highest bidder. Even if golf was contemplated in summer, it would not have been possible. Golf did not raise money, but grass did. Only much later when golf raised revenue, could the links, inches, haughs and parks be reserved generally for the game in summer.

The Land

By the 1700s, the links of the coastal towns usually belonged to the town, rather than to local landowners. The mediaeval Scottish kings had made gifts of land to the towns, in return for the town's political support and a promise of a supply of soldiers to the King when necessary. The King supported his 'Royal Burghs' to neutralise the power of the neighbouring land-owning barons. The towns received their land to be held in common for the citizens, and its use was governed by local Town Councils. The common land gave space for agriculture, pasturing of animals, and many other activities, including sport and golf. Common ownership of the land also meant that the town authorities kept records of any matters relating to the links. These documents tell us something about early golf and other sports.

These precious ancient gifts of land were later partly sold off by the towns in the financial difficulties of the period of the late 1700s, and municipal sport was thereafter threatened. The towns had a remarkable second chance later in the late 1800s, when repurchase of ancient land was encouraged by government, and Scottish collective town sport was restored.

Other Use

The earlier golfers had to mingle with many other users and activities on the links, nor was golf the only sport there. In early prohibitions, football and golf were usually banned together, and there was also horse racing from earliest times on many of these links, and the Town Councils of Scotland often owned and presented the main silver trophy for these meets. At Leith Links a great race meeting was held annually, with two silver cups available for competition. The earliest Scottish meeting was the Silver Bell trophy at Haddington from 1552, held in November. In May there were race meetings at Dumfries, Peebles, Stirling and an earlier one at Cupar in April. The race-courses involved were often found on the town links, notably at Aberdeen, Musselburgh, Montrose and Perth, and for the next two centuries the race-goers and golfers co-existed unhappily.

Users of the Links

The links had many other uses and many users. Tradition allowed that the turf of the links could be sliced off, and these 'divots', as they were called,

The ancient Links at Burntisland, a Fife fishing village. After the town expanded, the golf course and club moved inland to its present position.
From BOUNDARY COMMISSION REPORT 1832.

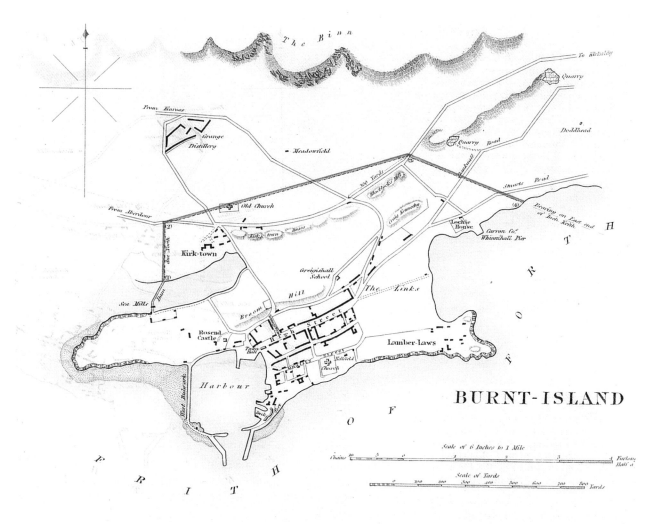

BURNT-ISLAND

The early Scottish Links had many uses and users. Paul Sandby's *Horse Fair on Bruntsfield Links* shows the annual horse trading in Edinburgh in 1750.

By courtesy of NATIONAL GALLERY OF SCOTLAND.

were used by the townsfolk for roofing, or after drying as a form of fuel. On the links, women laid out clothes to dry and bleach; fishermen dried their nets and the citizens could pasture their cattle and sheep. Other users of the links were owners of travelling fairs, who made a regular circuit of the towns, setting up their stalls and booths. The links might also be used for burials after epidemics or battles and Musselburgh Links were used for this melancholy purpose after the battle of Pinkie. Other military use was common. Armies camped and exercised on these flat sandy areas and the open links were also the site of many battles and sieges. On the North Inch at Perth, a natural place for golf and sport, there was also a famous gladiatorial battle in 1396. In 1560 the English army had a large encampment on the Links of Leith, and made trenches and gun emplacements for a siege of the town. The remnants of these earthworks could still be found two centuries later, and the 'Soldiers Lines' were mentioned in the earliest rules of the Leith golfers. The Covenanters also mustered here at Leith under Leslie.

The links were a natural place for the citizens to gather and in Aberdeen in 1625 a muster of 'fensibil persons' was called on the links.[5] Dunbar's extensive links have repeatedly attracted military visits throughout Scottish history. Cromwell's army camped here for six weeks prior to the battle of Dunbar, and much later, during the threat of invasion by Napoleon, the town was the scene of defensive activity, and a huge encampment of militia was assembled in

1802. In the Second World War, Dunbar links were also defended with trenches and minefields against possible invasion.[6] At Carnoustie similar military use occurred, since the area near the present second hole was used for gunnery practice until 1900. At Peterhead, use was made of the links for shooting during the Second World War, and alternative holes were available for the golfers. Such flat land was also suitable for airfields, and in this war, the Turnberry golf courses were taken over and levelled for this use.

Other Life on the Links

Familiar inhabitants of the links were, and are, oyster catchers, plovers and terns, protective of their nests. Rabbits, sheep and other animals, now thought to be a nuisance, were familiar sights on the links, and important in the stability of the little ecosystem of the links. Rabbits had a natural habitat on the links and had sanctuary in the whins: rabbit numbers at St Andrews and elsewhere were controlled by hunting each November.[7] Not only did the numerous rabbits fertilise the land, but they added valuable fibre, and cropped the grass, at a time before grass-cutting equipment had evolved. This 'organic golf' may have meant an exceptional quality of turf. The extravagant praise found in historical records of the 'velvet links', particularly at Dornoch, Montrose and St Andrews, may not have been an exaggeration, and might be credited to the influence of these useful animals.

The rabbits probably gave the Scottish game of golf its characteristic feature, namely aiming for a hole in the ground. On the links, a target was required for the game. The fine grass and expensive equipment gave the possibility of

Leith Races was a festive annual event on the Links and sands of the town. By courtesy of CITY OF EDINBURGH COUNCIL, CENTRAL LIBRARY.

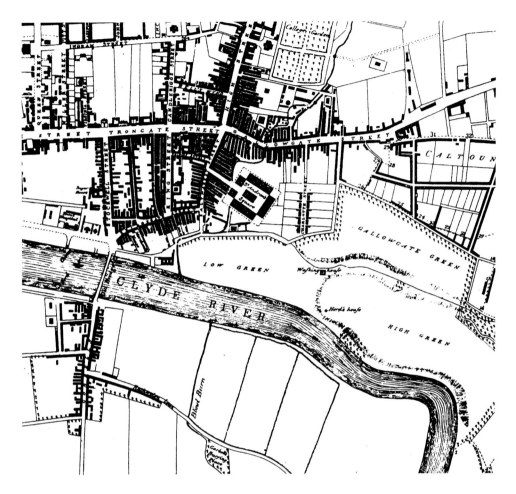

accurate play, and rabbit holes may have offered such a target. These holes led to another early routine in golf. To tee up the ball for the first long shot at the next hole, a pyramid of sand was perfect for the purpose. The early golfers plunged their hand into the sand holes to gain the necessary handful.

These sand holes, the ancient homes of Scotland's east coast rabbits, are now the essential feature of the international game. Not only did the rabbits' holes enter into the game, but in their endless search for new burrows, the rabbits made tentative scrapes on the fairways and dunes and opened up breaks in the ground. Erosion could widen these to form the broad open bunkers, the essential hazard in golf.

The Links and Golf

The modern game has been moulded by its origins on the links. The area of land occupied by the Scottish links beside the coastal towns is not round or square. The links instead form a long, thin strip of land, shadowing the beach and necessarily of the same form, snaking out from the town. Golf was naturally played out from the town and then back again. Two halves of the course and of any game or any match naturally existed - the holes 'out', and the holes 'in' or 'back' and to this day, this terminology persists from the Scottish east coast links origins of golf. The game of the links also meant that the ever-present, ever-changing wind added to the challenge. Play on the narrow links, out and back, meant dealing with the wind, against or behind, from left to right, and from right to left. In winter, the golfing season, the wind was ever-present, and changed with the time of day, giving testing shots into head winds and the exhilaration of playing down-wind. The full challenge of the Scottish game in winter is seldom now experienced in summer.

The hard, undulating links also gave an unpredictable bounce and run to the ball. This created a game which involved some degree of chance and luck. The links had from the start their 'fairways' - the fisherman's term for a safe passage. Golf was a serious journey out and back, occasionally unpleasant but as rewarding as the winter deep-sea fishing of the towns. It was a voyage out and back in rough weather, and full of hazard.

The Charter given to the town of St Andrews in 1552 allowing, among other things, for golf on the links.
Courtesy of FIFE COUNCIL

The Hazards

From the ancient Scottish linksland came the hazards of the modern golf course and those which naturally met the early golfers on the links are those still used by golf course architects today.[8] On the dunes beside the ancient fairways were whins, heather and heavy grass, the 'rough' of the golf course. Small streams and burns crossed the links on their way to reach the sea or to join the larger rivers. These streams, often tidal and meandering, were and

continue to be, prominent hazards on the Scottish golf links. Some named streams and burns are part of the lore of golf, so dominant is their role at crucial holes on some courses. The Swilken Burn at St Andrews guards the 1st (and extra 19th) hole: the tidal Barry Burn at Carnoustie crosses and recrosses the 1st, 17th and 18th holes. Other well-known streams are the burn at the 18th at Leven, and the Pow Burn at Prestwick with its magnetic attraction at the 4th hole. Less celebrated water - the Clynelish Burn - is well known to the Brora players, and other burns are found at the 17th and 18th at Tain, and the 2nd at Machrihanish. The Brodick golf course twice crosses the tidal Rosa Burn, and Shiskine's 2nd hole is called 'Twa Burns'. The Alton Burn guards the 17th green at Nairn and the Dee and Don rivers ran close to the ancient Aberdeen Links. These and many other streams and burns all have their place in local golfing lore. The golf course architects of the modern period copied these water hazards: if no flowing water was available, then ponds and lakes were constructed.

And bunkers were, above all, the essence of a golf course.

The Bunkers

These ancient, sandy hazards appeared when erosions in the links widened to give open sandy areas. The breaks in the ground formed naturally, perhaps started by cattle or sheep or rabbits, and then were widened by the wind. Thereafter the golfers may also have encouraged the more subtle type of fairway bunkers found in the hollows of the links. Perhaps as the golfers repeatedly played shots from the same depression, they opened up deepening sandy erosions. Having opened a much-frequented scar, its position naturally had almost magical attractions for golf balls. As the bunker became established, repeated play from it deepened it to a pot shape. The sand splashed out built up a mound on the forward, green side of the bunker. This pot and mound, entirely natural in evolution, is seen throughout the Old Course at St Andrews. These sand hazards have been copied wherever golf has spread throughout the world. If no sand was to hand, it was brought to the new courses to make bunkers: golf without bunkers might not be golf at all.

As golf has spread, the designers have faithfully copied the natural Scottish hazards – humps and hollows, rough, water and bunkers. Absent from the early Scottish links were some other hazards, such as trees. The travelling Scottish designers of the late nineteenth century were not keen on trees: if they found them, they cut them down.

But though golf and the links seem inseparable, the early documents regularly reveal another puzzling location for golf. The early records regularly refer to golf in the streets and churchyards of the towns. This game can be studied first.

Text References:

The numbered references given in the text can be found at the end of the book.

Intran

Johne Littill servitor to Robert

Carloos Nicholsaill

Andro Littill his brother sone

Dilaitit of the burning of Mr David Loittis in

the kirk of Borne Within the abbacie of

Sanct day of July — Jay vii Monthis Wyn

Corsbar

Sir Thomas Gorpus Craighall

kingis barnot his mat{er} aduocat

for his hienes interes

The pannell offerit hame selfis to the

contriot in the termined with produ

wer brought freehess Waird out of the fol

pannell Dilaitit and aronsefia of airt an

in at the instance of their possessouris

beris 6 to albyrille armo oute hairgs

farde contentia sin and hardey

The instro contineis the said dyet

and Andro Littill for the tryme first said

and ordanit the said Capitane Tho

Littill of Borne To remane cautionry fra his

and his committis vpoun testonis darbs Warn

this brightne and vpoun thirdbr of darbs

vndoely the call for the tryme mentionit

of Wa the said inne contrmes 6 the art of

of the said the Mwentie Agne darbs

Intendroz the said Capitane Thomas Gor

CHAPTER TWO

THE MYSTERIOUS YEARS

In 1632, a death occurred in a sporting accident at Kelso, an inland market town in the Scottish border country. The short, laconic legal record of this accident says that some players were at a 'bonspill', a sociable sporting gathering. They had met in the churchyard at Kelso, and it is likely that the day was Sunday. From ancient times the rural population gathered on that day, not only for the church service, but also for recreation. The legal report says that one participant hit a spectator with 'ane golf ball' near the 'lug' [ear] and there was 'a great effusion of blood'. The victim died. The ball which inflicted the fatal blow was 'struckin out with ane golf club'.[1]

What were they doing playing with golf clubs in the narrow confines of a churchyard so far from the links? Was this golf as we know it? If not, what was the game played? In solving these puzzles, we can come to a new understanding of early golf in Scotland.

Ancient Games

The human race has always sought recreation.[2] From childhood to adult maturity, sport and play have been used to rehearse for the more serious business of life and living. Young animals and children organise their play

OPPOSITE: The legal record of a death during a game of 'golf' in a churchyard in Kelso in 1632. By courtesy of the SCOTTISH RECORD OFFICE, JC2/7.

seriously: sport is part of growing up, and a preparation for hunting and fighting. Games are life in miniature, and games establish those who can lead and those who will follow, separating the brave from the timid. For most of the history of the human race, these preparations were essential for the hunt and for feuding, fighting and war. Early sport was for the fighters and hunters - the men. Women were not expected to appear for these rehearsals for killing.

Later, games evolved to be sports to be enjoyed for their own sake. These activities were more kindly, and rules appeared to prevent innocent misfortune or injury, and to allow recovery from blameless error. Unlike life, games always had fresh beginnings.

And some of these games were played with sticks and balls.

Egypt, Greece and Rome

It is likely that the human race has never been without stick-and-ball games. Man differs from monkeys in his use of tools and man was the first animal to use sticks for sport. Egyptian sports appear in their records and murals, and some stick-and-ball games are found.[3] In Greek times, sport achieved a prominent part in the life of nations. Greek sports, notably those of the Olympic

A stick-and-ball team game from ancient Greece.
By courtesy of the NATIONAL MUSEUM OF GREECE.

The Roman paganica was a hair-filled ball.

Games, were athletic meetings of importance and these contests involved games, largely of strength. Ball games were not prominent, and no team sports like hockey are obvious at the Olympics, nor can games like handball be found. Outside of these organised events, however, there is evidence from Greek sculpture that a team game with stick and ball, not unlike hockey, was being played in the fifth century B.C.

Roman games and sports are also well described. Although stick-and-ball games do not appear prominently, a game with a handball was a favourite. The ball used is of interest: it was a leather sphere stuffed with feathers or hair - called the *paganica*.[4] This use of hair-filled balls can be followed with the spread of the Roman Empire, and similar balls were used in later European games.

After the collapse of the Roman Empire, good historical records of all kinds disappear, and not until mediaeval times do the first brief descriptions of any sport re-emerge.

The Essence of Golf

When looking in the surviving patchy mediaeval records for the origins of the game called golf, the game we seek is a stick-and-ball sport played by teams of one or two persons. The ball is stationary when hit, and is struck by clubs to reach a target some hundreds of yards away. This target, though distant, is a hole in the ground, not a large object like a door. To win at golf, there is no race to the hole, nor can the opponent defend the hole or interfere with the opponent's ball. In golf it is simply the number of strokes taken to reach the hole that counts. Golf combines strong, long preliminary shots with more precise strokes as the small target is neared. A variety of clubs is used, and the ground played on is not flat or featureless. Instead, to reach the hole there are hazards to be avoided *en route,* and these hazards may mean that a variety of strokes and skills is required, even far from the hole.

The Claimants

In searching for the origins of golf there are, not surprisingly, a large number of closely related games to be considered. Golf has many antecedents and relatives, numerous first cousins and claimants to kinship. The early stick-and-ball games merged, diverged and blended repeatedly, and the early records are not good enough for us to sort out these evolutions. And evolve they did: one game changed into another with time, moulded by custom, circumstance and local preference. It is a mistake to believe that, some day, a tenacious historian will uncover formal rules for these early games, and find an exact description of an earlier primitive game which was clearly the fore-runner of golf.

The reality is more prosaic: rules of early games were neither laid down nor written down. Instead they were well known to the players, through habit and custom, as are children's playground games today. The games and their rules were malleable and varied from country to country and from town to town. To imagine that any single, widely-played game existed in any mediaeval European country, with standardised equipment and agreed rules is to misunderstand social life in pre-industrial society. People were born, lived and died in small, closed communities. They handed down their local traditions, and the accepted conduct of their local games, from generation to generation.

Many of these games used sticks and balls, and we can look at what little is known of some of these games from these times.

Stick-and-Ball Games

From the mediaeval period onwards in Europe and elsewhere, some stick-and-ball games are increasingly mentioned in the scattered records. We should be careful about any conclusions drawn from these few flimsy accounts, particularly about concluding that any of these games were necessarily an early form of golf. An early English document notes that the sports at King Alfred's coronation in the year 872 included 'driving balls wide over fields'.[5] We do not know what this game was, nor do we know anything of the game shown in the famous stained-glass window from Gloucester Cathedral from the mid-fourteenth century, where a player with a club is aiming at an

From the Book of Hours *Tres Riches Heures du Duc de Berry* of 1414 showing shepherds with metal-headed sticks not unlike Dutch colf clubs.

By courtesy of the MUSÉE CONDÉ, CHANTILLY, FRANCE.

apparently stationary ball. All we know from these and other records is that some citizens were hitting balls, which might have been stationary, with clubs. Where they were hitting to, and who else was playing, is far from clear.

However, in England in the fourteenth century, there was one such game played by enough people to be noted in a number of records. The game was called *cambuca*. It was well known at the time and may have been the game in the Gloucester window. Rymer's *Foedera* of 1363 says:

> *Cambuca known to all is the game of the curved stick or curved club (baculum incurvatum) or playing mallet, with which a small wooden ball (globus ligneus) is propelled forward.*[6]

The target in cambuca is unclear and it may even have been an adversarial game, with a player defending and one attacking.

Other related games from this time are stowball and, surprisingly, early cricket. In early England this was played with a curved stick, not a straight bat, and one player defended a crude target from the attacker's ball: cricket and cambuca may be first cousins.

In Europe

The Belgian game of *chole* also involved a defensive strategy: chole was not golf, but was close to it. The records suggest that two players or more played a ball each, and the defenders were allowed to 'dechole', i.e. hit the attacker's ball away, as the ball approached the target. The kinship of chole with yet another game - croquet - is evident. Another form of chole is suggested by this account:

> *When the harvest is almost cleared, men, women and children and everyone drives his ball as he pleases, and there is nothing cheerier than to see them filing on a Sunday, like a flight of starlings, across potato fields and ploughed land.*[7]

This reveals chole as an autumn community game played on rough ground

Chole players in France in 1497 from an engraving by Adriean van der Velde.

By courtesy of THE NEW YORK PUBLIC LIBRARY

on Sundays. The French stick-and-ball game *jeu de mail* came in a number of forms. The noble version used a formal, customised court, but a rural version was played with a two-inch wooden ball driven over a long course, using country roads and tracks, and ending by hitting an agreed stone in the road - the 'touchstone'.[8] Illustrations of other unnamed European stick-and-ball games are still emerging, and in the early Book of Hours *Tres Riches Heures du Duc de Berry* from France in 1414 an illustration shows a shepherd with a club and ball. An illustration of players with stick and ball on a short course in a German castle has also been found.[9]

There is even evidence of a game played by shepherds hitting pebbles with sticks.[10] In Germany in 1338, shepherds could claim grazing rights into the forest as far as they could hit a pebble with one stroke. These limits were marked by boundary stones or *'Hirtesteiner'*. The Swiss still have a stick-and-ball game variant called *hornussen*, and in Spain's vigorous *pelota*, the ball is hurled at a wall using a deeply scooped basket. Each primitive stick-and-ball game can be seen to have elements of others, and the cross-linkage of each, and their historical evolution can easily be imagined.

Stick-and-ball games were part of everyday mediaeval life and entered into everyday speech. The theologian Duns Scotus, of Scottish origin but domiciled and writing in Europe about 1285, could illustrate the power of God with a sporting analogy: *'sicut manus movet baculum et baculus movet pilam'*. The preacher's flock, familiar with sport, saw the analogy: just as players move a ball by means of the club, so God influences human events through his church.[11] An early Scottish manuscript also refers familiarly to a stick-and-ball game played by town children with 'goiff stafs'.[12]

Beyond Europe

Nor were early stick-and-ball games confined to Europe. Records showing play with clubs to a hole come from the Song dynasty in China (960-1279). This game of *chuiwan* (meaning 'beating-a-ball') is described in detail and illustrations of it have survived on pottery and in murals. These show a singles game of some kind in progress.[13] Centuries later, travellers in the Dutch East Indies noted natives at play

A page from the Book of Hours *Les Heures d'Adelaide Duchesse de Savoi* showing two forms of noble European stick-and -ball games from circa 1450.
By courtesy of the MUSÉE CONDÉ, CHANTILLY.

A stick-and-ball game noted in Chile by the French traveller Frezier in his *A Voyage to the South Sea* of 1717. Called 'sueca, jeu de croce' in the original French, the English translation was 'La Sueca, a Sort of Bandy'.
By courtesy of the MITCHELL LIBRARY, GLASGOW.

A group of ladies playing at chuiwan or 'beating the ball' a stick-and-ball game from China in the Ming Dynasty, circa 1430.

By courtesy of BOB GRANT.

with stick and ball, as did explorers in Chile in the nineteenth century. In contemporary Samoa the game of *kiri-kiti* is played with home-made bats and a latex ball. Teams of up to one hundred face each other in a tribal contest in which one village plays another.[14]

Each of these discoveries of primitive or ancient stick-and-ball games need not excite us too much, nor stir up new controversy about 'who discovered golf'. Instead, each of these fragments merely strengthens the view that all human societies, at all times and in all parts of the world, turned in moments of leisure to hit balls with sticks. These local games showed endless variation, and enthusiasm for such sport waxed and waned over centuries.

Close Contenders

But there are three mediaeval European games, well documented, which can be examined more closely for their part in the evolution of modern golf. The first is the Scottish team game of *shinty*, and its Irish antecedent *camanachd*.

Early cricket used a curved bat, not unlike other stick-and-ball games. Francis Hayman *Cricket in the Artillery Ground* 1743.

By courtesy of the MIDLAND COUNTY CRICKET CLUB.

The second is *colf,* the game of the Low Countries, and the third game to be examined closely is perhaps a surprise. It is early Scottish *'golf'.* The early Scottish game called by this name, as played by the humble citizen, may *not* have been the modern game called golf.

Shinty, Shinny, and Camanachd

Stick-and-ball games, as we have seen, were not prominent in early Mediterranean society. Such games flourished in early Ireland, and a team game with stick and ball became a national obsession from earliest times: its modern version still thrives.[15] The antiquity of this game — camanachd – is considerable, and a manuscript from twelfth-century Ireland records that in the rule of King Conchubhar, at the time of the birth of Christ, he

> *settled the affairs of state early in the day then divided the remainder into three - the first third of the day is spent watching the youths playing games and camanachd, the second in playing board games, and the last third of the day is spent in consuming food and drink, to the lulled music of minstrels and musicians, until sleep comes on them all.*[16]

This early game of camanachd evolved and changed slowly over centuries. Ancient camanachd was a winter team game, played with the ball close to the ground among the many players. The stick used was called the 'caman' and the legends have clear descriptions of how to make a stick for play. An elder tree growing sideways out of a bank gave, when trimmed, the ideal shape of club, since the growing shaft curved up towards the light away from the horizontal root. The ball used had a central core of cork, wood or wool, then covered by leather, and made up by shoemakers.

One village was pitted against another. Camanachd was a slow-moving game played with large teams and the game might be deadlocked from time to time, with the ball stuck fast beneath the ruck. These games were held on Sundays, holidays and feast days: violence, on and off the pitch, was common, as was heavy drinking. Camanachd persists in modern Ireland, having evolved into *hurling,* a fast-moving game similar to hockey and with smaller teams, a softer ball and more aerial shots.

But it is the variants of camanachd that are of interest to golf historians. One legend tells us that a form of the game existed which involved single players hitting the ball at a target. On one day when King Conchubhar visited the field of play he watched not a team game like camanachd, but a variant - the 'hole game':

> *...he saw something which astonished him: thrice fifty boys at one end of the field and a single boy at the other, and the single boy winning victory from the thrice fifty youths. When they played the hole game (cluiche poill) and when it was their turn to cast the ball and his to defend, he would catch the thrice fifty balls outside the hole and none would go past him. When it was their turn to defend and his to drive, he would fill the hole with all their balls and they would not be able to prevent him.*[17]

The evidence of this document, even when treated with the necessary scepticism, shows that as well as the *team* game called camanachd, the players could change mode to a game in which players, with a stick, hit a ball towards a hole, a hole defended by others with sticks.

The club, or caman used in early Irish camanachd as shown on an early gravestone.
By courtesy of the OFFICE OF PUBLIC WORKS, DUBLIN.

Scotland's Highland ball-and-stick team game of shinty, from J&F Tallis' *Map of Scotland* 1851.
By courtesy of the NATIONAL LIBRARY OF SCOTLAND

There is other evidence that the caman and ball might be used in a more personal game in this way, since another Irish legend tells of a widower Irish king who married again and fathered a second son. His new Queen favoured this, her own son, and gave the boy a golden caman and a silver ball. The King's son from his first marriage received only a wooden club and ball, but, the story goes, when the two played, the King's first son, with the simpler equipment, managed to beat his better-equipped younger half-brother. The game played by the boys could not be team camanachd: it was a singles stick-and-ball match of some kind.[18]

In summary, we know that Irish players used sticks and balls in a plurality of games. The best-known sport was the noisy, robust, team game of camanachd. But there is more than a hint that play could revert to less well-known forms, in which individuals played with the same sticks and balls against each other in personal, peaceful contests. One of these was known as the 'hole game'.

Scotland and Ireland

These ancient Irish games are important in Scottish history. Irish missionaries, notably Columba, travelled to Scotland, bringing with them not only their new Christian faith, but also their Irish customs. Even Columba's departure from Ireland had involved sport, since he had quarrelled with the King following a dispute over the cirumstances of a death on the field at camanachd. It is not surprising that a team game similar to camanachd developed in Scotland. It was initially called by the same Irish name of camanachd, but increasingly the name changed to *iomain* or *shinty*, and this game of shinty still survives vigorously in the Highlands of Scotland.

20

Shinty also has a golf-like variant which is described in the Celtic legends. The Irish warrior Cuchullin travelled in the Highlands of Scotland (giving his own name to the mountains in Skye). He is said to have halted his journey from time to time, and taking his shinty stick, hit a silver ball over the moors.[19] In the story of 'The Herding of Cruachan' a singles match with a golden ball and silver stick is described. Another similar early legend from the Highlands is that a Gael, Gaisgeach na Sgeith Deire (the Hero of the Red Shield) went out with his three foster brothers to 'play the ball'. He competed against the three combined and 'put a half shot down and a half shot in on them'. This arcane but tantalising fragment might suggest some form of adversarial stick-and-ball play with shinty sticks.[20]

Though shinty is now regarded as a Highland game, it is easily forgotten that in mediaeval times the game was also played widely in the Borders and Lowlands of Scotland. This observation increases our interest in shinty as a possible relative or precursor of the early game of golf. Two scraps of information from Glasgow, a Lowland town, show this link. In 1595 the Town Council of Glasgow acted to ban 'golf, carrick, and shinty' as nuisances in the town, revealing that shinty was as popular as golf with the ordinary citizens.[21] As late as the 1700s, shinty was a favourite with the lowland university students. Murray's lively social history *The Old College of Glasgow* says that shinty was popular at that time in Glasgow and that 'every boy had to find his own shinty stick'.[22] Murray says that in consequence, there was steady damage to the local hawthorn hedges in Glasgow, as the boys made up their own sticks from the bent hedge saplings, the traditional way of making a sporting club. These young College players, mostly from well-off lowland families, probably also used these clubs for golf as well as shinty. The curved sticks shown in the early illustrations of shinty are not unlike early golf clubs, and the construction of the hair-filled shinty ball is similar to the later descriptions of the feathery golf ball. Shinty even appears in 1671 in the town records of North Berwick - a town in Scotland far from the Highlands.

A Highland chief with a single-piece tree stick starting a game of shinty.
From R. R. McIan *The Clans of the Scottish Highlands* 1845.

> Reported some of the East and West Gait [Gate] to have played at the schinne on Sabbath last in the afternoon...[23]

Lastly, even the most remote part of Scotland - the island of St Kilda - had its stick-and-ball game. Martin Martin, who toured and published an account of his tour of Scotland in 1697, recorded of the islanders:

> They use for their Diversion short clubs and balls of wood; the sand is a fair field for this Sport and Exercise, in which they take great pleasure, and are very nimble at it; they play for Eggs, Fowl, Hooks, or Tobacco; and so eager are they for Victory that they strip themselves to their Shirts to obtain it.[24]

The St Kilda game may have been shinty or it may not: play for a prize suggests an individual rather than a team game.

Sticks - for Shinty and Golf

Making wooden sticks, tools and utensils was a routine part of mediaeval life. Early rural communities used and made a range of wooden artifacts - creels, boats, baskets, fiddles, fishing rods, bagpipes, barrels, household utensils and walking sticks.[25] Hazel was the most versatile of the woods used, and was cultivated in coppices as a valuable crop: every part of the hazel tree had a niche market. Other trees had their own uses, and each type of wood had its own characteristics.

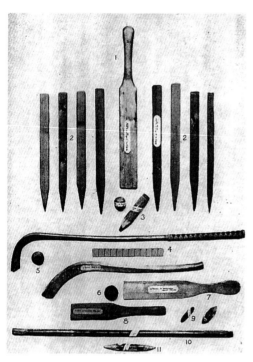

Wood was also used for bows, arrows and sporting clubs. For all of these, the desiderata were a long, straight unbranched stem or branch from wood which was strong yet flexible. For ball games, a curved, hard, expanded head was desirable, avoiding the need for complex reshaping. Young hawthorn trees had this particularly valuable feature, since beneath the soil it had a thickening - the club root. Golf and shinty players had always looked for suitable young thorn trees which were accidents of nature, growing sideways out of a bank, and in this way a strong, single-piece club, usually curving gracefully at the head, was obtained which required little extra trimming. An alternative was to fell a mature tree and pick a long side branch, follow it back to the trunk, cut a rough head from the main trunk at the base of the branch, and then finish it as desired.

Clubs, sticks and balls for rural games played in nineteenth century Argyll showing a variety of stick-and-ball sports.
From R. C. Maclagan
The Games of Argyllshire
Glasgow 1900.

Later Links with Shinty

These close and unexpected links between golf and shinty can even be traced into the nineteenth century. Bob Ferguson, Open Champion 1880-82, described starting golf as a boy in Musselburgh using a shinty stick, as had 'Old' Willie Park. Even in his prime, Park could take out a shinty stick to play and beat lesser golfers and demonstrate his mastery of golf. His biographer described his early play:

> In the summer evenings the caddies began to play on their own account. It was difficult at first for Willie [Park] to procure clubs and balls... When he could not get a club he found a substitute in the shape of a large thick stick, hooked at one end - in other words a shinty. With this, Willie made such progress that in a very short time his opponents with the aid of the more orthodox weapons were no match for Willie with his shinty.[26]

Alex Herd, Open Champion in 1902, is known to have started playing golf as a boy using 'shinties' cut from trees in the woods near St Andrews, and played with cork balls made from champagne corks rescued from the bins behind the R&A clubhouse, balls which were weighted with screws driven into the cork.[28] Even Vardon in Jersey later started his play with a 'tree stick',[29] and James Barrie's *Historical Sketch of the Hawick Golf Club* of 1898 starts

> Don't bounce about your dog's of war
> Nor at our 'shinties' scoff, boys;
> But learn our motto - 'sure and far',
> Then come and play at Golf, boys.

Finally, a remarkable finding is that primitive stick-and-ball games, hardly changed from the early Irish games described above, or from the east coast caddies' game, persisted in a number of forms in remoter parts of Scotland to the twentieth century. The folklore expert Dr Maclagan in his seminal work *The Games of Argyllshire* describes in the late 1800s not only shinty (and a form of cricket) played with simple home-made equipment, but also a stick-and-ball game remarkably similar to the 'hole game' mentioned in the ancient Irish records. The Argyll game was called 'Cat and Dog' or *caddog* in gaelic, with variations called *stracair* and *iomairt air a bhall-Speil* and this game is noted elsewhere in Scotland.[30]

For shinty in Argyll he describes an early great match each New Year's Day on the part of the links at Machrihanish where the championship golf course now starts. Even the name Machrihanish comes from the ancient Machair-an-Iomain - 'field of the shinty'. Upwards of a thousand people might gather, players and spectators, and the game was played on a pitch stretching over a quarter of a mile, land which is now the first hole of the golf course. The game started, not in mid-field, but between the goals or den, and the defending team struck the ball off from a tee or 'cogy' of earth at the goal.

Modern golf did not start at Machrihanish until 1876 and it was at first only a gentleman's game. But humble players with stick and ball had been out on these velvet links for centuries before. Shinty and golf may have been more closely related than has been thought.

Early Scottish Golf

From mediaeval times onwards there is a game mentioned in Scottish records called *'golf, goff, goif, gof, gowffe, golve* or *gouff.'* These different names need not perplex us nor detain us: the spelling of the day was variable and flexible. Nothing can be made of this linguistic abundance, and two forms of the word could be used in the same document, such was the low regard for standardised spelling, though it does suggest that the 'l' was not used in speech, and that instead the spoken name of the game might well be 'gouwf'. The derivation of the word is also unclear. Those who have favoured a Dutch origin of the game point to the related word in the Low Countries *kolf* or 'club'. However, there are equally ancient Scots words – the verbs *golf, golfand* and *golfing* meaning 'to strike'. The name of our game may have come from these words.[31]

The earliest use of 'golf' and its variants is found in public records, in the Acts of Parliament in 1457, 1471 and 1494, in the Aberdeen Town Council Records in 1565 and in the Glasgow Town Council Records in 1595. They show that the game called 'golf' was popular with the ordinary townspeople, popular enough and troublesome enough to warrant the attention of the authorities.

But the strange finding is that this game called 'golf' was a sport of the churchyard or street: and it was a winter, Sunday game.

Golf, Gouf, *n.*¹ Also: golfe, golff, goulf; goufe, gouff(e, gowf, gowff(e, gauff; goff(e, gofe, goofe; goif(f. [Prob. ad. Du. *kolf*, the club used in a game similar to golf.] The game of golf.

(a) At the fut bal ande the golf be vtterly criyt done and nocht vsyt; 1457 *Acts* II. 48/2. It is thocht expedient..at the futbal & golf be abusit in tym cummyng; 1471 *Ib.* 100/1. To the King to play at the golf with the Erle of Bothuile, iij Franch crounis; 1504 *Treas. Acc.* II. 418. Certane horsmen of Edinburgh..past to the links of Leith, and thair tuik nyne burgessis of Edinburgh playand at the golf; *Diurn. Occurr.* 285. Walter Hay..accusit for playing at the boulis and golff upoun Sondaye in the tym of the sermon; 1596 *Elgin Rec.* II. 46. William Stokis,..Thomas Craig, quha war playing at the goulf upon the Sabbothe day; 1608 *Kinghorn Kirk S.* 14. James Rodger [etc.]..were complained upon for playing at the golf upon ane Lord's day; 1651 *Misc. Maitl.* C. I. 440. The King went to goulf in..(Spittle) Feilds; 1662 BRODIE *Diary* 240. *attrib.* I send thé here a playand ball, And ane golf staff to driffe the ball vithe all; *Alex.* (Taym.) 54 b. That thai..playit in the golf feildis..[in] tyme of fast and preiching; 1583 *St. A. Kirk S.* 515.

(b) That in na place of the realme be vsit fut bawis, gouff, or vthir sic vnproffitable sportis; 1491 *Acts* II. 226/2. Being accusit for prophaning of the Saboth day in playing at the gouf eftir nune; 1598 *St. A. Kirk S.* 846. To play at the goufe ..the tyme of sessioun; 1599 *Ib.* 913. Playeris at gouff, bowllis, kyillis or any vther pastyme on the Saboth day; 1604 *Aberd. Eccl. Rec.* 38. He exerciset the gowf, and oftymes past to Barry lynkes, quhan the wadfie vas for drink; *Reg. Panmure* I. p. xxxii. Thair sall be na public playing suffred on the Sabbath dayes, as playing at..archerie, gowfe, &c.; 1610 *S. Leith Rec.* 8. That the schollers be exercised in lawful games, such as goufie, archarie, and the lyk; 1642 *Mun. Univ. Glasg.* II. 466. Ife..you have a mind for a touch at long gauff tomorrow, lett mee know; 1690 *Seafield Corr.* 64.

(c) At the goiff, because thai war partismen wyth the said Jhone in wynning and tyinsell [etc.]; 1538 *Aberd. B. Rec.* (MS) XVI. (J). Sic playis wnlefull, & speciallie cartis, dyis, tabillis, goif, kylis, bylis, & sic wther playis; 1565 *Ib.* XXVI. (J). Keipand the said..rod quhill it come to the fuird of the goiff burne; 1615 *Aberd. B. Rec.* II. 325.

(d) For archerie and goff, I haid bow, arrose, glub and bals; MELVILL 29. Playing at the goff in the park on the Sabboth

The Oxford English Dictionary entry on the word 'golf'.

Sporting Gatherings

Mediaeval Sundays were important for sport. To attend church, people came considerable distances by foot to the scattered townships, and on that day they enjoyed company and entertainment. Before the Reformation the churchgoers used this occasion - the only opportunity for meeting during the week - for a convivial day out, with meetings, drinking and sport before and after the services. Feast-days and holidays were particularly enjoyed in this way. The church and taverns were in the centre of the villages and the church-yard was a natural gathering place, with land available for sport. The Church's benign attitude at that time to these festivities was more than simple tolerance. On special feast-days, the church made money for its funds by selling the drink consumed – 'wakes and ales'.[32] At other times the Church had needed civilian military support for its Crusades, and archery practice was required: sports were to be encouraged.

The Sunday games played could be of many kinds, and took place on the flat grassland round the church. Football was popular, and as we saw above, in 1595 the Glasgow Town Council had to ban 'golf and shinty' from the 'High and Blackfriars Yards'. The High and Blackfriars were the principal churches in Glasgow, and the yards were their churchyards. Since golf and shinty were banned together, this increases the likelihood that these were two forms of one game played with the same club (shinty) and ball. Perhaps many of the Sunday sportsmen brought along a club, and if enough players

A stick-and-ball game played in the Dutch manner on the frozen river at Largs on the Firth of Clyde. This 'Winter' car-touche is from the painted ceiling of the Skelmorlie Aisle in Largs.
By courtesy of
HISTORIC SCOTLAND.

appeared, team games like shinty were played. But if few appeared or few wished to play, they reverted to the simpler, personal, stick-and-ball game of 'golf', to the displeasure of the authorities. On the long walk home, neighbours might enliven the journey with a cross-country stick-and-ball game.

But what was this churchyard game called golf? The poor of Glasgow and elsewhere (to whom these regulations were addressed) could not afford the elegant golf clubs and balls. Played in the churchyard with simple equipment, golf could only be a short game, perhaps towards a broad target, like the door of the church itself. Further hints of golf as a churchyard game come from Aberdeen in 1613:

Jhone Allan, cutler, convict, and Jhone Allane buik binder, convict for setting ane goiff ball in the kirk yeard, and stricking the same against the kirk.[33]

The mistake made by the players which brought disapproval is not clear: perhaps they broke a window or damaged a crumbling wall, after previous warnings. Whatever they were up to with the 'goiff ball', it certainly was not the long golf game of the links. They were playing a short game of some kind in a churchyard.

Other evidence of churchyard sport is found in the Kirkcudbright Town Council Records for 1580, in which there is a prohibition of playing 'keich ball' (a handball game like fives) - in the churchyard. Like the game of fives, it was commonly played against a wall, notably the north wall of a church, where there were no graves.[34] Churchyard games were important and common at the time.

The Dangers of the Game

The puzzle of the Kelso tragedy described above - the death in the churchyard from a blow by a golf ball - can now be explained. The Kelso game was not unusual, but was rather typical of sport at this time and of one form of early Scottish golf. It was a 'short' game played with simple home-made sticks and balls, with close encounters and contact in the confines of a churchyard. Though called golf, it may not have been a sedate game with careful shots, but more like shinty.

There are other scattered reports of deaths and injury in which the instrument was a golf club, and some of these are earlier than the Kelso incident. One comes from Stirling in 1561, and even earlier in Brechin, in 1508, John Thowless killed a man with 'a stroke of a golf club'. He was absolved from a murder charge. Another case from Falkirk in 1639 says the victim had been struck with a 'golfeclub and bloding of him thairwith upone the face'.[35]

Falkirk prosecution involving a 'golf club' as a weapon in 1639.
By courtesy of the SCOTTISH RECORD OFFICE, SC 67/67/1.

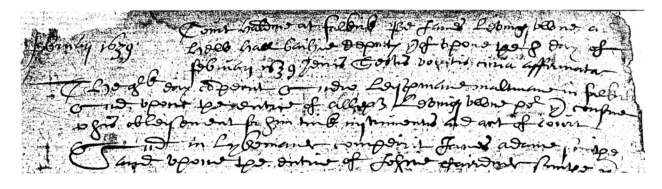

Any sporting gathering at this period could be noisy and violent, and feast days were notorious for disorder and trouble from the the drunken mobs. A diarist in Duns, near North Berwick, had little time for the traditional town sports on the Scottish festival of Fastern's E'en in February, since

all idel people in that burgh were usually conveened by touck of drum to play at football, which did always end and determine in the effusion of blood among the inhabitants.[36]

One death from assault by such a sporting mob is recorded. Sir John Carmichael, on his way to hold court in the Borders in 1600, ran into a rabble returning from a Sunday football gathering and was attacked and killed. The murderer was traced and convicted: after having a hand cut off, he was hanged and his body suspended in chains.[37]

Sunday, the King and Sport

Knowing the existence of the short Sunday golf played by the ordinary citizen, we now turn, with interest and new insight, to the best-known and earliest of the golf records, an Act of Parliament of 1457: this is the text of the original hand-written document:

Anent Wapinschawing

Item it is ordanyt and decretyt that wapinschawing behaldin be the lordis and baronys sprituale and temperale four tymes in the yeir And at the futbawe and the golf be vterly criyt done and nocht wsit And at the bowe markis be maide at all parochkirkis a paire of buttis and shuting be wsyt Ilk Sunday...

The Act was printed, for the first time, in 1566 and later in 1597 and the text continued to change slightly, while retaining the original intent.

*65. Weapon-schawings, Fute-ball, Golfe and Archers.
ITEM, It is decreeted & ordained, that the weaponschaw-ings be halden be the Lords and Barrones Spiritual and Temporal, foure times in the zeir. And that the fute-bal and golfe be vtterly cryed downe, and not to be used. And that the bowmarkes be maid, at ilk Parish Kirk a pair of Buttes, and schuting be vsed. And that ilk man shutte sex schottes at the least, under the paine to be raysed upon them, that cummis not, at least twa pennyes to be giuen to them, that cummis to the bowemarkes to drink...[38]*

The difference in the text reflects changing use of the language and that the original hand-written text had been copied many times for the benefit of the 'Barronis' and that many informal versions of the Law, now lost, were available. With this uncertain start, it seems the famous act was doomed to be treated with disrespect by golf historians there-after. A recent version of it reads that the game

be utterly cripit downe... the bowe merkis be mude at ilke proch Kirk a pair of batts and schiting be usit...[39]

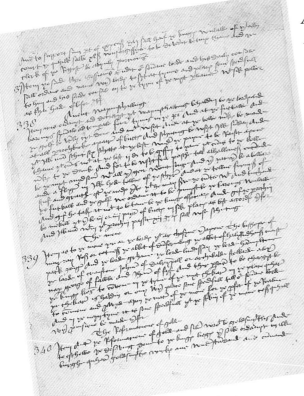

The Act of Paliament of 1457 contains the famous attempt to discourage golf and football and support archery instead.

By courtesy of the SCOTTISH RECORD OFFICE.

The Original Act

But there is no mistaking the intention of the original Act. Such Acts of Parliament, though impressive, did not then have the force they had later. Central power was not strong: power lay with the local barons and enforcement of any national proposals required their co-operation. The existence of such an Act meant there was considerable national concern and that national compliance was to be attempted. The reason for the encouragement of archery was that Scottish archery was poor, and had been responsible for earlier military defeats. These preparations were also of domestic importance. In 1460 Scotland attacked England, recapturing Roxburgh in the Borders, and Scotland was also helping France's military campaign by sending soldiers.

To encourage practice at archery, the new law shows that targets were to be set up outside each parish church on Sundays for at least four practice sessions a year, and this was to be encouraged in place of the usual football and golf. An ingenious and probably workable punishment is suggested: those not turning up were to be fined and the money given to those attending to purchase drink.

This brief law is the earliest surviving mention of golf in Scotland. It confirms that Sunday was the important day for general gatherings, and it also shows that the citizens on that day, when left to themselves, would prefer to play golf and football. The Act confirms that golf was a game popular with the ordinary people who would be the foot soldiers of the army.

Fourteen years after the 1457 Act, golf was again banned in an Act of James III in 1471. The Act reaffirmed and echoed the earlier prohibitions, namely that

The futbal & golf be abusit [abandonned] in tym cummyng & the buttis maid up and shot vsit [used] efter the tenor of the act of parlyament.

This Act suggests that the earlier exhortation to practise archery had been unsuccessful or had lapsed, and that the hoped-for improvement in archery had not resulted.

It is sometimes stated that this Act applied also to the nobility, and that they were also discouraged from playing golf, advice which they ignored. But the laws did not apply to them: the barons made their own rules.

Noble Golf

This evidence shows that in mediaeval pre-Reformation Scotland, there was a game called 'golf', a churchyard game widely played by the ordinary folk, far from the links.

But other records show that another smaller group were already out on the links and also playing a game called golf. This noble game of golf appears in other records in quite different settings. The game does not appear to be played as part of convivial group sport on Sundays. Instead this form of golf was a game played by the kings, court and aristocracy on open parkland or the sea-side links. These golfers used expensive custom-made equipment rather than the ubiquitous shinty stick, and they used expensive balls.

This raises the possibility that *two* forms of golf existed at this time - the 'short' golf of the humble churchyard players, and the noble 'long' golf of the

James IV was known to be a golfer from his purchases of balls and clubs, and a tradition of sporting Scottish monarchs continued thereafter.

Artist unknown: by courtesy of the SCOTTISH NATIONAL PORTRAIT GALLERY.

links. If this is true, then the word golf was used in mediaeval Scotland to describe a range of stick-and-ball games in which the ball was hit at a target. The humble players may have used the word golf for their short simple game in imitation of the long game of the nobility.

The Skilled Long Game

This aristocratic game makes its first documented appearance in an Account Book of the Lord High Treasurer, who disbursed the royal pocket money. In an entry fifty years after the 1457 Act of Parliament which dealt with humble golf, James IV spent some money thus:

Sept 21 1502 - Item to the King for clubs from the bower at St Johnston [Perth]...xiiij s [fourteen shillings].[40]

In 1503, five months later, there are these entries:

Feb 3 1503 - Item to the King to play at the golf with the Erle of Bothuile [Bothwell] ...xlij s [fortytwo shillings]

Item to golf Clubbes and Balles to the King that he playit with ix s [nine shillings].[41]

In the following two years there are two more specific items:

1505-6 Feb 22. Item for xij Golf Ballis to the King...iiij s

1506 July 18. Item for ij Golf Clubbes to the King...ij s.

These brief extracts are surprisingly informative. The King was on his usual restless travel round the land, moving from palace to palace, when these financial items are recorded. His bases when the golf matches are recorded were Perth, Stirling and Falkland Palace in Fife. The entry for Falkland Palace in 1503 is of interest. In detail, the match with Bothwell had been on 3rd February, and on that day the King gave money to the Bishop of St Andrews. Three days later he bought more golf balls and paid an innkeeper.

This suggests that the royal party had perhaps travelled far from the palace for the game, and perhaps it was St Andrews that was favoured. The game played by the King and the nobles sounds more like the modern long game. They did not play in the churchyard, as part of the Sunday golf and football melée, and with the sophisticated equipment they looked for space and freedom beyond the churchyard. The King's expenditure probably included a bet with the Earl of Bothwell and to pay for caddies and entertainment afterwards. The outing seems to have been a personal match, not a team game or a solitary pleasure. It sounds like a singles match-play with expensive equipment, at St Andrews, as early as 1503.

The King's expenditure in 1503 while at Falkland Palace in Fife included purchase of golf clubs and balls. These entries also suggest a golfing trip to St Andrews, staying overnight in the town.
From J. P. Paul *Accounts of the Lord High Treasurer* Edinburgh 1900.

FEBRUAR.

Item, the first day of Februar, to Alexander Wardlaw, be the Kingis command, ... xviij s.
Item, the secund day of Februar, to Gareoch pursewant to pas in Ingland with the Kingis writing, . . xxxvj s.
Item, [the thrid day of Februar], to the gysaris of Edinburgh that daunsit in the Abbay, v Franch crounis; summa . . . . . iij li. x s.
Item, to the King to play at the golf with the Erle of Bothuile, iiij Franch crounis; summa . . . xlij s.
Item, be the Kingis command, to Johne Barbour with the Beschop of Sanctandrois, x Franch crounis; summa . . . . . . vij li.
Item, to the priestis of Dunblane that singis for Margret Drummond, thair quarter fee of Candilmes, . v li.
Item, the ferd day of Februar, to the lard of Inchmertynis man brocht ane halk to the King, be the Kingis command, ... xxviij s.
Item, [the vj day of Februar], to George Robison, for mail quhair the King occupiit in his innys, iiij Franch crounis; summa . . . . . lvj s.
Item, to Pasing, armorar, to the bigging of the harnes myln, ... xlij s.
Item, for golf clubbes and balles to the King that he playit with, ... ix s.
Item, the vij day of Februar, be the Kingis command to Rountas the cornut quhen he passit away in Ingland, x Franch crounis; summa . . vij li.
Item, the ix day of Februar, to Johne Forman of the Wardrob, for xvij turs of bent, . . . xxxiiij s

The Scottish Court
required to move from
place to place to govern
the land, and Falkland
Palace offered a base for
many sports for the nobles,
and included a tennis
court. The golf links in Fife
were also at hand.

Painting by Alexander
Keirincx, by courtesy of the
SCOTTISH NATIONAL PORTRAIT
GALLERY.

The Bowmaker's Clubs

The King's clubs were not cheap and home-made; they were expensive
items purchased from a skilled artisan. The King's accounts show that he
purchased more than one club at a time - strong evidence that he was playing
a long, skilled game, requiring a variety of shots, unlike the short, churchyard game. The golf club was made for him by a 'bower', a craftsman skilled
in making the strong, flexible bows for war. These clubs were sophisticated
instruments: they were certainly not suitable for shinty or a rough churchyard knockabout.

Bowmaking was a serious business. Anyone could make a simple bow, but
for war the bowmaker's skills were required and their work was a deadly
serious business. The makers strove to achieve strength and power in the
bow's construction: archery won and lost wars. The bowers had skills in
shaping a bow with a strong central section and pliant extremities. But at
some point unknown, the ancient bowmakers had tumbled on the secret of a
better bow. Single stems or branches from a tree made reasonable bows. But
since symmetrical halves were the ideal, seldom was this naturally possible:
no amount of trimming and planing was ever satisfactory. Instead, the
advance in bowmaking was for the bower to select *two* stems closely
matching each other, and join them with glue in an overlapping joint in the
middle of the bow, covering the glued junction with a leather piece for the
hand-grip and adding a horn inset for the arrow track.[42]

The similarity of this two-piece bow to the construction of the older form of
golf club is striking. It is highly likely that these skills allowed the bowmakers, at a time unknown, and in Scotland alone, to use a similar strategy to

make a composite golf club for their noble patrons, a two-piece club which propelled the ball further. This composite club could also use different wood for the head and shaft, using wood with whip (e.g. ash) for the shaft, and tough inelastic durable wood (e.g. apple) for the head. The two parts were united by a glued joint, the 'scare' joint, also covered in some way, and horn was added to the sole, to protect from damage from the turf. These were the skills used by bowmakers to make bows. Since the two-part bow for archery dates from early mediaeval times, it may be that noble golf in Scotland is as old as skilled archery.

The Makers

The names of early bowmakers and clubmakers of the time are unknown to us, and the bowmaker at Perth who supplied the clubs to the King in 1503, cannot be identified. But some bowmaker/clubmakers from a little later confirm the linkage between these skills. First to be recorded is the bowmaker Alexander Dais who died of the plague at St Andrews in 1585 and whose estate contained not only bows and arrows 'made and unmade', but also 'certain club heidis and schaftis'. Another was William Mayne, appointed in 1603 as 'Maister fledger [arrow-maker], bower [bowmaker], clubmaker, and speir-maker to his Hienes.' Next was George Gibson, 'bower burgess of Edinburgh', who when he died in 1622 left 'fiftie tua golff clubis' in his estate.

Another was Donald Baine, 'bower burgess of Edinburgh', whose workshop goods listed after death in 1635 included a remarkable entry – 'clubheids and clubschaftis ane thousand made and unmade'.[43]

The bowmaker Mayne's title shows that he was not only a clubmaker, but also an arrow-maker, and spear-maker. This arrow and spear work may have given these men other skills which aided the production of golf clubs. In making arrows they had to join feathers to the arrow shaft with whipping, and doubtless they used this skill in covering the scare joint of wooden clubs. In making spears, axes and arrows, they also had to fit wooden shafts into metal heads tightly and securely. The most commonly used axe in the sixteenth century was the 'Leith axe', suggesting skills among the artisans at Leith in the work of fitting shafts to axe heads. Mayne and other bowmakers were therefore well placed to make, and finish, the other golf club - the clumsy iron-headed golf clubs for trouble shots, the 'bunkard club' mentioned in early documents. In making this club, metal heads were obtained from the blacksmith and secure shafts fitted to these heads. We do not know if the bowmakers did make the early 'bunker' clubs, but they certainly had the skills to do so.

A bill from a St Andrews clubmaker and bowmaker, in which charges for bows, arrows and golf clubs are mixed together, showing that these early crafts were combined.
By courtesy of COWIE COLLECTION, ST ANDREWS UNIVERSITY LIBRARY, photographed from documents in the Auchterlonie papers.

Beyond the Churchyard

There were a number of places where these aristocratic golfers could have played a satisfying game. On the occasion of purchasing clubs in 1502 at Perth, the King may have played on the ancient golfing site of the North Inch. About the time of the King's purchases of golf equipment, there is a record of another noble golfer, Sir Robert Maule who 'exercised the gouff' at the 'links at Barry [Carnoustie]'.[44] Mary, Queen of Scots, played 'golf and pall mall' in 'the fields beside Seton', probably the links at present-day Cockenzie.

Other well-known golfers also sought the open links for their play rather than visit the churchyard. We know of some Edinburgh burgesses who visited Leith in 1575 to play golf.[45] Royal play at Stirling was in 'the park' near the castle. But conditions for a satisfying long game - namely a fine links and a dry day - might not always be available. In between, the noble golfers moving from castle to castle had to make do with a rough field or park, with long wet grass totally unsuited to their equipment: perhaps on occasions the cruder balls and clubs of the short game sufficed. At inland Dunfermline, royal play is traditionally supposed to have been at Golf Hill, a ridge of rough ground to the north of the town, near the street now called Golfdrum.[46]

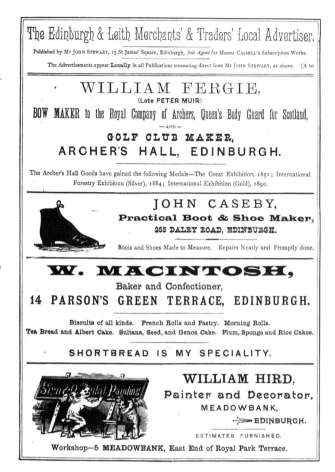

Bow-making and club-making crafts combined in Edinburgh as late as the 1880s.

The nobles and merchants had another reason to seek to play on the links, or in nearby parks. There they could avoid the rucks and close encounters of the churchyard sport, and the drunkenness of the bonspeils, at which their enemies might have a chance to harm them. But in these troubled times, even while at their sport on the links, the prominent citizens were not safe. On Barry Links at Carnoustie, Sir Robert Maule was attacked and wounded while at golf in 1560, and some Edinburgh burgesses were pursued by horsemen on Leith Links and murdered in 1575. Lennox and Sandilands, two noblemen, were attacked on their way to golf from Edinburgh to Leith at about the same time, but fought back and survived.[47]

Feathery Golf Balls

At some time unknown, the noble and well-off Scottish golfers began to use a feather or hair-filled ball, a ball which flew further than others, and which suited the jointed wooden clubs. This ball's construction used the ancient principle of the Roman hair-filled ball. A small, wet, leather sphere was stuffed with wet feathers and when dried out, gave a hard, elastic ball which flew and bounced well. But the feathery, like the older golf clubs, had a short life. Long golf was expensive. King James IV also bought golf balls in the purchases recorded by the Lord High Treasurer. We can surmise that these golf balls were featheries and not crude wooden balls, judging by the expense of his purchases. The price of the King's clubs and balls can be calculated from the 1505-1506 entries at perhaps 1/- each for clubs and 4d for each ball. This gives the club price as about three times the price of balls.

The craftsmen making the early feathery balls were the cordiners - the shoe-makers. Accustomed to working with leather, they had stitching skills and golf-ball making was a natural extension of their craft. The cordiners also made footballs of quality, judging by the payment made by Glasgow Town Council about 1600 to a local cordiner for a football for the traditional match on a festive occasion.[48] It is likely that this football was an air or hair-filled ball, in the Roman style, since there was a warning to players that, if disturbances occurred, the ball would be 'cut' and made useless.

Our first mention of ballmakers in Scotland is a reference to the 'cordiners and ballmakers of North Leith' who, in 1554, had a dispute with the cordiners of the Canongate in Edinburgh, but no names of the early makers have survived.[49] King James IV purchased his balls in 1503 at Stirling. There are a number of records of golf balls stocked by traders, and as early as 1567 the estate of a merchant in Stirling showed that, at the time of death, he had a stock of three dozen 'gof bawis'. Other merchants' estates in Stirling and Edinburgh show holdings of balls by the dozen, as if local traders regularly had balls in stock for sale.[50] A legal action in Haddington in 1576 records that a merchant had failed to pay a local supplier for, among other things, a dozen golf balls.[51]

Foreign Balls

A feature of the history of the ball in Scotland is that golf balls were imported from the Low Countries in mediaeval times.[52] The links between Holland and Scotland at this time were close. Travellers and traders from Scotland were frequently found in the Low Countries and the port of Veere specialised in this Scottish trade. The Scottish presence in Veere was big enough to support a Scottish chaplainry, endowed in 1541, and in 1612 this congregation was formally linked to the Presbytery of Edinburgh. The Low Countries and Scotland were politically close and were never at war: Scots soldiers often served with the armies of the Low Countries.

Another link was that fishermen from the Low Countries followed the shoals of herring as they moved across the North Sea to reach the Scottish coast. These fishermen docked frequently in the Scottish east coast ports and villages, and might stay in harbour for long periods. Scottish east coast houses built about this time may show this continental influence. Traders from the Low Countries also attended the great St Andrews Fair, lasting for two weeks in spring of each year from 1350 to 1580, and the harbour and bay were thronged with vessels.

The balls made in the Low Countries were quite large and filled with hair, not feathers: this imported ball was a cheaper product, perhaps a compromise between the superior, expensive feathery and a dull wooden ball. All the evidence points to a variety of balls being used in Scotland according to purse and circumstances. Detailed records of exports of balls from the Low Countries have survived from the years 1487, 1494, 1495 and 1497. Up to six barrels of balls per year destined for Scotland are recorded, and this odd bit of trading was typical of the Scottish economy at the time. Scotland was rich in the raw materials (hide and hair) but lacked the manufacturing tradition.

The Low Countries and Golf

The two Scottish games we have studied so far are shinty and the game or games called 'golf'. The third game of interest is the game of the Low Countries called 'colf'. This stick-and-ball game has attracted the interest of historians, and in colf some scholars see the origins of modern golf. However, a closer look at colf shows fundamental differences with the Scottish long game. At best it can be claimed that colf and short Scottish 'golf' are related.

Historians of sport studying the Low Countries' stick-and-ball game are fortunate. They have more local records available than in Scotland: colf is shown in many illustrations, in paintings and drawings, and on tiles. Scotland, poor and backward, had little tradition of painting or decoration, and the Church in Scotland after the Reformation became hostile to painted images, and many existing paintings, murals and other images were destroyed.

Studies by Steven van Hengel on colf in the Low Countries have produced a new account of this game.[53]

The Game called Colf

His study of the Low Countries stick-and-ball game discards the various names for the game used by earlier historians, notably 'het kolven'. The game of the Low Countries, like the Scottish game, was found to have variable terminology in the original sources – *spel metten colve, den bal mitter colven, colven, Kolven, colffven, colfslaen,* and other variants. Van Hengel sensibly proposed that these names be replaced, for historical discussion of the game, by the simple core term *colf*, though this typographical closeness to *golf* invites confusion and immediately presumes that a close relationship exists.

Colf seems to have been, in its simplest form, a street game, a pastime popular with children. It did not seem to have particular favour with royalty or with the court in the Low Countries. The majority of the paintings show young players involved with the game, and Halma's *Dictionary* of 1708 says it was

> a children's game played in the great squares and market places. They make little heaps of sand or snow on which they place the ball, and thus striking it underneath, they can send it a great distance.[54]

The young colf players are usually shown with hands placed wide apart on the shaft, pushing the ball, rather than striking it. A street game is also suggested by the action taken by the town authorities in 1587 and 1590 at the coastal town of Brielle (now den Briel). They banned colf players from the town because the sport was causing damage and nuisance.[55] The Naarden authorities also banned the game from the churchyard in 1456. Earlier, in 1401, the Dordrecht authorities had enacted that 'nobody shall play any ball games whatsoever... nor in churchyards, nor in churches, nor in cloisters, nor to throw balls, nor to play balls with the club...'[56]

If anything, colf resembles the short Scottish game of the churchyard, and study of the colf equipment supports this.

DE TOL VAN IERSEKEROORD

DOCUMENTEN EN REKENINGEN

1321—1572

DOOR

Dr. W. S. UNGER.

'S GRAVENHAGE
verkrijgbaar bij MARTINUS NIJHOFF
1939

Unger's research showing that there was export of balls from the Low Countries to Scotland in the fifteenth century.

Colf: Clubs and Balls

Colf clubs and balls are shown in many illustrations, and some club heads and balls have survived: unlike the Scottish game, we have no need to debate the size, shape or construction of the mediaeval colf equipment.

The colf clubs and balls were not simple home-made artifacts. The many available paintings help in reconstructing the appearance of the intact colf club. The shafts look short and stiff, and were apparently made of ash or hazel. The grip is woven and decorative, and does not look robust enough for heavy, regular use. The surviving club heads confirm the appearances in the contemporary pictures. An upturned toe juts out and the compact head has a broad base. All the clubs have a loft, perhaps that of a contemporary five iron, both on the front and on the back, suggesting that the clubs were made to suit both right- and left-handers, or were used for reverse shots by players. The unchanging loft suggests that little variety of shot was employed. Some club-heads have been found which show a maker's mark; some of the heads are made of lead, the others of iron.[57]

The head was moulded to the wooden shaft in a curious way. A branch from a hazel tree was used, trimmed to a stout side branch close to one end, and onto this side branch the metal head was moulded and fitted. This junction was not strong, and a powerful full shot at a ball does not seem possible: the broad base also seems a hindrance and would drag on the ground. Perhaps the bigger ball and the use of a tee, as mentioned above, is the key to this mystery, and the ball was routinely hit without contact with the ground. The club would make a poor shinty stick, nor could the colf club serve for accurate putting.

These iron-headed clubs appear repeatedly in paintings and other illustrations, and show little variation in style. But occasionally other clubs are evident. At least three paintings showing wooden clubs of the long-nosed variety are shown in use in the Low Countries. One shows a Christmas present of such a club to a child, another shows Scotsmen, in kilts, at play with long-nosed clubs, and many others show players with such clubs, playing an open game like ice hockey. These wooden clubs were referred to in the Low Countries as 'Scottish cleeks'. Even the colf players acknowledged that these elegant clubs belonged to a different game, and perhaps had no regular place in their usual short street game.[58]

Colf club heads.

By courtesy of ARCHIE BAIRD.

Colf Balls

The balls used for colf in the Low Countries are also shown in illustrations, and some have survived in historical collections. These leather-covered balls have a core of wood or hair. The leather template is different from the Scottish feathery pattern, and the balls are bigger. The records of the Low Countries show that specialised ballmakers existed, and in 1520 in Leyden the 'club-maker's alley' was named, and still is called, the Kolfmakerssteeg. The illustrations given by van Hengel are of an elm ball 5 cms in diameter and an estimated 40 gms original weight.[59] The modern ball is 4.2 cm in diameter and 46 gms weight. These colf balls are bigger and lighter than Scottish featheries and could not be propelled any great distance.

All the evidence is that colf was a short street game, probably played towards a large target, and that the teed ball may have been scooped into the air by the youthful players.

Colf Variants

Like all early stick-and-ball games, colf was not standardised. The usual form is described above, and as always there is evidence of some variety in the game according to local custom and circumstance. Colf on ice is shown in some paintings with the target as a hole or post in the ice. On those special days (possibly quite rare) when the canals were frozen and safely weight-bearing, the inhabitants enjoyed a sociable sporty gathering, playing with their colf clubs and balls, at gatherings similar to the rare Scottish curling bonspiels. Colf on ice was rare enough and colourful enough to catch the attention of painters and illustrators in the Low Countries. Colf on ice must have been a slippery, entertaining, occasional lottery unrelated to the game of the links.[60] The clubs shown in use on ice are invariably long-nosed woods, not metal colf clubs.

Colf on ice in Holland. From Barent Avercamp (1612-79) *A Winter Scene with Figures on Ice.* By courtesy of the BRIDGEMAN ART GALLERY and JOHNNY VAN HAFFTEN GALLERY, LONDON.

In another unusual mode we see some kinship of colf with Scottish golf. One illustration suggests play to a hole in the ground. In a *Book of Hours* from the Low Countries in about 1530, a marginal illustration does show players at a stick-and-ball game apparently approaching a hole in the ground. They are each playing with one club. It is held awkwardly and the ball seems to be pushed, rather than hit, with hands well apart on the club.

Lastly there is evidence of a rare 'long' variety of colf played on special occasions. From 1297 onwards, the villagers of Leonen played a cross-country game, once a year, to celebrate the anniversary of the relief of the local

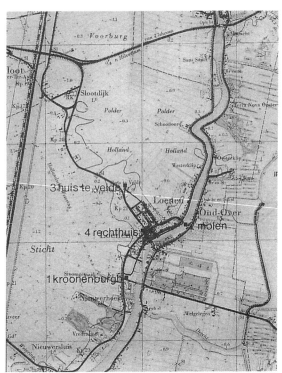

A form of cross-country colf was used on a special anniversary near the town of Leonen.

By courtesy of the late STEVEN VAN HENGEL.

Kronenburg castle after a prolonged siege.[61] There were four 'holes' played, totalling over 4,950 yards, i.e. over 1,000 yards each. A large number of villagers took part and the game was played over rough ground: the target is not mentioned but was probably a broad one like a door or a tree. It may have been an outing with a single ball pursued by all players, rather than a game with an individual ball. A similar game was played over a rectangular course outside the town of Haarlem in 1450, and these games may have involved a race to reach the target. They have all the appearances of mass, festive, participation sport, confined to a single day. They were not typical of colf and, if anything, instead resembled jeu de mail or chole. These rare early cross-country outings do, however, have something of the spirit of long, Scottish golf.

Colf Abroad

Colf was exported by the Dutch. At their colonies at Fort Orange and at Albany in New York, records of colf exist in 1657 and 1659.[62] Other evidence comes from the cargoes of two Dutch ships wrecked off the north coast of Scotland. The ships were the *Lastdrager* and the *Kennermerland*, and when passing along the treacherous northerly routes out of the North Sea from Holland to the Dutch East Indies or elsewhere, they were wrecked off the Shetland Islands.[63] Parts of the cargoes have been brought up by divers, and some objects were recovered and eventually recognised to be colf club heads.

The End of Colf

But colf did not last. The game died out in the Low Countries in the mid-1600s. Street colf probably became impossible in the increasingly crowded towns. The streets became narrower, muddier and more crowded, and other towns, like Briell, banned dangerous colf.

After the Reformation, in the Low Countries as in Scotland, all sport was less favoured and Sunday sport in particular was discouraged. In Scotland discreet use of the town's links was tolerated. In the Low Countries there was nowhere else for the players to go. The towns were inland on the inland seas and waterways, and winter was severe. The coast, though blessed with linksland, was far away. Street colf disappeared, and no serious park or links game emerged. But in Scotland, the links with their natural short grass were available, adjacent to the towns, and winter was mild.

Instead, a new game emerged in the Low Countries. This new stick-and-ball game has been much studied and is well documented. It was called *kolf*, and closely resembled the English game of pall-mall and the sophisticated French game of mail(e). Kolf was played with elegant mallets and large wooden balls, on a short, custom-built court which resembled the layout required for pall-mall. Kolf was fashionable and expensive and was to survive, supported by a small group of wealthy enthusiasts.

In Summary

It is likely that Scottish golf before 1600 took at least two forms. The well-off minority played a long game with specially-made clubs and feather balls, seeking maximum length with their shots, and they sought to play on the links when possible. This superior game and equipment may date back at least to the earliest days of composite bowmaking. The common people had another form of golf, a short game of the town streets and churchyards, which was played with home-made sticks and cheap balls. Colf, the early game of the Low Countries, resembles this Scottish short game. Both short golf and short colf faded out in the mid-1600s.

But in Scotland the game of long golf not only survived but prospered.

FURTHER READING

Accounts of the early history of golf are usually taken from Robert H.K. Browning *A History of Golf: the Royal and Ancient Game* London 1955, and Guy Campbell in Bernard Darwin (and others) *A History of Golf in Britain* London 1952; less commonly consulted are Harold Hilton and Garden C. Smith *The Royal and Ancient Game of Golf* London 1912, Geoffrey Cousins *Golf in Britain: A Social History from the Beginnings to the Present Day* London 1975 and Tom Scott *The Story of Golf: from its Origins to the Present Day* London 1972. General histories of golf, particularly coffee-table books, have largely recycled material from these books in *précis* form.

However, scholarly research in special areas has resulted in important new texts recently, notably Ian T. Henderson and David I. Stirk *Golf in the Making* Crawley 1979, Alastair J. Johnston and James Johnston *The Chronicles of Golf: 1457 to 1857* Cleveland 1993, Steven van Hengel *Early Golf* Bentveld, Holland 1982, and Alastair J. Johnston *The Clapcott Papers* Edinburgh 1985, and these texts have been of assistance in this book. The history of the golf ball is given in John S. Martin *The Curious History of the Golf Ball* New York 1968, and early golf clubs are described in David Stirk *Golf: the Great Clubmakers* London 1992. For detailed accounts of local Scottish golf history see David Hamilton's 'Early Golf' series *Early Golf in Glasgow* (1985), *Early Aberdeen Golf* (1986), *Early Golf at St Andrews* (1987) and *Early Golf at Edinburgh and Leith* (1988). Scholarly interest in early Scottish shinty is found in Roger Hutchinson's *Camanachd!: the Story of Shinty* Edinburgh 1989, and Hugh Dan MacLennan *Shinty!* Nairn 1993. For the persistence of stick-and-ball games into twentieth century Scotland, see R. C. Maclagan *The Games of Argyllshire* London 1900. Lastly, for insight into Scottish mediaeval sport, see F. P. Magoun (1931) 'Scottish popular football 1424-1815' *American Historical Review* vol 37, 1-13.

For early sport in general see Robert Scott Fittis *Sports and Pastimes of Scotland* Paisley 1891, William J. Baker *Sports in the Western World* Totowa 1982, and Peter Moss *Sports and Pastimes Through the Ages* London 1962. The best general social history of early Scotland is T. C. Smout's *History of the Scottish People 1560-1830* Glasgow 1969.

The game of Mail shown in *New Rules for the Game of Mail* Paris 1717. The upper and lower engravings show a golf-like variety of shots; long approach shots were followed by a precise stroke to 'shoot the pass.'

By courtesy of RUARI MCLEAN.

The King's Majesty's Declaration to his Subjects, lawful Sports to be used[1].

Imprinted at London, by Robert Barker, Printer to the King's Majesty; and by the Assigns of John Bill. 1633

[Quarto; containing twenty pages.]

———————

By the King.

OUR dear father of blessed memory, in his return from Scotland, comi cashire[2], found that his subjects were debarred from lawful recre days, after evening prayers ended, and upon holidays; and he prudently if these times were taken from them, the meaner sort, who labour hard all have no recreations at all to refresh their spirits. And after his return that his loyal subjects, in all other parts of his kingdom, did suffer in the sa perhaps, not in the same degree; and did, therefore, in his princely w declaration to all his loving subjects, concerning lawful sports to be use which was printed and published, by his royal commandment, in the y tenour which hereafter followeth:

By the King.

WHEREAS, upon our return the last year out of Scotland, we did sure, touching the recreations of our people in those parts, under our causes us thereunto moving, we have thought good to command these ou given in Lancashire, (with a few words thereunto added, and most ap parts of our realms,) to be published to all our subjects.

Whereas we did justly, in our progress through Lancashire, rebuke so

THE TURBULENT CENTURY

At the time of the mid-1500s, Scotland entered a time of social unrest. The Church and its clergy were under increasing criticism, and advocates of sterner religious practice and probity in public conduct were gaining political strength. Allegations about misuse of Church properties and finances circulated, as did stories of neglect of duty by priests.

The established Roman Catholic Church was challenged throughout Europe shortly afterwards, and in Scotland the Reformation was particularly intense. The new fundamentalists planned not only for a new church but for a more puritanical lifestyle. Their attitude to sport and the Sabbath was clear. Sunday was for worship and not for fun: fun had heathen or popish origins. Action was proposed against Sunday sports, and the legal records of some of these proceedings survive. When shorn of their penal aspect, they give us, for the first time, vital information about the golf of ordinary citizens, and about where and when they were playing. The Reformation of the Church may also have had one major effect on golf: it may have driven the common, short Scottish game of golf away from the churchyard and onto the distant links.

After the Reformation

The Reformation meant the overthrow of the Roman Catholic Church in Scotland. The new church acted quickly, and in 1561 issued its plans for social

OPPOSITE: A later reprint of the 'Book of Sport' issued by James VI of Scotland and I of England in an attempt to reduce the strict Sunday observance brought in by the Puritans.

engineering as a new moral code – the *Book of Discipline*. Further clarifications were to follow. Two years later, in 1563, the policy on dealing with the sin of adultery was issued and in 1567 the punishments for fornication were announced. Having dealt with these priorities, Sabbath observance was considered in 1579. Measures were taken to ensure strict Sunday observance, and breaches were to be dealt with by the church and the local town authorities - not, as previously, by the noblemen. All Sunday activities were curtailed: the worst offences were dancing, drinking and swearing, and all forms of work and labour were outlawed. The reformers were not only determined to stamp out the lax and cheerful Sundays of old, but they also targeted festivals and holidays - Christmas, Easter and ancient pagan holidays like Beltane (the first day of summer), New Year's Day and others. These holidays were made ordinary working days, thus preventing the traditional celebrations. Banning Sunday sport and reducing the number of holidays effectively prevented the ordinary people from playing sport at all.[1]

Sunday Observance

Each parish and town sought to enforce the Church's new rules. Edinburgh Town Council prohibited all games on Sundays, and the citizens were not to be seen at 'ony gamis within or without the toun upon the Sabbath day, sic as golf, airchery etc'. This campaign by the Edinburgh authorities was conducted in a single-minded way, and it may have had the effect of driving the players out of Edinburgh and down to Leith where the authorities were more tolerant.[2] The frequent mention of golf in these Sunday limitations reveals the popularity of the game among ordinary people: this game was not a minority sport of the privileged.[3]

Even in St Andrews, the Kirk Session took action against the Sunday golfers:

St. Andrews Kirk Session, Dec 18th 1583

This quilk [same] day, it was delatit [charged] that Alexander Milleris two sonis [sons] ar inobedient to him, and that thei, with Nicholl Mane, William Bruse and otheris, thair complices, playit in the golf fields Sonday last wes, tyme of fast and preching, aganis the ordinances of the kirk. The sessioun ordanis thame to be warnit and accusit theairof.[4]

This prosecution tells us much. It shows that golf at St Andrews in 1583 was popular and was sufficiently established for there to be an area known as the golf fields, certainly the links we know today, and mentioned in earlier statutes. The accused were young boys, the sons of a local citizen, and they had a group of golfing friends. Their play was in winter, in December, a season which, we will see later, was important for sport, and other 'Sunday golf' prosecutions confirm that the ordinary citizens of the Scottish towns played golf at this time. In Stirling an apprentice was accused of playing golf in the park on Sunday.[5] Apprentices were the poorest of all those at work, and were paid little or nothing. Yet they, like the St Andrews boys, played golf. There is no chance that they played golf with the expensive feathery balls and equipment of the nobility.

One noble golfer at St Andrews also made himself prominent at this time. The reformers of the new church claimed that the Earl of March had diverted the income of the local St Leonard's Parish Church, spending it liberally instead on 'goff, archerie and guid cheir'.[6]

Sunday Play

At first, the accusations of breach of Sunday observance involved play during the church service. The boy players mentioned above were out in the 'golf fields... tyme of fast and preiching'.[7] Play later on Sunday *after* the church service seemed permitted. But the regulations soon tightened, and action was taken also against golfers who were out 'eftir nune'.[8] In Aberdeen by 1604 the ban on sport had extended to the whole of Sunday, and even in smaller towns like Kinghorn in Fife the Sabbath ban was total by 1608. Even lax Leith had a total Sunday ban by 1610, when the South Leith records crisply announced that sport was outlawed 'fra morne to evin' on Sundays.[9] Even playing at the time of the mid-week Kirk Session meeting (the local management committee) was prohibited in St Andrews in 1599.[10]

Enforcement and Evasion

The protestant reformers' plans for a pious Sunday may have been difficult to enforce. The numerous prosecutions suggest that, far from being successful, the rules were regularly flouted. The ordinary people may have been out of sympathy with the fundamentalism of the leadership. Instead, the new Sabbatarianism may have forced the ordinary people to play their Sunday games away from the churchyard, moving to more distant areas where they might play without censure or detection. No-one would now risk play in the churchyard or streets on Sundays. Perhaps for this reason, ordinary golf and other sports of the humble migrated out of the town to the links outside. Only the coastal towns had such suitable adjacent playgrounds, and it was there that golf prospered. The short game of golf is no longer mentioned as played in the churchyard or streets: those caught playing golf were far from the churchyard.

Other noisy Scottish sports such as shinty or football were also easy targets for censure. The violence and drunkenness associated with these sports had always attracted critics, who now had powerful support from the Church. After the Reformation, these mass sports were severely discouraged. But dispersed, quiet small groups of golfers were less obvious and caused no nuisance, and this pressure towards discretion favoured individual, low-profile sports. This may have been a powerful factor in Scotland in changing the pattern of recreation in the Lowlands away from violent tribal confrontations towards personal, good-mannered games like golf.

Things get Better, then Worse

King James VI, King of Scotland also became King of England in 1603, changing his title to James VI and I. He moved from Scotland to London and made only an occasional return to his native land. But in

James VI of Scotland as a youth, holding a hawk, indicating his love of sport. By courtesy of the SCOTTISH NATIONAL PORTRAIT GALLERY.

John Knox's reformed Church brought in a stern Sunday observance, and a ban on all sport on that day.

1618 on his way back from one of these rare visits to Scotland he was sympathetic to complaints made to him in Scotland about the new strict Sunday observance:

'With our own ears' he said 'we have heard the complaint of our people that they were barred from all lawful recreation and exercise upon the Sunday afternoons after the ending of all divine service. For when shall the common people have leave to exercise if not upon the Sundayes and holydayes, seeing that they must apply their labour and winne their living in all working days?'[11]

The King was entering the delicate area of the relations between Church and State. He was King, but could not intervene on the issues in the province of the Church. He did hint at a compromise, and he clearly favoured a return to the original partial ban on Sunday sport - a ban only at the time of the church service. There is some evidence that relaxation did occur. But this did not last, and it may even have been seen in Scotland as English laxity. In December 1638, the Rev Robert Hamilton, a minister in the Scottish Borders was convicted, being

according to the English fashion, a prophaner of the Sabbath, provoking and countenancing his parishioners at dancing and playing at the football on that day.[12]

Events moved rapidly. The Covenanters and Cromwell then both restored the severity of Sunday observance in Scotland, banning once again all recreation and entertainment. The ancient non-Sunday holidays, such as Christmas, were again abolished and regulated by a new wave of puritanism. A diarist wrote of Christmas Day in Aberdeen in 1641:

Now this day no preaching nor such meitings with mirrieness, walking up and down; but contrair, this day commanded to be keped as ane work day... feasting and idlesett forbidden out of pulpits... the people wes otherwise inclined, but durst not disobey.[13]

The gloom had settled once more. And now there were two services and two sermons on Sundays, one in the morning and one in the afternoon; other activities were being squeezed out. But some of the citizens and even the clergy may have resisted the bans. In 1640, as an example to others, the assistant minister of a church at Dunbar was disciplined and disgraced 'for playing goufe' on a Sunday.[14] He may have been getting away with it before this. Shortly afterwards, in 1651, at Humbie - well inland in East Lothian - a church deacon was also deposed for playing golf on Sundays.[15]

These new edicts from the Church leaders were again perhaps only patchily observed and enforced: the Church, though strong, still had problems enforcing general rules. As the confused times of the 1600s continued, the ordinary people's inclinations resurfaced time and again. The Puritans were overthrown eventually and a less stern Sunday returned when the monarchy was restored, but the Kirk in Scotland was steadfastly against relaxation.

The Rules Relax

Church prosecutions eventually ceased by the 1700s. The last known such prosecution for Sunday golf was of John Dickson, the Leith innkeeper and clubmaker. In 1724, to his surprise, he was charged with giving food and assistance to some Sunday golfers.[16] He disingenuously suggested to the court that the men had been out only for a walk on Leith Links with some golf clubs under their arms. His plea reveals the new liberal mood in Scotland and suggests that the Church's rules were by now flouted widely. He was found guilty, and this was the last formal action in a period of 150 years of strict Sunday observance.

Sunday observance runs in a cyclical manner throughout Scottish history - a slow waxing and waning of tough rules on Sunday behaviour. Liberal in mediaeval times, attitudes became strict in the 1600s. Relaxation followed in the 1700s, but Sunday observance returned a century later in the late 1800s and lasted another 100 years until the 1950s, when Sunday sport slowly reappeared.

The Highlands

In the 1600s, the development of the Highlands diverged from that of the Lowlands, not for the first time. The Reformation had penetrated the Highlands only with difficulty, and failed to reach some parts of the north - including a part of the Outer Hebrides, which remains loyal to the Roman Catholic Church to this day. The Highlands retained the older style of Sunday even in the 1600s and traditional Sunday sports continued, in spite of the puritan revolution in the Lowlands. The cycle of liberalism to fundamentalism and back again was to operate thereafter in the Highlands, but with a different rhythm.

A Turbulent Period

It was a violent, turbulent world for Lowland noblemen. Scotland in the 1600s was wracked by internal feuds and religious wars. Mary, Queen of Scots was executed and Montrose was hanged, drawn and quartered; Charles II was tortured. Logan of Restalrig, a landowner and golfer, subjected his tenants at Leith to arbitrary harassment, torture and robbery.[17] John, Earl of Cromartie, one of the Foulis golfing clique at Leith, became Viscount Tarbat in 1684 and a Law Lord. Known as a 'convivial and entertaining companion', in 1691 he joined in a fight over a woman in a pub at Leith. In the melée, a man died.[18] Involving yourself in golf in the seventeenth century could even have hazards for the poor, and local justice could be harsh. In 1637 the Town Council of Banff, a town on the Moray Firth, recorded that 'ane boy of ane evill lyffe' was hanged for the theft (among other things) of 'some golf ballis, some of which he sauld to Thomas Urquartis'.[19]

Noble Golf in the 1600s

When the ordinary people left the churchyard and used the links instead for recreation, they joined the noble golfers already playing there. As we saw earlier, the King and nobles were habitual users of the links, playing there with their sophisticated equipment. In the 1600s there are further records of distinguished golfers out at play. The great Duke of Montrose deserves attention, not simply because he played, but because he seems to have played so seriously. Montrose's diaries show that he played golf on 9th November 1629 prior to his wedding the next day, and immediately after the ceremony he had another game of golf. On the ninth day after his wedding, he despatched a man to St Andrews for 'sax new clubs, dressing some auld anes and for balls'. In the next few days there were also payments for stabling a horse while 'my Lord was in Montrose at golf'.[20]

Early golf at St Andrews, showing three or four players, and caddies, in the late 1600s. The town is seen behind and the players are at about the present 16th hole. The clothes worn are cut-away jackets with breeches and cocked hats. The caddies have about six clubs each and all or almost all are woods.The painter is unknown.

By courtesy of the ROYAL AND ANCIENT GOLF CLUB, ST ANDREWS

Children of the nobility were also encouraged to play, and golf found approval at least with the University of Glasgow teachers who enacted in 1642 that the 'schollers be excercised in lawful games, such as gouffe, archerie and the lyk...' The sons of the Duke of Hamilton, a golfing family, attended the Glasgow Grammar School and were provided with golf equipment. James VI was fond of golf and played at Perth and Dunfermline. When he left Scotland after the Union of the Crowns in 1603, and went with his court to London, he started playing golf at Blackheath near London, and as a farewell present, James was given a set of two clubs by the Laird of Rosyth.[21] Other noble golfers were found in court circles at this time and from London, James sent back the Duke of York to rule in Scotland. The Duke took this tricky role seriously, and to ingratiate himself it is said that he became a regular member of the golfing cliques on Leith Links. On these links there was a famous match between the Duke of York and his partner - a humble Edinburgh shoemaker called John Patersone, said to be the best player in Scotland - and two English noblemen attached to this Scottish Court. As a shoemaker, i.e. cordiner, Patersone was probably also a ballmaker and caddie. Patersone, the famous story goes, built a house for himself with his winnings from the match, such was the level of the stakes.[22]

Noble Long Golf

How old was the noble, long game of the links? Was it the long game of golf played with a variety of clubs towards a series of holes, as in the modern game? The Scottish short churchyard golf and Dutch colf used only a single club. There is clear evidence that, by contrast, the early noble Scottish golfers used more than one club in their play. The Treasurer's accounts for King

James IV show that he bought a number of clubs in his single purchase from the bowmaker at Perth in 1502. Montrose also purchased clubs in 1629, six at a time, and it seems that a set of clubs was used among the gentry at least. When the much-disliked Bishop of Galloway was seized by a vision on the Leith Links (as described later) in 1603 he threw away his 'clubs', not 'club', before he fled from the links.[23]

There is also a clear description of the existence of different types of club in this period. A manuscript from the early 1600s contains the description of a set of four clubs and lists them as 'a bonker club, an irone club and twa play clubis'.[24] In 1636 an Aberdeen latin vocabulary lists the 'baculum ferreum' and translates it as 'bunker club'.[25] Later in the century a letter dated 1690 says that the writer 'does not doubt that his friend made good use of the putting club',[26] and Alexander Munro, a professor at St Andrews, wrote in 1691 to a friend sending him 'ane dozen of golfe balls and some clubs, viz ane play club, ane scraper, and ane tin-faced club'.[27] These players clearly played with a variety of clubs, and were probably playing a form of the modern game.

How long this long game had been established in Scotland is the most important question in the early history of golf, and it is likely that it preceded the King's interest in the game in the early 1500s.

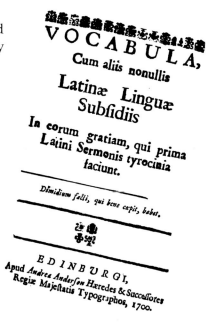

Wedderburn's Aberdeen *Vocabula* first published in 1636 used every-day phrases to teach latin, and included a section on golfing terms known to his young pupils at the Grammar School.

By courtesy of ABERDEEN UNIVERSITY LIBRARY

Clubs and Balls

About this time in the 1600s evidence emerges which shows that the expensive wooden clubs used for the long game did have a hybrid two-piece construction similar to the mediaeval professional bow. About 1650 a biographer said that

> the eminent [St Andrews] preacher Mr Blair is said to have illustrated the relations of our Lord to the Church by a homely simile drawn from the clubmakers art, the whipping and the glue which unite the head and the shaft.[28]

This analogy seems to have been familiar to his congregation, and it is the vital first evidence which shows that the clubmakers were, as thought earlier, making a composite club, joining a head and shaft with a splice, in which the wood of the head was selected for strength, and the wood of the shaft for flexibility. This joint was called 'scare' from the 'scarfed' joints used to mend broken masts of ships.

Clubmakers known in this period of the 1600s were Pett, Mill, Roddie and Thomas Comb.[29] These craftsmen were part of the crafts of the town, and they had many of the ancient customs and traditions of craft and guild life. Training was by apprenticeship: son followed father in the business.

The Golf Ball

The noble game had, for centuries, sought to develop clubs which would propel a ball further and further on the links. In the search for length, the hybrid clubs had evolved early, and the ball that flew furthest was also desired. If a clubmaker or ballmaker could devise a better club or ball, then the great and good of the land would seek him out. Neither the simple ball of the churchyard game, nor the inelastic shinty ball, nor the hair ball of the Low

Countries was ideal. Instead, trial, error and experiment seem to have produced a ball unique to Scotland, a leather ball stuffed with feathers. No other stick-and-ball game in any other country is known to have regularly used such a ball. Empirically, the Scottish players and craftsmen had evolved a ball which flew far, bounced and ran on. This ball was to last until about 1850 as the optimal and most satisfying golf ball for the game at its best. But it was very expensive. Not only was the feathery expensive, it lasted only for one round. On a rainy day, it became rapidly unusable: even wet grass would eventually dull its performance, and the cover of the ball, wet or dry, was easily split by a poor hit.

Ordinary golfers had to use other balls, and cheaper balls were available for those who were prepared to do with less, through poverty or lack of skill. An Edinburgh merchant's last will and testament in 1610 lists his holding of expensive balls, but also lists 'five score twell [twelve] flok goif ballis'.[30] This stock of 112 cheaper golf balls stuffed with wool or hair suggests that cheap golf balls were often available for purchase: the merchant's huge stock suggests they were popular.

Some other literary sources confirm that golf could be played at a variety of levels at this time according to the equipment used. Sir Patrick Waus wrote to a friend in 1585 asking him to 'remember to bring with yow ane dossen of commoun golf ballis' and in 1664, the exiled Rev John Carstairs wrote from Ireland to St Andrews to obtain 'a dussen and a halfe of good gouffe-balls' for a friend. These literary sources suggest that a variety of balls from 'common' to 'good' was available. Lastly, a description of the siege of Orkney states that the cannon balls of the besiegers were 'broken like golf balls, and cloven in two halves'.[31] A wooden ball would break in this way: a feathery would instead burst and extrude feathers.

Long and Short

With a range of balls available, the type desired had to be specified. Even the game played may then have been called 'long' or 'short' golf at this time. The Seafield correspondence in 1690 reveals James Ogilvie writing from Boyne Castle in Banffshire to his cousin at Cullen, also on the Moray Firth, who says:

Ife you have a mind for a touch at the long gauff tomorrow lett mee know this night wher I shall waitt on you with a second, or if yee would do me the honour to come this lenth, because the links ar better and we shall see ife ye cannot make better use of a club in this country then ye did at Eden. This is not that I doubt but ye made good use of your short putting club there.[32]

The ball, and to a lesser extent, the clubs, determined the level of play. Cheap balls and clubs meant short distances achieved and a short game. The best balls and best clubs attained length for a long game.

The Prices and Makers

The price of golf balls varied greatly, again suggesting that a range of balls was available for play. At the upper end of the market, the price of 5/-(shillings) appears repeatedly in the later 1600s. The Kincaid and Foulis diaries give this figure, as do the Montrose Accounts. The older Mackenzie

TWO STUDENTS

AT

ST. ANDREWS

1711-1716

Edited from the Delvine Papers
by
WILLIAM CROFT DICKINSON, D.Lit.

Published for the
University Court of the University of St Andrews

OLIVER AND BOYD
EDINBURGH: TWEEDDALE COURT
LONDON: 98 GREAT RUSSELL STREET, W.C.
1952

The Mackenzie family's student golf expenditure at St Andrews was recorded in their tutor's accounts.

student at St Andrews, mentioned below, played regularly with balls costing 4/-, and which lasted only one round. In the middle range for price came a 2/- ball used by the younger Mackenzie student. This ball also lasted only for one round and is also likely to have been a feathery. Its cheapness might have been the result of the use of cheaper feathers or simpler methods in manufacture. Perhaps they were reject balls, judged imperfect after production, or even repaired balls, discarded after play by wealthy owners.[33]

To compare the price of the best feathery at 5/- with other goods at this time, the Montrose Accounts mention that a chicken cost 8/-, and a chopin of claret (a quart - i.e. two pints or 1.14 litres) was 7/-, a sum which would also buy 1 pound of candles. But cheap balls, very cheap balls, are also noted. In 1676 the young son of the Marquis of Atholl sent back accounts from the University of Glasgow, and balls at 1 penny are included.[34]

Players went out with a number of balls ready for loss during play. In 1685 an estate mentions 'a leather pock with some gouff balls'. This suggests that featheries were taken out on a round in quantity in a bag perhaps to protect against the rain.[35]

Ballmakers and Family Firms

In the early 1600s, there was a family of ballmakers called Dickson (William and Thomas) working at Leith, and in 1632, the civil records of Leith contain the name of a John Dickson, who, when he married, gave his occupation as 'maker of golf balls'.[37] Also about this time, yet another (or the same) John Dickson of Leith was encouraged to settle in Aberdeen in 1642.[38] In 1643, at St Andrews, the Solemn League and Covenant was signed, and the names included a further Dickson - Andrew, a 'ballmaker'.[39]

In this short period of time in the 1600s, we therefore know of four ball-making Dicksons - William, Thomas, John and Andrew. Another Dickson, first name unknown, was said to be a forecaddie in the famous match between the Duke of York and two noblemen of the court in Scotland in 1681.[40]

This trail suggests strongly that a family of ballmaking Dicksons based on Leith existed in the 1600s. Perpetuation of skills through a family was the practice of the day, and these Dicksons may even have been the 'cordiners of Leith' involved in the dispute in 1554. The Dickson dynasty seem to have carried on into the next century, changing to clubmaking, since a son and grandson of John Dickson were traced later at Leith as clubmakers.

Another dynasty may have been the family of Paterson who were involved as ballmakers of Leith in the dispute in 1554.[41] A John Patersone was the ballmaker in Leith in 1681 who played in the celebrated golf match mentioned above.[42] However by the 1700s no Patersons are found in the lists of makers of clubs and balls.

Legends say that a poor Edinburgh caddie/shoemaker called Patersone played with the Duke of York in a match at Leith in 1681, and from the winnings of this aristocratic match he bought this tenement 'Golfer's Land' in Edinburgh.
From Clark's *Golf: A Royal and Ancient Game* 1875.

The Golfer's Land

globum. Arbiter, *a braundie.* Judices arbiter, Arbiter mihi
affentitur, Mihi addicit v&oriam, Incommodoceffit, *It hath
lucked ill with me,* Commodè hic lufus ceffit.

R E G U L U S,

BAculus, Pila calvaria, *a coulf ball.* Fovea, *a goat.* Percute
pilam baculo. Nimis curtàfti hunc miflow, *this is too fhort
a ftroke*

a ftroke, Pila tua devia eft, procul excuffifti pilam, *that is a good
ftroak,* ftatumina pilam arena, *Teay your ball on the fande* Statu-
men, *the teay,* Fruftra es, *that is a mifs,* Vel irritus hic conatus
eft, percute pilam fenfim, *give the ball but a little chap* Appo-
firè *that is very well.* Immiffa eft pila in foveam, *the ball is
goaled.* Quomodo eam hinc eliciam ? Cedo baculum ferreum,
det fee the bunkard club, J m iterum fruftra es, *this is the fecond
mifs.* Tertia quarta, &c Bene tibi ceffit hic i&u*, that is well
ftricken,* Malè tibi ceffit hic i&us. Huc rectà pilam dirige. Dirige rectà verfus foramen, *ftrike directly upon the hole.* Percute
pilam furium verfus. *ftrike up the hill.* Percute deorfum verfus, *ftrike down the hill.* An præterlapfa eft foramen. Factum
quod volui, I *would not wifh a better ftroak,* Immiffa eft in paludem, *it is in the mire.* Rectè evolavit, *It hath flowen directly
in.* Baculi caput, *the head of the club.* Baculi caulis, *the fhaft of
the club.* Baculi manubrium, *the handle where the wippen is.*
Bacul filum, *the wippen.*

N A V I S.

NAvis ad littus noftrum hac no&e appulfa eft: Tres hac
no&e naves ir wortus dela æ funt; Jam navis eft in portu, portus eft plen*·   ·*: Ex alto in portu tevchitur: E
portu in altum tv   ·*lwit è portu navis: Jam an-

Male tibi cessit hic ictus.
recta versus foramen —
Huc recta pilam dirige. Dirige
[The full rendering is *'This stroke has turned out badly*
for you. Aim the ball straight in this direction. Aim it
straight for the hole.']   29

strike directly upon the hole

Percute pilam sursum versus —
strike up the hill

Percute deorsum versus —
strike down the hill
[The Aberdeen links still have, to this day, broad sand
dunes and hillocks of some size.]

An præterlapsa est foramen. Factum quod volui —
I would not wish a better stroak
[A full translation of this is 'Can it have slipped past the
hole? It has turned out as I wanted'. This may describe
holing out in one.]

Immissa est in paludem —
it is in the mire

Balls from the Low Countries may have been cheaper. In 1618, a man called James Melville, quarter-master in the Earl of Morton's private army, managed to catch the attention of the King and convince him that too many golf balls were being imported into Scotland. Melville obtained a monopoly in his name, and his partner William Berwick was to be the maker. The King, who raised money by these monopolies, rationalised this award by saying that it would bring down the cost of balls and discourage imports. It is doubtful if the monopoly was enforceable, and the effect seemed to be that Melville was also entitled to tax other golf-ball makers. Eleven years later, in 1629, Dickson of Leith complained that Melville was claiming a tax on every ball made in Scotland. Melville had sent round some thugs to Dickson's house, and took away balls which were ready for the King's use, so Dickson said in evidence.

This murky episode was decided in the courts against Melville and his monopoly, and he had to repay £5 for the nineteen stolen balls, i.e. about 5/- each, confirming the earlier price estimate for the best balls in the 1600s.[43]

The Holes

Proof that aristocratic Scottish golfers were playing the long game we know now prior to 1500 is lacking. All we have is the suggestive evidence that these noble players had sets of expensive jointed clubs and used a sophisticated ball which travelled far. Golf is a game of a series of holes and no early evidence of this exists. But in the early 1600s, shortly after the Reformation, we have the first partial descriptions of play on the links.

In Aberdeen in 1625 the local records mention the military exercises 'in the principal parts of the links betwixt the first hole and the Quenis Hole'.[45] The use of the word 'hole' gives joy to the golf historian - surely here in 1625 is direct evidence of the game of golf as a series of holes on the links. But some caution is required: the word 'hole' may simply have meant sand-pit, or quarry. About this time also there are some documents and two important diaries from Aberdeen which partly satisfy our curiosity about how the early long game was played. The first source is a grammar school teacher's textbook - Wedderburn's *Vocabula* – published about 1636.[46] The book was written to help his reluctant, but well-off, students in their classical studies by the familiar device of using latin words and phrases for everyday events. Wedderburn used golf to illustrate his teaching of latin, and the golf section of the book not only gives us much valuable information on the game, but also shows that his young grammar school pupils were keen players, keen enough to understand golf jargon. From the text, much emerges about the game. It is clear that the players teed up the ball on sand to play their first shot, and the text mentions sliced shots, missed putts, and balls in bunkers. This is our modern game with a variety of skills, playing to a hole, and even the use of iron clubs to recover from bunkers is described, and they played a series of holes. Here in 1636, we have, for the first time, definite evidence of the game in its modern form, on the Aberdeen links, and played by the grammar school boys. They were not the first players of the long game with many holes; they are the first known to us.

Golfing Routine

Day-to-day golf in the later 1600s can be studied in half-a-dozen diaries and account books of the times. Starting in 1671, Sir John Foulis, a sportsman and owner of Ravelston, an estate near Edinburgh, kept a diary and careful financial accounts.[47] He travelled regularly to Leith to meet up with his cronies and play golf, one of his many sports. He recorded his daily expenditure, and we can work out a little of his golfing routine. His outings were entirely in November, December and February. The clique met usually on Saturdays but sometimes on Mondays, and only in winter. He paid 10/- for the return journey coach fare from Edinburgh to Leith, and spent money mostly on new balls and clubs, replacing those broken or worn out, and he had dinner at Leith after golf with his friends. He lost money on bets, sometimes heavily. He paid 2/- for a caddie, and on one occasion hired a set of three golf clubs. One visit to play at Musselburgh rather than Leith is mentioned and there he played with his friend 'Gosford' from the estate nearby. This is the first hint that, at this time, Musselburgh also had a reputation for fine golf links.

Another diary from this century is of interest. It is the diary of Thomas Kincaid, an Edinburgh medical student, who recorded his introversions as he tutored himself on golf and medicine. The diary gives us further evidence on the play at Leith, but at a humbler level than Foulis.[48] Oddly, Kincaid preferred Mondays for his game, but much of the rest of his routine confirms the Foulis pattern. Kincaid's diary confirms the coach price of 10/-, but adds that it was cheaper if the coach was shared with others. Kincaid sought the perfect golf swing and struggled to master 'pathologie'. He entered this advice to himself in his diary:

1687 February 9. I rose at 7. I thought upon the method of pathologie and in playing the golve, I found that in all motions of your arms ye most contract your fingers verie strait...

Foulis's account books from 1671, showing numerous golf and sporting entries.

By courtesy of the NATIONAL LIBRARY OF SCOTLAND, MS 6154.

He paid the same price for balls as had Foulis, at an Edinburgh pub, and the same fee for a caddie - a 'boy'. Kincaid names the Leith pubs used by the golfers as Captain Brown's and Rose's. At Leith they played golf until 5pm on a February day. He visited a pub in Leith for dinner, then another in Edinburgh, where they had 'collips' (i.e. meat), and he was sick afterwards.

Kincaid repaired his own clubs and added horn insets to the heads, probably on the sole. He gives us our first direct description of a handicapping system, meditating on the best way to make a match equal.

Crowded Links

Another historical fragment from about the same time shows that the links at Leith were busy. Sir Robert Sibbald, the great Scottish physician, whose autobiography was so much admired by Samuel Johnston ('the plainest account any man gave of himself') was visiting a patient in Leith in 1690:

> *I was coming from Sir Robert Milne his house in Leith where I had been visiting... as I was going downe to passe the ditch to goe to the links wher I left some company playing at goufe, and my servant following me, neither he, nor I nor the boy adverting, I was strucken by a boy (said to be Captain Taylor his son) of fourteen or fyfteen years, with the back of the club with much force betwixt the eyes, at the root of the nose... I bled much and took a coach and came up [to Edinburgh].*[49]

Sibbald's famous clarity of exposition confirms the popularity of Leith golf with his friends from Edinburgh, and with the impecunious youth of Leith. The golf links were crowded and busy: busy enough for a pedestrian to be hit by a teenager's practice swing. The distinguished physician could have easily avoided solitary players.

"*Even at his paſtime.*"—Ibid. line 3 from bottom.

Within a day or two after this, being at his paſtime* (for he loved that all his lifetyme verie much, ſo that that part of the Biſchops' Verſes, "*Ludos Gallowa*,"* is his ſhare) in the Linkes of Leith, he wes terrified with a viſion, or ane apprehenſion; for he ſaid to his play-fellows, after he had, in ane affrighted and commoved way, caſt away his play-inſtruments, (*arma campeſtria*,) "I vow to be about with thoſe two men quho hes now come vpon me with drawen ſwords!" When his play-fellowes replyed, "My Lord, it is a dreame! We ſaw no ſuch thing; theſe men have bein inviſible." He wes ſilent, went home trembling, tooke bed inſtantlie, and died, not giving any token of repentance for that wicked courſe he had embraced.—It ſeemes he hath died in a fitt of deſpaire; but, *raro vidi Clericum penitentem* is not ſo old as true.

Biſchop of Galloway.

1608.
Terrified in a viſion.

Died impenitent.
In deſpaire.

The disliked Bishop of Galloway's panic attack while at golf on the Links of Leith in 1608, from Rowe *Historie of the Kirk in Scotland* 1842.

Another Scottish professional man who enjoyed playing at Leith at this time was the Bishop of Galloway. In this troubled period, Scotland had, for a while, an imposed system of bishops. This liberal Bishop, like others, was famous for his love of sport, but in his controversial position he was subject to panic attacks. One day while at golf at Leith, his critics recalled

he was terrified with a vision, or ane apprehension; for he said to his play-fellows, after he had in a frightened and commoved way, cast away his play-instruments, 'I vow to be about with those two men who have now come upon me with drawen swords'. When his two play-fellowes replyed 'My Lord it is a dreame: we saw no such thing; these men have been invisible.' He was silent, went home trembling, tooke to bed instantlie and died, not giving any token of repentance for that wicked course he had embraced...[i.e. becoming a Bishop in Scotland].[50]

All these literary accounts confirm that Leith was a busy golfing area.

Student Golf at St Andrews

Yet more information about golf emerges towards the end of the century and the beginning of the next, notably from the diaries and accounts from

Pages from the Mackenzie family students' accounts from St Andrews University in 1712.

By courtesy of the NATIONAL LIBRARY OF SCOTLAND M5 1480.

1712-15 of some St Andrews students. The boys were sons of Mackenzie, the Laird of Delvine. He had an older son and younger twins, and all attended St Andrews University. From there, their private tutor sent back details to their father of their expenditure, and the invoices give clear evidence of a variety of clubs and balls available, according to the skill and budget of the player.[51]

The older son played well and was allowed expensive feathery balls at 4/- and three clubs at 12/- each. This 1:3 ratio in cost of good club to feathery was unchanged from mediaeval times. The accounts show that these expensive clubs lasted on average only ten rounds before breaking. The feathery balls were discarded after only one round.

But the younger twins were given only one cheaper club each at 7/- and these proved more durable than the 12/- club, but doubtless were less effective. The boys also played with a cheaper ball at 2/-, half the cost of their older brother's ball. It was clearly a feathery, a cheap feathery, or even a hair ball. All the clubs were repaired regularly and the horn insets on the sole were replaced frequently, since this horn edge protected the club during play on the rough links. These privileged students also took part in archery. St Andrews University had an annual silver arrow archery competition and one of the twins won the trophy.

There is more than a hint in the letters and accounts that golf was a useful accomplishment for these young men from wealthy backgrounds. If they entered into the professions, Edinburgh would be their base: in the capital of Scotland, golf was a social asset.

ACCOUNTS 1713			lib s d	lib s d
			Alexander	K & Th
September	2nd	for 2 balls to K & Th	—	04 00
	8th	for a ball to Alexr	04 00	—
		for a Clubshaft to K	—	04 00
	9th	for 2 balls to K & Th	—	04 00
	13th	for 2 balls to K & Th	—	04 00
October	14th	for 2 balls to Alexr 8s/and one to K: 2s	08 00	02 00
	21th	for 2 balls to Alexr	08 00	—
	26th	for a ball to Th	—	02 00
	29th	for a ball to Alexr 4s/ & for 2 to		
		K & Th 4s	04 00	04 00
February	1714			
	2nd	for 2 balls		04 00
	9th	for 2 balls		04 00

A summary of the entries for golf clubs and balls purchased by the Mackenzie students: from David Hamilton *Early Golf at St Andrews* 1989.

The North

Golf at Leith and St Andrews was popular, but golf was played at numerous other places. In Orkney some soldiers stole golf balls from a shop in 1614, suggesting there was a local demand for balls.[52] At Dornoch the links were admired in 1616 as 'fitt for Archery, golfing, ryding and all other excercise; they doe surpasse the fields of Montrose or St Andrews'.[53] This shows indirectly that Montrose was highly esteemed at that time by experienced players. At Kinghorn in Fife there was a prosecution of Sunday players[54] and also at Dunbar.[55]

In particular, the enthusiasm along the Moray Firth, from Inverness to Fraserburgh, should be noted, showing the vitality of Scottish golf in many places before any golf club was formed: formal clubs did not emerge on the Moray Firth until 200 years later. At Elgin a ballmaker was mentioned in 1649,[56] and at Banff, a little along the Moray Firth, some golf balls were stolen in 1637.[57] There was a prohibition on Sunday golf at Fraserburgh in 1613,[58] and golf was noted at a spa at Burghead near Elgin in 1672. A visitor there was first to record the addictive qualities of golf:

> I was this night at Burgi. Mr Colin Falconer [Episcopal Bishop at Forres] drank
> wi me and we recreated the bodi at Golf... Lord let this be no snar[e] to me.[59]

This is a remarkable list of golf activity, considering the poverty of the records surviving from those times. It suggests that the lure of golf was indeed a snare to the inhabitants of the entire east coast of Scotland in the 1600s.[60] In studying the surviving local records from this period, golf is quite commonly mentioned.[61]

Summer and Winter

Of particular interest is that in the 1600s, and earlier, golf was a winter game, not a summer sport. Study of the diaries of this period shows, with remarkable consistency, that play was almost entirely in winter. The medical student Kincaid's trips to Leith were in January, and all Foulis' games with his Leith friends were between November and February. In the previous century even Mary, Queen of Scots' single recorded game was in February 1567. Of King James IV's five recorded outings, four were in winter months. But the most convincing evidence for winter golf comes from the many prosecutions for Sabbath-breaking by golfers. Invariably these show winter play, usually in December and January.

This unexpected seasonal reversal of participation in sport make sense when the needs of the agricultural society are understood; *winter* was the time of leisure. In this pre-industrial society the people in summer tended their crops, took in the harvest and fattened their animals; they were too busy to spend time at sport, even with the long daylight hours of summer available. The harvest was of crucial importance, and dominated the yearly calendar. If the harvest failed, a difficult winter followed. If a second crop failure occurred, then famine and disease could and did result.

The Seasons

The agricultural year started then, as it does now, with planting and lambing in spring; thereafter, work quickens until the serious business of harvest time and the race to get the harvest in before the weather deteriorated. Harvest is followed by ploughing, and in ancient times by the necessary slaughtering of animals, not only to give winter food, but also to save on scarce fodder. Thereafter outdoor work was not possible in the cold winter, and the land was wet and heavy: wheeled carts could not be used. Winter was a time of low activity for farmers.

Fishing communities also were inactive in winter. Their busy season was the summer, when better weather, calmer seas and the longer hours let them seek the fish stocks and earn a living. The early industries - bleaching and dyeing - were also seasonal and discouraged by the cold damp of winter. Even war was a summer activity; armies moved by foot at this time and their supply vehicles and armaments followed by road. In winter, hostilities ceased, armies were disbanded, and the soldiers and gentlemen officers had returned home and had time on their hands.

Winter was accordingly a time of leisure. Farming and fishing came to an end, and only essential travel was attempted. Military campaigns were temporarily halted. But the turf on the sandy links remained in good condition in the Scottish winter. Rain, though common, drained quickly from the links, and snow and ice were and are uncommon at the Scottish coast in winter, protected by the warming effect of the North Sea and the Gulf Stream current. In winter, the links were temporarily free of the clutter caused by other summer users - grazing animals, soldiers on excercise, fishermen drying nets and those bleaching cloth. Wheeled vehicles were less common on the links in winter and travelling fairs did not appear. Everything encouraged winter sport in general and golf in particular, on the short smooth winter grass.

Even those who might wish to play in summer faced a surprising difficulty. In summer, the links might be used for growing grass, a valuable crop auctioned off by the towns.

The Weather

One of the unsolved mysteries about early golf is whether or not the golfers played in rain. The clothes of the winter golfers were thick but not waterproof and little other protection was available. Were our early golfers daunted or undaunted by the winter weather? The evidence suggests that they probably did not venture out - but not because of their clothing. The problem was the feathery ball, which rapidly deteriorated in wet conditions, losing performance and bursting easily. Such was the vulnerability and expense of the featheries, that golf in the rain was probably not contemplated.[62] However, this is nowhere explicitly stated. The only hint about weather is one remark later from Smollett, who qualifies his description of golf at Leith by saying that it only took place 'when the weather permits'.[63] This hardly solves the mystery. However, it should be noted that the rainfall on the east coast of Scotland in winter is remarkably low, and about one quarter that of the west coast. Edinburgh and St Andrews had cold but dry winters, entirely suitable for golf.

East and West

In this early period, golf seems more common on the east coast of Scotland than on the west. This geographical difference remains a puzzle, since both

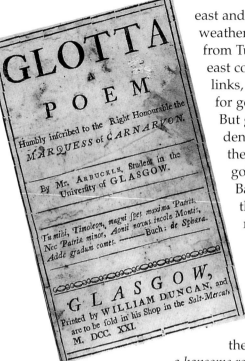

Frontispiece to the Glasgow poem *Glotta* by Thomas Arbuckle in 1721, largely about the Clyde, but mentioning golf on Glasgow Green, well before the foundation of the first club in Glasgow. By courtesy of the MITCHELL LIBRARY.

east and west have the same coastal terrain, and the west has warmer weather, notably in winter, the season for early golf. The west coast links from Turnberry through Prestwick to Ayr and Troon, are as good as the east coast terrain. Further north, on the west coast, are vast expanses of links, machair and dunes, suitable and largely unused then and since for golf.

But golf was not absent from the west coast of Scotland. Well-off students at the University of Glasgow had used Glasgow Green for their sport, including golf, from earliest times.[64] We know there was golf in early times in Ayrshire, since in the late 1500s the Laird of Bargany had his nose broken by 'ane straik of ane goiff-ball, on the hills of Air in reklesnes' and there is a local tradition that a monk at Crossraguel Abbey played a grudge match against the Laird of Culzean, the stake being the monk's nose, and that the match was played on the 'linkes at Ayre'. Other play was noted on the 'linkis callit the grene of Ardstinchell', later known as Ballantrae, south of Turnberry, and natural links for golf. It was from Ayrshire that the landowners Hamilton and Montgomery went out to Ulster in 1603, taking golf with them. And in 1723 a document describes the town of Ayr as

a hansome royall brugh and place of trade beautified with pleasant greens, to the east and west wher hore [horse] courses are run playing at goufe and severall other manlie divertisements'.[65]

But there is no doubt that golf in early Scotland was markedly an east coast game.

Edinburgh in Winter

It might be thought that the east coast's ancient links with Holland gave golf an early impetus there, but another explanation exists. The main reason for the east coast's involvement in golf (and the apparent lack of interest in the west) is that in winter, the golfing season, there was a migration of landowners from the rest of Scotland to Edinburgh.[66] Literary sources show that from the 1600s onwards, the Edinburgh capital attracted these men in winter, once their crucial harvest was gathered in. First they settled their sons to university - often St Andrews. In 1717, for instance, the University of St Andrews decided to start the term on 20th October 'so that gentlemen who had legal business in Edinburgh would be able to put their children to college beforehand'. In Edinburgh the gentlemen sought help for their financial affairs, and indulged in another favourite pastime - litigation. Chambers *Traditions of Edinburgh* said of Edinburgh at the time

it had no [royal] court, no factories, no commerce; but there was a nest of lawyers in it, attending on the Court of Session; and a considerable number of gentry gave it the benefit of their presence in winter.

The migrants enjoyed Edinburgh's convivial winter. The houses were smaller and warmer than their country houses, and entertainment and company were at hand. In Edinburgh they joined the company of talented merchants, lawyers, teachers and doctors at a time when Edinburgh was increasingly confident and successful and much admired in Europe.

And Leith was at hand. Leith was a wealthy, cosmopolitan port serving Scotland's trade with Europe. The lifestyle of the Leith merchants, and their wine cellars, were much admired by the Edinburgh citizens. Leith was self-confident and independent, and made its own rules. Only two miles separated the capital from its port, and Scotland's first 'haikney coatch', which took Foulis and Kincaid down to play at Leith Links, served the Edinburgh to Leith route from 1660. Many of the wealthy winter migrants enjoyed golf and travelled to Leith with their cronies for a sociable sporting gathering, where the winter coastal weather favoured golf.

After the harvest was in, the landowners left for Edinburgh and perhaps autumn was their *first* big gathering of the Edinburgh season: there is some evidence that their spring meeting in March was the *last* golf gathering before they returned home. Back at their estates in the west coast, and even in Ayrshire, East Lothian and Fife, golf was forgotten for the summer.

In the west the humble players had no gentlemen summer golfers as exemplars; and in winter the gentlemen players were absent in Edinburgh. Little humble golf can be detected in the west at this time.

Scotland and Ireland

As early as 1606 we have the first evidence of something the Scots were to do so successfully later - export golf. James VI and I had taken the game to London, and thereafter there are scattered but persistent references to royal and other golf in London at Vincent Square (Upfields) and Spittle Fields. From this time on Scottish travellers took the game with them wherever they went,

Charles I hears of the Irish rebellion while on Leith Links in 1641.

and they played if weather and terrain permitted. The Scots travelled throughout the world, and even at this early date within this Scottish diaspora, there were little cliques of golfers including some enthusiasts in Ireland and London.

In 1606, King James encouraged Scottish 'plantations' in Northern Ireland as a deliberate encouragement of Protestant emigration, luring suitable persons with a generous allocation of land. Two noblemen from Ayrshire were already there - Hamilton and Montgomery - in 1603.[67] A historian of the time recorded that:

> *His Lordship (Montgomery) also built the quay or harbour at Donaghadee (in County Down on the east coast of Ireland), a great and profitable work, for public and private benefit, and built a great school at Newton, endowing it, as I am creditably told, with twenty pounds yearly salary, for a Master of Arts, to teach Latin, Greek and Logycks, allowing the scholars a green for recreation at golf, football and archery.*

The game had reached Northern Ireland, or perhaps could be said to have returned to Ireland. The Montgomery estate was devastated by the Irish Rebellion of 1641, and curiously enough, Charles I heard the news of this rebellion while he was at golf on Leith Links.[68]

Transient Interest

The game did not take root and grow thereafter in these distant sites. Instead, when the Scots moved on, the game disappeared; the time was not yet ripe for golf to survive independently, unless Scotsmen were present. But one notable group of emigrant Scots did not play, as far as we know. In the 1600s, large numbers of Scottish students travelled for further study to the Low Countries. In particular they were drawn to study medicine at Leyden during the winter terms under the great teacher Boerhaave. Like the Edinburgh student Kincaid, many of them would have been golfers. Very good records and many diaries survive from this Leyden link, but there is no description of stick-and-ball games played by these visitors at Leyden or elsewhere. This finding strengthens the idea that the game of the Low Countries was not a long game of the open links, but a street game, unattractive to Scottish visitors, and that these visitors did not find conditions suitable for their long winter game of the links as at home.

Golf Emerges

By the end of this period, from the Reformation to 1700, we have only this dim and incomplete understanding of golf in early Scotland. The short game of the churchyard in inland Scotland was dying out, as was colf in Holland. An increasing number of documents show that the gentry, professional men and merchants were playing the long game on the east coast Scottish links with elegant clubs and feather balls.

This increasingly popular long game of golf was to flourish in the 1700s, and the first golfing societies emerged. No other European stick-and-ball game survived beyond the mid-1600s as part of national life. But in Scotland, 'long' golf prospered and took on most of its modern features in Enlightenment Scotland, a golden era of Scottish life and letters.

FURTHER READING

The numbered text references are given at the end of the book.

Early secondary works are Robert Clark *Golf: A Royal and Ancient Game* Edinburgh 1875, Robert Browning *A History of Golf* London 1955, Bernard Darwin (and others) *A History of Golf in Britain* London 1952 and I. T. Henderson and D. Stirk *Golf in the Making* Crawley 1979. For an illustrated account of early Scottish sources on golf see Olive M. Geddes *A Swing Through Time* Edinburgh 1992. The documents of the period are examined in Alastair J. Johnston and James Johnston *The Chronicles of Golf* Cleveland 1993; see also David Hamilton *Early Golf in Glasgow* Oxford 1985, David Hamilton *Early Aberdeen Golf* Glasgow 1988, David Hamilton *Early Golf at St Andrews* Glasgow and Oban 1989 and David Hamilton *Early Golf at Edinburgh and Leith* Glasgow 1990. For comments on the early Scottish golf links see Geoffrey Cornish and Ronald Whitten *The Golf Course* Leicester 1981. Few golf club histories add to knowledge of early golf in their area, but see R. C. Brownlee *Dunbar Golf Club: a Short History 1794-1980* Dunbar 1980. For curling history see David B. Smith *Curling: An Illustrated History* Edinburgh 1981.

Sunday observance and sport are discussed in T. C. Smout *A History of the Scottish People 1560-1830* Glasgow 1969.

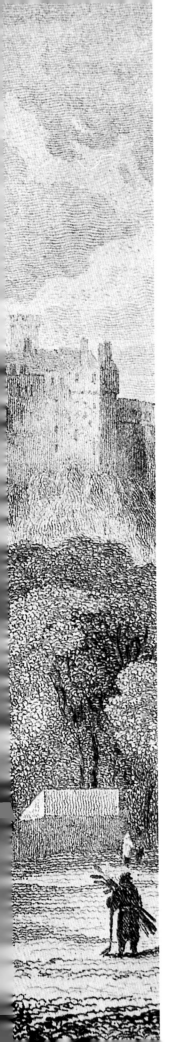

CHAPTER FOUR

TRANQUIL TIMES

The eighteenth century was a period in Scotland's history without parallel before or since. It was tranquil, self-confident and successful. The religious strifes of the 1600s were rapidly put aside, and violence, civil and personal, almost disappeared. Instead, Scotland became dominant in Europe in matters of learning and the arts. Scottish philosophers, chemists, doctors and engineers pioneered the new learning: her painters, poets, writers and architects were widely admired.[1] And the economy blossomed, after a delay. The Union of Parliaments in 1707 meant that Scotland could now venture into the former English colonies, and the merchants of Scotland's west coast were not slow to take up the advantages of their geographical position in opening up trade with the Americas and elsewhere. And where the Scots went, they took golf with them.

In this period of progress and optimism, the disorders of the 1600s were replaced by order and conviviality. The golf clubs and their cheerful camaraderie were but one part of this liberal society which respected the law, and it was natural for the golfers, for the first time, to draw up regulations for conduct, both when at play and in company. Because the golfing societies kept written records, we know much more about golf and golfers, the state of the links, and day-to-day play.

OPPOSITE: Edinburgh Castle from Bruntsfield Links. Edinburgh's eighteenth century was illustrious and tranquil, and it was in Edinburgh and Leith that the world's first golf clubs were formed.
By courtesy of EDINBURGH PUBLIC LIBRARY.

Scotland's Progress

The political events leading to these events in Scotland were initially unpromising. The King had left Scotland in 1603, hardly to return, and the Union of Parliaments in 1707 had taken away from Scotland a powerful cadre of aristocrats, the normal patrons of important activities. After the Union, the country continued to be poor, and the town of Edinburgh in particular was in decline. Even the military garrison was withdrawn from the capital.

In an attempt to try to fill this cultural and political void, local initiatives were proposed: some of these succeeded beyond any reasonable expectation. Local leaders in Edinburgh fostered a medical school which became well known: the town's support for sporting meetings at archery and golf at Leith had a similar impact. In place of the missing aristocracy, a group of talented professionals had taken the initiatives, and led Scotland into a central role in European culture. Edinburgh became the 'Athens of the North'.

Leisure was taken seriously and indulged in unselfconsciously. The Union had brought peace: 'golf not war' was the theme of the poem *The Goff* of 1743. Scotland made her own rules in much of the business of life, and when at play. The citizens ate and drank well, they set up clubs and societies of distinction, and they played golf.

Life was simply more pleasant. Life expectancy rose, and the epidemics of the 1600s had disappeared. During the plague visitations of the 1600s, the Burgh Muir in Edinburgh (Bruntsfield Links) was a place of burial, and in the next century, the links at St Andrews were also used in 1832 for this melancholy purpose. But in the tranquil 1700s the links were undisturbed by mass burials. Food was rarely scarce, and distribution of food by road during dearths had improved. The road system was expanded to deal with Jacobite Highland risings, and ancient tracks gave place to the first turnpike roads. The first link of this new road system reached out from Edinburgh to Cupar and on to Perth. From Cupar, then the most important town in Fife, a network of lesser turnpikes radiated out, including one to St Andrews.[2]

It was even possible that the weather was better in the 1700s. Preceding this century, geographers have described a 'Little Ice Age' from 1500-1700, and in this illustrious century winter, the season for golf, may have been more kindly.

The Sportsmen

The mood of the times is caught in a remark in Dr Alexander Carlyle's *Autobiography*. Born in 1722, this distinguished Scottish minister of religion (and golfer) knew of the old strict days but had lived into this liberal period. He wrote with amusement of the constraints on previous generations of ministers, notably the attitudes of the famous preachers Drs Robertson and Blair (born circa 1600). In their time, Carlyle remarked

> *...the common people thought to play with cards or dice was a sin, and everyone thought it an indecorum in a clergyman... they [Blair and Robertson] could neither of them play at golf or bowls and far less at cards or backgammon. This made them unhappy in their friends' houses in rainy weather.*

Carlyle's generation was different. In the 1700s, clergymen could and did play sport and join in the conviviality. Nothing characterises this period of the

Enlightenment more clearly than the new attitudes to Sunday sport, which was actively banned in the previous century. But in the 1700s there were no such rules: a sensible personal code of conduct had been substituted. Historians have concluded that 'for most of the century, private sport was common on Sunday in most of the country. But *spectator* sports avoided Sundays.'[3]

The Highlands

In the Highlands of Scotland, as noted earlier, a paradox continued. The Reformation failed to reach the Highlands, and a relaxed attitude to Sundays in general, and sporting Sundays in particular, had been normal and had persisted from mediaeval times into the 1700s. Sunday gatherings, particularly for shinty, had carried on through the 1600s as if Knox and his Lowland movement had not existed. But in the 1700s the new *literati* in the Lowlands concluded that the highlanders, supporters of Prince Charles, with their own religion and language, were hostile to the new order and an embarrassment to the newly patriotic and sophisticated Lowlanders. The Highlands were to be disciplined and evangelised. The Society for the Propagation of Christian Knowledge set forth to bring the Reformation, at last, to the Gaels in the north. Some missionary ministers tried to introduce prosecutions against Sabbath-breaking, familiar to, but declining in, the Lowlands. A new minister in Speyside in 1747 was only supported on the locals' own terms:

> For hours before public worship began, the young men of the parish met and played shinty before the arrival of the clergyman, who, nolens volens, was compelled to join the players, otherwise he was given to understand that he would have to preach to empty benches. So, after a hail or two, the shinty clubs were thrown aside, and a large congregation met to hear the new doctrine...
> Immediately the services were over, shinty was resumed, and carried on until darkness put an end to their amusements, when many retired to neighbouring crofts and public houses...[4]

Thus the Highland Sunday continued much as before. It was not until the next century that puritan fundamentalists there were to gain control, and the Highlands became identified with strict Sunday observance through to the twentieth century.

The Lowland Game of Golf

Why did this stick-and-ball game of golf prosper in Scotland alone, while other stick-and-ball games in Europe faded out? It is remarkable that every other game with any kinship to golf - colf, chole and cambuca - all declined elsewhere after about 1650. A number of factors were involved and the finding that golf was a winter game is important. The Scottish towns and cities, notably Edinburgh and St Andrews, were on the coast and close to suitable links which had excellent turf in winter. In Europe and England the main towns were largely inland, and in their severe winters the play areas became muddy spaces in the town. The Scottish coastal climate, the winter golfing season and the position on the coast of important towns like Edinburgh and St Andrews with distinguished winter inhabitants are vital parts of the explanation of this important historical question.

From 1700 onwards, nothing more is heard in the Lowlands of golf in churchyards or on the long grass of the parks. Golf from now on was played entirely on the coastal links or at a few suitable, similar inland places. These early golf courses were not designed; they just grew. No-one marked out the holes at St Andrews or Musselburgh or North Berwick. Earth was not moved in quantity and no plan was made. The subtleties arose over centuries, as generations of players adjusted the layout to pose challenges appropriate to their skills and their equipment. The courses were malleable, and nothing was sacred; if clubs and balls and players changed, so did the layout.[5]

Holes, Names and Numbers

The records show that on the early golf links a variable number of holes made up a round. At Leith Links there were never more than five holes and this circuit was played at least three times in a serious game. At early St Andrews there were twelve holes, and the players played to the same hole going out and coming back, making 22 holes played in all. At Musselburgh there were initially six and eventually nine holes. At Aberdeen there were five, but 13 at Montrose, and North Berwick had seven. Only later did St Andrews settle on an 18-hole round and this was later copied throughout the world - except at a few Scottish courses of independent outlook. Well-defined greens did not exist in early golf and it is likely that the holes were cut in favourable areas of the links, where the ground was flatter or in a green hollow where the grass was optimal for putting. There were early experiments with artificial, durable holes, since some blocks of stone with holes suggestive of golf holes have been found at the golf links at Rosehearty and Fraserburgh, of uncertain age.[6]

The early holes of the golf courses were sometimes named or numbered, with the usual 'first hole', 'second hole' etc but if a name was used it tended to be taken from the hole (in the ground) just played *from*.[7] At Leith the first hole was called the 'Thorn Tree Hole' not because this tree was at the first green played to, but because this famous tree was found near the hole beside which play started. Leith had a curious supernumerary hole which was the first played in any first circuit of the five holes, but not in subsequent rounds. This may have been a device to prevent a cluster of newly arrived players gathering beside the final hole (in the ground), and to which players were also approaching. Prestwick's original course may also have had a short practice hole to start the round.

Golf's Supporters

It was to the links that the gentlemen and the humble citizens increasingly resorted for their golf in the 1700s. There they mixed fairly amicably with the other users, but because of the involvement in the game by the gentry, golf on the links had powerful local support. In 1726, for instance, the Town Council in St Andrews gave William Gibb a licence to raise rabbits on the wider links, but the links were 'not to be spoiled where the golf is used'.[8] Later at St Andrews in 1769, 'after examining old men', the traditional permitted route of golf play through the wider Pilmour Links was marked out by march stones (still to be found on the Old Course) to preserve the turf there 'from pasturing

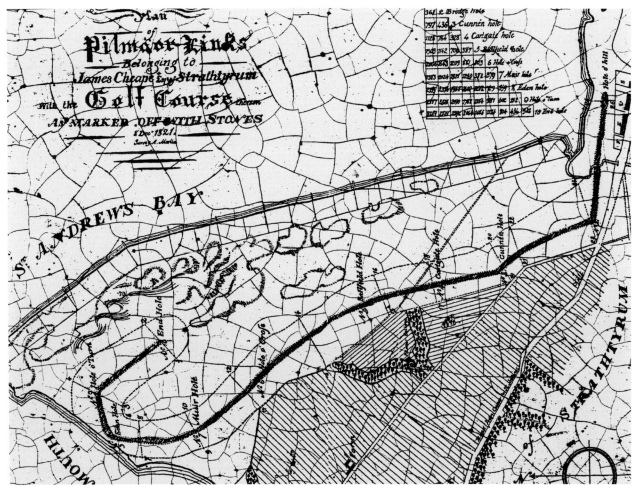

or cutting up for divots'.[9] In 1695 the Edinburgh authorities allowed some quarries to be dug at the Burgh Muir (now Bruntsfield Links), with the proviso that they were not to disturb 'the playing of golf'.[10] In 1797 the Nairn Town Council allowed the growing and sale of the grass on the links, with the condition that such a project 'shall not prohibit the gentlemen of the town or others from playing golf on the whole links at pleasure'. In 1770 the Marquis of Lorne reviewed the Earl of Albermarle's regiment of dragoons at Musselburgh Links, and then went on to review the 22nd Regiment at Leith Links. Afterwards his officers were 'elegantly entertained in the new Golf House'.[11] The public golf links had many users: some of them were golfers with political influence, and they defended recreational use of this land.

Golf was, and is, a dangerous sport for players and others using the links. Play in public places needed the tolerance of local citizens, and in Scotland this was given, based on traditional use of the links for golf by many. The assumption in Scotland was that the onus was on those on the links to avoid being hurt, particularly if a warning shout was given. This assumption was not shared later when golf spread elsewhere. In vain the golfing pioneers in England and America cited the Scottish tradition, but outraged victims unschooled in the meaning of the shout of 'fore' were not happy to be hit by golf balls. Beyond Scotland, golf on public land did not prosper.

Map of Pilmour Links from 1821, then owned by the Cheape family of Strathtyrum House. The route of the golf course was marked out by 'march stones', many of which can still be found on the Old Course. The yardage and names of the holes are shown.

Winter and Summer

In the 1700s, golf was still a winter game and the harvest was still important. In 1703 the provost of the town of Fortrose, north of Inverness, sent to Edinburgh for some golf clubs and balls, privately confessing that he should not have been playing at the harvest time.[12] And the grass of the links was a summer crop. In Perth a golfer and his clubs are briefly described in the early 1700s. He played on the North Inch

where the citizens for ages have exercised themselves during the spring and autumnal seasons with golf-clubs and balls. The pastime is interrupted during the summer season by the luxuriancy of the grass which affords rich pasture for the milch-cows belonging to the inhabitants.[13]

Summer was also a closed season for golfers at North Berwick in this century. On 27th March 1728 a ruling by the magistrates (reaffirmed in 1775) closed 'the town green [the east links] after the 25th of this month [March] till the first of September next, and so on yearly without liberty asked...'[14] The summer links crop of grass was often too important and fetched a good price: other users came second. At the end of this century, the minutes of the Glasgow Golf Club (founded 1787) mention that a match was to be played on the first Saturday 'after the Green opens for the winter season'.[15] And, as we shall see, even the pioneer golfing societies at Leith and St Andrews still played in the winter.

Inns and Taverns

The inns of the towns played a role in early golf, and were an important focal point in the life of the town and its sport.[16] The inns provided food and drink for local inhabitants, accommodation for travellers, horses for hire and space for meetings. At night there was entertainment, and here some ladies of the town were available. It was at the inn that the passenger coaches arrived (with the mail) and departed for distant towns. At Leith, the town's officials were elected at a tavern, and there they held their local court.

Sport was encouraged in the vicinity of the inn - cockfighting, boxing and games of chance - and it was natural that the innkeeper had a role in early Scottish golf. At the inn, the golfers dined before and after play, and kept their clubs, and the publican also sold balls and hired out clubs. It was at the inns that the golf clubs of the 1700s had their early meetings and conducted their business. In these pubs after play they drank, sang, arranged their meetings and made their bets. Clubhouses came later: much later.

The early golfing records repeatedly mention these inns by name. By far the oldest known golfing pub was the Golf Hall or Hotel beside Bruntsfield Links. It was patronised by the Bruntsfield golfers long before formal golf clubs appeared. At Leith the golfing pubs in the 1600s mentioned by Kincaid in his diary were Captain Brown's and Rose's and by the mid-1700s Mrs Clephan's establishment at Leith was popular with the first clubs.[17] Later the Gentlemen

The 'Golf Hotel' beside Edinburgh's Bruntsfield Links was used as a clubhouse. The frontage was later modified to make the present Golf Inn. The outside stair on the right led to the golfers' upstairs meeting room.
From Aitchison and Lorimer *Reminiscences of the Old Bruntsfield Links Golf Club* 1902.

Golfers used Straiton's pub, before building their own Golf House in 1768, and leasing it as a pub to a tenant, retaining use of part for their own meetings. At St Andrews, Baillie Glass's tavern is found in the golfing records, and at Musselburgh Mrs Sheriff's, Mr Ward's, Thom's or Kedzlie's appears in the records of the 1700s.[18] A mysterious early club at Scotscraig near St Andrews met at Pryde's pub at Tayport, and at Leven the celebrated Caledonia Inn was used by the golfers. At Burntisland a club played over the town links and a 'Golf Tavern' remains there to this day, long after the town's golfers have moved elsewhere. The list of founders of Crail Golf Club included 'the owner of the Golf Hotel' showing that golf had been well established, and their meeting place fixed, before the formal club appeared. The early Glasgow golfers used the Prince of Wales, Buck's Head, the George, Johnson's, or the Tontine inns near Glasgow Green.[19]

A Mass Game?

It is asserted occasionally that only a small number of gentlemen golfers played the game at this time in Scotland and that they, and their tiny number of clubs formed in the 1700s, alone kept the game alive until the boom in golf in the mid-1800s.[20] The historical record is to the contrary: all the records suggest that golf was widely popular with Scottish citizens before and during the 1700s.

The evidence is, firstly, that many ordinary golfers were brought before the church courts in the previous century, for playing on Sundays, and the offenders singled out by the Kirk Sessions were not men of substance, but ordinary citizens - tailors, masons, apprentices and others. Young men and boys also feature in the Church's actions. Secondly, at this time some towns like Elie and St Andrews had ancient charters which protected the play at golf by the 'inhabitants', 'citizens' or 'neighbours'. Such regulations were unnecessary if only the local lairds were at play. Thirdly, in the 1700s, direct evidence of golf as a widely popular game appeared. Pennant's *Tour of Scotland* of 1769 says that the sports of Moray, on the north-east coast, were 'hunting, firing at marks, football and club-ball'.[21] But the most important evidence relating to this controversy is from John Chamberlayne's *Magnae Britanniae*, a survey of British life in 1708, and he says of Scottish sport that he found

> not to mention Hunting, Hawking, Setting, Horse-Racing, Fishing, Fowling, Coursing, Bowling and such manly Sports, proper only to the Nobility, gentry and their attendants; the sports called Football playing, and Golf, were the usual recreations of the Common People.[22]

Chamberlayne's conclusion is clear: the game of golf was a mass game, a game more popular with the ordinary people than with the gentry. Smollett in his *The Expedition of Humphrey Clinker* makes this same point in his description of golf at Leith in 1766. Of golf he says:

> Of this diversion the Scots are so fond, that when the weather will permit you may see a multitude of all ranks, from the senator of justice to the lowest tradesman mingling together in their shirts, and following the balls with the utmost eagerness.[23]

LETTERS
FROM
EDINBURGH;
Written in the Years 1774 and 1775:

CONTAINING
SOME OBSERVATIONS
ON THE
Diversions, Customs, Manners, and Laws,
OF THE
SCOTCH NATION,
DURING A SIX MONTHS RESIDENCE IN
EDINBURGH.

Non hic centauros, non gorgons, harpyasque
Invenies, Hominem pagina nostra sapit.

LONDON:
Printed for J. DODSLEY in Pall-mall.
M.DCC.LXXVI.

Topham's *Letters from Edinburgh* describes golf by all sections of the community in Edinburgh.

Topham's account of his visit to Scotland in 1774 gives much the same picture, adding that 'they [the Scots] instruct their children in it, as soon as they can run alone'. Even at the end of the century a local description of the game at Leith describes the same situation. *The Statistical Account* of 1793 says grandly that

the greatest and wisest of the land were to be seen on the links of Leith, mingling freely with the humblest mechanics in pursuit of their common and beloved amusement. All distinctions of rank were levelled by the joyous spirit of the game. Lords of Session and cobblers, knights, baronets and tailors might be seen earnestly contesting for the palms of superior dexterity, and vehemently but good humouredly discussing moot points of the game, as they arose in the course of play.[24]

This vision of a vibrant classless game of the links is perhaps overstated. But it gives no support to those who consider that early Scottish golf was an aristocratic preserve, an élite game of the few. Instead it does seem to have been a widely popular game, though perhaps one lacking sophistication when played at the lower levels.

What is the origin of this aristocratic myth? Most golf historians have equated golf activity with membership of a club, an understandable assumption from an English viewpoint later. In studying Scotland they have only noticed the numbers of golfers who were *members* of the early golfing societies. Instead, the vast majority of players were not involved in any club, society or golfing clique: many golfers, rich and poor, simply went out and played on the links. The formalities of a club were not desired, nor necessary, for most players in the 1700s.[25]

Long and Short

The many ordinary golfers out at play lacked the elegant equipment of the gentlemen's game - the feathery balls and the brittle hybrid clubs. It is likely that the humble players were using simpler equipment, hitting the ball less far, and a full round of the links might have been an ordeal. This suggestion is strengthened by finding 'short' golf holes and 'short' golf courses, suited to the simpler equipment, at a number of places, plus continuing references to short holes or short play. In the Seafield correspondence of 1690 in the north-east of Scotland, mentioned earlier, there is a hint of this: 'Ife you have a mind for the long goff, lett me know'.[26] Similar language is found in 1786 when a correspondent in Edinburgh wrote to a friend on the island of Mull:

I meant to send you a Doz golfe clubs and half a Doz balls to play round the Green at short or long holes as you chose - if I thought it would be agreeable to you to have such - as it would be a new exercise in Mull.[27]

Short courses for short golf with inexpensive equipment are hinted at surprisingly often in early documents. At Leith near the start of a circuit of the links, there was a short course called the Braehead Holes, and to the left of the first hole there were also the 'Scholars' Holes'. At St Andrews there were also the 'Scholars' Holes' near the 17th green and today the Scholars' and Progressing Bunker persist nearby as a reminder perhaps of these short holes. At Musselburgh there were the 'caddies holes' near the 5th hole. Carnoustie later had a 'Duffers Course', and North Berwick had its 'Tree Holes', a name which raises the possibility that these holes were played by those with tree clubs, i.e. home-made shinty sticks. In the 1770s both a long and a short course were found at Elie.[28] These were not putting greens but a set of golf holes of modest length.

These all testify to the existence of a simple form of golf played with simpler equipment by the humbler players on shorter courses. It was the short churchyard game, evolving onto the links, where the gentlemen golfers were a familiar sight playing the long game. But before looking at the important changes in the 1700s in the skilled long game, one other noble sport - archery - deserves attention, since this sport still had links with early golf.

Archery

Archery competitions have considerable antiquity in Scotland, arising out of the military significance of the weapon.[29] A Peebles trophy for archery, presented by the Provost of that town, dates from 1628. There were similar competitions in Selkirk and Stirling from the 1660s, and St Andrews University had its own 'arrow competition' from 1618. In 1668 the ancient and famous archery competition at Kilwinning was formalised and a new handsome silver trophy was presented as their prize.

But the Royal Company of Archers in Edinburgh owned the earliest known Scottish archery trophy - the Musselburgh Arrow - dating from 1603, and they had all the activities we associate with the later golf clubs. Musselburgh, also featuring in the early golf records, was a convenient half-way meeting place for the sporting gentlemen of East Lothian and Edinburgh. The archers dined together after their competitions and wore uniforms at play. In 1709 the Royal Company of Archers approached the Edinburgh authorities, in much the same way as did the golfers later, and were granted a silver arrow by the Edinburgh Town Council, to be shot for on Leith or Bruntsfield Links. This trophy was carried through the town prior to the match, as was the golfers' trophy some years later. The event was a popular piece of sporting theatre, and the winner was the 'captain' of the Company for the year.

Allan Ramsay, the poet, described an Archers' competition at Bruntsfield:

> First striving who shall win the bowl
> And then gar't flow with wine
> To Bruntsfield Green lets hy
> And see the Royal Bowmen strive.[30]

He says that the archers were then competing for a silver bowl to be filled with wine - exactly the type of prize played for by Leith golfers, in the famous poem *The Goff*, which describes play there before the first club and the first formal competition were organised.

The Goff

In 1743 a poem was published in Edinburgh with details of a match at Leith. *The Goff* is the first literary work devoted to golf, and one of the most interesting of all works on early sport.[31] Two

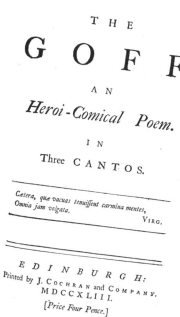

Frontispiece to the Edinburgh golfing poem *The Goff* of 1743. By courtesy of the MITCHELL LIBRARY, GLASGOW.

young Edinburgh men apparently play a personal golf match. But the text merges with details of play by a distinguished golfing clique. The winner of the golf competition among the group on the day was awarded a silver cup filled with punch by the others. Experienced caddies were present and the best St Andrews feathery balls were used, and the clique kept a handsome bets book in which golfing exploits were recorded. The structure of the competition is dimly perceived, and odd to modern eyes. Rapid match-play on one day was probably involved, leading to a final singles match, and the poem's assumptions are that this was an ancient, unchanging way of play at Leith. It is clear that the golfers were a familiar sight on the links, and drew a knowledgable crowd of humble golfing citizens, who followed the play closely.

Cliques and Clubs

Out of one of these Leith golfing cliques, possibly the same one as in the poem, emerged a golfing society later known as the Honourable Company of Edinburgh Golfers.[32] It was the world's first known golfing society with a formal organisation, though this group was probably an old clique playing for a new trophy. And the new trophy came from the generous Town Council of Edinburgh.

Edinburgh's problems of morale and reputation at this time after the Union of the Crowns led to several civic improvement proposals to counter this decline of the town. Some were remarkably successful, and became a regular part of town life, but other initiatives foundered. A golf competition might be a public entertainment, and the civic authorities were supporters of the idea. The Royal Archers' public tournament had been successful, and in 1724, a golf match between Alex Elphinstone and Captain Porteus for 20 guineas was 'watched by the Duke of Hamilton, the Earl of Morton and a vast mob of great and little beside'. Noble golfers on parade with servants, caddies, forecaddies and playing with expensive clubs and balls drew in the crowds, who were knowledgable about the game and probably played the game themselves. The golfers, calling themselves in their application 'the Gentlemen Golfers', petitioned the Town Council in 1744 to provide a trophy for a golf competition. A display of skilled golf with elegant equipment by Scotland's great and good (including the nation's most famous judge) would be worth watching. The Town Council concluded that a golfing competition might provide games, if not bread, for the inhabitants of Edinburgh and Leith. They also thought, wrongly, that distinguished players from a distance might attend.

The Silver Club

The Edinburgh Town Council agreed to the Gentlemen Golfers' request for a trophy. A silver club seemed appropriate, one reminiscent of similar trophies for archery and racing.[33]

All the evidence is that the town intended the competition to be an open one. The invitation to compete was to 'noblemen, gentlemen or other golfers of Great Britain and Ireland.' Perhaps the town hoped for a national entry, in the way that race meetings and archery brought sportsmen from afar. In the

event, no entries from distant nobility or
gentlemen were received. Nor were entries
received from the skilled local Leith ballmakers
and clubmakers. A deterrent to these 'other golfers',
if any was required, was an entry fee of 5/-, about
three times the cost of a golf club: the winner also
had the expense of affixing a silver ball to the
trophy. The constituency for the trophy was
very limited: it was to be a display of noble,
long golf, and in the event the only players to enter
were the existing Leith group of players.

The Town Council supported the event in other ways, and
arranged for their Town Guard – some elderly military pensioners – to parade the trophy through the town shortly
before the competition with 'tuck of drum', a routine local
way of drawing attention to coming civic events.[34]

The Rules of Golf

The arrangements for play for the new
trophy forced the Gentlemen Golfers for the
first time to make some written records. These
minutes were not about domestic matters such
as their own outings or office-bearers, or bets.
Their first records are simply the rules for play
on the competition day, and a list of the
entrants for the trophy. Other formalities of their
clubbiness emerged slowly on paper, but later.

For play on the day, the Town Council and the Gentlemen Golfers (as they
called themselves) drew up regulations in order to decide the winner. This
victor was also to be the Golfers' 'captain' for the next year, with the minimal
duties of adjudication about any disputes in the following year's competition.
To have a winner from a one-day competition among players accustomed to
match-play seemed to pose difficulties. The rules for play for the silver club
seem precise, but looked at more closely are ambiguous, and are quoted here
in full. This puzzle of the format of the Silver Club competition has engaged
and baffled historians of golf for 250 years, the main mystery being whether
the first competition was stroke-play or match-play.[35]

After the lots were drawn for partners the rules stated:

*the SET or MATCH beginning with No.1, &c., shall goe out first, with a Clerk to
mark down every Stroke each of them shall take to every hole; AND when the
Match is ended, a Scrutiny of the Whole Clerk's Books or Jottings is to be made,
and the player who Shall appear to have won the greatest Number of Holes shall
be declared to be the Winner of the Match; And if there shall be two, three, or
more, that are equal, then these two or three &c must play a Round themselves...*[36]

At first, the 'jottings' seems to indicate stroke-play competition. But stroke-
play was little known in Scottish golf until a century later: to this day the
descendants of the Leith Golfers - the Honourable Company of Edinburgh
Golfers - avoid it if at all possible. More suggestive of match-play is that the

Detail from an engraving
of David Allan's portrait
of William Inglis, the
Captain of the Edinburgh
Golfers, showing the Silver
Club being paraded and
announced by 'tuck of
drum' by the Town Guard
in Edinburgh prior to the
annual event.
From Clark's *Golf* 1875.

Minutes of the Town Council of Edinburgh reporting the Rules for the Gentlemen Golfers' Silver Club Competition in 1744.
By courtesy of EDINBURGH CITY ARCHIVES.

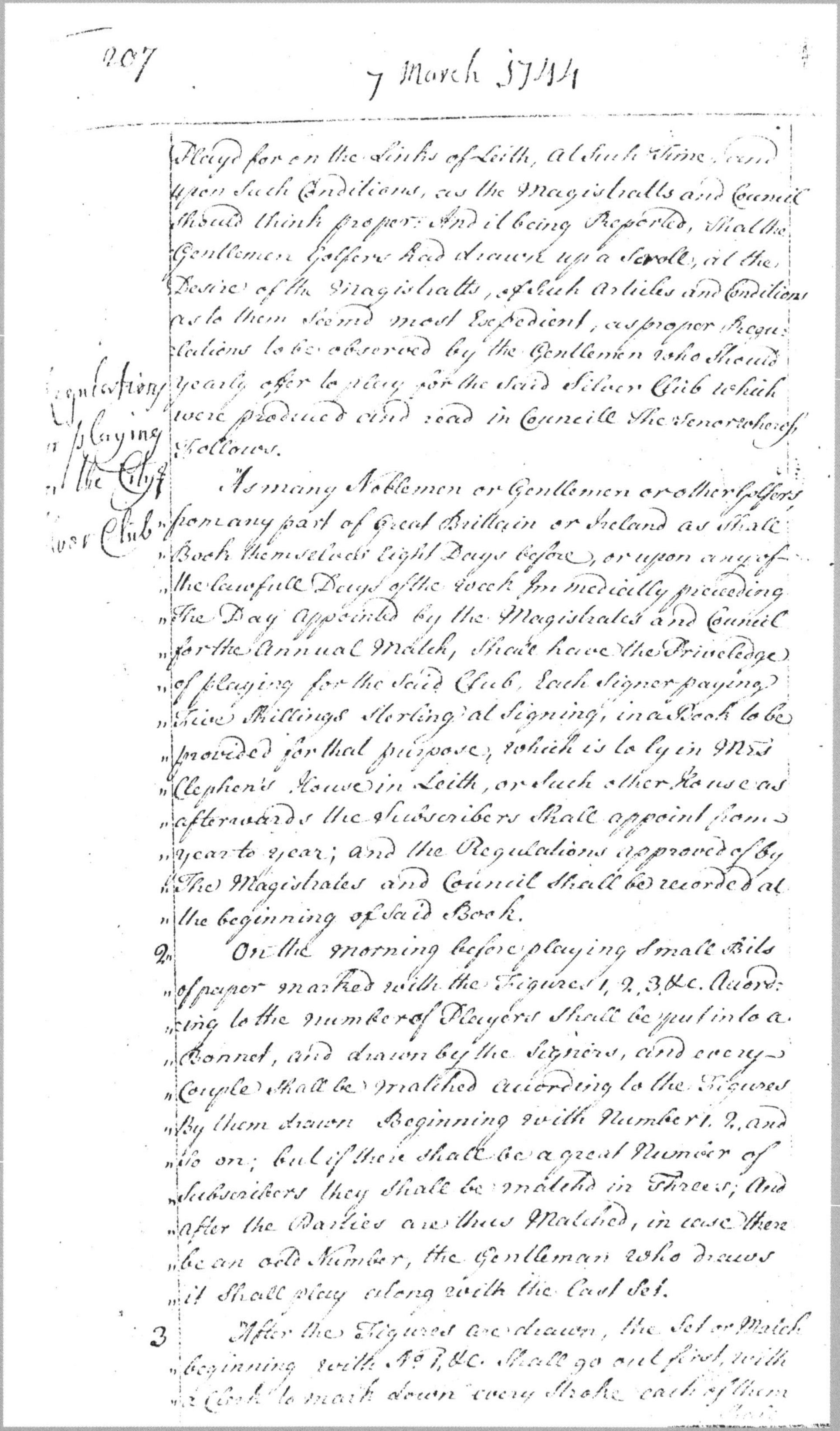

207

7 March 1744

Play'd for on the Links of Leith, at such time and upon such Conditions, as the Magistrates and Council should think proper. And it being Reported, That the Gentlemen Golfers had drawn up a Scroll, at the Desire of the Magistrates, of such Articles and Conditions as to them seem'd most Expedient, as proper Regulations to be observed by the Gentlemen who should yearly offer to play for the said Silver Club which were produced and read in Councill The tenor whereof follows.

Regulations of playing of the City Silver Club

As many Noblemen or Gentlemen or other Golfers, from any part of Great Brittain or Ireland as shall Book themselves eight Days before, or upon any of the lawfull Days of the week Immediatly preceeding The Day Appointed by the Magistrates and Councill for the Annual Match, Shall have the Priviledge of playing for the said Club, Each Signer paying Five Shillings Sterling at Signing, in a Book to be provided for that purpose, which is to ly in Mrs Clephan's House in Leith, or Such other House as afterwards the Subscribers shall appoint from year to year; and the Regulations approved of by The Magistrates and Councill shall be recorded at the beginning of Said Book.

2. On the morning before playing Small Bits of paper marked with the Figures 1, 2, 3 &c. According to the number of Players shall be put into a Bonnet, and drawn by the Signers, and every Couple shall be matched according to the Figures By them drawn Beginning with Number 1, 2, and so on; but if there shall be a great Number of Subscribers they shall be matched in Threes; And after the Parties are thus Matched, in case there be an odd Number, the Gentleman who draws it Shall play along with the last Set.

3. After the Figures are drawn, the Set or Match beginning with No 1, &c. Shall go out first, with a Clerk to mark down every Stroke each of them

70

winner is considered to be the player who won 'the greatest Number of Holes' as if all entrants were matched against each other retrospectively from 'the jottings' of the Clerks. To reconstruct match-play between all the players would be tedious indeed, but some historians have considered that this was the case and the winner was the player beating all others in this retrospective analysis. With this system, ties were likely and the regulations concede that a play-off would result.

But this was to be a public occasion for the town, and such an exercise on paper hardly made for any sense of drama, unless there was a tie. The local spectators would expect the usual excitement of match-play among the gentlemen. Perhaps it was expected that the jottings/match-play system would usually produce a tie, and the drama was in the play-off, as in *The Goff*. But the evidence from *The Goff* is that a small group of players could indeed manage a form of rapid match-play in one day. *The Goff* mentions preliminary 'heats' then a final, singles match-play. Help is at hand from the early history of the R&A. They copied the rules for their first competition verbatim from the Leith rules of 1744, including the use of the mysterious 'jottings'. Five years later, the R&A changed the rules.

> *In order to remove all disputes and inconveniences... in all time coming whoever puts in the ball at the fewest strokes over the field... shall be declared and sustained victor.*[37]

Clearly the original silver club system was not working at St Andrews, and simple stroke-play was substituted, doubtless with reluctance. It does sound as if a complex multiple match-play format had been attempted. Some help is also given from the rules of another Edinburgh club - the Bruntsfield Links club, who also attempted a match-play outing.

It may be that we should not take these early Leith regulations too seriously; they may never have been used nor have been needed, because the original, wide scope of the competition was never realised in practice. Perhaps the Edinburgh golfers hoped for a large entry, and an unusual device was needed to declare a winner from a large field in one day. In the event they probably quietly reverted to their own customary 'heats and play-off' system of *The Goff*.

Duncan Forbes of Culloden, golfer and judge, played in the early Leith silver club competitions, and was a regular player at Leith Links.

By courtesy of the SCOTTISH NATIONAL PORTRAIT GALLERY.

The First Winner

In the first competition, only twelve players entered, and presumably the players were old friends.[38] Of the eleven entrants, six are mentioned in *The Goff* – Forbes, Dalrymple, Rattray, Biggar, Crosse and Leslie. But four serious golfers listed in *The Goff* did not play for the silver club, nor can be found as members

15th January 1764

[Manuscript petition to the Council of Edinburgh, in two columns of handwritten text, concerning the regulations for the Silver Club competition.]

Change in rules in 1764 for the Silver Club competition which abandoned the idea of an open competition in favour of one restricted to the local members.
By courtesy of the CITY OF EDINBURGH COUNCIL.

of the Honourable Company later – MacDonald, Stewart, Brown, and Alston. Also not competing was young Francis, 5th Earl of Wemyss (1723-1808), who purchased the estate of Gosford to indulge in his passion for golf. Also missing from the entrants were any of the distinguished aristocratic golfing families of Hamilton and Morton, whose members had attended the famous challenge match at Leith in 1724 and had played at Leith in the Foulis clique in the 1680s, together with Lord Gosford. These findings do raise the question whether *other* distinguished cliques existed at Leith, possibly bonded by common political or other links. It is highly likely that members of the Hamilton, Morton and Wemyss families were still active players. Perhaps they had their own, aristocratic, outings and that the silver club players were from the professional and merchant class.[39]

John Rattray the surgeon was the winner of the silver club on the day. He is the world's first known golf trophy holder. The suggestion that a bigger, open competition had been hoped for, but did not emerge, is supported by later events. In 1764 the Golfers went back to the Town Council, and pointed out that their own group alone was playing for the trophy. The Golfers claimed that in any case, the regulations

> *were too broad for by it any person whatever from any part of Great Britain or Ireland is entitled to play for the Silver Club whereby persons of bad fame or such as are not fitt company for gentlemen may play for and winn the Silver Club...*

The Town Council agreed to the Gentlemen Golfers' application to change the rules and limit the competition to their local society. This also removed the risk that a humble outsider could win and be in charge of the activities of the club as captain.[40]

The Players and the Rules

Some of the early Gentlemen Golfers are of interest, and two were involved with Prince Charles Edward Stuart's 1745 rebellion, one year after the silver club competition, though taking opposite sides. Duncan Forbes, the great law-maker (known to play at Leith even in the snow), opposed the Jacobites, but John Rattray, the surgeon, joined Prince Charles in the 1745 rising. Rattray went out to tend the wounded when Prince Charles' army, moving towards England, had met and defeated Cope at Prestonpans near Edinburgh. In that year Rattray had won the Edinburgh Golfers' silver club for the second time, and he travelled to Derby with the Prince. He then came back with the retreating army to defeat at Culloden, where he was taken prisoner, but was freed with the help of fellow-golfer Forbes. These military and political events, an important and romantic part of Scottish history, had little effect on day-to-day Edinburgh life. Lowland life simply carried on, once the armies had passed through. Both Rattray and Forbes were back playing for the silver club in 1748. Prince Charles escaped to Italy, and a visitor to him later found him moodily practising his short game.[41]

Other Clubs

The Silver Club competition had forced the Gentlemen Golfers to organise some of their activities and thereafter they slowly metamorphosed into a golf society. Other golf clubs began to appear from 1744 onwards, and became increasingly important in the game. Some changes in eighteenth-century society led to formal societies of all kinds evolving, with rules, common finances and office-bearers. These clubs grew out of the informal groups which had previously happily managed without such internal organisation.

The new golf clubs of the gentry and merchants subtly changed the evolution of the game. Though much golf continued outside the societies on the public links, the new clubs increasingly took it upon themselves to look after the common land, its golf holes and turf, though they did not own it. Their organisation meant that they had some funds held in common and they could employ others to tend the links. The clubs could act in other ways to protect the interests of all golfers on the links, taking legal action if necessary. The Scottish links supported many activities, and had multiple users. Friction was inevitable, and such matters might need professional help.

Prince Charles Edward Stuart was an occasional golfer.
By courtesy of SCOTTISH NATIONAL PORTRAIT GALLERY.

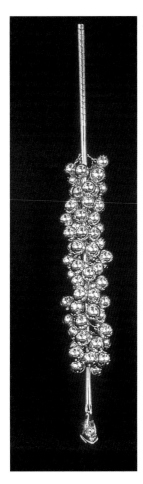

The First Club?

The claim of the Gentlemen Golfers - later known as the Honourable Company of Edinburgh Golfers - to be the world's first golf club is not undisputed, however. A rival claim comes from others, notably the Royal Burgess Golfing Society of Edinburgh. The first entry in their minutes, from 1773, state that the Society was 'currently in poor shape' and that 'many of the old members were dead and others neglected to attend the meetings of the Society'.[42] This has led to suggestions about an earlier existence of this club. As we saw, non-club golf at Bruntsfield had been well established. In 1717, the Golf Hall Tavern at Bruntsfield Links was well known and golf at these Links was mentioned by the poet Allan Ramsay at this time:

When we were wearied at the gowff
Then Maggie Johnstone's was our howff.

She died in 1711. Golf was popular enough on these links to catch the poet's eye. This type of evidence allows advocates for the Burgess golfers to claim they were indeed active prior to 1773, possibly much earlier, prior even to the formation of the Edinburgh Golfers.

This dispute cannot be settled, and is in the end a little futile. We have seen that groups of golfers at both Leith and Bruntsfield were playing together informally for a considerable time prior to drawing up their formal association. There is no doubt that there was golf at Bruntsfield Links in the early 1700s, but this was poorly organised. It is only reasonable for us to take the evidence of formal association, e.g. surviving minutes, as the point of foundation of any club. By this criterion, the Honourable Company's claim to be the first golf club in the world, founded in 1744, is upheld, with the proviso that active, group golf did not suddenly spring into existence on this important occasion.

The Royal and Ancient Golf Club

If we judge the Honourable Company to be the world's first golf club, without suggesting that a golfing group was a new idea, then the Society of St Andrews Golfers (known later as the Royal and Ancient Golf Club of St Andrews) was certainly next to be founded. In 1754 they also obtained a silver club for competition. While the Edinburgh golfers obtained their club from the town authorities in Edinburgh, the St Andrews golfers paid for a trophy by subscription from their 22 members. They still had civic responsibilities in mind, since in forming the Club they recorded that it was to help 'the interest and prosperity of the City of St Andrews', and the St Andrews silver club competition also was initially open to all-comers. St Andrews, like Edinburgh, had suffered after the Union of Parliaments, and the Fife town had declined from its important role as the ecclesiastical centre of Scotland. For their event, the St Andrews golfers slavishly copied the regulations for the Leith competition, matching them paragraph by paragraph: the St Andrews rules even absent-mindedly included local Leith landmarks like 'The Thorn Tree Hole'.[43]

The explanation for this inadvertence probably arises from the remarkable amount of cross-membership between the two clubs, in spite of the distance between them. The Society of St Andrews Golfers had many local players drawn from east coast lairds and aristocracy, but they also had Edinburgh members. The St Andrews Golfers also invited the Leith society to their early competitions, and advertised the St Andrews meetings in the Edinburgh newspapers. The harmony of the two sets of rules was to be expected.

Golf in Scotland outside the Clubs

These important events in Edinburgh and St Andrews should not conceal that golf continued to be played in the rest of Scotland by a host of humble players who left little or no record behind them. There were also patrician golfers at play on the links at many other places in Scotland, joining together without forming a club. Some other cliques may have continued at Leith outside the Gentlemen Golfers' group. Smollett's account of his visit to Leith in 1766 describes some players:

Among others I was shown one particular set of golfers the youngest of whom was turned of four-score. They were all gentlemen of independent fortunes who had amused themselves with this pastime for the best part of a century, without having felt the least alarm or disgust; and they never went to bed without having each the best part of a gallon of claret in his belly.

This was a small group of wealthy senior citizens, well enough known to be pointed out to the writer. They do not sound like the Gentlemen Golfers, who were a bigger group of younger, professional men. Earlier evidence showed active noble golf at Dornoch, Montrose and Carnoustie. Other golfing groups appear without a formal club in this century. At Fortrose, north of Inverness, gentry were noted at play on the Links:

Chanonry Nefs projects a good way into the fea and forms a fine curve which makes it a beautiful object. It terminates in the Links of Fortrofe, about an Englifh mile in length, and fmooth as a carpet. This is fine ground for the golf, which is often played here by the gentlemen of the town and country.[44]

As noted above, in 1702, the Provost of Fortrose, one of the gentlemen of the town, sent for golf clubs to Edinburgh. Further north, at Cromarty, a regular gentlemen's golf outing on the natural golf links was recorded, and further north, in Orkney, golf was again described at this time. Later, at Fraserburgh, documents relating to a golf club in the period about 1777-86 have recently been found. At Elie, in Fife, golf is also recorded in the mid-1700s and the players were described as 'incomers from as far as Edinburgh [who] made a constant practice of playing golf on the links'.[45] There was student golf in Glasgow as in the poem *Glotta* of 1721 and noble golf at Nairn is mentioned in 1797.[46] And there was golf on the lovely links at Dubbieside near Leven, where in 1745 there was a famous incident in which the revered schoolmaster, J. Grubb, was hit on the leg by a golf ball. Thrombosis followed and the leg was amputated, with recovery.[47]

And it should be remembered that golf continued at Musselburgh in the 1700s, having been visited by Foulis in 1672. Duncan Forbes of Culloden played there with his son, and the country estates at Gosford and Seton, east of Musselburgh had natural golf links, a golfing area now concealed by the coastal road and wall. At Gullane, a little further along the coast, there was an ancient golf match of a tribal nature on Auld Hansel Monday between the weavers of Dirleton and those of Aberlady.[48] Later a shadowy clique of golfers

The original Silver Club given to Edinburgh's Gentlemen Golfers: from Wood's *Golfing Curios.*

is noted at Dunbar in 1794, long before the club was formed there. Even on the west coast of Scotland, old maps show the 'Golf Fields' at Irvine beside the estuary of the River Irvine, though there was no golf club until the mid-1800s. At Dumfries in 1762, a prisoner was allowed out of jail to play golf on the haughs on the river nearby at Kingholm, giving unexpected evidence of golf in the south-west of Scotland.[49] At Glasgow the golf interest continued, and the Town Council minutes contain references in 1760 to the 'Golf House' on Glasgow Green, prior to the appearance of the golf club.

Non-Club Golf

This is an impressive list of golf sightings in the 1700s and is of the greatest interest. It is important to realise the scale of Scottish golf outside the small number of celebrated clubs formed in the 1700s. The absence of a club in a town does not mean that golf was absent. All over the country there were not only ordinary players out on the links, but little groups of country sporting gentlemen who were well known to each other and who gathered regularly for sport including golf. Golf historians have been preoccupied with the early formal clubs and their small number of members. At all of the above golfing sites like Orkney, Glasgow, Cromarty, Brora, Fraserburgh, Elie, Gullane, Leven and Dumfries, no clubs were to be formed for 100 years or more.[50]

East and West

Though golf was mainly an east coast game, some of the gentry in the west of Scotland did play and were prominent players.[51] Instead of playing golf on the entirely suitable west coast links, they contented themselves with winter sport when in residence in Edinburgh. This paradox was to continue for almost two centuries. One of the greatest of west of Scotland sporting families was the Eglintons, with extensive estates in North Ayrshire, close to Prestwick. The earls were golfers, active in the Honourable Company and the R&A but they never played in the west in the 1700s. When at their estates in the west in summer, life was too busy to consider regular golf, even though the attractive Prestwick and other classic links in Ayrshire were nearby. West coast golf was to emerge later, only when the preoccupation with the harvest lessened and summer golf emerged in the mid-1800s.

Golfers' Routine

The routine play of the early golf clubs, notably at Leith and St Andrews, when examined closely, shows that, as in previous centuries, play seems to have been mostly in winter rather than summer, and the important meetings were in spring and autumn. The day of the week favoured was not necessarily Saturday. The Honourable Company's now famous silver trophy was played for on the first Monday in April, hardly the optimal time for golf on the east coast of Scotland. Monday was a favourite day for play at Leith, traditionally a leisure day for lawyers and the courts, and the judge Duncan Forbes of Culloden, one of the members, played at Leith on Mondays.

The ordinary play for the Gentlemen Golfers and the St Andrews players started at mid-day or earlier. The meeting day of the club was predictable, as a fixed day of the month, and a reminder to members was often placed in the

Archibald William, 13th Earl of Eglinton and Winton, had an Ayrshire estate, but played his golf on the east coast links.

Edinburgh newspapers at the last minute. At the Burgess Club in Edinburgh a messenger was sent round to ask members if they would be playing and dining. The winter game required speedy play to finish the matches before the sun had set. It seems likely that the clubs, with their small membership of a dozen or so, decided their early competitions by rapid match-play.

Caddies or servants accompanied the players on their round. Forecaddies were sent ahead on the busy public land to signal where the ball lay and to warn other users of the links of the approach of the golfers. The 1775 Leith rules mention that the caddie could remove the ball from a hazard, suggesting that one role of the forecaddie was to pluck the vulnerable feathery from water before it was thoroughly soaked. At North Berwick in 1775 the Town Council enacted that

> no person shall be permitted to play at Golf over the Castlehill without a runnner before to warn passengers [pedestrians] passing or repassing to keep out of harm's way.[52]

Forecaddies also guarded the feathery balls from being stolen - 'taken up' - as the early rules charitably put it. Also liable to be taken up were flagsticks, and the holes were usually not marked. At best a large feather was inserted, or a 'boy' stationed at the hole: only later were the club's own flagsticks purchased, for use during competitions. These were put out for the day's play, by each club, and gathered in again later.

For routine outings, the local pubs or the clubs held stocks of balls for sale, which were bought in bulk at a discount, and the pubs also rented out clubs.[53]

For the club's meeting a club- and ballmaker might be invited to attend, who would sell clubs and balls and arrange for repairs. In the late 1700s, McEwan travelled from Bruntsfield to the coast and took a boat to Fife and thence by road to St Andrews to attend the golfers' meetings.

Scoring in the 1700s

We have little knowledge of the quality and speed of play, but the normal score in the 1800s for each of the Leith 400-yard holes was probably six to seven shots for a good golfer. Eye-witness accounts of play in the eighteenth century are not available, but one record from Perth from 1837 may describe the traditional ways of play. The match took one and a half hours to play and the holes - the number played is not mentioned - measured 300-400 yards. Each hole had a boy stationed at the flag, and a dozen competitors played, each with a marker. At night 120 members and guests sat down to dinner. New members introduced at the meeting had to kiss the golf balls attached to the club's silver club, a hollow club which was then filled with wine for the golfers to drink. After the dinner and toasts, songs were sung by professional singers, and music provided by fiddlers.[54]

Handicapping

Match-play was the dominant format in early golf. The first formal stroke competition to appear among the St Andrews Golfers did not appear until 1776. Other clubs procrastinated, and not until 1837 did the Honourable Company inaugurate a stroke competition. Left to themselves, the Scottish golfers of the time preferred match-play, often the sociable, speedy two-ball foursomes - i.e. 'Scotch' foursomes. Modest matching of the four players could produce a thrilling, fast, close game well suited to winter play, without the need for handicaps. Later, singles match-play and stroke-play competition gave pressure for formal handicapping systems.

There are hints at earlier systems of the giving and taking of strokes. A primitive form of handicapping is described as early as 1687 in the Kincaid diary, and formal handicaps appeared at the Burgess club in the early 1800s. In the arranged matches, the handicap jargon used is 'one half', or 'one more' etc. Even so, the minutes of the first clubs make no mention of handicaps. It seems that the usual form of club golf was matches arranged within these informal groups of golfers with such knowledge of the players' capabilities that matches were nicely organised to pit equal against equal, particularly in two-ball foursomes.

The *esprit* of the 1700s also meant that many unusual matches are recorded, such as one player playing only with an iron, and other exotic challenges like golf versus archery, or golf versus throwing the ball only. Bets on individual performances were also made, often paid out in drink.

The Rules

There were no *written* rules of golf until 1744, but this is not to say that before this time there were no rules. Shortly after the Silver Club competition was inaugurated, the Edinburgh Golfers put down on paper their regulations for play - in addition to the conditions of the competition. Doubtless these rules of golf were not a novelty, but were the agreed tradition of play by the early Scottish golfers and the Leith cliques in particular. These rules probably had some antiquity.[55] There was no need for a written code in early Scottish golf: in match-play the customary practices were well known and any disputes could be settled quickly among friends and gentlemen, with regard to equity and good sportsmanship.

These written rules of the Gentlemen Golfers appeared to meet the needs of the new competition at the inauguration of the Silver Club competition in 1744. The organisers were expecting entrants from afar, and needed to clarify the 'form' at Leith. It was a crucial moment in the history of golf. It was the first *written* rules for the game. This pioneer code was lost for many years and was not included in the book *Rules of the Ten Oldest Clubs* published in 1935 by C. B. Clapcott. This first set was not discovered until 1945, again by Clapcott.[56]

Sets of rules similar to those of the Gentlemen Golfers' were to be adopted by other clubs. These codes were similar and they hardly changed in the 1700s, suggesting that the core rules were widely used and agreed by oral tradition. The technical aspects of these early rules are discussed elsewhere. But selected rules indirectly give us much information on eighteenth-century golf and the game as played then. The prose used is direct and clear:

The first rule tells us something about the lay-out of the early courses:

RULE 1:
'You must Tee your Ball within a Club's length of the Hole.'

Golfers restarting on a new hole did not go to a distinct, distant teeing area. Instead they teed up within one club's length of the previous hole, and since only wooden clubs were in use, little damage to the turf resulted. There may even have been a practical advantage to this rule: the golfers used sand to tee up the ball and this continuous dispersal of sand close to the hole may have contributed to a higher quality of turf and a smoother surface round the hole, hence aiding putting.

RULE 3:
'You are not to change the Ball which you Strike off the Tee before that Hole is played out.'

This prohibition confirms that damage to the feathery ball was likely at any time, if cut by a poor shot or by a rut iron, or soaked through in wet weather. There may even have been a temptation, even in spite of its great price, to change a ball in the middle of playing a hole. The Honourable Company sensibly decided to discourage such an extravagant practice. Substituting a new feathery for a deteriorating ball at the next hole was expensive enough.

RULE 4:
'You are not to remove any Stones, Bones or any Break Club, for the sake of playing your Ball, except on the fair Green, & that only within one Club's length of your Ball.'

Anything that might break the precious long-nosed clubs could not be removed from the links, except close to the hole - the 'fair green' or putting area recognised as a special area as early as this. Clearly, stones and bones were often found on the links. 'Break club' did not mean the discarded parts of a damaged club, but instead meant any object liable to damage a club. In

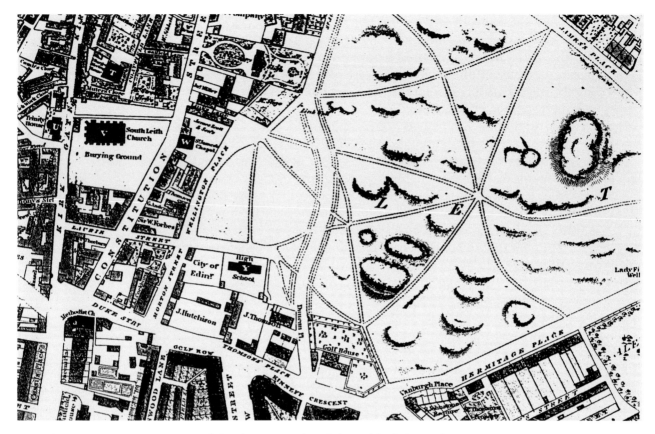

Map of Leith Links in 1817 showing the Golf House, the first purpose-built golf clubhouse to be constructed.

By courtesy of EDINBURGH PUBLIC LIBRARY.

spite of the danger to the club and ball from these loose objects, the Gentlemen Golfers had decided to stand firm against any improvement in the lie of the ball.

RULE 5:

'If your Ball come among Watter or any wattery filth, you are at liberty to take out your Ball & bringing it behind the hazard and teeing it, you may play it with any Club and allow your adversary a stroke...'

This 'lift and drop' rule with a one stroke penalty shows that there were burns, casual water and cow dung ('wattery filth') on the links.

RULE 8:

'If you shou'd lose your Ball, by its being taken up or any other way you are to go back to the Spot, where you struck last, & drop another Ball, And allow your adversary a Stroke for the misfortune.'

Dealing with a lost ball proved to be a difficult situation to legislate for, and the rule changed a number of times into the next century. At times, the rules said the stroke should be replayed with no penalty (i.e. distance loss only) and at other times a penalty of one shot plus distance was in force. This charitable attitude to a lost ball might be explained by the roughness of the links and the ever-present whins.

But the rule also mentions that the ball might be lost by being 'taken up'. Dogs and small boys in Scotland have always been in the habit of 'taking up' any well-hit ball at a distance from its owner. To penalise such a loss would seem harsh and the early rules did not always enforce an extra penalty.

RULE 11:

'If you draw your club, in order to strike & proceed so far in your stroke, as to be bringing down your club; if then your club shall break in any way, it is to be accounted a stroke.'

This confirms the fragility of the early clubs, and that the shaft could break on the downswing.

RULE 13:

'Neither Trench, Ditch or Dyke, made for the preservation of the Links, nor the Scholar's Holes or the Soldier's Lines, Shall be accounted a hazard, But the Ball is to be taken out Teed and play'd with any Iron Club.'

This rule shows that partial relief from these other hazards - notably earthworks for improvement of the links - was allowed. This was the first acknowledgement of the later principle that relief could be allowed from 'objects and events foreign to the essential golf course'. The Leith golfers allowed the ball to be lifted without losing a stroke, but an interesting small penalty had to be accepted, namely that an iron club shot then had to be played, thus losing distance, though the ball could be teed up. The iron club was carried for other reasons - notably dealing with ruts, tracks, bunkers and poor lies. Its use was for extraction, not for distance shots, and its obligatory use here meant a shorter shot.[57]

There was no rule dealing with unplayable lies. The ball could not be lifted, other than at the water or ditches and dykes mentioned above. In the match-play ethos the ball had to be hacked at wherever it lay: if not extracted eventually, the hole could be conceded. The crude iron club was essential for this trouble shot or series of shots.

This rule also reveals something of the terrain at Leith Links and that the golfers had been involved in early greenkeeping in 1744. Trenches, ditches and dykes had been made to improve the links. The 'Soldier's Lines' were possibly the trenches from ancient sieges or more recent military exercises. Of great interest are the 'Scholars Holes', the short course for the young or beginners close to the school on the west of the links, and they are further evidence that golf at Leith was not simply for the well-off.

Finally, the rules consistently give another valuable insight: they assume that golfers were involved in match-play at all times. Penalties were always allowed 'to the adversary'. The rules give no hint that stroke-play existed: all penalties were awarded to the opponent, not added to the score.

The Rules Spread

In 1754, the St Andrews Golfers had copied the Leith code word for word, doubtless because the code was common practice among the players on the east coast. The Leith rules also had been drawn up by Scotland's best legal brains. But thereafter the St Andrews Golfers seem to have taken an independent line when considering changes, and a major reorganisation of their rules was first made by the St Andrews Golfers in 1809 and, as described below, the authority of this club in these matters became steadily greater as the vitality and authority of the Honourable Company went into temporary decline in the 1800s. The R&A had a more cosmopolitan membership, and the town had visitors and university students who played on the links and took back the rules

RULES

OF

The Thistle Golf Club;

WITH

SOME HISTORICAL NOTICES

RELATIVE TO

THE PROGRESS

OF

THE GAME OF GOLF

IN SCOTLAND.

EDINBURGH:
Printed by James Ballantyne and Co.

1824.

Rules of The Thistle Club, one of the golf clubs at Leith Links in the early nineteenth century.

to other parts of Britain. Outside of Scotland, the St Andrews club increasingly became identified with golf and its rules. The Honourable Company at Leith necessarily remained a local, albeit prestigious, society.

But golf was only part of the life of the clubs. Conviviality drew the golfers together, and the new clubs developed a rumbustious lifestyle that was to reach its peak in the late eighteenth century.

Clubbiness

Of this time, the historian of the Burgess Society wrote:

In Scotland by the end of the seventeenth century, the inhabitants of many places had a prescriptive right of playing golf on certain areas usually termed commonties [common land]. Already possessing this right, there was no need of a club to provide it, and of that the early golfers took advantage and excercised their rights. But obviously congenial society and private matches at specified times were essential for complete enjoyment. The players would dine together at a convenient inn, where as regular clients they would be regarded as a society of golfers and given the personal attention accorded to consistent customers... of course no-one had need for rules except as to regulating the payment of the dinner bill and perhaps bets. This may have been the beginning of some of our prominent clubs.

Robbie's succinct summary of how the golf clubs evolved cannot be bettered.[58] The emergence of the golf societies did not mean the emergence of a new sport: it meant merely a sophistication of existing practice as a result of changes in social life. The golf clubs were but part of an enthusiasm in Scotland, and elsewhere, for promoting clubs and societies. There was a rapid rise of political clubs, literary clubs, scientific clubs, and medical clubs. The towns were now enlarging, and there was new leisure, plus confidence and prosperity. In this century, noisy eating and drinking no longer attracted censure. Winter was still regarded as the time for relaxation, a reward for the agricultural exertions of the summer, and Edinburgh in particular still had its additional winter influx of visitors. The old cliques of political, social and sporting cronies now felt the need to evolve into organised clubs, with precise membership, common finances and a division of labour among the office-bearers. For some reason, the old informal arrangements between friends no longer sufficed.

Clubhouses and Dinners

The Honourable Company (then called the Gentlemen Golfers), the first golfing society with formal organisation, kept up the initiative in mid-century. In 1768 it changed from using Straiton's pub and erected its own clubhouse at Leith, the first known custom-built golf clubhouse. The domestic arrangements were interesting. The club raised money among the members to build their Golf House, but then rented it out as a pub to a landlord, while retaining space for their own use.[59]

In this way, the club's dinners moved from the taverns to their own premises. Attendance at dinner was required of the members, and those who did not appear had to subsidise those present, a useful discipline when the membership was small, active and exclusive. At this time, the R&A also required that members meet every fortnight at 11 o'clock and dine together in the evening at Baillie Glass' inn and pay a shilling for dinner, 'the absent as well as the present.' If there were any limits on the membership numbers, it was on account of the capacity of the inn and the limited winter playing time, and there seems to have been no pressure within the early clubs to exceed a membership of about 25. Dinner started early, namely three or four o'clock in the afternoon, after golf finished at winter sunset. The golfers' clubs might be taken home or put away in the tavern until the next meeting.

Dinner was followed by business. Matches were arranged for the next outing and bets placed on the outcome. Other bets were made on golfing feats or on any of the political or military issues of the day. Songs were sung and poetry of variable quality recited. Semi-serious fines on members' indiscretions were recorded and exacted, the debts and fines paid in drink for the others. New members would be admitted and for this a high proportion of the members had to be in agreement. Later a 'black ball' system was introduced which would allow even one or two members secretly to exclude a new applicant.

On the special competition days, a preliminary procession in the town might be added. These public parades by the members prior to their main competitions are well known in the history of golf at Leith and St Andrews. The events prior to Royal Musselburgh's annual competition for their silver bowl are less well known, but suggest that this was part of a familiar ritual throughout Scotland:

First the trophy had to be brought by last year's winner to the tavern which was the club's rendezvous for the day. What a hubbub, to be sure, would be about the door of Mrs Sheriff's, or Widow Cochrane's as the cup would be brought in and honoured by the military officers, the local gentry, the clergy, the doctors, and other personages of importance in the 'Honest Toon', who formed the club membership. What a clamour of little barefoot caddies with their cries of 'Ca'ry for ye, Sir John,' 'Me, sir!' 'Me, sir!' and the like. Presently the procession would be formed. In front stalked the drummer, beating his merriest, for was he not to get three shillings and something to drink for his trouble! Then followed the club's officer carrying the cup, glittering in the April sun-blink, and jingling with its medals. Thereafter, side by side, would march old Sir John Hope, Bart. of Craighall, and Colonel Charles Stewart, who had entered to play for the cup. Following them would come the other members as blythesome as the lark soaring over Pinkie at the moment. And in the rear, ragged but happy, a jostling crowd of caddies. What a subject for a picture with Musselburgh's quaint old Tolbooth and High Street as background! Then when the links had been reached and the feather balls swiped from the tee, how charming in fancy to follow the game stroke for stroke around the course, flanked by threatening whin. What excitement! What betting of sixpences, or of half-crowns, or of bottles of wine or of dozens of wine or of legs of mutton! And when the play was o'er and the procession reformed with the cup winner, now captain or preses-elect for a year in the place of honour, how pleasant to march back to Widow Cochrane's or Mrs Sheriff's and join in the revelry and hear the annual grant made 'according to the articles of the club' of eleven and a half dozen golf balls to the boys of the Musselburgh Grammar School, which had to be played for by the scholars under the eye of their Rector...[60]

Club Budgets

The early golf clubs had no entrance fee, and no annual subscription. Their finances revolved entirely round the dinners; these were their only serious source of income and their only major expenditure. Slowly the clubs found it useful to drop the tedious gathering of dinner money for each meeting, and instead introduced an 'annual subscription' to cover the finances of the dinners. In 1785 the Musselburgh club decided on an annual fee of 6/- for the cost of nine dinners.[61] This income was added to by small fines on non-attendance at the dinners, and also by a small levy on the many bets on future matches made at the dinners. Slowly in the late 1700s, the clubs found another source of revenue. As the clubs became popular and membership desirable, an entry fee could be exacted from eager aspirants. In 1764 the Leith golfers decided on a half-guinea entry fee. This item rapidly became important in their budgets and was increasingly relied on to underpin the club's annual revenue: this change was to give great difficulty later.

The 'Cock of the Green', Alexander M'Kellar was a familiar figure on Bruntsfield Links as a passionate golfer. He carries five woods and no iron clubs. He has breeches, a waistcoat and a two-part hat. His shoes look ordinary, and he has the closed stance typical of play in the feathery era. From Kay's *Portraits* 1837.

The price of the club's dinner was fixed and food prepared for those expected. There were two problems for the club treasurer. The first was if members did not appear. The second was if drinking got out of hand. The first nuisance was dealt with throughout the century by charging those members who did not turn up: the second potential overspend was mentioned repeatedly in the minutes. It seems that, on the morning after, the clubs often faced a drink bill which was unexpectedly large and that no funds were left to meet this overshoot. To prevent embarrassment, a simple strategy was widely in use among the clubs. To the 'Preses' – the Captain – was given the task of watching the progress of the dinner and, knowing his budget, he could judge when an overspend on drink was imminent. He had to be watchful and call for the club's bill from the landlord once the subscribed money had been used up: thereafter the drouthy members had to buy their own drinks. The Gentlemen Golfers at Leith in 1779 recorded a rule, one reinforced many times later

the proper regulation by which the preses is bound to call a bill after a Chopin bottle [two pints] of Claret has been called for each person.[62]

Enough money was promised ahead for this adequate consumption, but in the event of the Captain failing to call for the bill within the proper time, the members decided on a simple solution, to concentrate the captain's mind, namely that 'the surplus shall be paid by himself'. The Dunbar Golfing Society later had an even simpler strategy: 'when expenditure at dinner rose above 2/6, the club shall be dissolved'. These sensible, self-regulating, workable procedures were typical of this relaxed century.

A bill for one of the Gentlemen Golfers' dinners at Leith for 14 members was:

Dinner	£2 0 0
Bread and Biscuit	£0 2 0
Porter, Ale, Spruce	£0 8 0
Gin and Brandy	£0 6 8
Port and Sherry (7 bottles)	£1 13 6
Claret (16 bottles)	£5 12 0
Tody, Glasses, Wax,	
Lights and Servants	£0 11 2
TOTAL	£10 13 4

The amount of wine, spirits and ales consumed on these occasions was considerable.[63] As mentioned above, the Leith Golfers' captain had to call the bill when one quart bottle of claret each had been served. In the bill for this Leith dinner, fourteen members had a chopin of claret (two pint bottles) each plus a half- bottle of fortified wine (sherry or port) each. Two bottles of gin and brandy were also on the table, together with an unspecified amount of ale and porter. One drink conspicuously missing from these lists is whisky. This may not be because Scotland's own drink was uncommon, but because it was so common. Whisky drinking was part of daily life in Scotland: it was cheap and not highly regarded. It is just possible that whisky was freely available at the golfers' dinner, but was hardly worth mentioning. In short, all the evidence suggests heavy drinking at the golfing dinners - very heavy drinking.

The extent of this indulgence, though accepted at the time, was embarrassing to the temperate and polite society which followed in the 1800s. Attempts were made to ignore and even hide the evidence of this conspicuous alcohol consumption of the 1700s, and later, pride was taken in this tidying up of Scottish behaviour. Dean Ramsay wrote in 1872 of this evolution that 'the next change in manners which has been effected in the memory of many still living regards the banishment of drunkenness from polite society. Indeed it is scarely possible to realise the scenes which took place seventy or eighty years ago [i.e. about 1800]'.[65]

The food at golfing dinners of the time also appears lavish and the menus apparently show a feast of many courses. However, the many items listed were not eaten one after the other, as might appear. The eighteenth-century style was to serve all dishes simultaneously, rather than as separate courses, and most items were cold, not hot. The available menus were probably meagre by the standards in the well-off golfer's home, and Scottish tavern food was not highly regarded. Some golf clubs, like the North Berwick Club later, by-passed the tavern food and organised their own dinner, each member bringing a dish of his own choice.[66]

Broken Rules

The clubs' disciplinary records show the spirit of the times. The golfers of the mid-1700s often had their tongues firmly in their cheeks when writing their minutes: punishment for breaking rules in the 1700s was often measured by the bottle. A member convicted of playing without his uniform was fined six pints of claret, and 'having confessed the heinousness of his crime, at his request he was fined 3 pints more'. These nine pints were doubtless immediately placed on the table: society was urbane and tolerant.

Even the chaplain to the club took part in this unselfconscious revelry, since the minister said the grace *after* the dinner and not before. Nor did the office-bearers take themselves too seriously. A secretary to the Honourable Company, 'Singing James' Balfour, was in the habit of lurching homewards from Leith, betting passing citizens to a race to the next tavern. The bet was the expected bottle of claret, to be drunk on arrival. His members in the club seem to have shared his ribald attitudes. The inscription on the membership certificates of the Edinburgh Golfers in the eighteenth century had the motto *'Stiff Shafts and Hard Balls.'* At any other time in Edinburgh's history this flippant motto would have attracted adverse comment by serious-minded persons, but this motto survived the 1700s, and its cheerful crudity was removed from the Company's official papers only when the solemn and temperate 1800s arrived.

Other Edinburgh clubs at this time shared this outlook. The distinguished Harveian Society of Edinburgh, founded in 1782, took itself seriously in later years, but its founders stated that they would

> gather annually on 12th April to commemorate the discovery of the circulation of the blood by the circulation of the glass.

This medical club of the 1700s had an inner élite club within a club, proudly calling itself the Dissipation Society. It disappeared in the sober and self-conscious 1800s.

Domestic Affairs of the Club

The Edinburgh Golfers had been first to make formal arrangements for their golfing society and first to have their own clubhouse. A third innovation is less well known but is important. Some funds of the Gentlemen Golfers' society found their way towards the upkeep of the Leith golfing links: they were the first club to tend their own links.

As noted above, the 1744 rules of the Gentlemen Golfers mention 'dykes and ditches for the preservation of the links', showing that some elementary drainage had been attempted. The first entry relating to such greenkeeping is in the Golfers' minutes of 1758, which reported a levy on the members for 'the upkeep of the links'. In 1762 the Golfers raised further money for a major drainage scheme at Leith, and from 1764 onwards an annual levy was in force to 'keep the links in good order'. Further schemes followed. In 1787 the minutes record that they had had

> very considerable expense in making drains; one of them in the year 1778 cost above £28 sterl. and they have been at a constant yearly expense in repairing and cleaning of drains, beside carting of Earth, sowing Grass Seeds, and many other articles not necessary to be mentioned.[67]

The Gentlemen Golfers were the first greenkeepers. But they went further. In 1787 they obtained a lease of the Leith Links for about £37 per annum, and became the first club to have some control over its golf course. The golfers were a little reluctant to take on this pioneering expense; instead the innovation was forced on them. The golfers did not want to have the burden of a rental of ground which was freely available for use to them and any Leith or Edinburgh citizen. But others in Leith were also asking to lease the links from the town in order to pasture animals. The golfers were tolerant but did not like the prospect of unrestricted numbers of cattle on the links. Sheep and rabbit dung were acceptable, but, as they minuted:

> *The dung of black Cattle, of all others, is most hurtful to Golfers; even in dry weather, it smells and is encrusted, but so thinly that a ball lighting upon it will break it, will sink and be out of sight;...*[68]

Accordingly, they took on the burden of a lease of the links, if only to save their precious featheries from the damp cow pats.

These actions of the Edinburgh Golfers show them as a pace-setter in a range of golfing matters. The Golfers had been first with a formal club organisation, first with a clubhouse, and they had been first to tend a municipal links. With a rental now of the links, albeit reluctantly, they were first to have some degree of possession of their own course. These actions give the Edinburgh Golfers additional claims to importance at the time and give them additional historical respect. These events set them apart from any other club particularly those which have claimed earlier foundation.

Dress and Uniform

An interesting discipline within the golfers' societies in the late 1700s was the wearing of the club uniform. The style of these uniforms, unique to each club, was unmistakably military, and appeared when Britain had become heavily involved in war abroad.

The early part of the century had been untroubled by hostilities at home or abroad. But by the 1780s, Britain faced not only rebellion in North America but thereafter the threat at home of invasion by Napoleon. Large numbers of volunteers were raised in Britain under the Defence of the Realm Act, and of these 15% came from Scotland, a country now convinced of the need for British patriotism in defence of an agreeable post-Union lifestyle. The golf club uniforms became popular during this active military period of the fifty years from the 1780s onwards and the uniforms entered general use among the members of the golf clubs. Thereafter, the uniforms entered into a part of golfing mystique and tradition, but lapsed later as the origins were forgotten.

As military preparations became essential in the late 1700s, many of the golf club men had seen active service or were volunteer officer reservists. The clubs copied the habits of the regiments in seeking a uniform and this gave an *esprit de corps* among the club members. It is sometimes said that the Scottish uniforms were worn to warn the ordinary users on the links of the approaching golfers, but this analysis fails to satisfy. Such warnings were not required to be given by gentlemen: noble golfers had no need to warn the lower orders that they were advancing on the links. Instead, the uniforms were an ostentatious show of power and rank, to which others naturally deferred and the golf club members at play were watched with new awe. In any case, the mass of other humble golfers were just as dangerous, but had no uniform. Later, in the golf boom in England, the pioneer golfers on the common land did present a danger to the citizens, and in this situation, the uniform worn at play made sense and was often required.

The uniform had a practical additional justification. It was suitable for protection from the wet, cold Scottish winter weather. It was designed for military combat in all weathers in the open and to allow free use of the arms and legs. It solved a problem for the winter golfers of the eighteenth century: the best the golfers could do in wet weather was to dress up as for war. The thick heavy cloth kept out the rain – for a while.

The Choices

The colours and the decorative parts of the uniform were characteristic of each club, as they were for any regiment. The variables were the colour of the coat, the colour of the collar, and the type and decoration of button. The members might have two uniforms, even of different colours, one for play and one for dinner at night. Perhaps the golfers were prepared to be soaked while at play and kept a change of formal dress. The uniforms of each club are recorded with pride. The Honourable Company at Leith ordered their first uniform in 1787 – a scarlet coat with blue collar, plus blue club buttons. These colours are seen in some portraits, and that of William Inglis, captain in 1782-1784 shows his uniform to be not dissimilar to that of the military Town Guard behind. Other golf clubs had similarly colourful uniforms: the Burgess Club playing over Bruntsfield Links had a scarlet coat with a black collar and badge from 1789. Though red was the favourite colour for the coat, and was to be regarded later as the only golfing uniform, not all the clubs used red. The Glasgow Club had a grey coat, the Innerleven Club used Prince Charles tartan, and the Kingsbarns Club chose blue.[69]

General use of uniforms began to decline in the mid-1800s. The continental wars were finished, and uniforms were considered outmoded and expensive. As use of the uniforms on the links declined, dressing up was only enforced at dinner. When this tradition also declined in turn, by the end of the century only the Captain was required to put on the old display by wearing a red jacket at dinner, a tradition still maintained in a number of clubs. One tiny vestige of the generality of club uniforms has survived. In some clubs, club buttons are still available for use on blazers and jackets, as the last trace of an old custom.

The early golfers had to protect their heads, and it seems likely that they used their everyday hat or bonnet. The portraits of golfers from this time show such headgear or a three-cornered velvet hat. A top hat is shown in some illustrations from the early 1800s, and records show that these were worn routinely by the Aberdeen golfers on their outings. Golfing gloves seem to be as ancient as the game itself, particularly to grip the unprotected, slippery handle in wet weather. The early golfing gloves were made of kid, and the early portraits show them on the right hand of the golfers, and not on the left. Sensible breeches are shown in the golfing portraits of the time. No special footwear is described, and one early rule hints that the golfers used ordinary leather soles and that these gave a problem. The early Aberdeen rules forbade any improvement of stance, but did allow deliberate 'wetting of the golfers soles', probably to improve their grip. Golfing boots with tacks were still to come.[70]

A Hidden Club?

Most gentlemen golfers were members of another club - the masonic lodge. Freemasonry had started in Scotland in the 1500s when the stonemasons' craft attracted outside social members who patronised and gentrified the town craft and encouraged its initiation rites. To this they added conviviality and benevolent activities. By the 1700s many gentlemen were masons, and many gentlemen were also golfers: thus we need not be surprised that many gentlemen golfers were freemasons. But the suggestion has been made that the eighteenth-century golf clubs were a facade concealing secret masonic lodges and that the clubs' evening gatherings were thinly disguised lodge meetings. This view further suggests that golf was not the most important nor the most serious part of the day's outings. Further suggestions are that the gaps in the early historical records of the golf clubs resulted because the golfing masons destroyed their early secret minutes and records.

This thesis is thinly supported by the evidence. Instead of a conspiracy of destruction of minute books, the evidence is of the usual loss, decay and muddle. Any analysis of any activity in the eighteenth century is hampered by such loss of records. Indeed the Honourable Company's records and those of the R&A, the most important of the century, are remarkably well preserved. These records also show that, far from the dinner being the high point of the day, and essential for masonic cohesion, the Gentlemen Golfers' organisation was plagued by the converse - the dreary problem of lack of interest. The members tended to play golf, and many then departed for Edinburgh without taking dinner at Leith. As for secret rituals, privacy could hardly be great in the back room of a popular pub at this time, and any rites involved in the admission of new members, such as complex oaths of allegiance, would be difficult to conceal.

In any case, the evidence is that such activity would not be concealed. The Lodges had a high profile and were often involved in public ceremony, when their members and procedures were on open display. At Leith, on 2nd July 1768, the foundation stone of the Edinburgh Golfers' new clubhouse was laid with 'masonic ceremony'. But this does not prove the masonic link. When the Royal Infirmary of Edinburgh was opened in 1741 there was also a masonic procession and ceremony, and a little later the foundation stone of Aberdeen Royal Infirmary was ceremonially placed by the local 'Society of Free and Accepted Masons'. Masonic activity was simply part of public life in the 1700s: obsessive secrecy and concealed activity was to come later, when, in Europe at least, the masons furtively opposed the traditional power of the aristocracy, hoping to elevate their own interests. By the time this happened, the early Scottish golf clubs were badly attended and in decay, and incapable of any influence, secret or otherwise. It is unlikely that our early club golfers had a hidden agenda of masonic activity.[71]

The Weather

Searching the records of golf from this period, there is little comment on the weather. Golf was still a winter, east coast sport, a game played without waterproof clothes in cold weather which intruded daily into life and sport.

But the east coast, as noted above, had the driest winters of any part of Scotland, and for this reason play was regularly possible even with the damp-sensitive feathery ball. Comments on the weather are suprisingly rare. One Silver Club competition of the Honourable Company was postponed in 1776 from a Friday in January until the next Tuesday because of the weather, but when they gathered again, because 'the Weather continued stormy the captain and Councill adjourned playing for the Cups *sine die*'.[72] Another summer minute says that the Honourable Company proposed the date for the Silver Club competition, adding 'if the weather is good'. But how good was 'good' for these early unprotected winter players?

Alexander and James, sons of the chief of the Clan Macdonald, shown against the background of the Island of Skye, and as sportsmen with golf clubs and gun. The wooden golf club shows the 'long-nosed' design. The various tartans they wear confirm that no specific tartan was attached to any clan at that time in the 1750s.

By courtesy of the SCOTTISH NATIONAL PORTRAIT GALLERY.

Clubs and Clubmakers

There are no surviving wooden or iron clubs from the 1600s, except one nicely finished wooden club-head possibly made in Leith in 1682, but there are a few surviving golf clubs that can be confidently said to come from the 1700s. These, plus some descriptions of clubs from this time, and a few illustrations, allow a sketchy description of the clubs for eighteenth century play.

The clubs for routine play were the woods. The head was of dark thorn with a flat lie, and the long, thin head suited the flat sweeping swing of the times needed for play with the feathery ball. In the head was a substantial lead insert which gave power to the impact. The sophisticated golfer of the 1700s played, as before, with a small set of clubs, usually about three or four woods and one iron. The shafts of the woods were long, dark and elegant and were made from ash or hazel. The shaft was subject to torque, and the clubface opened slightly on the downswing. To neutralise this, these ancient wooden clubs had a closed face, with the toe in advance of the heel, thus connecting squarely with the ball on impact. These clubs determined the swing; all paintings and illustrations from this time show a remarkably closed stance.

Many wooden clubs had a strip of horn or bone added, not to the face as later, but to the sole, to protect the club from the turf and from any loose objects on the links. It was not to protect the club from the feathery ball, which was kind to the club face. The accounts of the day show steady payments for replacement of this horn to favourite clubs.[73] The clubmaker applied red keel, an iron-based dye made in the Lothians, to protect the head and to show grain – varnish was to come later, in about 1810. The head might be 'tinned' to waterproof it. The shaft was joined to the head in the traditional way at a splice 'scare' joint which was glued and strengthened by enclosure in a wrapping of fisherman's twine plus more glue. The thick leather grip on the handle covered an under-wrapping of thin cloth off-cuts, discarded by furniture makers.[74]

Iron Clubs

The single iron club carried by the players was a club not for routine use but for emergencies. Known simply as the 'iron club', or 'bunker club' or 'scraper' at this time, it was only later in the century that the term 'rut iron' or 'track iron' was applied. Its crudity and lowly place in the golfer's equipment contrasts with the elegance of the wooden clubs. The iron clubs were more expensive at 2/6d at this time in the mid-1700s, as against 1/2d for a wood, but the iron club required little attention or repair: it was robust and little used.

Not until 100 years later did the iron club emerge as the club for accurate approach play. In the 1700s this heavy, awkward club was used to get the ball out of trouble, bad lies or from bunkers. The links were ungroomed, and there was no out-of-bounds. To attempt recovery shots from heavy ground with the precious woods was foolish and risked a broken shaft. On the other hand, the use of the robust iron club for such shots endangered the feathery ball. Our noble golfers of the eighteenth century therefore had a costly choice to make when in a rut, bunker, rough or cuppy lie. The ball had to be played where it lay, and the hole had to be finished with the same ball. Doubtless many holes were simply conceded in match-play.

An early rut or track iron from the eighteenth century, used for trouble shots, with a heavy head and stout shaft lacking the grip. By courtesy of the PEOPLE'S PALACE, GLASGOW.

But the iron club had one little role of its own, a foretaste of its future rise to importance. As noted above, the rules of the golfing societies allowed for balls to be lifted from certain hazards - e.g. the dykes and ditches on Leith Links - and dropped. Instead of a penalty shot, the stroke was played with the iron club only, thus forfeiting some distance.[75]

The Clubmakers

The clubmakers of the 1600s were mentioned above, and we know a little more about their equivalents in the 1700s. As before, the clubmakers did not make golf balls: nor did the ballmakers make clubs.

The clubmakers of the eighteenth century are increasingly identified in the growing number of golfing records.[76] In 1735 a clubmaker called Andrew Bailey is noted at Bruntsfield. The next well-known maker there, and one who founded a family of clubmakers, was James McEwan who came from Stirling to Edinburgh in 1770 to be clubmaker to the Bruntsfield Club. Other club-makers of the time were Jackson in Perth, Patrick at Leven, Davidson at Montrose, and Ballantyne in Musselburgh. Clubmakers at St Andrews are not well known, but a family called Lindesay calling themselves 'spoon-makers', flourished at this time in the 1700s, giving about ten clubmakers known in Scotland. Some of these were found in locations not otherwise known for golfing societies, such as Leven, Perth, Montrose and Musselburgh. This confirms other suggestions that there were gentlemen golfers playing golf far from the better-known golfing links, and that they were active enough to support a local maker, without any formal golf clubs locally.

BELOW AND OPPOSITE: Play and rut iron clubs of simple construction from the early 1800s.

By courtesy of PHILLIPS, CHESTER.

Golf Balls

At this time, the long game of golf was played, as before, with the feathery ball. It lasted only for about one round, eventually losing resilience and performance. If wet, it rapidly soaked with water; if struck badly with an iron, it would split, and the caddies went out with a number of balls, ready for all possible problems. This limitation of the ball is hinted at in some of the bets recorded in the minutes of the early clubs, and some wagers among the Gentlemen Golfers were for games in which the players were limited to one ball each; doubtless they had to make the ball last as long as possible, by cautious play.[77]

Ballmakers known at this time were Robertson of St Andrews and in that town there was also a ballmaker called David Lindesay and his son John.

Feathery ball from the early 1800s.

By courtesy of PHILLIPS.

Making the Feathery

The making of a feather ball was a tedious business, and a quality maker could produce only about 50 or 60 per week. Appropriate templates of horse or bull's hide were cut, three pieces in all, wetted and partly stitched together, leaving an entrance hole. This shell was turned inside out, to conceal the stitches. Wet bird feathers (goose breast if possible) were inserted forcibly. The last feathers were pushed in with a *brogue* - a ramming device strapped

That *Fury* now from our blefs'd fields is driv'n,
To fcourge unhappy nations doom'd by heav'n. 20
Let *Kouli Kan* deftroy the fertile Eaft,
Victorious *Vernon* thunder in the Weft;
Let horrid war involve perfidious *Spain*,
And GEORGE affert his empire o'er the Main:
But on our plains *Britannia*'s fons engage, 25
And void of ire the fportive war they wage.

Lo, tatter'd *Irus*, who their armour bears,
Upon the green two little pyr'mids rears;
On thefe they place two balls with careful eye,
That with *Clarinda*'s breafts for colour vye, 30
The work of *Bobfon*; who with matchlefs art
Shapes the firm hide, connecting ev'ry part,
Then in a focket fets the well-ftitch'd void,
And thro' the eylet drives the downy tide;
Crowds urging Crowds the forceful brogue impels, 35
The feathers harden and the Leather fwells;
He crams and fweats, yet crams and urges more,
Till fcarce the turgid globe contains its ftore:

The dreaded falcon's pride here blended lies
With pigeons gloffy down of various dyes;
The lark's fmall pinions join the common ftock
And yellow glory of the martial cock.
Soon as *Hyperion* gilds old *Andrea*'s fpires,
From bed the artift to his cell retires;
With bended back, there plies his fteely awls,
And fhapes, and ftuffs, and finifhes the balls.
But when the glorious God of day has driv'n
His flaming chariot down the fteep of heav'n,
He ends his labour, and with rural ftrains
Enchants the lovely maids and weary fwains:
As thro' the ftreets the blythfome piper plays,
In antick dance they anfwer to his lays;
At ev'ry paufe the ravifh'd crowd acclaim,
And rend the fkies with tuneful *Bobfon*'s
Not more rewarded was old *Amphion*'s
That rear'd a town, and this drags on
Such is fam'd *Bobfon*, who in *Andrea*
And fuch the balls each vig'rous hero

Text from *The Goff* (1743) describing the manufacture of feathery balls.

to the maker's chest. Tradition says that a single ball contained about a top hat full of dry feathers. The stitching was then completed, and the ball was dried, becoming tense, hard and round as the shrinking leather compressed the expanding feathers. To make the ball spherical, some gentle hammering might be required.

There is evidence, as we saw above, of a range of prices of feathery balls. It may be that the best balls used the best feathers. Even so, the balls were remarkably expensive, bearing in mind the low costs of the materials. At the other end of the price range, less expensive feathers and less labour perhaps were involved in the cheaper balls, and damaged balls might be repaired and sold on to less demanding players.

For an important match, the gentlemen doubtless sought the perfect ball. The Leith players in *The Goff* used St Andrews balls, 'the work of Bobson', i.e. Robertson of St Andrews. These serious players were prepared to by-pass any local Leith ballmakers, such was the quest for the tiny advantage of the best ball available.

A lyrical and informative account of feathery production is found in Mathison's *The Goff*:

And thro' the eyelet drives the downy tide;
Crowds urging crowds the forceful brogue impels,
The feathers harden and the leather swells;
He crams and sweats, yet crams and urges more,
Till scarce the turgid globe contains its store.

Feathery ball from the early 1800s.

By courtesy of PHILLIPS.

Kincaid's diary makes comment on the leather used for featheries and says that 'the pores should be able to admit a pin'. This interesting technical point is not discussed elsewhere, and raises interest in the role of these channels in the leather cover. If the pores were too big, perhaps the ball let in water too easily during play: and too small a pore prevented drying out during manufacture. Whatever the reason, after this drying, the ball was then coated with thick white oil paint, or white lead, to make it as waterproof as possible.[78]

The Cost

The price of featheries in the 1700s was about 6d in post-Union money, which roughly corresponds to the 5/- in Scots money earlier. Clerk of Penicuik's son at school in Dalkeith in 1731 was given balls at 6d each, in the English currency, and John Dickson of Leith sent balls at about 6d to the Marquis of Annandale in 1722.[79] A Scottish flax merchant in Riga wrote home for golf supplies in 1748, and clubs were sent back to him from Scotland on the good ship *Helen of Methil* with this invoice:

We have sent you by captain Lumisdaine a box containing 17 play clubs at 14d each; 3 iron clubs at 2/6 each and 6 dozen golf balls at 4/- a dozen...[80]

At this price for a dozen, allowing for a discount, single balls might cost 5d each. As late as 1789 the Kilmarnock retailers Samson's catalogue listed golf balls at 6d each.[81] Surprisingly few club prices have survived from this period, but a nobleman near Inverness paid 1/6 for a new club, a price which fits well with the 12/- price in old money before the Union.[82]

Caddies

When noble golfers appeared on the links in earlier times, their clubs were carried by servants. If not, there was always the local clubmaker or ballmaker to oblige, and if all else failed, there was always a 'boy' at hand. These boys appear, on cue, to carry clubs in the earliest literature of golf. Montrose paid a boy to carry for him in 1628, as did Foulis in 1692 and Kincaid in 1687.

The word 'caddie' does not appear until the mid-1700s. Early golf historians and commentators have suggested that the word came from the French word 'cadet' – which means the youngest son of the family - one sent to learn a profession or trade. This may have been the original derivation but instead, all dictionaries of the Scots tongue show the word is used in a different and much more plausible way. The 'caddies' of Edinburgh in the eighteenth century were a semi-official band of porters and messengers who hung about the centre of Edinburgh, touting and picking up what work they could. They carried luggage, took messages, knew the town, directed visitors and were acquainted with the local low life. Topham's *Letters from Edinburgh 1774 and 1775* describes the caddies as

CADGELL, *s.* A wanton fellow. V. CAIGIE.
CADGY, CADY, *adj.* V. CAIGIE.
CADGILY, *adv.* Cheerfully, S. *Ferguson.*
CADIE, *s.* 1. One who gains a livelihood by running errands, or delivering messages; a member of a society in Edinburgh, instituted for this purpose, S. *Ferguson.* 2. A boy; especially as employed in running errands, or in any inferior sort of work, S. 3. A young fellow; used in a ludicrous sense, S. *Burns.* 4. A young fellow; used in the language of friendly familiarity, S. *Picken.*—Fr. *cadet,* a younger brother.
CADOUK, CADDOUCK, *s.* A casualty. *Monro's Exped.* L. B. *caducum,* haereditas, (from *cad-ere,*) something

Jamieson's *Dictionary* from 1808 is in no doubt about the Edinburgh origins of the word 'caddie'.

a group of poor messenger boys organised under a captain called the constable of the caddies. They were a society of men who constantly attend the cross in the High Street and whose office it is to do any thing that any body can want...whether you stand in need of a valet de place, a pimp, a thief catcher or a bully, your best resource is to the fraternity of caddies.[83]

These men were usually from the Highlands of Scotland, since another traveller in 1817, also interested in this Edinburgh service, noted that

'the breed [caddies] was kept up by continual levies of fresh recruits from the same rugged wilds. Every year brought [recruits] from the fastnesses of Lochaber and Braemar'.[84]

A certain amount of discipline was exerted by the 'chief caddie' and the group had some reliability. Being employed to carry luggage round Edinburgh, they doubtless were prepared to take clubs down to Leith and having done so, would naturally be hired to go out on the links carrying these clubs.

Ordinance from the Edinburgh Town Council regulating the Edinburgh street caddies - the town's porters.

By courtesy of SCOTTISH RECORD OFFICE H 9/14/114.

Their name has thus been passed on to the bearers of clubs.

One such caddie is described in 1743 in *The Goff*, and given the classical name of 'Irus'. First, he tees up the ball, or rather both balls, for the two players:

Lo, tattered Irus, who, their armour bears,
Upon the green two little Pyr'mids rears;

The caddie then warns others out on the links:

The Chief, assigned to Irus who, before,
With frequent warnings fill'd the sounding shore.

Lastly, the caddie goes ahead as a forecaddie and reports back on the drive:

Swift as a thought the ball obedient flies,
And Irus to the Chief the welcome tidings sends.

The poem reveals much of the ancient duties of the caddies at this time. In addition to watching for the flight of the ball, they might warn any others on the links that there were advancing players. In acting as forecaddies, they also prevented the ball being stolen, and perhaps rescued the feathery ball from water.

It was the tradition to give the caddie any surviving ball after play, and there is evidence later of caddies then reselling these if they 'werna owre muckle disjeskit'.[85]

Women and Golf

In the early game of golf, there were no prohibitions on play by anyone. Young and old used the public links of the towns for golf and other sports, without formality. The male golfing societies founded in the 1700s were but one group in this range of activity on the links. Anyone could play golf on the links, and there were no organisational obstructions to women playing the game at this time, but it is clear that women were not playing the game in any number. Only two scraps of historical information describe women playing golf. Mary, Queen of Scots was a player and as Queen she seems to have taken up royal sports. Perhaps she was a woman in a man's world and played the male sports of the Court. This came to notice when her detractors gossiped about her play at 'golf and pall-mall' at Seton shortly after the death of Darnley. That women did not play golf or other sports in this early phase of golf development could only be the result of the widely held assumptions in society of the day.

The second notice of women's golf is from much later, and is a description of a competition at Musselburgh involving the townswomen in 1810. A new creel and shawl were awarded to the best female golfer in this annual event in January, the 'competition to be intimated to the Fish Ladies by the officer of the [Musselburgh] club'. It seems likely that this was a winter festive gathering, and that similar ones were held on other important holidays. It does not give evidence of any all-year-round interest in golf by women in that town. It also seems that they were unusual women. Dr Carlyle studied the Musselburgh women and concluded...'as they do the work of men, their manners are masculine... On holidays they frequently play golf; and on Shrove Tuesday there is a standing match at foot-ball between the married and unmarried women'.[86]

Otherwise the total dearth of historical records on golf by women does, for once, appear to mean that there was no regular golf played by women in the 1700s.

Golf Furth of Scotland

In this successful and productive eighteenth century, Scotsmen travelled the world in greater numbers than ever before, and numerous visitors came to tour or study in Scotland. The new and successful Scottish west coast tobacco trade with America meant a continuous interchange of merchants and trade between Glasgow and the Carolinas. On the east coast of Scotland, Edinburgh University attracted students from many countries, and, once trained, they returned to North America and the colonies, as well as to England and Europe.

It is not surprising to find traces of the playing of golf in the parts of the world reached by the Scots. We find hesitant starts for golf in America, Ireland, England and elsewhere. The third edition of the poem *The Goff* in 1793 was dedicated to to 'all the lovers of goff in Europe, Asia, Africa, and America'. These émigrés required golf equipment and wrote home for the best available. Noted above was the Scottish merchant in Riga, on the Baltic, who felt deprived of golf in 1767. Also in 1767, the Scottish representative at a wine merchant's business in Bordeaux, sent home for golf balls and clubs.[87] A native of Brora in Sutherland, exiled in Jamaica, wrote home frequently for balls and clubs, and another wrote home from Philadelphia to Brora in May 1763 thus:

I must desire on receipt you may get bought twenty dozen golf balls of the best St Andrews kind for me from 28 to 32 and 34 drops each, which order in a small box to London, directed to Mr Angus MacKay, with particular directions to forward

Mary, Queen of Scots, Scotland's first known woman player, shown on a medal from 1565 with Lord Darnley.
Courtesy of the SCOTTISH NATIONAL PORTRAIT GALLERY.

me per first opportunity. Depending you will get the best sent. You
tled to a quart claret for your commission.[88]

Doubtless there were many other groups of golfing expatriates i
diaspora who have left no record. Even Sierra Leone saw the gai
1773. Two botanists at Bense Island recorded that 'we amused ou
Goff, a game played in some particular parts of Scotland and at E
Two holes are made in the ground at about one quarter of a mile (

And in England, play continued in a small way at Blackheath. T,
enthusiasm there, as elsewhere, was derived from exiled Scotsmen
indigenous enthusiasm can be detected in England at the time. Not
the initiative for golf come from the Scots, but sustaining the interes
depended also on the Scots.

North America

Of these early scattered golfing activities, the tentative foundation of golf
societies in America is of special interest. The arrival of these clubs was, as
usual, preceded by evidence of play without such formality. Forty years
before the first golf club in America was founded, a Leith Customs Account
Book from 1743 lists the cargo on the *Magdalen* bound for Charleston, South
Carolina as not only sailcloth and salt from Anstruther, but also two boxes
with '8 doz golf clubs, and three gross golf balls'. Shipments of clubs and balls
by the dozen from Greenock on the west coast of Scotland for Virginia also
appear in other Customs books in 1750-51.[90] These exports confirm the early
existence of the game in the American South prior to any organised clubs. The
export of balls and clubs in round dozens often suggests export to a merchant,
with customers waiting, rather than to individual golfers. There was a merchant in Charleston who stocked Scottish goods, and when he died in 1764
there was in his inventory a dozen 'goof sticks and balls'.[91]

But the numerous student visitors to Scotland were themselves cool about
playing the game. One famous medical student was Benjamin Rush, pioneer
of American medical teaching, who studied in Edinburgh before returning to
Philadelphia. His many writings in America include a recommendation of the
healthiness of golf: there is no evidence that he took his own advice.[92]

South Carolina

The first club golf in America emerged in South Carolina
some time after these exports of golf equipment are recorded.[93]
The established American planters and gentry in that area had
favoured racing, but the incoming Scottish merchants and
tobacco dealers had other assumptions, and started a golf club
in 1786 on Harleston's Green, linksland near Charleston. They
met in mid-week, with business meetings at William's Coffee
House and with dinner at 3 o'clock. Their main meetings were
in May and September, a timetable determined, as at home, by
the harvest. The club was active for at least 23 years, judging
by newspaper reports and advertisements.

A neighbouring port is Savannah, Georgia, and newspaper advertisements
show that there was also an organised golf club here from 1797. The meetings

Anniverſary of the South Carolina

Golf Club

WILL be held at Williams's coffee houſe, on Thurſday, the
29th inſtant, where the members are
requeſted to attend at two o'clock pre-
ciſely, that the buſineſs of the club
may be tranſacted before dinner.
September 20   *tuthſru ſt*

Announcement of a South
Carolina Golf Club meeting.
By courtesy of GEORGE C.
ROGERS JR. and his *The Carolina
Low Country* (1980).

were in autumn, and the players gathered in a hotel or coffee house, or even in a marquee in the manner of the North Berwick Club at home. Analysis again shows that Savannah golf was not patronised by the social élite or the very wealthy. Golf was for the merchant class.

SEAFIELD, near BRAY.

O be Tet for a Term of Years, and entered upon immediately, being a genteel Country Seat in complete Repair, within nine Miles of Dublin; the House is convenient for a large Family, and hath Locks, Grates, with all neceffary Fixtures in every Room, befide the Kitchen; one of the Parlours is large, with a Bow Window to the Sea; there are 31 Acres of choice Land well divided and quicked, with a large Garden walled round, and planted with Fruit Trees, Offices of all Kinds ftrongly built and flated; it is near the Church, Market, and two yearly Fairs at BRAY, well fituated for the Goats Whey, for Bathing, Boating, and Fifhing, bounded on the Eaft by a Common, famous for that manly Exercife called GOFF. Inquire of Mr. Thomas Cufack, Auctioneer, in Montague-ftreet, Kevin's-port, who can fhew a Map of the Premises.

Irish golf at Bray in 1762
By courtesy of WILLIAM GIBSON.

Ireland

As mentioned above, golf was first taken to Ireland in 1603 just prior to the Scottish protestant plantations, and golf seems to have continued there in a small way.[94] In 1762 golf at Bray was noted and a new golf club appeared. It met to dine at the house of a Mr. Charles Moran, with Elias de Butts Esq. from a Huguenot family as chairman. About the same time a house was advertised in Bray

well situated for the Goat's Whey, for Bathing, Boating and Fishing, bounded on the east by a Common, famous for that manly exercise called Goff.[95]

Clearly, golf was well known in this area at this time.

Fin de Siècle

But this scattered use of golf outside Scotland was to disappear. In America about 1808, the vitality of commerce declined and the Scots went home. Harleston's Green at Charleston was encroached on, houses built, and the railway later ran through what remained of the open ground. Golf simply disappeared with hardly a trace, and when it revived later it was considered an entirely new game.

None of the other metastatic golf ventures in the rest of the world came to anything. Golf at Bordeaux never flourished. Golf in Ireland also faded out and golf at Riga still remains to be developed. Sierra Leone was and is not prominent in pioneering African golf. Golf in the 1700s and early 1800s still required the presence of Scotsmen, and golf came and went with them.

But there was another reason for the eclipse of golf beyond Scotland at this time. At the end of this tranquil and illustrious century, we can detect a lessening of interest in the game of golf, even in Scotland. One statistic is important. By 1786 the membership of the Honourable Company at Leith had risen to 132 members, but then the membership started to decline. This was the first sign of a loss of interest in golf, and even in sport in general, in Scotland. Life in Britain was to be more serious, and leisure less available or enjoyable. The American colonies were lost, and there were revolutionary events in Europe which threatened the old order at home. Some sports were marginalised, and became the indulgence of the few, until the revival in the mid 1800s.

FURTHER READING

The numbered text references are given at the end of the book.

The important specialised texts on early golf clubs are I. T. Henderson and D. I. Stirk *Golf in the Making* Crawley 1979, and the history of the golf ball is discussed in John S. Martin *The Curious History of the Golf Ball* New York 1968. The older histories of golf are fairly sound on the eighteenth century – see Robert Browning *A History of Golf* London 1955, and Bernard Darwin (and others) *A History of Golf in Britain* London 1952. Robert Clark's *Golf: A Royal and Ancient Game* Edinburgh 1875 (facsimile edition 1975) has lasting value, particularly as many of his sources have disappeared, and John Kerr *The Golf-Book of East Lothian* Edinburgh 1896 is full of interest. Alastair and James Johnston's splendid analysis of the earlier texts of golf is *The Chronicles of Golf 1457-1857* Cleveland 1993 and for a new history of the rules see Kenneth G. Chapman *The Rules of the Green* Chicago 1997.

Some original source material has yet to be studied in depth, notably the minutes and records of the oldest Scottish golf clubs and the *Statistical Account of Scotland*. The emergence of the caddie is dealt with in David Stirk *Carry Your Bag, Sir: A History of Golf's Caddies* London 1989 and the clubmakers are described in Stirk's *Golf: the Great Clubmakers* London 1992.

Histories of individual clubs are variable in quality. The best source for this period is the affairs of the early Honourable Company in the essays of Clapcott as gathered by Alastair J. Johnston in *The Clapcott Papers* Edinburgh 1985. Also of merit is J. Cameron Robbie *The Chronicle of the Royal Burgess Golfing Society of Edinburgh* Edinburgh 1936, a work assisted by Clapcott. See also H. S. C. Everard *A History of the Royal and Ancient Golf Club* Edinburgh 1907, J. B. Salmond *The Story of the R and A* London 1956, Charles Smith *The Aberdeen Golfers: Records and Reminiscences* London 1909 and Stewart Cruden *Bruntsfield Links Golfing Society* Edinburgh 1992. For early golf at St Andrews and Carnoustie see Stewart Hackney's excellent, but unreferenced *Carnoustie Links: Courses and Players* Dundee 1988 and *Bygone Days on the Old Course* Dundee 1990. For Leith see James S. Marshall *The Life and Times of Leith* Edinburgh 1986, and early golf in the southern States of America was carefully researched by Charles Price and George C. Rogers *The Carolina Low Country: Birthplace of American Golf* Charleston 1986.

For the links and golf see Robert Price *Scotland's Golf Courses* Aberdeen University Press 1989 and Geoffrey Cornish and Ronald E. Whitten *The Golf Course* Leicester 1981. Archery is described in Margaret Buchanan *Archery in Scotland: an Elegant and Manly Amusement* Glasgow 1979 and for curling see David B. Smith *Curling: An Illustrated History* Edinburgh 1981 and W. H. Murray *The Curling Companion* Glasgow 1981.

CHAPTER FIVE

THE INTERLUDE

I t is observable that those gymnastic exercises which constituted the chief pastime of the Highlands forty or fifty years ago, have almost disappeared. At every fair or meeting of the country people, there were contests of racing, wrestling, putting the stone etc, and on holidays all the males, young and old, met to play at shinty... These games are now practised only by schoolboys...

So concluded the *Statistical Account* for the Parish of Moulin in Perthshire in 1793. But the decline of the sport was not restricted to these ancient Highland games, nor to the Highlands. In the first half of the nineteenth century, all sports in Scotland, including golf, entered a period of difficulty.

The causes of the decline in sport are not far to seek. In the Industrial Revolution, the towns of Scotland were expanding, and encroaching on the links with loss of traditional play areas. The Scottish town finances deteriorated, and many sold their ancient links or rented them out to private owners, and the town centres decayed, with growing overcrowding and poverty. Serious epidemics returned for the first time since the plague visitations of the 1600s, and, as in those horrific times earlier, the links were again used for mass burials. Industrial society demanded long hours of work, both in summer and winter, with only Sundays allowed for leisure. Overtime was attractive and this extra work further diminished leisure time.

The weary majority had little time or energy for sport. Nor did employers encourage sport: it brought injury, violence, drinking and gambling.[1]

Changes on the Land

The rural population declined as mechanisation reduced the labour force needed for agricultural work, particularly at harvest time. The ancient hierarchy of labour - shearers, gatherers, bansters and rakers - found their work increasingly replaced by machines. Industrialisation pulled the rural work force into the new factories of the towns, with loss of traditional rural winter relaxation and recreation.

OPPOSITE: Leith Links circa 1840. The links are rough and have many users; carriages and horses are seen crossing the links.

The old Montrose golfing course, circa 1822, reduced to a narrow strip by surrounding new buildings. The course moved to its present position at the edge of the beach later, leaving a clubhouse stranded in the town. From Wood's *Plan of Montrose* 1835.

The new factory working hours were long and the week well filled. The factories were heated and illuminated by gas and were kept open throughout the year, thus abolishing traditional winter leisure. For the owners and managers, industry involved the financial problems of booms, slumps, borrowing, lending, insecurity and bankruptcy. Fortunes could be made, but old money was eroded by a period of serious inflation in the early 1800s, and private means were devalued. For all, leisure was less enjoyed or enjoyable.[2]

In the Lowlands, the towns' golf links were surrounded and constricted by new industry, such as the rope works built close to the Leith Links. At Leven, shipyards and coal mines narrowed the velvet Dubbieside Links, necessitating the first 'out-of-bounds' rule in 1820. Leven's Scoonie Burn 'where once there were fish' became polluted and lifeless. Glasgow Green and Bruntsfield Links were later surrounded by new residential building. Some of the remaining town links like Glasgow Green were 'improved' - i.e. flattened and organised - removing the traditional golfing challenges of rough terrain, hazards and whins. The links and greens were increasingly crowded by the presence of other users and by citizens going to their business in the newly-busy adjacent town. At St Andrews, North Berwick and Monifieth, house building extended along the landward side of the links, again narrowing the ancient strips of sporting turf. The ancient start and finish of all these golf links were precariously maintained and remained as charming, narrow golfing alleys with houses on the town side and usually the beach on the other. At Montrose, the golf course was well back from the beach, and soon it was also narrowed by house building on both sides.

The links were also looked at anew by farmers in the 1800s. In the European War to 1812, there was a new demand for grain, and prices soared, encouraging the landowners to grow this crop, rather than to pasture animals. The benefits of crop rotation were now known, and landowners with linksland wished to use it for a crop and dig it up every four years. This strategy might not allow a return to grassland: rain eroded the ploughed land, and wind could sweep away the broken topsoil from the sand beneath.[3]

Civil Unrest

The old lifestyle was also interrupted by calls to arms. There was first a fear of invasion by Napoleon, and then nervousness that a French-style revolution might emerge at home. Street demonstrations made the authorities edgy, and troops opened fire on citizens in some British towns. The Highways Act of 1835 was primarily intended to reduce public gatherings, but it also abolished street football, and cockfighting was outlawed in 1849, suggesting official hostility to sport. Even public holidays were reduced, from 47 in 1761 to only four in 1834, days which had been traditional occasions for public sport. The old habits of the clubs, sporting and otherwise, were increasingly inappropriate and interest declined. Historians of sport conclude that the nadir came about the year 1830.[4]

In the new industrial society this decline and crisis in golf was but one part of a general contraction in sport. Shinty was fading out in the North,[5] though curling may have been popular.[6]

The loss of interest in golf at Leith, home of the Honourable Company, and a major golfing venue for many citizens, is the most prominent event in this shrinking golf world. But the problems at Leith were not simply brought about by local loss of amenity. They were part of a national shift in use of waking hours, a shift away from sport, towards a new work ethic. Moreover, golf was more expensive. Clubs, balls and uniforms, never cheap, now increased in price during this time of inflation, and the price of a feathery rose from the 6d level in the 1700s to reach 2/- by 1840.

Loss of public recreation space in Edinburgh in 1791 was resisted when the Town Council turned down a request from the Trustees for High Roads for a major road through Bruntsfield Links. Health considerations were used by the Burgess Club in their opposition to the road.

By courtesy of EDINBURGH CITY ARCHIVES.

The *Edinburgh Advertiser* 10th November 1786 carried an advertisement announcing the annual Silver Club competition. There was the added warning that prosecution for horse riding on the Links was possible, an early indication that the Leith Links were becoming over-crowded.

ROUND, OR GOLF LENGTHS,

IN

LEITH LINKS.

ROUND PREVIOUS TO 1821.

	FEET.		YARDS.
1st hole,	1242	=	414
2d . . .	1383	=	461
3d . . .	1278	=	426
4th . .	1485	=	495
5th . .	1305	=	435
	6693	=	2231

PRESENT ROUND, 1824.

	FEET.		YARDS.
1st hole,	975	=	325
2d . . .	1221	=	407
3d . . .	1278	=	426
4th . .	1485	=	495
5th . .	1305	=	435
	6264	=	2088

The yardage of the ancient five holes on Leith Links, and the contraction in the course due to the expansion of the town. From *Rules of the Thistle Club* 1824.

The Decline at Leith

The golf crisis at Leith, Bruntsfield, St Andrews, Glasgow and North Berwick can now be examined: the pattern of decay in these celebrated, confident golfing areas is remarkably similar. One hint of early loss of confidence at the Burgess Club at Bruntsfield came in 1824 when Peter McEwan, clubmaker and 'officer' of the club, said he could

no longer be absent from his business on Saturdays between 1 and 3 to carry the captain's clubs and would send his son instead.[7]

The Bruntsfield Links Club, also playing over these links with the Burgess Club, had serious loss of support about this time, and by 1812 it had only seventeen members. It lost four more in that year, and these members had all been three years in arrears with their subscription. Other difficulties emerged. At Bruntsfield Links construction of a racecourse was proposed in 1811, and though this did not appear, a 'Royal Riding School' did result and its horses were a nuisance. The Burgess Club, shrinking in size, protested without much authority, at the damage done by the horses to the links. The club was in decline, as was its lobbying power.

Campbell in his *History of Leith* of 1827 paints a similarly gloomy picture of the new situation at Leith:

in days of yore it [golf] was conducted with a degree of frank and free hilarity which has long since ceased to animate the modern practice of this manly pastime. The solitary parties of players who may now occasionally be seen wandering over the links go through the business of the game with a coldness and heartlessness of manner which announces that the true and ancient spirit of the game has gone.[8]

What had happened at Leith and its pioneering golf club and clubhouse? The crisis which overtook the Honourable Company is well documented.[9] The factors involved not only falling interest on the part of the members: the Company had decided on a risky financial policy. To balance the books, they used the new substantial entry fees as annual income. This policy could only succeed if the membership renewed itself steadily, and the evidence is that interest in golf was falling. The vital revenue from entry money did decline, the Company started to postpone paying its bills, and fell years behind in paying for its lease of Leith Links. In spite of this, the Company took on new projects, including drainage works, and they spent freely, notably on an expensive portrait of the Captain by Raeburn.

The start of the final crisis arose out of an apparently minor nuisance - the use of the links by the military. In 1803 the minutes note that

contrary to all precedent the Mid Lothian Volunteers and other Cavalry assumed to themselves the right of excercising and even riding upon the Links at pleasure.

But to protest at this illegal use of the links at a time of preparation for war was unpatriotic, and a ban by the golfers on such manoeuvres was impossible to sustain in practice. Worse was to follow. The local inhabitants,

who had been kept off the links by the vigilance of the golfers, saw this
military use as a signal to reclaim their earlier general use of the land.
The minutes record that

*from this time forward horses and even carriages of every description had paraded
the links in all directions.*[12]

In vain it was ordered that

*Placards against trespassing on the Links be Renewed and those
convicted prosecuted.*

But the invasion of the golfers' haven was unstoppable, and the costs of
ineffectual prosecution of non-golfers added to the Company's outgoings.
The links were badly damaged, and the Golfers had to record that

*the Links had been patched so as in a great measure to destroy them as a
golfing course.*[13]

The damage and loss of turf must have been great: even the sheep-grazing
sub-tenants declined to pay their rent to the Company, adding to the club's
downward spiral of debt. The Golfers allowed their arrears of rent to the City
of Edinburgh to grow, and this reached £113 by 1806. Further burdens multi-
plied. Simon Cossar, their professional, went bankrupt and his debts had been
partly guaranteed by the Company. The Golfers also were forced to rescue the
debts of the tenant publican in the clubhouse and pay his outstanding bills to
wine suppliers. Further imprudent litigation was begun, in attempting to
defend the rights of the Company to lease the bleaching green adjacent to the
Golf House, but the Leith authorities successfully claimed an ancient right of
the inhabitants to bleach clothes on this area and on the whole Green. Soon
the arrears of rent by the Honourable Company to the City rose to £377.

The Crisis

In 1824 the Golfers had to raise a bank loan on the security of their Golf
House for £500: four years later another loan of £200 was required, at a time
when tradesmen alone were owed £250 by the Golfers. Internally, the
Company was in disarray and the members dispersing. Substantial losses on
dinners which were ordered, but not taken, reveal an uninterested membership. Fifteen changes in the post of secretary are recorded in as many years in
this unhappy period and eleven in the treasurer's position. One secretary fled
the country, leaving behind personal debts, and money was missing at the
club. Overall, the picture is of poor supervision, lack of interest and low
morale, at a time of general national unrest and uncertainty.[14] Interest on the
debts mounted, and in 1833 the club's creditors forced a humiliating public
sale of fixtures and fittings at the clubhouse, including the Golf House's magnificent paintings. The enforced sale raised £106. Many items were bought by
members, and many have never been traced since. Finally, in 1834, the Golf
House itself was sold for £1,130; the Honourable Company thereafter was
reduced to an inactive shell.

In retrospect, the accumulation of these huge debts was the product of over-
confidence. The Company had taken on novel responsibilities. This advanced
thinking at the club brought considerable liabilities, which could not be sustained in difficult times. It was a golf club too far.

The Honourable Company survived the crisis in a modified form. They were not the only Leith club to suffer: the important Thistle Club (of *'Rules'* fame) - founded in 1815 - did not survive, and disbanded at this time, never to reappear.[15] The Royal Company of Archers in Edinburgh was also in debt, and was weakened by internal strife and allegations of cheating at cards.

St Andrews

But the most important evidence for a general decline in the game in Scotland at this time comes from St Andrews. The town and its favourite sport of golf were in trouble. Carnegie's poem *Golfiana* of 1833 starts:

> *St. Andrews! They say thy glories are gone*
> *That thy streets are deserted thy castles o'erthrown...*[16]

The rot had started in 1797. About then, the university's reputation began to sink and by 1850 a critic recalled that

> *the University of St Andrews numbered only a hundred students; its buildings*
> *dilapidated; the professors, with a few eminent exceptions, were old and anti-*
> *quated, and contended with each other after the manner of dogs.*[17]

In the late 1700s, the town had to sell part of its extensive common land, land which included the golfing links. Though protection for golf was agreed in the conditions of sale, the new owner then passed the lease of the land on to a third party uninterested in golf. Rabbit breeding on a large scale was established, and golf was seriously impeded by the proliferating rabbit holes and scrapes. A triangular struggle between the golfers, the owner and the tenant ensued. The defence of the links succeeded eventually, but only after tedious litigation, which reached the House of Lords. The golf lobby was just strong enough to support a claim of ancient 'servitude' of golf on the links, i.e. a right established by ancient usage and custom.[18]

At the first court hearing in 1804, evidence emerged of the diminishing interest in golf at St Andrews. A caddie said that in his early days

> *there were 20 balls played then for every one now... this was due to the College*
> *being much better attended then than now.*

His evidence confirms that the students were an important part of St Andrews golf, and confirms the loss of status of the university. Another caddie mentioned that he had work in winter at St Andrews and travelled to Leith and Bruntsfield in summer, as if St Andrews play was still mainly in winter and associated with the university term. In the *Delineations of St Andrews* of 1807 it was calculated that there were about one dozen balls made locally per day. Even if most of these were used at St Andrews, this suggests only about ten to twenty rounds played each day, perhaps only five to ten singles matches or the equivalent in foursomes. This estimate is confirmed by the diary of a visitor to St Andrews in the autumn of 1842 who saw only four players out on the links, and was assured that 'up to 20 might play on a good day'.[19] Other literary sources confirm the low numbers out at play. As late as 1849, Roger's *History of St Andrews* says

> *formerly the golfers held monthly meetings to enjoy the game, but of late these*
> *have been discontinued, and only the two great meetings are held (i.e. May and*
> *September).*[20]

Cockburn, the eminent judge, wrote of St Andrews at this time in his *Circuit Journeys* that 'they have a local pleasure of their own... this is golfing...'[21]

Cockburn was a judge based in Edinburgh and one who travelled widely in Scotland. His detached description of golf assumes that it was an unusual game, and a local curiosity. For an Edinburgh judge to speak of golf in these terms confirms other evidence that the game in Edinburgh, Leith and Musselburgh was in near-terminal decay.

A temporary decline of the R&A club started about 1827, confirming other evidence about St Andrews golf, and the club recorded at one point that their 'funds were not sufficient for expenditure'. By 1832 the minutes reveal an unhappy society, with letters of complaint and resignation. The club severed the old link with MacEwan, their supplier of clubs from Edinburgh, who found it was not worth attending the St Andrews meetings from 1819 onwards. Instead this gave a chance to Philp, the local furniture maker, to start making clubs, and these products were, and are, much admired. His output could not have been great, since in the 1831 census he described himself as a 'wright' not a clubmaker.[22]

But the R&A survived. Another St Andrews club did not: the St Andrews Golf Club, founded in 1810, disbanded in 1839.

Decline in the West

The east coast was not alone in turning away from golf. The Glasgow Golf Club, founded in 1787, disbanded completely in 1794, prior to the Napoleonic Wars of 1795-1803, when nine regiments were raised in the city, taking many gentlemen golfers away to serve. Interest fell away and for those remaining, golf on Glasgow Green was unpleasant, not only because of the difficulties caused by increased use by non-golfers, but also because of the municipal drainage and levelling scheme of 1813. Peter's *Letters* describe his visit to Glasgow and on the Green he saw a curiosity - 'several elderly citizens playing at the old Scots game of golf'. In 1809 the club revived temporarily but dispersed again in 1835. The last captain, J. P. McInroy sensibly took possession of the club's elegant silver club trophy for safekeeping, in case the club might rise again. His verdict was that this was unlikely.[23] In 1854 the *Glasgow Herald* reminisced: 'we have lost one of the oldest of our Scotch games, viz. the Golf, which used to be regularly played upon the Green of Glasgow, not only by boys, but also by many of our first-class citizens.'

Elsewhere in Fife

Even in the smaller towns of Scotland the game was largely abandoned. At Crail, a Fife fishing town, unchanged and unchanging for centuries and where the celebrated club was formed in 1786, golf was in eclipse. Crail's perceptive historian noted a change in the minutes from the early 1800s:

> The old order has changed and this is borne out by the Minutes, which have not the charm of the first fifty years. One senses a change in the social side. True, there are many references to conviviality and good-fellowship, but these are more formally expressed than in the past.[24]

The Glasgow Golf Club ceased existence in the general decline of golf in the early 1800s, and its silver club was taken to a place of safety by a far-sighted member.
From Colville *The Glasgow Golf Club* 1907.
By courtesy of the MITCHELL LIBRARY GLASGOW.

This shows that the convivial Crail club was fading out slowly but surely, as were the clubs of the towns at the time.

The first hint of trouble at Crail was a light-hearted minute in 1789 encouraging 'no members to absent themselves on pretence of tea drinking'.[25] Clearly, the members were beginning to excuse themselves from golf and the noisy dinners, and were even joining polite tea-drinking society instead. By 1811, the minutes show that attendance was falling off, and other excuses were given, notably the demands of the harvest. In 1812 there were only ten active members left, and only eight in total next year, when a decision was made to dissolve the society. Like most other clubs which closed at this time, Crail was to revive strongly later in the century.

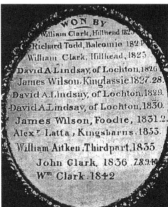

The irreverent text on this medal from the short-lived Kingsbarns Club in Fife incorporates the spirit of the early 1800s before the club disbanded.
From Wood's *Golfing Curios and the Like* 1911.

Pressure Elsewhere

Even at North Berwick, the golf club was on the wane. The town's status had declined and in 1832 it was described as 'a decayed fishing village with little prospect of improvement'. About this time another set of users of the links achieved ascendancy: the North Berwick fishermen were granted unimpeded use of the links to dry their nets on Saturdays. This Town Council decision was reversed in 1859, but not before the golf club almost closed in 1848. In a legal action in the town in 1863, witnesses were produced who said they had never seen golf played on the ancient (though less active) golfing area on the east links at North Berwick.[26] At Dunbar close by, the golfers were driven from the Common, and the municipal land was sold to pay for the new harbour for the town. Even at Gullane there were closures: one club, the East Lothian Golf Club, had disbanded.[27]

Much further north, the pattern was the same. At Aberdeen in 1825 the business meeting of the club, founded in 1780, was called but only the secretary turned up. 'There was', wrote Farnie in 1857 'a club at one time in Aberdeen, but whether or not in existence at the present time we cannot say.' Elsewhere, discouraged golfers also had to deal with those who wished to change the use of the land. The links were valuable farming land and the golfers' lobby was less effective than before. At both Fraserburgh and Montrose in 1785 the tenant farmers planned to plough up the links, but were dissuaded.[28] At Elie and Earlsferry, the tenant also intended to plough, but legal action prevented the plan, since an ancient 'servitude' of play was successfuly claimed in the courts. At Scotscraig, north of St Andrews, the owner proposed to plough the links, and did so, and the local golfers moved elsewhere. To the south, between St Andrews and Crail, lies the village of Kingsbarns and the sophisticated Kingsbarns club was founded in 1823. It had a sturdy existence and a full range of activities, including play over natural linksland for some delightful silver medals. It disbanded in mid-century, its records disappearing without trace, and never revived. The village and links exist to this day but the position of the former golf course is not known.[29]

Other clubs, little known now, flourished briefly at this time. A gentlemen's golfing society at Burntisland in Fife is mentioned in the 1791 *Statistical Account* but has never appeared in conventional histories of golf. Further to the north of Burntisland another sporting group met to play for the 'Bow of Fife' prize. Their society has not appeared in any records, but the trophy survives. North of Aberdeen a 'Cruden Golf Club' has been traced in 1791, but disappeared thereafter, leaving nothing behind, other than their ballot box.

The Curlers

The Scottish curlers were in better heart and curling was still popular. But the curlers lost one battle for continuation of their ancient customs. In 1850 the curlers of Lochwinnoch were denied access to Castle Semple Loch for a Grand Match. The case was taken to court, but the Law Lords ruled that although the landowners had 'for time past the memory of man' given regular permission to play on their land, this did not constitute a right of play - a servitude. As described above, only with difficulty was the corresponding servitude of golf established on some of the ancient golfing sites.[30]

Furth of Scotland

This eclipse of golf in Scotland seemed to remove, at a distance, the fragile hold gained by golf elsewhere in the world. The game in South Carolina and Georgia disappeared about 1815. Golf in Ireland also vanished and later was thought by some never to have existed. A golf club set up at Manchester in 1818 also suffered a reverse.[31] The better-known Blackheath club in London also entered a period of difficulty in 1843, and its associated club, the Knuckle Club, had earlier disappeared for ever in 1825.

This shrinking of the tiny international golfing diaspora was not by a mysterious action at a distance: it is easily explained. Scottish merchants, military men and others had travelled the world, and on their travels had played their favourite game. At home, the Scots were no longer interested in golf, and now no golfing travellers planted or maintained the game outside Scotland. Only some Scottish soldiers doggedly founded golf clubs while on service in the Empire, and in Bengal, Major Hugh Lyon Playfair, a talented St Andrews man, set up a club at Dum Dum. Playfair was to return to Fife and assist in the revival of the fortunes of the town, and its golf.

Like other clubs to appear outside Scotland, the Manchester Golf Club had a Scottish founder, George Fraser.

By courtesy of MANCHESTER PUBLIC GALLERY.

A Sporting Clique

As the Scottish clubs struggled to survive, one group of leisured sporting gentlemen came to prominence. These players seem confident, wealthy and worldly, in contrast to the demoralised ordinary players at this time. Many of these men played at St Andrews and some are seen in Charles Lees's panoramic picture *The Golfers* of 1851 and some also appear in the poem *Golfiana* of 1833 by George Fullerton Carnegie, one of this clique.[32] There is more than a hint of decadence about this group, who maintained an exuberant eighteenth-century style in the new nineteenth-century circumstances. They were awkwardly out of their time, but have prominence in this golden twilight of old-style golf. One hint about this group's behaviour is the careful verdict by Lord Cockburn on the St Andrews golfing set he encountered - 'a guttling lot' - commented the judge in his *Circuit Journeys* of 1844.[33]

These gentlemen golfers were men of means and leisure, playing golf frequently, and not only on competition days. They had multiple membership of

The early 1800s were a time of decadence with heavy drinking on and off the course, as shown in Lees's painting *The Golfers* of 1841.

Tinted engraving by courtesy of ROBIN SCULTHORPE.

the few remaining clubs, and indulged in racing, hunting and curling together with drinking and cards in the evening. In Stewart's *Golfiana Miscellanea* the author describes St Andrews at this time as the 'Doncaster of golfing'.[34] This racing analogy is an insight into the assumptions of the remaining club golfers. Doncaster and St Andrews were indeed the high points of their sporting circuit.

The dominant clubs in this small, elegant sporting and social whirl were St Andrews, Perth and North Berwick. Of the four principal golfers in Lees's St Andrews golf painting, all were wealthy, mobile North Berwick players, and numerous Perth gentlemen are also shown.

The Meetings

The structure of North Berwick golf meetings at this time, as in other clubs, was not dissimilar to a race meeting. The two-day North Berwick meeting saw a variety of golf matches, hearty lunches and big dinners: ladies were prominent in the social events. The money involved in the competitions was considerable; and the prize money played for at North Berwick at this time was £70, a huge sum of money.[35]

After this golf gathering, the members then moved off elsewhere. This may have started the habit of keeping golf clubs in a sturdy box, which prevented damage to these much-travelled, elegant clubs. As golfers became less restless later, and multiple club membership declined, these boxes increasingly resided in one clubhouse.

John Kerr in his *Golf-Book of East Lothian* later in the century reconstructed the mood of the North Berwick meetings:

Each country house within driving radius had its contingency of visitors, who generally arrived on the scene a day or two before the meeting of the club. On the morning of the meeting, parties drove down in great style and the town was quite on the 'qui vive' over the arrival of the golf equipages, caddies and forecaddies...[36]

These golfers also played more golf in summer. Perhaps with their independent means they were not so tied to the land as before, or perhaps they neglected their responsibilities. The burden of the harvest had been lifted from them, or they ignored it. The North Berwick meetings slowly changed from winter gatherings to playing instead on the first Wednesday in May, June, July and August.

Because of the multiple memberships, the North Berwick golf meetings were co-ordinated with meetings of the R&A, and later with the plans of the Prestwick and Carnoustie clubs, but not with the Honourable Company at Leith, which still seemed to have modest support from working professional men rather than a leisured sporting membership. The clubs in the circuit were also careful with their calendar not to clash with major race meetings in England and Scotland, and the golf gatherings would be at the time of local race meetings and musterings of local militia.

The R&A golf meetings had a high local profile, and Rogers *History of St Andrews* says that at the two great meetings (May and September) 'the golfers walk through the town in procession, preceded by a band, drums and flute'. A description of these golfing gentlemen assembling for an R&A meeting, is also given by a lady traveller in July 1838:

> *Dearest Mama,*
> *Arrived here [St Andrews] between 5 and 6 and found all the Inns full of golf playing gents, Mr. Campbell of Saddell, Clanranald, and many of the same kind - so we had to hunt all over the town for Lodgings.*[38]

The ladies may have been lucky to have avoided some of these men. Something is known of Saddell and Clanranald and some of the others of 'the same kind', notably George Carnegie, the sportsman and poet whose poem, mentioned above, described his golfing clique at play. Some, though blessed with inherited land and income, came to unfortunate ends. Of Carnegie, their laureate, this stern obituary was written:

> *Carnegie no sooner came into possession [of his inheritance] than he commenced a gay and extravagant life. There was then living in Edinburgh a very wild set of young men who played for high stakes, hunted, kept racehorses and so on. Of this set Carnegie became a well-known member. Carnegie in a very few years had his estates in the hands of his creditors, and was under trust.*[39]

Carnegie's income had been £5,000 a year, a huge sum of money. Of the other golfers, Campbell of Saddell was then described as 'a Magnus Apollo with the fashionables of his day', and was a bachelor living with Clanranald (Macdonald of Glengarry). Clanranald, denounced by some as a impostor, also went through his fortune. Old money and old families were under stress during this period of unrest and inflation: the feckless did not survive.

The Wagers

Carnegie's poem describes heavy betting by this group of gentlemen golfers. Even during the match a fresh bet of £5 at 15-1 was made on the last few holes, and the recording of wagers can be seen in Lees's painting. This, like the £70 prize money at North Berwick, was a large amount of money, and greatly exceeded the stakes in the previous rumbustious century, when a guinea was the routine bet among the golfers at Leith.

GOLFING.—St Andrew's Golf Meeting.—In our paper of the 20th ult we announced that Sir David Baird had won King William the Fourth's gold medal and Mr George Condie the club's gold medal; but as the latter had gained the silver cross in May, it was necessary that he should resign it, as the club rules do not permit a member to hold two honours in the same year. Seventeen members therefore started to compete for the silver cross on Thursday, and, after some fine play, Captain H. Maitland (who had tied the day before) was found to be the winner, he having holed the round in 98 strokes. One of the great events of the meeting then came off, namely, a match which had been on the *tapis* for some time, Sir D. Baird and Mr Goddard against Mr G. Condie and Mr R. Hay. The stakes were said to be £50 a side, and the result was looked forward to with great interest. The betting, about two months before it was decided, was in favour of Sir David Baird and his partner at the odds of 6 to 4; gradually they fell to 5 to 4, and then the betting became even; and on the day of the match at least as many were ready to back Mr Condie and his friend at evens. The match was to consist of 36 holes (two rounds), and about twelve o'clock they started, surrounded by a goodly muster of friends and admirers of our national game. The play was very even, but at the conclusion of the first round Sir David Baird and partner were two holes ahead. The second round commenced, and when only seven holes were to play the younger players were still behind. They now made a vigorous effort, and the game was brought to all even, and two holes to play. Here a great mishap befell Sir David Baird; in striking off his teed ball it fell into a *bunker* (sand hole); in getting out of this difficulty it fell into a whin bush, and the hole was gained by Mr Condie and his partner. The last hole was halved, and the match gained by Mr Condie and Mr Hay by one hole. Some other excellent matches were played; and on Friday week a match for £25 a side was made, Allan Robertson and Thomas Morris against William and James Dunn of Musselburgh; the play commenced on Saturday, about eleven o'clock, and, after as fine an exhibition of play as could have been seen, the St Andrew's men were the winners by two holes; they holed the round in 89 strokes. When this match was over William Dunn was backed against Thomas Morris to play one round, when the latter was defeated by one hole. Thus ended the excellent meeting of October, 1850.

Similar huge bets by sporting gentlemen were recorded elsewhere. The *Montrose Review* of 1829 described that a Major Cruikshank and Captain Bertram played against Mr John Wood and James Hay of Leith in a match over two days for £100 a side. These men were 'amateurs' in the later use of the word. Some years earlier Cruikshank was involved in another match within the racing and golfing clique, in which he played Lord Kennedy 'during the [Montrose] race meeting over three holes at night for £500 a hole', using servants with candles to illuminate the course.[40] Cruikshank's partner, Captain Bertram, had earlier been noticed by the Scottish newspapers as playing for high stakes against a Mr Marshall of Aberdeen at Montrose in 1817 'with considerable bets depending on the match'.

At Carnoustie, near Montrose, there are hints of the same mood, and Charles Robertson of Buttergask, founder of the Carnoustie Caledonian Union Golf Club in 1848, was known as the 'great Falstaff of the game', and had multiple club memberships. These men were the greatest golf gamblers ever, in the twilight of old-style golf.[41]

But attitudes to the sportsmen were changing. In 1838 the minister of the Church of Scotland at Inveresk, beside Musselburgh Links, made it clear that the gambling golfers in Scotland were drawing attention to themselves:

Newspaper report of the Royal and Ancient Golf Club meeting in 1850. Heavy betting among the gentlemen is noted in their additional, personal matches as well as on the professional contests.

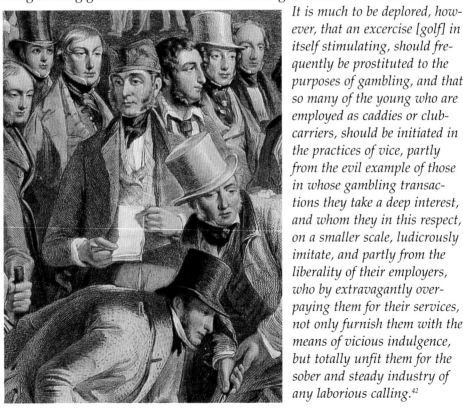

Lees's painting The Golfers shows a number of spectators taking bets and making up a book as the match progressed.

By courtesy of ROBIN SCULTHORPE.

It is much to be deplored, however, that an excercise [golf] in itself stimulating, should frequently be prostituted to the purposes of gambling, and that so many of the young who are employed as caddies or club-carriers, should be initiated in the practices of vice, partly from the evil example of those in whose gambling transactions they take a deep interest, and whom they in this respect, on a smaller scale, ludicrously imitate, and partly from the liberality of their employers, who by extravagantly over-paying them for their services, not only furnish them with the means of vicious indulgence, but totally unfit them for the sober and steady industry of any laborious calling.[42]

This sermon confirms the extent of routine wagering on golf and also the generosity of caddie fees. It shows that the moral mood was changing, and that puritan assumptions were about to return and set a new rectitude in public and private behaviour.

But this rather unattractive group of sporting and gambling golfers kept the long game alive in the early 1800s, and they supported professional caddies and artisans in the last years of the use of the feathery ball, at a time when golf and sport in general were in decline.

The Gentlemen's Caddies

As the century progressed, more serious-minded gentlemen players emerged at St Andrews and elsewhere who had less exuberant discourse and manners. Carnegie was gone, and the new group seem more mature - and less restless. They may still have had membership of the other clubs at Perth and North Berwick, but the group became increasingly identified with St Andrews alone - and the players include Maitland Dougall, Whyte Melville, J. O. Fairlie, Moncrieff and Condie. Many of them were still active after the gutty ball had arrived, and the feathery had gone, and the game was becoming popular. They also, like the earlier clique, kept alive the skills of golf's artisans - the ballmakers and clubmakers - but added to this by employing and encouraging the play by some caddies, particularly at St Andrews.

Until the early 1800s, we have few descriptions or names of regular caddies or skilled humble players. But towards the mid-1800s the gentlemen started to employ regular personal caddies, men who were to gain their place in golf history - Robertson, Morris, Kirk, Herd, Pirie, Andrew and others. Under the patronage of their masters, these caddies had regular employment.

Professionals of the late feathery era at St Andrews, with some visitors from Musselburgh. From Everard's History of the Royal and Ancient Golf Club *1907. Left to right - James Wilson, Willie Dunn, Bob Andrew, Willie Park, Tom Morris, Allan Robertson, Jamie Anderson and Bob Kirk.*

The portrait of John Whyte Melville of Mount Melville near St Andrews. Active in the R&A Club, he was captain in 1823. He is shown about to drive off from beside the 17th green, playing the 'backward' route on the Old Course. The clubs carried are four woods and two irons. The feather ball is placed on sand.

By courtesy of the ROYAL AND ANCIENT GOLF CLUB, ST ANDREWS.

The gentlemen bred and raced racehorses and kept fox-hounds, and they employed jockeys and huntsmen. To this group they now added professional golfers to assist their masters on the links and partner them at play. And play by the caddies on their own account was encouraged. Having fostered a player, matches between these 'professional players' were arranged by the gentlemen, as they were accustomed to do with their racehorses.

Campbell of Saddell first employed Bob Kirk as his regular caddie, and later Saddell was patron to Sandy Herd. Allan Robertson was regularly seen with

Sir John Muir MacKenzie and Sir Thomas Moncrieff. Later J. O. Fairlie had Tom Morris as his assistant. Sandy Pirie carried for Maitland Dougall, Andra Strath for Sutherland and Herd later for Whyte Melville: Sir Hope Grant used Sandy Philp. James Condie, the sporting Perth merchant, had his caddie Bob Andrew on his firm's payroll, as office messenger, but he was free to play each afternoon. Later Robert Chambers the publisher and George Morris were inseparable for 25 years.

Most of these partnerships are detected at St Andrews: no similar arrangements are obvious at Musselburgh or Leith or even North Berwick. These steady pairings were perhaps inevitable when golf was so neglected. The caddies had little other work, and welcomed such patronage. The gentlemen in return had the reliable assistance of talented players always at hand, and the sportsmen had a group of increasingly skillful players to pit against each other in a new piece of golfing excitement - the money matches.

Gentlemen golfers and caddies at St Andrews in the late feathery age, namely George Whyte Melville, Maitland Dougall, George Glennie, James O. Fairlie and Sandy Pirie. From Everard's History of the Royal and Ancient Golf Club *1907.*

The Challenge Matches

The gentlemen of St Andrews encouraged the professional challenge matches which were to be an important part of mid-nineteenth century golf. Sporting gentlemen wagered on anything - racing, running, and pugilism: now golf offered some additional sport. The large money at stake in the professional challenge matches which they were to sponsor did not, as it might appear, go to the professionals. It was not a prize for the players, but was the sum wagered by their backers, money put up ahead by both sides, and the winning gentlemen took the pot for their syndicate. The winning players were rewarded informally by the successful gentlemen. As Andra Kirkaldy put it later after a win, 'the gentlemen were vera findfu'.[43]

The first evidence of such play comes from St Andrews. After the autumn meeting of the R&A in 1819 the minutes note that a 'caddies tournament' was held, and a sum of money raised for play - the 'input.'[44] There is no description of the mode of play. Perhaps it was stroke-play, but this would be unusual, since all the great professional challenge matches of the later century were match-play. This mode is more capricious and more thrilling and it suited the betting man: new bets can be made at any point. Though the records are silent on the details of these early caddies' tournaments, it is likely that they were rapid match-play encounters.

But the St Andrews gentlemen golfers had a problem. Among the caddies, Allan Robertson was now supreme, and was perhaps the greatest golfer of the time. His ability to beat all-comers must have inhibited the organisation of well-matched professional challenges. The solution was to leave him out from the caddies' match, as was done from 1842 onwards.

The gentlemen were also prepared to play for money with professional partners in challenge matches. In 1844 Moncrieff and Allan Robertson played Tom Morris and J. O. Fairlie in a notable match. In 1852 Robert Hay, an amateur (in the later sense of the word), won the R&A's King William medal, and then challenged the world to play against himself and Willie Dunn. Only later did a distaste arise for amateurs and professionals joining together in such golfing challenges.

The Humble Game

In this period of golfing decline it is not clear if ordinary golfers had also lost interest in the game, since the main sources about early golf come from the activities of the well-off golfers and their societies. But the lack of golf played by *anyone* at Leith Links at this time, mentioned above, does suggest a general decline in interest in golf throughout society, and that even the humble form of golf was no longer popular.

But humble golf still survived, perhaps in a small way, at least at St Andrews. The gentry supported the local caddies and this encouraged the boys of the town to play the game. 'Old' Tom Morris, born in the town in 1821, said that as a child he was hitting stones about the streets with a stick, and at the age of eleven he was playing on a set of short holes at the railway station, near the seventeenth green. There are hints of two clubs in Montrose pre-dating the better-known mill-workers Mechanics' Golf Club of 1846. Known as the Weaver's Golf Club and the Flaxdressers' Club, their members must have played with simple equipment.

And the tribal, mass golf game also survived, at least once a year. In the early 1800s, an annual New Year's golf match is noted at Fraserburgh, when the men of the town played the neighbouring fishing villages at golf, with attendant revelry. At this same time of year, there was an ancient mass golfing match of a similar kind at Gullane: the short game was not entirely abandoned along the east coast of Scotland.[45]

The Interlude

This crisis in sport had started about 1800, and the trough was reached about 1830. About 1840 signs of recovery can be seen: no more golf clubs disappeared, never to revive. The surviving clubs gained strength, and a few new ones appeared. Club golf in the crisis seems to have been perilously maintained mainly at St Andrews, Musselburgh, Aberdeen, and Montrose. To survive, the clubs made sensible alterations in their habits to suit the new circumstances.

One such reorganisation was to acknowledge the change from the old agrarian society to the new industrial structure, and that summer golf was possible. At Crail there was an early acknowledgement of the new importance of summer play and that some members might work during the week. Struggling to survive, the golf club changed its meeting from Wednesday to Saturday, and the monthly meetings were extended from winter to include play in the months of May and August. But the harvest was still important, and summer golf might, on occasion, take second place. In 1824 and 1825 the Crail club had to bring forward the August meeting 'because of the harvest advancing rapidly'. The R&A about this time also regularly brought forward its August meeting, if the harvest was to be early.

Revival

By the 1840s Europe was at peace. The possibility of revolution in Britain had passed and the economy improved. Even the cholera epidemics were less violent than in the 1830s, and then slowly faded out. The nation's morale had steadied and recovered. Real wages rose after 1840 and again from 1870. After 1850 it became statutory in the textile industry to allow regular time off from work - two weeks' annual holidays and a half-day off on Saturdays. Work in the factories continued in summer and winter, unlike agriculture, and society now had a choice of when to take holidays. There was no real choice - summer was more attractive.

The Victorians knew that the expanding cities and towns were unhealthy, not only for the body but also for the mind, and they were concerned about the return of epidemic disease. Seaside holidays and sport were considered antidotes to ill-health. The laureate of Innerleven Golf Club could write:

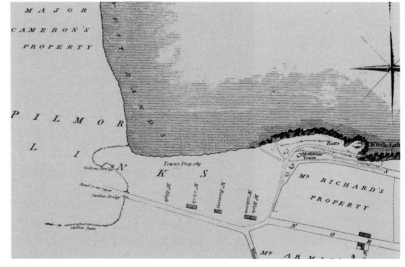

St Andrews Links circa 1830 in Wood's *Town Plan*, prior to the new interest in golf.

> *Whae wad be free from doctor's bills,*
> *From trash o' powders and o' pills*
> *Will find a cure for a' his ills*
> *On the links o' Innerleven.*

The society emerging from the unsettled times had different objectives and a sterner morality. The Reform Act of 1832 had extended the vote to the middling classes of society, who now increasingly influenced parliamentary legislation, which was previously the preserve of the landed class. The new voters had a new seriousness in response to the unsettled times and they had a work ethic, in which orderly use of time, and attention to health and sobriety were important. They were critical of the idle rich and the feckless poor. In Glasgow

> *the heavy drinking and swearing of the eighteenth century disappeared from polite society... sober culture was fostered by the Glasgow Literary and Commercial Society... The pious youth of the city was called to a life of philanthropic service in Sunday Schools, Bible Societies, systematic visiting, charitable education and rescue work.*[46]

Exercise, healthy exercise, now also had increasing support.

Sport Revives

The middle classes now allocated a modest amount of time to leisure. The demand for sport came from an increasingly well-off group who now had good regular wages. Service industries like insurance companies and banks thrived, as did their new managerial class. Professionals like doctors and lawyers also prospered and all sought to imitate the habits of the older monied and leisured class.

But the traditional and expensive field sports of the gentry were not attractive. Instead came a new interest in athletic sport, and a re-emergence of golf. Sport was seen as healthy, and encouraging virtues required by leaders in the new industries, the Empire, and the armed forces. Sport was thought to develop not only physical fitness, team discipline, and leadership, but also patience, self-discipline, and resourcefulness in emergencies. Schools, starting with public schools, encouraged sport in the young.

Golf did not quite fit into this paradigm. But it had a place. It was played in the newly fashionable open air, unlike the increasingly discredited indoor billiards and card games. Golf was not violent and no animals were hunted or killed. It could be played into maturity, well after normal athleticism had passed. Foursome play or the handicapping system produced a thrilling game between players of widely differing skills, and people were living longer and had leisure time after service in the armed forces or in the Empire. Golf gave a good day out, and a little betting on the side was not discouraged, and helped the excitement. The game was healthy, cheap and innocent: ministers of religion could and did play.

Golf also attracted informed professionals and eventually not a few politicians. The golfing community grew larger in numbers and was now prepared to do battle with difficult landowners and farmers. This golf lobby not only preserved golf on the links from other predators, but also allowed St Andrews, North Berwick and other Scottish burghs via an Act of Parliament to purchase back their ancient golf links, the land sold in the late 1700s, to increase the sporting amenities of the towns, particularly for visitors.

The Coast and Sea

For Victorian society, escape to the country and to the sea air of the coast for sea-bathing was considered to be particularly health-giving. Scottish fishing villages which the world had forgotten, if they had ever known them, now found themselves thriving. John Kerr noted that in his time

> *the fishing villages have become fashionable sea-side resorts and hundreds of acres*

*formerly useful for nothing but rearing rabbits have become a great golf
sanatorium to which thousands resort every year for health.*[47]

One decision made Scottish holidays important. In 1852 Prince Albert bought
the 17,000-acre Balmoral estate, and the Royal family were thereafter to make
this their summer home. They took notice of local sport, and patronised the
local Braemar Highland Games, now reviving as part of the Highland redis-
covery of allegedly traditional sport. The aristocracy had always retreated to
Scotland for their field sports, but the added Royal approval meant that
Scottish holidays of any kind became widely fashionable. The peaceful,
charming, seaside towns and Highland villages, untouched by industrial
change, were now sought out by the town-dwellers, and they prospered.

Bathing and the Coasts

From the early Christian period, swimming and bathing had been con-
demned. The liberal 1700s saw a relaxation in this, as in other matters. At
first, sea-bathing was promoted as a therapeutic measure, followed slowly
by the rise of bathing as a recreation.[48] At Leith in 1750 a bathing machine
was set up in the shallow tidal water, but subsequent machines were mobile
and the bathers were taken out inside them to reach the sea. Later, machines
were fixed on the beach and used simply for changing clothes. In time, even
the machines were ignored, and this changing on the beach caused adverse
comment. Bathing by women irritated the genial judge Lord Cockburn:

*I never saw sea bathing performed by ladies in Scotland even with common
decency. Why the devil can't they use bathing machines, or go to retired places or
wall or pale off enclosures?*

This interest in bathing and swimming was a town-dweller's enthusiasm.
It was not shared by the locals: Scottish fishermen have always been non-
swimmers. Scotland had beaches in abundance, and this brought in visitors.
If there were no beaches, an outdoor pool was constructed, and indoor sea-
water baths followed later. The sea-bathing enthusiasm had started before the
golf boom, and the two were linked. Both were the result of a revolution in
transport.

The Railways

In this period, there was a quickening of travel within Britain. Earlier, horse-
drawn coaches, willing but unpredictable, ran on the ancient muddy tracks,
which were improved in 1800 when Telford's roads and McAdam's smooth
surfaces brought in the 'Golden Age' of coach travel from 1820 to 1840.[49]
By then about thirty coaches left Edinburgh for London daily, and the famous
Edinburgh to Aberdeen coach *Defiance* was so punctual and predictable on the
new roads that country people judged the time of day by its passage up the
east coast.

But many journeys were slow and awkward. Before 1800, to travel from
Edinburgh to St Andrews meant an uncomfortable journey by sea to Fife and
thence by horse or personal coach. Even travel from Edinburgh to Musselburgh
was tedious, by coach or horse, though an omnibus started to run from
Edinburgh to Musselburgh from 1845. The coming of the railways was to
transform transport, and lead to important social changes, not least in sport.[50]

One of the first railways in Scotland to carry passengers ran on the flat, short journey between Irvine and Troon on the west coast in 1812. In 1839 this line was used to bring in spectators for one of the world's great sporting flops - the Eglinton Tournament - where rain and mud defeated the knights in armour. Glasgow and Edinburgh were linked by rail in 1840, and in Fife the network reached Leuchars. From there a branch line was built to St Andrews in 1851. Glasgow and Ayr were linked in 1848, as were Carnoustie and Dundee. The railway to Musselburgh from Edinburgh opened in 1847 and pushed on to reach North Berwick in 1850. In 1848 rail travel obtained reluctant royal approval when Queen Victoria's usual sea journey from Aberdeen to London was delayed by fog, and she took the train instead thereafter. The line from Aberdeen to Inverness opened in 1858, and Moray Firth towns like Nairn and Lossiemouth - reached by rail in 1852 - and blessed with a dry sunny summer climate, began to prosper and expand, successfully promoting themselves as resorts and retirement areas; even the chilly waters of the North Sea were considered part of the attractions. But railway expansion then hesitated and did not immediately reach much further north than Inverness. Teams playing in golf matches between the Lossiemouth and Dornoch clubs travelled by sea across the Moray Firth until the 1890s. With the railways came hotels, and with the hotels, came more golf. Feeding into the main lines, little branch lines were constructed, many reaching towns with suitable golf links. Dornoch was eventually reached by the line from Embo, and thrived, as did Machrihanish, served by the Campbeltown Light Railway.

Influence of Rail

The arrival of the railway meant a rapid influx of visitors and improved trade. The new railways took the coastal route, avoiding the central mountains and hills of Scotland, and after reaching the fishing villages, distant markets could be supplied with fresh fish. Regular visitors, having come for holidays, might return for retirement, and some towns prospered remarkably. In 1832, before the railway came, North Berwick was linked to Edinburgh only on alternate days by a horse-drawn noddy. By the end of the century, the railways and golf had made North Berwick the 'Biarritz of the North', patronised by the famous and known for its fashionable hotels, soaring house prices and its six resident teaching golf professionals. These changes in transport also meant an intermingling of the Scots and English as never before. To the Scottish coastal towns and their golf clubs came English customs and attitudes. And these pensioners and valetudinarians were active in sport, as they had been all their life.

Not for them were the rigours of winter golf. After a life in the heat of India, summer sport was dominant. To this day, the golf clubs founded in this era have a colonial and military flavour, not least the names of their prizes, holes and bunkers - Redan, Malakoff, Calcutta, Bombay, Rorke's Drift and others.[51] And these golf club members often distanced themselves from the local humble players, using familiar methods.

Railways and Golf

The importance of these changes in travel to sport in general and golf in particular can hardly be exaggerated. The new trains easily bettered road travel for comfort, speed and economy. Travel was now available to many, having previously been an indulgence of the few, and there was a double bonus for noble golfers. Not only could they indulge in their sport, but those who had sold land to allow the railway to pass through had the right to stop and use any passing train. Some sportsmen, like the Earl of Eglinton near Prestwick, used this dispensation to reach his play at the Ayrshire links in style, as did the Earl of Seafield at Castle Grant near Grantown, when he wished to play at the Moray Firth.

Many of the golf clubs near the railways developed close arrangements with the local stations. Special exits from the platforms were constructed and warning bells in the clubhouse alerted the members to a train departure.[52] The railways were mindful of the golfers. Later, many golfers' 'specials' and concession books of tickets were issued and the rail journey to golf by many regulars was considered a convivial part of the outing. Saturday golf was a bonus to the railways, since it used the spare capacity outside the working week, and the railway companies were glad to sell concession tickets to golf club secretaries. The railways might help in other ways and the golf links used cast-off sleepers to face bunkers and steps, in spite of the dangers from rebounding balls. The railways broadened the horizons for local golf ball-makers and clubmakers, who, thriving on the new interest in the game, could now transport their products cheaply and efficiently over great distances. These Scottish artisans rose to the opportunities of the times and they and their golfing products became household names in Britain in the late 1800s.

Railways and the Links

The railways on the Scottish coasts now seem to run obtrusively through the links. This was no accident. Railway lines were easily laid out on the hard, flat linksland, also loved by the golfers. At St Andrews the new track ran uncomfortably close to the edge of the ancient links, and the railway sheds jutted awkwardly into the ancient 17th hole. The rail track at Leven, now abandoned but still very obvious, ran straight through the links, dividing one ancient part from another, and altering the golf course. To the south, railway sidings obliterated part of Leven's Dubbieside links. At Banff the golf links were severely reduced by the railway and at Cullen nearby, the necessary huge viaducts destroyed the amenity of the beach and golf links.

Only occasional protests at this intrusion by the railways can be detected at the time. One of Farnie's many grumbles in his pioneer *Golfer's Manual* was that the Burntisland links were 'curtailed and spoiled by the Northern Railway crossing one corner'. Few agreed with him. This lack of resistance to the coming of the railway is easily explained. The golfers, like the other townspeople, welcomed the railway without reservation, and any loss of amenity was a small price to pay for the gains to the town. Railways were a good thing.[53]

The New Ball and the Revival

It probably never occurred to the ballmaking craftsmen that the ancient, expensive feathery ball, which had stood the test of centuries of play, could be

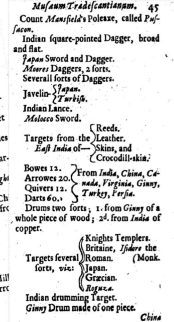

Asian malleable rubber - 'mazer wood' - made its first appearance in Tradescant's Museum in London. This collection later formed the core of the Ashmolean Museum, Oxford and reproduced by their permission.

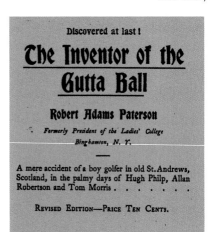

Advocacy for Paterson as inventor of the gutty ball: a pamphlet by Robert Paterson in 1910.

improved on, or made cheaper, and still maintain the traditions of the long game. Perhaps no effort had been made. The crisis in the game in the early 1800s may have made the search for cheaper materials essential, as did the revival of interest in golf in the 1840s. Whatever the reason, a new cheap ball was made and used. There are a number of claimants to the title of inventor of the new, revolutionary 'gutta' or 'gutty' ball. Though its provenance is controversial, the timing of its arrival is quite precisely known. Charles Roger in his *History of St Andrews* of 1849 says that 'gutta-percha arrived one year ago' i.e. 1848. Peter's *Reminiscences* state, as do others, that he saw the ball on sale in Edinburgh in 1848. It seems agreed that 1848 was the year, the revolutionary year, of the gutty ball.

One finding may be of relevance to this controversy. Gutta percha had been around in Britain, and widely used, for a considerable time before 1848. It was commonly available, and many users employed it for other purposes. Many may have shared in the making of the new ball from this familiar material.

Gutta Percha

This hardened juice was obtained from thirty varieties of trees growing in the Malaysian peninsula, notably the giant *Dichopsis gutta*. Mature trees grew to a height of 80 feet, with a diameter of up to four feet. Gutta percha was collected from the trees after the rainy season and collection required felling the tree, cutting the bark, and collecting the emergent juice. The juice was heated to remove resins, cooled and moulded, and, often adulterated with stones to increase weight and hence its value, the blocks were exported to Europe. There it was refined by heating, and the impurities separated out.

Gutta percha was noticed well before its use in golf in 1848. In 1822 a surgeon in the East India Company's service, Dr William Montgomerie, is said to have observed its use in the manufacture of whips in Singapore, and in 1842 he suggested to the Medical Board of Calcutta that the material might be of utility in making splints and other medical equipment. He sent specimens to the London Society for the Encouragement of Arts, Manufactures and Commerce, and on his return to Britain in 1844, two years later, he was awarded this Society's gold medal for his innovation. But he was not the first to bring gutta percha to Britain. One year earlier, Dr Jose D'Almeida had brought a similar specimen to London, and shown it to the enthusiastic Royal Asiatic Society.

It was then realised that a specimen called 'mazer' in Tradescant's Museum of London, opened in 1656, and which was moved to form the core collection of Oxford's Ashmolean Museum, was also of gutta percha. The ancient catalogue stated crisply that the 'plyable mazer wood, being warmed in water, will work to any form'.[54]

And so it could. The ancient mazer wood, or gutta percha, now suited the flexible needs of the new manufacturing society. In the 1840s it was worked into long bands or ropes and was also a splendid insulator of electricity; being inert and impervious, it also made excellent hollow pipes. It had good acoustic performance and was used for stethoscopes, aural tubes, speaking tubes and telephone hand-sets. It was resistant to corrosion even by acid and made admirable storage bottles and cylinders; it also made hard covers for books and dependable dentures.[55]

In short, the versatile gutta percha had been available, and patents taken out for its use, for about four years before its time came in golf. If there was an inventor of the gutty ball, it was perhaps the new railway network.

The Claimants

There is a remarkable array of claimants to be the inventor of the new ball.[56] The best, most romantic, and least likely story, is that of the Rev Robert Paterson of St Andrews, who received a statue from India by mail about 1845. The statue, last seen in possession of the University of St Andrews, is of an Indian god. The packaging for the journey to Britain included strips of gutta percha, and the minister's son, it is said, studied the material and found that it made useful soles for shoes. When warmed gently, it became soft and malleable and young Paterson later made a golf ball, of sorts, from the material. But Mr H. T. Peters, a well-known golfer at the Innerleven Club, claimed to have used a gutta ball first in 1848, having purchased one at a shop in Edinburgh, and shown it to Allan Robertson and 'Old' Tom Morris. Also in 1848, James Balfour and Maitland Dougall, playing at Blackheath, were told about the new ball and they interested Gourlay, the ballmaker, in it. Gourlay himself has a different story, and said that it was Sir Thomas Moncrieff who brought gutta percha to him from London. Of the other 'inventors', James Balfour of Musselburgh claimed to have used gutta first in Scotland, having obtained a supply from London in 1848. At Musselburgh, a Mr William Smith, watchmaker and inventor, later confidently stated that he made first use of gutta percha, about 1846, making a ball out of a whip handle shown to him by a carter.

This remarkable confusion may have a simple explanation. The material was widely available, but a simple sphere of gutta made a poor ball. Many golfers may have made such a ball before 1848, and put it away, disappointed with its use. The simple sphere simply did not fly. The golfing world, brought up on the smoothness of the feathery ball, had not suspected a paradox. Only when the first versions of the gutty ball were experimented with further was the empirical observation made that this cheap, easily made ball, though dull in play, performed better with repeated use. The dentable gutta sphere, when roughened and scored by the iron clubs, flew better, and held better on fast greens. The essential feature for success - still necessary for the modern ball - was to provide the surface of the ball with irregularities.

There were therefore two stages to the evolution of the gutta ball from a familiar household substance. Many persons may have attempted to make a useful ball, and desisted: others persisted with the reluctant smooth sphere, modified it and evolved the new ball. Many, in retrospect, could reasonably claim their priority in this important innovation.

The Luddites

Not everyone was pleased with the gutty, nor saw its potential. Nor was the eclipse of the feathery as sudden in 1848 as might seem. Three years on, in 1851, Gourlay's brother still won an award for traditional feathery ball manufacture: but by the following year the gutty was dominant. To some of the ballmakers and professionals, who were gaining a modest place in the reviving golfing world, a new cheap ball seemed a threat. Allan Robertson and 'Old' Tom Morris, still a young man, were then in partnership in the ball-making business and Allan, the senior of the two, was hostile to the new ball. He, like others, argued that the cheap ball would ruin their livelihood. Old Tom started using the ball, and recorded later that 'we had some words and this led to us parting company'. Allan Robertson also attempted to organise a caddies' strike to oppose the new ball, but introduction of the gutty proved to be irresistible. Allan had not realised that the game could now spread beyond the group of sportsmen familiar to him.

In the event, the great increase in the popularity of the game brought remarkable rewards to the golfing equipment makers. The gutty ball and the cheaper clubs allowed a greater participation in the game and this established the club-makers and ballmakers more securely in their trade than before, and opened new opportunities for them as professionals. This availability of the long game to those of modest means was noticed at the time. A commentator noted that the game was now

> extended to our youth and tradesmen who were to a certain extent excluded from joining the game of golf from the price of balls.

This change was also noted in the *Dundee Courier* of 1859, not without regret at the passing of the old ways:

> The St Andrews links are crowded with careless multitudes luxuriating in the pastime cheapened to them by the discovery of the gutty perch; and the game is popularised at the expense of its stately traditions.[57]

Making the New Ball

The early ball was called a 'gutta': the later composition balls had additives to the gutta percha and were properly termed 'gutty'. The gutta/gutty ball was hand-made during much of the remaining century, and a rough shape of the material was first prepared, then heated and shaped to a proper sphere. On cooling, it was hammered with a sharp edge, usually with about 250 strokes. The balls were kept for six months to harden, then painted white. The brown gutta took this paint badly, lost its coat quickly, and the dark ball was difficult to find when lost. The new balls cost 10/- per dozen or 1/- each, compared with 2/6 for featheries. They had a characteristic click when hit, and this click became part of the lore of golf. But it was durability which made the gutties so economical and desirable: the ball was almost indestructible and if damaged or misshapen could be easily remoulded.

Variants on the Gutty

There were all sizes and weights of the gutty ball: a standard ball was not enforced. The commonly used ball was 28 'drops' in troy weight. A bigger ball had a higher weight at 29 and there were a number of lighter ones at 26, 27 and 27½. These balls included later a 'floater', which would float on water. Other variants immediately tried had lead or iron filings in the centre and the Eclipse ball later had an additional outer skin.

By the 1880s, as the game became popular, moulds to make gutties appeared. The credit for constructing the first of these devices goes to a Mr J. G. Orcher, captain of the Dalhousie Club in Carnoustie. Using this machine, the balls could be made in quantity and be provided with indentations from the start.

The Gutty in Play

The gutty ball was more symmetrical than the older feathery. Though it did not fly any further, the gutty ran more truly on the greens and the lottery of putting on bumpy greens with the ovoid feathery ball had gone. This gave the stimulus to seek a truer putting surface through better greenkeeping.

Another property of the gutty had important consequences. At the end of its flight, the gutty 'fell like a stone' and the traditional Scottish pitch-and-run shot now had a rival in the chip-and-stop philosophy. With the new, almost indestructible ball, the iron clubs could be used without fear of damage to the ball and the way was open for routine use of the iron clubs in approach play. Manufacture of suitable clubs was encouraged and they were eventually to overthrow the ancient supremacy of the wooden clubs. The shot with a lofted iron club, hitting downwards into the turf through the ball and imparting back-spin, and from which the ball cleared trouble and drew up sharply on the green, was now favoured. It was Allan Robertson who showed the way, and his skill with this new shot earned a new and permanent popularity for this method of precision short play. In Allan Robertson's obituary in the *Dundee Advertiser* he was described as the pioneer of the use of iron play near the hole:

> *Previous to about 1848 or 1849, short wooden clubs, the baffing or short-spoons were used for this important shot - both difficult and frequently inaccurate. But Alan employed the cleek to jerk up his ball, however badly it might lie, it was all the same and this killing game, destructive to a certain extent to the green, is now all but universal.*[58]

This taking of a divot was quietly deplored. Farnie wrote in 1857 'we would suggest deferentially that the beginner wishing to acquire this peculiar use of the iron should do so when his ball is off the course...' The new ball changed other assumptions. In match-play in the feathery era, a player in a hopeless lie would concede a hole rather then risk slicing into his precious ball. But a shot with the gutty was always possible: this may have encouraged the transition to stroke-play.

The New Clubs

For the ordinary golfer at this time, in the mid-1800s, there was still a simplicity about the set of clubs carried. All historical sources are in agreement

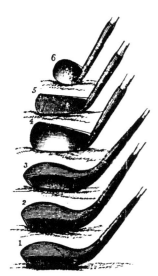

Various Forms of Club-heads.

The clubs available in 1862 for routine play showing three woods and three irons. Two of the irons were for trouble shots from bunkers or ruts, and routine play from tee to hole was with wooden clubs. From Chambers *A Few Rambling Remarks on Golf* 1862.

that three or four clubs, as used in the previous century, were all that the player required. Lees's painting shows players with about four or five clubs each, and as late as the 1880s *Golfiana Miscellanea*, the source of advice for new players, could recommend two woods and an iron club as sufficient for a decent outing:

> *It is almost indispensable for a player to have at least two clubs ... a long one for driving and a short one for putting near the hole; and on the links at St Andrews where there are many sandholes or bunkers, as they are termed, a club with an iron head is required.*

This simplicity was to last for much of the century. The historian David Hay Fleming of St Andrews recorded his first golfing outings carefully: '28th May 1888. Bought a driver, putter, cleek and four balls from Tom Morris...15/-.' In Sandy Herd's first attempt at the Open in 1885 he used four clubs only.

The New Iron Clubs

The crude early irons - the 'bunker club', 'track iron' or 'rut iron'- had heads made by the blacksmiths, but were only made as an occasional part of their trade.[59] These iron heads were handed over to the traditional clubmakers, i.e. wooden clubmakers, to add a shaft. The book *Golfiana Miscellanea* was dismissive and unimpressed with the iron clubs:

> *the irons are obviously of an unchanging character and so simple in form that it puzzles the most theorising enthusiast to invent another or a better mould.*

Endless 'theorising enthusiasts' appeared shortly after, and continued, with allegedly better moulds, with increasing tempo up to the present day.

The Cleekmakers' Marks

To receive the shaft, the earliest iron club heads had a moulded socket formed round a mandril by the blacksmiths. The shaft was inserted into this socket (hosel) by the wooden clubmakers, and held there by hand-crimping the edge of the metal socket onto the wood. The union was finished by hammering a peg through a hole in the hosel and into the shaft.

These clubmakers were considered to be the superior craftsmen, since their skills included customising shafts, and it was considered at this time that the shafts had to be fitted to the player. Just as a gentleman ordered suits from his tailor and his shoes and gloves were also made to measure, so his golf clubs were to be fitted to him. Hence the wooden clubmakers held a top place in the hierarchy of golfing artisans, and dealt directly with the customers.

The low reputation of the iron club, and its humble status in the golfer's equipment also induced humility in the makers of these heads, far into the

From the mid-1800s, use of cleekmakers' marks in Scotland grew in popularity. By courtesy of DAVID STIRK.

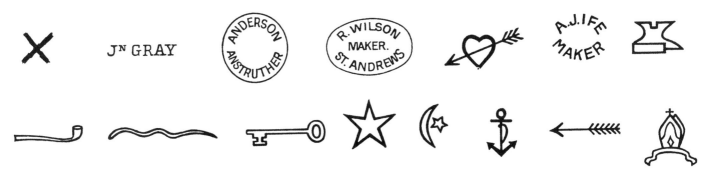

126

nineteenth century, and the early iron heads had no maker's mark. As the demand for irons increased, some blacksmiths evolved into full-time cleek-makers; and added their mark to the clubheads. Much later they began shafting their own clubs. Some started to achieve a reputation for their irons, sold direct. These iron heads were made by hand almost until the First World War. Then drop-forging methods appeared and mass production of heads commenced.[60]

The Markings

A delightful and arcane subject is the markings on the early iron club heads, as they emerged from the dark ages of the use of unmarked rut irons to the era of precision play with matched sets in the twentieth century. The earliest iron-head maker to identify himself was Alex Carrick of Musselburgh, a blacksmith and toolmaker from the late 1700s, and the earliest heads made by him have a simple small cross on the rear as his mark. Another early identifi-able cleekmaker was John Gray of Prestwick. His irons were the first to bear the maker's name, rather than use a mark. Born in 1824, he had a blacksmith's training and started forging iron heads in 1851. He was one of the original members of Prestwick St Nicholas Golf Club, and in spite of his success as a clubmaker, on his death, age 80, in 1904, his gravestone gives his occupation as blacksmith.[61]

As iron club manufacturing increased, the humble cleekmakers, previously content to put a small mark or name only on the back of their iron heads, started to add more elaborate detail. The heads were still passed to the shafter (clubmaker) who also added his name to the increasingly informative rear surface of the iron head. These shafters, who included a large number of club professionals, also put their name on the shaft near the grip. The obliging cleekmaker might even pre-stamp his heads with the future shafter's name prior to delivery, and cleekmakers held a full range of such stamps for their regular customers. By the end of the century we see a cluttered rear face of the iron club, perhaps displaying the name of the club (e.g. mashie), the cleek-maker's mark, the cleekmaker's name, plus the shafter's name. By contrast, the face of the iron club at that time was entirely smooth.

The first man to be successful as a cleekmaker, i.e. a specialist quantity supplier of iron clubs, was Robert Wilson of St Andrews, who was first to give up his blacksmith's work to supply the other clubmakers in St Andrews with iron heads. But even in the gutty era the iron clubs were carried in limited numbers and range. Until about 1900, the most lofted club carried was the five-iron equivalent.

127

The Shafts

The traditional long, slim, whippy ash shafts of the feathery era did not suit the new iron heads. Lancewood had the required stiffness and spring, but was heavy and brittle: greenhart was similar, but found a niche as the shaft for putters. But hickory had all the properties required of a shaft for the new iron clubs. It was tough, elastic, light and waterproof. It was to dominate club-making for eighty years.[62] The first use of hickory in golf club manufacture is difficult to trace, but Philp clubs surviving from the 1800s show such hickory shafts. A letter in the *Sporting Magazine* of 1828 mentions that hickory was used for the golf club shafts and also for billiard cues, axe handles, pit props, rakes and wheel spokes. Hickory had to be seasoned, i.e. dried slowly, before use, reducing the moisure content to less than 10%. The wood came from the Southern States of America, and the best centre cuts of hickory trees had a straight grain through the shaft. Not only was hickory strong, but it had less torque during the downswing; hence the old closed-face wooden clubs gave way to more open-faced designs. Above all, the hickory shaft absorbed the impact of the club when hitting the ground in the new divot-taking golf stroke.

The Heads

To suit the gutty ball, the heads of the woods became deeper and shorter, leading to the emergence of the 'bulger' shape of clubhead. This was less pointed than the older, long-nosed clubs, and the face was flat rather than concave, and might even be convex.[63] Claimants for invention of the bulger were Willie Park, and Simpson at Carnoustie. The new harder gutty ball could damage the face of thorn, apple or pear clubheads and the wooden clubs now required protection, which was supplied by placement of protective shallow insets of horn or ivory into the face. Beech and the even harder persimmon wood now found favour for heads and these were soon dominant in club pro-duction from the 1880s onwards. Persimmon was so hard that it might require no insets on the face.

With the cheap, durable ball, and tough, indestructible shafts and club-heads, golf was inceasingly economical and could now be played by anyone. Some thought that a golden age of perfection had arrived.

The Effect on Play

The increasing use of the iron clubs brought with it a new problem. Wooden clubs had taken no divot of turf from the links: but the turf was now damaged with each iron shot. In 1793 an early warning was sounded when the Honourable Company took a stand against over-use of iron clubs.

The minutes record:

It is the unanimous opinion of this company that no member shall play on the links with irons all without the consent of the Council, and it is recommended by the meeting that they will not grant the desire of such application.

The Burgess Club passed a similar resolution in the same year. The phrase 'irons all' suggests that the ban was on those going out to play only with iron clubs. This odd rule may have had its origin in the many unusual and extravagant bets made within the clubs at this time, including some contests for play with iron clubs only, clubs which could not hit the ball any distance. This struggle against the iron club, as the enemy of the links was, in the end, lost. So useful were the iron clubs that the battle against them failed, and golf has had to live with the damage done to the turf ever since.

The new gutty ball had to be hit: the feathery had been 'swept'. The new ball and the new swing may also have altered the stance of the players. All the early illustrations of play in the feathery ball era show a very closed stance. The new clubs and ball changed this stance to a square one. A bent elbow at the top of the swing appeared with a full pivot, giving the player a full arc of club movement, and the ball was hit with force. Only later, with the next ball, the Haskell, came the straight left arm, and a shorter swing, and it was commented at the time that the passing of the gutty 'took some of the athleticism out of the game'.

The effect of this change in equipment on the game in the mid-1800s can be measured. The winning scores in the medal competitions of the Royal and Ancient Golf Club of St Andrews are available and they show an improvement about 1850, when these changes in ball and club appeared.

Improved medal scores seen after the arrival of the gutty ball in 1848.

The Royal and Ancient

WINNERS OF THE SILVER CROSS
Presented by Colonel J. Murray Belshes of Buttergask

		Strokes
1836	James Condie, Esq., Perth	110
1837	John H. Wood, Esq., Leith	100
1838	C. Robertson, Esq.	108
1839	Do.	104
1840	Samuel Messieux, Esq.	109
1841	Robert Haig, Esq.	104
1842	Do.	104
1843	Captain David Campbell	103
1844	Robert Haig, Esq.	111
1845	Captain A. O. Dalgleish	99
1846	Robert Lindsay, Esq.	110
1847	Captain David Campbell	104
1848	Robert Hay, Esq.	101
1849	J. O. Fairlie, Esq., of Coodham	100
1850	George Condie, Esq., Perth	96
1851	George Glennie, Esq.	99
1852	Captain W. H. Maitland Dougall, Scotscraig	96
1853	Henry Jelf Sharpe, Esq.	96
1854	J. O. Fairlie, Esq., of Coodham	95
1855	Captain W. H. Maitland Dougall	98
1856	William Playfair, Esq.	102
1857	W. C. Thomson, Esq., Dundee	96
1858	Sir Thomas Moncrieffe of Moncrieffe, Bart.	95
1859	James C. Lindsay, Esq., Broughty Ferry	101
1860	James Ogilvie Fairlie, Esq., of Coodham	99
1861	Thomas Hodge, Esq.	92
1862	Henry Mackechnie, Esq.	94
1863	Gilbert Mitchell Innes, Esq.	97
1864	William C. Thomson, Esq., Dundee	95
1865	Gilbert Mitchell Innes, Esq.	98
1866	William C. Thomson, Esq., Dundee	92
1867	Robert Clark, Esq., Edinburgh	92
1868	Major Robert T. Boothby	92
1869	Robert Clark, Esq., Edinburgh	92
1870	Do.	92
1871	Henry A. Lamb, Esq.	93
1872	Ross W. Ochterlony, Esq.	98
1873	Henry A. Lamb, Esq.	99

Other Changes

After the middle of the century, the itinerant, sporting golfers became less restless. The social sporting circuit became less intense and multiple club membership started to decline. The golfers' boxes of clubs also moved about less, and instead stayed regularly in the same clubhouse. Initially the boxes were stored flat, then for tidiness the boxes were stacked vertically, and eventually were screwed to the wall. Thus evolved the club locker, and as membership of the golf clubs increased, problems of identification of clubs, when fetched by the caddie masters, arose.

This appears to have been solved by the evolution of the golf bag, which had the owner's name or initials prominently displayed. The bag may not have evolved primarily for carrying clubs, but for storage, enabling collection and delivery of the correct clubs from the lockers and boxes to their owners on the links. Andrew Kirkaldy credits a Dr Trail with the introduction of the golf bag. The caddies still held the clubs and bag head down under their arms as they always had done, initially ignoring the opportunity to carry the bag, even if a strap was attached. The earlier golfers probably avoided play in bad weather, but the new gutty ball and tough waterproof hickory shafts meant that play in rain was possible. A bag also helped to keep the shafts dry.

The swing in the early gutty era was full and athletic, with a bent left arm and flying right elbow. From Chambers A Few Rambling Remarks on Golf 1862.

Mid-century Play

A St Andrews diarist tells us about playing the game about the middle of the nineteenth century, just as the new popularity started:

It is not yet eleven, that great hour of cause on the Links. Groups of caddies are prowling about: a clash and rattle of clubs are heard as you pass the club-makers' shops. One or two golfers are putting idly at the starting hole with their burnished cleeks. 'Where's Allan?' - the cry is repeated by telegraphic caddies right up to the champion's little garden. A minute elapses and down comes the champion in hot haste to the Club House. Now the match is arranged. Allan has evidently got to nurse an elementary golfer. It is a foursome: Allan and his partner against two rather good hands.[65]

This is no longer the St Andrews of the sporting gentry; there is a different atmosphere in this vignette. The players are humble innocents, waiting for the gracious professional to organise them, not the reverse. In the new revival, Robertson is arranging the day's play, and will play with a beginner himself. Play still starts close to the last hole (in the ground) and practice play into the hole is evidently permitted. Play by the group starts at 11 o'clock, and the links are not crowded.

From other diaries we get more information on play at St Andrews in mid-century. The games started at the traditional time of eleven in the morning, 'the hour of cause'. This ritual of a slow morning start is puzzling: perhaps the newspapers had to be read after a large breakfast and cigar. Two rounds were played quickly in the day. The morning matches, singles or foursomes, were followed by lunch at the Union Parlour, or later at the R&A clubhouse. If, on the other hand, the match finished at a distance from the last hole, the players would cut over and start a second game on the outward holes. It was for this reason that the famous ginger beer stall arose. This mobile booth sold food and refreshments, notably ginger beer and brandy, at the present 4th hole. It was a resting place, and a meeting place where matches were started afresh, and old photos suggest that balls and clubs could be purchased there. The hole is called Ginger Beer to this day, and the large bunker there gave shelter during this pause in play.

These two rounds of match-play were completed by four o'clock. Two rounds plus lunch, probably a leisurely one, in five hours was the norm for most of the century, and other figures confirm this speed of play, one which continued until the end of the century. The starting times for club competitions in the mid-1800s were only four minutes apart: even stroke-play golf was a fast game. Match-play was the dominant mode and was probably even faster. Though the ancient clubs did have trophies and competitions for stroke-play, it was remarked by a lofty traditionalist at the R&A, that stroke play at this time

was confined to two days in the year... the mere securing of the medal by strokes was not dwelt upon. It was a necessary evil at the time... but nobody remembered it a week later...[66]

The Scottish links were all uncrowded in this period. The layout of Prestwick (founded 1851) testifies to the sparsity of the players on the links at this time. Old maps of Prestwick show endlessly criss-crossing holes - 'cross routes' - with some greens used many times. St. Andrews still retains a single subtle cross-over at the 7th/11th holes.

The Royal and Ancient membership list from 1854 as printed in the *Edinburgh Almanac*. The membership is still largely from the east of Scotland, but a number of distant members are noted, the beginnings of the club's national role in golf.

Summer Play

In this new era the ancient tradition of winter golf was also slowly disappearing. The players, new and old, were less involved with agriculture and the land, and more with commerce. Rarely was the links grass crop in summer now more important than golf. But Farnie's *Golfer's Manual* of 1857 lists a number of courses unsuitable for play in summer, notably Cupar and Bruntsfield Links, because of long grass. Even at North Berwick, Farnie summarised the suituation that

> *because of the thick growth of grass, mole-heaps and absence of hazard, the play is very monotonous. The principal time for play is autumn and spring.*[67]

The golfers' calendar still gave a pride of place to the Autumn and Spring Meetings, but in the improving golf courses, various ways were found to allow summer golf. The crop was taken in early, by scything, and sheep were then allowed on the links to make a professional job of trimming the grass. This use of the links for grazing compensated for loss of the grass crop. Golf became a holiday sport and summer play by the visitors increased at St Andrews, North Berwick and a host of other seaside resorts. This new holiday summer play did not entirely suit the older gentlemen golfers, who were accustomed to Scottish field sports, particularly grouse shooting, from 12th August onwards. It was said at St Andrews that those golfing gentlemen who had not been invited to a grouse moor by the 12th would hide for a few days and then reappear slowly on the links, such was their embarrassment.

Another group of golfers found summer golf much to their liking. On the west coast of Scotland, the estate owners found that they were no longer obsessed with the harvest and could join the new summer golfers occasionally. These golfers also knew that their local west coast links, particularly in Ayrshire, were as good as those on the east, where their forebears had played during their winter migration. The most important development was at Prestwick. The local Ayrshire golfers, already prominent in the membership of the R&A and the Honourable Company, started to use their local links at home in summer, and Ayrshire golf was to prosper for the first time and to thrive thereafter.

Dress

The new summer golfers still followed the dress of the noble golfers. They dressed as if playing in winter. In 1857, a St Andrews golfer could complain that

> *the old Scottish club dress is about the most uncomfortable garment that the golfer could endure. The staring red colour alone is enough to give anyone a fever on a hot day.*

Though the traditional military-style coats were rapidly disappearing, the substitutes were still unsuitable. Tight coats, buttoned high, waistcoats and broad hats were the fashion. The professionals wore even heavier attire. A thick tweed jacket and strong working trousers made them look ready for winter weather, even in summer. Their hats were more sensible and look snug and functional, unlike the noble golfers' top hats. Heavy-nailed boots with spats were worn: the more powerful swing with the new clubs required more anchorage.

From 1800 on, the ancient ceremonial dress of the golf club members had proved hard to enforce both on and off the links - perhaps because of expense. Various light-hearted fines are noted in the club minutes in attempts to compel the discipline of dressing in uniform for dinner, but the wearing of the uniforms could not be maintained. The Honourable Company in particular struggled hard to maintain the tradition, but by 1888 had to admit the force of events and reluctantly declared that only the Captain need appear in uniform, and the rest could do as they pleased. A historian of the Honourable Company could record later that thereafter no-one dressed up for golf, and on the course 'only the coverings of the head and feet differed from that of Princes Street'.

Greenkeeping

In this recovery period there was a new interest in the quality of the turf used for play. The Scottish links had probably changed little in 200 years, and the golfing area was little tended, since human feet and grazing animals did all that was required to keep the grass short and fertilised. The healthy grass gave a springy, brassie lie at all times. The greens were rough, by later standards, and the bunkers were but huge irregular breaks in the links moulded by the wind, rain and burrowing animals. Horses were freely admitted to the links, and golfers and their supporters might use ponies while out playing. Some paintings from the time show these mounted spectators and players.

The quiet mid-century links at St Andrews from Clark's *Royal and Ancient Game* of 1875.

As we have seen above, there had been the first experiments with the skills of greenkeeping at Leith in the earliest days of the Gentlemen Golfers' society. In the 1700s they had repeatedly attempted to improve Leith Links by drainage schemes, and later they moved whins and earth, and replanted and seeded open areas. The new interest in golf in the mid-1800s led to greater use of the golf links, and the need to restore the turf. A new desire for precision

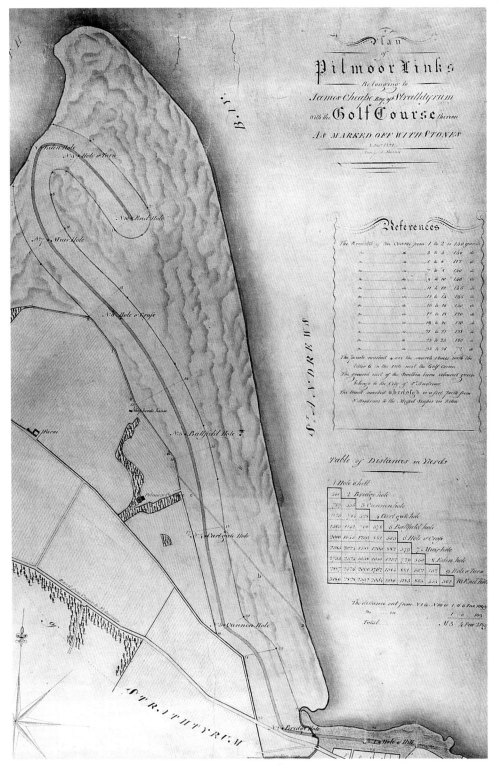

The holes of the St Andrews golf links circa 1820. The holes in the ground were named and the first hole is described as played from 'The End Hole' to 'The Bridge Hole', i.e. the present 17th green. This terminology came about from the habit of playing off close to the last hole played to, and the round started close to the final hole. There were ten holes in the ground, eight of which were played to twice, making eighteen holes in all at this time.

By courtesy of the FIFE DISTRICT COUNCIL and the SCOTTISH RECORD OFFICE.

arose, probably from the rise of the gutty ball and use of iron clubs. There was interest in the new technology available, notably for cutting grass. So the links fell under the gardener's eye. The Aberdeen golfers took the initiative in the matter of the putting green, and ruled in 1815 that the putting surface was to be fifteen yards round each hole. New technology was also used to make new implements. The hole-cutter appeared in Montrose in 1825, Musselburgh in 1829 and at Aberdeen in 1849, and iron bands to support the interior appeared at Elie in 1874. The same club purchased its first grass mower shortly afterwards in 1877.

To accommodate increased play at St Andrews, the playing area of the links was extended by an unusual strategy. Instead of creating new holes, the greens were expanded to make large double greens. It was announced in 1856 that

in consequence of the golfing course being much out of order by the greatly increased number of golfers and smashing with clicks, the Royal and Ancient deemed it necessary to vote a sum of £25 to have the turf and bunkers repaired. Although just about half the sum is yet laid out the course wears a better look... Along with this is another improvement, viz., two holes in each putting green, with the exception of the first and end hole, white flags going out and red ones coming in. The bent and whins have been cleared to widen the course when necessary.[69]

Thus the ancient narrow course was expanded, much to the sorrow of some old-timers. The pressure of the new popularity of the game led to the peculiar arrangement of the double greens, which remains to this day. Even the Musselburgh whins, as Hutchinson said, were 'going the way of all whins'. One consequence of this expansion at St Andrews was that, to rest the areas of heavy wear on the links, the course could be played backwards, i.e. 1st tee to 17th hole, 17th green to 16th hole etc. In the nineteenth century the St Andrews Old Course was still regularly played in this way and the links

Greenkeeping improved in all sports in the later 1800s, and cricket and golf benefited from use of scythes and rollers as did the Glasgow bowling green shown here. Grass cutting machines were to come.

could be played either right-handed or left-handed, with a change of mode every two weeks.[70] The Opens of 1873, 1876, 1879 and 1881 were played on the backwards course, as was the 1886 Amateur Championship, but thereafter the present anti-clockwise route became standard.

This flexible and sensible system was slavishly tried elsewhere. Early Carnoustie Links had double greens and North Berwick had a 'backward' version of play on the links. Even the Burgess Club tried (unsuccessfully) to reverse the use of their new parkland course at Barnton when they arrived there in 1900.

Keepers of the Links

Until the middle of the nineteenth century, the links had been largely untended. The successful little ecosystem relied mainly on the animals who cropped the grass and fertilised it, to which was added blown sand which renewed the surface. How much greenkeeping was involved is not clear. The great keeper of the links, 'Old' Tom Morris said that 'neither broom nor scythe' had been used at St Andrews until mid-century.

The older clubs had employed part-time help, often a caddie or professional, for the chores of elementary course management. At Bruntsfield, David Denholm, a clubmaker, was paid as 'keeper of the green' from 1809-20. Montrose employed a keeper from 1829. Earlier at St Andrews, Allan's father, Charles Robertson, was keeper of the links at St Andrews for 5/- a year, paid by the R&A. Towards the end of his term his salary was doubled because of the increasing problem with rabbits. Even earlier at St Andrews, from about 1785 to 1805, Robert Morris - Tom's father - was keeper. Later Tom Morris was also made keeper at St Andrews with a part-time salary, and he was 'to make the holes, look after the flags and mend the turf.' Later, on return from Prestwick to St Andrews in 1863, he was allowed 'one man for two days a week, plus barrow, spade and shovel'. At Bruntsfield Links earlier, the five golf clubs employed Douglas McEwan to help 'keep the green'. The instructions to the keeper of the links at Dunbar in 1859 stated he was to make 'new holes each Saturday, putting greens to be swept and sorted every Wednesday and Saturday, molehills to be kept down on the course and to be in attendance on medal days'.[71] There was no mention of cutting the grass. At St Andrews in 1863 the holes were changed weekly on Monday, or prior to big competitions. Sand may have been used liberally, placing it on rabbit scrapes and putting areas, and the early rules allowed the players to smooth down loose sand before putting. 'Mair saund, Honeyman,' urged Old Tom to his young assistant when any remedial work was required. The present elevation of some of the huge St Andrews greens above the level of the fairway may have been the result of Old Tom's policy.

Tom Morris' role in improving the St Andrews links has probably not been acknowledged; even to consider grooming the ancient course may have been a controversial novelty. Some players felt that the game should be played without changing the natural habitat, and there was eloquent defence of the variety of greens at St Andrews. One, the eleventh, was entirely surfaced at that time with close-cropped heather. This variety of surface had its supporters, and Morris' innovations were more radical than they might seem now. His changes included resurfacing such greens, tidying bunkers and preventing their erosion by formalising their edges. Later photographs of St Andrews show the bunkers to be faced with bricks of turf, or shored up with railway sleepers; St Andrews was leading the way. As late as 1864, a visitor to Carnoustie complained that:

> Though the links possess natural advantages unsurpassed by any other in Scotland, they are allowed to remain totally uncared for. The putting green is in most cases very rough... holes distended into huge triangles... no flags visible to guide the player and even one accustomed to the links cannot tell with accuracy the precise position of the hole until a few yards from it.[72]

Clearly, players' expectations were rising.

As the numbers of golfers rose and standards of play increased, through practice and the increased precision of play with iron clubs, so more interest appeared in the quality of the courses and their maintenance.[73] Cutting of fairways was posssible when horse-drawn equipment became available, and advice from cricketers and bowlers was obtained. The keeping of a horse was expensive and awkward, but by the end of the century this was essential for course maintenance. The horse was shod with shoes of canvas and wood when working on the course. In 1901 a guide book could say of the course at Aberfeldy, as if encountering a novelty, 'the grass is kept short by cutting it.'

New Societies

In this interlude before the great golf boom, new golf clubs started to appear, and old ones, which had succumbed in the crisis, re-emerged. Farnie's list of 1857 gives the following golf clubs: Aberdeen, St Andrews, Bruntsfield, Burntisland, Cupar, Crail, Dunbarnie, Innerleven, Kingsbarns, Leven, Monifieth, Montrose, Musselburgh, North Berwick, Perth, Prestwick, and Wemyss Castle Golf Club. In 1848 a club of significance appeared in a new area, at Carnoustie, by then on the main railway line north of Dundee. The Caledonian Union Club was formed by 'the best clubmen from St Andrews, Perth and Montrose' suggesting that the founders were some of the last of the circuit of sporting gentlemen. In the west, the Glasgow Club revived. Some St Andrews clubs had survived well through this difficult period, and now new ones appeared. From 1845 onwards, when the Mechanics Club was formed at St Andrews, a cluster of new clubs appeared in the town - the Artisans (1849), the St Andrews Operatives (1849), the Students (1855), the Madras (1857) and the Ladies (1867). As was usual in Scotland, most of these clubs had no clubhouse, blending their outings with general play on the links.

LIST OF SCOTTISH GOLFING CLUBS

WITH AN ACCOUNT OF THE VARIOUS LINKS PLAYED OVER; AND THE DATES OF THEIR RESPECTIVE MEDAL DAYS

[We regret that this list is not so complete as was anticipated. Considerable unforeseen difficulty occurred at the last moment in obtaining definite information from several clubs respecting their medal-days, &c; but all particulars received from the various secretaries, and from other sources, have been epitomised and arranged in the following account.]

ABERDEEN—This Links is very good golfing ground. It lies seaward; the soil is sandy, but does not abound in furze or whins. There are, however, very stiff hazards interspersed, and the links as a whole has all the elements of a good course. There was a club at one time in Aberdeen, but whether or not in existence at the present time, we cannot say.

ANDREWS SAINT—This is the Queen-Links. No one can be truly said to have tasted the ultimate pleasures of golf who has not played at St Andrews. The course is oblong and slightly winding and of great extent; hazards abound of every description; bunkers, whins, and inequality of ground occur every hole. This course is preserved by the Royal and Ancient Club who play over it, and is in consequence always in good order. This golfing club was instituted on the 14th May, 1754. It has since been remodelled and re-instituted so to speak. There are two annual meetings, for medal competition; one on the first Wednesday of May, when the Silver Cross and the Bombay (Silver) Medal are played for, and the other on the Wednesday nearest to the first day of October, whether that may fall in September or October, when members compete for a gold medal presented by King William IV, and also the Club (gold) medal. There is an imaginary competition at this latter meeting, for the silver club, which confers on the *nominee* the dignity of Captain for the year.

Another club plays over this Links; known as the St Andrews Golf

80

H. B. Farnie, the erratic St Andrews student, wrote his *Golfers Manual* in 1857, the first of the golf handbook genre.

136

Other sports revived and the first football clubs appeared. In the Highlands interest in shinty re-emerged and in 1849 the North of Spey Shinty Club, the first of its kind, was formed.

Club Competitions

In early sport, villages or parishes played their neighbours, usually at football, curling or shinty: occasionally this rivalry took the form of an annual tribal form of golf, as at Gullane and Fortrose.

GOLF TOURNAMENT.

THE grand golfing tournament, for which arrangements have been in progress for some time past, commenced on Tuesday, under highly favourable circumstances. The weather was everything that could have been desired, and the green was in first-class order. The attendance of spectators was considerable, and great interest was taken in the game, the fine playing of several of the professionals being much admired. Amongst those present we observed:—Lord Dupplin; Wm. Macdonald Macdonald, Esq., of St Martins; Arch. Turnbull, Esq. of Bellwood; Frank Sandeman, Esq. of Springland; Jas. Condie, Esq.; Hon. John Rollo; the Officers of the garrison; and many of the principal inhabitants of the city. The prizes played for on Tuesday were :—1st, £10; 2d, £5; 3d, £3, open to all competitors, either professionals or amateurs. No fewer than fourteen couples started, amongst whom were T. Morris, Prestwick; W. Park, Musselburgh; R. Andrews, Perth; W. Strath, St Andrews; G. D. Brown, Musselburgh; G. Morris, Carnoustie; W. Dow, amateur players; and other professionals. The bers of the Perth Clubs. The game was thre

The celebrated golf tournament at Perth in 1864.
From *The Perthshire Journal and Constitutional* April 21st 1864.

Professionals at the Perth Tournament of 1864. Young Tom Morris made an appearance in a boy's match, and is shown leaning on his father's shoulder in the top left of the picture.
By courtesy of ST ANDREWS UNIVERSITY LIBRARY, COWIE COLLECTION.

Improvements in travel now meant a revival of these cabalistic customs, the teams could travel to any contest by rail. Golf clubs, newly confident, could consider regular tournaments and challenges at the national level.

In 1830 we find the first minute of a formal inter-club match in the modern sense of the word when the Bruntsfield Links Golf Club played the Burgess Club at Musselburgh - where both clubs played their club outings. This match was further solemnised by a trophy presented in 1854. The first match involving travel to a distant venue may have been when St Andrews Golf Club visited Leven in 1849. The members of the St Andrews team were given expenses of 2/- each by the club, and returned home to a civic welcome after their victory. In 1857 the Prestwick Club took another initiative and the following clubs were invited for an inter-club tournament, showing which clubs were active at this time in mid-century: the R&A, the Honourable Company, Prestwick, the Burgess Club, North Berwick, the Bruntsfield Links Club, Innerleven, Montrose Royal Albert, Dirleton Castle (playing at Archerfield), Royal Blackheath, Perth and Carnoustie Panmure. The Glasgow Club was invited but, being inactive, did not attend.[74]

The first national tournament to be organised for club golfers was a match-play tournament in 1851 at St Andrews, and another was held there in July

Robert Chambers at the eighteenth green at St Andrews in one of the first amateur tournaments arranged in the mid 1800s.

1857, and repeated in 1858 and 1859. Foursomes and singles match-play was the format. The Blackheath Club performed well in these early tournaments, but this should not be taken as evidence of considerable golfing talent in England. Multiple membership of golf clubs was common; the Blackheath players were often Scotsmen and R&A members, part of a group well known to each other. Another celebrated meeting involving teams apparently travelling from a distance was the Royal Albert Tournament at Montrose in which a Blackheath team again did well. Professionals also took part in some events at these meetings and these joint outings allow comparisons of the skills of the gentlemen and the players. The scores of the good amateurs were about twelve strokes worse per round than those of the leading professionals.[75] The gentlemen players brought their own caddies to the tournaments, and having brought them, they then had some sport by putting up a prize for play in challenge matches involving the professionals after the main event.

One of the most ancient surviving amateur team trophies is the East Lothian County Cup. Started in 1864, this magnificent trophy for team play in the county was presented by the Earl of Wemyss.

The Rise of Musselburgh

The larger Scottish towns were expanding and their recreational space was shrinking. Golf at Glasgow Green was no longer pleasant and at Leven, heavy industry was threatening recreational use of the Dubbieside Links. But of all the traditional golfing areas, the pressure on Leith Links is the most interesting to study, and as Leith became less and less suitable for golf, the players looked for an alternative. They chose the Musselburgh Links.

The 'Honest Town' of Musselburgh, eight miles east of Edinburgh and twelve miles south-west of Gullane and Muirfield, is not highly regarded today. Yet this town rose to be the major Scottish centre of professional golf and the golf manufacturing industry in the later nineteenth century. For a while it eclipsed St Andrews as the home of golf, judging by the number of

Arms of Musselburgh Golf Club, later the Royal Musselburgh Golf Club. Though 1774 is given as the foundation date, a less formal club was in existence from earlier times at this ancient favourite site for East Lothian golf.

successful players and its golfing industry. In the 1874 Open at Musselburgh, 16 out of 42 entrants were local players, and in 1886 almost half the Open entrants were from the town. It was at Musselburgh that a new generation of golfers realised the potential for commercial development of golf equipment production and course design, and it was here that it was realised that advertising and testimonials would sell golf clubs, and that golfing goods could be marketed.[76]

Musselburgh's rise had been the result of the over-crowding of Edinburgh's ancient golfing areas. At Bruntsfield, such was the growth of the town that street lights appeared at the edge of the Links, and the Allied Club there made local rules to deal with the problem of broken lights. Other incidents occurred. Edinburgh citizens had always been hit by golf balls but the number of accidents increased. The golfers' defence was that the traditional shouted warning of 'fore' absolved them from any delict. About this time, Bishop Gillies was hit on Bruntsfield Links by a ball but took the matter no further. However, in 1863 a child was struck by a ball and required medical attention. Complaints were made to the authorities.[77] The Procurator Fiscal took an interest, and statements were taken from witnesses. Although there was no prosecution, clearly public opinion was no longer as tolerant of golf as before.

Musselburgh had golf links which were much admired. But its distance from Edinburgh had until now made these suitable only for an occasional outing. Now the railway changed this when the line reached Musselburgh in 1847. A period of uncertainty followed: some clubs remained in Edinburgh, but some moved to Musselburgh. Others hesitated. Edinburgh's Bruntsfield Links club, for instance, still played at Bruntsfield on Saturdays, but for week-day play, travelled by train to Musselburgh.

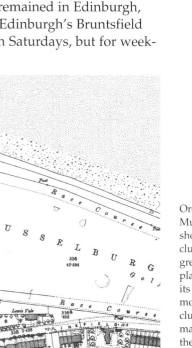

An early medal of the Honourable Company of Edinburgh Golfers, showing the Musselburgh Race Course stand, used as their temporary clubhouse on arrival at Musselburgh. From Wood's *Golfing Curios*.

Ordnance Survey Map of Musselburgh of 1893 still showing the abandoned clubhouses of the three great Edinburgh golf clubs playing at Musselburgh in its dominant era, before moving elsewhere. These clubhouses are still marked at the west end of the race-course - the Burgess, Bruntsfield and the Honourable Company.

Golf Moves Out

The decision by an Edinburgh club to go to Musselburgh permanently was made first by the Honourable Company and they moved in 1836. Other Edinburgh clubs, notably the Burgess and Bruntsfield, then started informal, intermittent play at Musselburgh. The Bruntsfield Links Club rented rooms from Gourlay the ballmaker in his Golf House when they first arrived at Musselburgh. Already playing at Musselburgh were the (Royal) Musselburgh Golf Club from 1774. It was a time of increasing prosperity for these clubs and the three principal clubs at Musselburgh soon had elegant clubhouses. The Honourable Company built one in 1865, Royal Musselburgh followed in 1873, the Burgess in 1875, and the Bruntsfield in 1886.

There was soon a mass of other little golfing societies visiting Musselburgh: at the height of the town's influence there were an estimated 60 such 'clubs without a clubhouse', but regularly playing there on the open links for trophies and prizes. Many were Edinburgh clubs, great and small. There was a mass of local golfers also playing, including caddies, without belonging to formal clubs, enthused by the influx of Edinburgh players. More and more of these local men began to make a living from golf; some were to be highly successful.

Professionals and Makers

Musselburgh had a developing golf industry from the early 1800s onwards. As the Edinburgh influence increased, so the club and ballmakers moved with them. McEwan moved from Bruntsfield to Musselburgh in 1847, and as noted above, the Musselburgh blacksmith Carrick had early success with his cleeks. Musselburgh now also had Douglas Gourlay - the best feather ballmaker of his generation - a shrewd and organised businessman, who had moved to the town in the 1840s. He was tenant of the racecourse grandstand and there he accommodated the Honourable Company and their golf club boxes when they first arrived. He was known as a 'perfect master of ceremonies' and was also asked to preside at the North Berwick club meetings. Another Musselburgh firm emerged - J. and D. Clark who made the famous 'Musselburgh' gutty ball. These golfing artisan families intermarried and thrived in the enthusiastic golfing milieu at Musselburgh. Initially the town had no player of stature to compare with Allan Robertson. But the rise of 'Old' Willie Dunn put Musselburgh into prominence. But Musselburgh seems to have had no high-profile cliques of gentlemen players, as had St Andrews: the town's patrons were less flamboyant.

Musselburgh's Players

As Musselburgh rose to rival the fame of St Andrews, in 1849 the chance of a sporting occasion arose. This, the first of the century's great golf challenge matches, was for one of the largest stakes ever put up, one not exceeded in the boom years of golf later. It was also watched by one of the great sporting crowds of the nineteenth century, itself evidence of increasing interest by all classes in the game, and a result of easier travel. 'Old' Willie Dunn and his brother Jamie Dunn of Musselburgh, played Allan Robertson and 'Old' Tom Morris of St Andrews. The stake raised was £400, a huge sum but not untypical of the gentlemen's gambling era then on the wane. As usual, the format was of one match at home and one away, and a third at a neutral links, using match-play with accumulated scores. Many side-bets on each leg of the game were laid. In the final 36 holes at North Berwick the Dunns started with a seemingly invincible lead of 13 up, but they immediately faltered and were only four up with 18 to go. In the last few holes, the St Andrews pair overtook the Musselburgh golfers and won the game.

The challenges continued, and Musselburgh continued to engage St Andrews in golfing contests. In 1854, at the age of twenty, Willie Park of Musselburgh and his brother turned up at St Andrews at the time of the R&A meeting. They and their backers challenged Morris and Robertson for the more modest wager of £100. Tom and Allan won.

Wille Park Jnr, Musselburgh's Open Champion, successful clubmaker, course designer and first professional of the modern era.

The Open Championship

In this period of recovery, one of the world's enduring sporting events was born. The present importance of the Open Championship should not conceal its humble reputation then. The Open was first called the 'General Open Competition' and had its origins in the rising enthusiasm for golf at Prestwick. These natural west coast links had lain largely unused for golf while it was a winter game played on the east coast. But now the Ayrshire gentry warmed to the summer game, and had other projects in mind also. Not only did they set up the Prestwick Golf Club in 1851, but they enticed the best man available - 'Old' Tom - away from his east coast roots to tend their links. The club soon owned their own land, one of the first to do so. And as part of this burst of activity, they inaugurated a tournament for professional golfers.

The activist in all these endeavours was J. O. Fairlie, an Ayrshire landowner who, like many of the founder members of Prestwick Golf Club was a regular player on the east coast, and a member of the R&A.[78] In 1860 he had a remarkable triumph on the clubmen's circuit, winning medals at Prestwick, St Andrews and North Berwick. A local Ayrshire laird, the Earl of Eglinton, was also an enthusiastic east coast golfer, active in the R&A and the Honourable Company, and Fairlie organised the sporting Earl to support the new golf club. Fairlie, using the Earl's name, busily assembled a club, and announced the first meeting for 2nd July 1851 to coincide with another local activity, namely 'the Ayrshire Yeomanry being on duty'. The second meeting in October of that year was timed to coincide with an Ayrshire race meeting - the Caledonian Hunt.

The club was a success. During its early years, Fairlie also organised the amateur tournaments at St Andrews from 1857 onwards. Fairlie and the Prestwick club then proposed that the older clubs should support a professional tournament at Prestwick in 1857, but they had little response from the other clubs contacted, and the matter was put aside. In 1860 they decided to organise a tournament themselves. Fairlie was again in charge and for the October meeting of the club he outlined his plans for an open tournament.

J. O. Fairlie, one of the best amateur golfers of his generation. He was the talented organiser of tournaments at St Andrews and then of the professional meeting at Prestwick now known as the Open Championship. A friend of Lord Eglinton, he is shown here in armour worn for Eglinton's controversial Tournament of 1829.

By courtesy of the ST ANDREWS UNIVERSITY LIBRARY, COWIE COLLECTION.

Writing on Eglinton Castle notepaper he drew up the proposal.

The Open was to be open to acceptable players only and the description of the event used the word 'caddie' and 'professional' interchangeably. The Challenge Belt was not mentioned in the circulars to the members and as late as ten days before the week of the October club meeting there was still a muddle about dates, such was the informality involved. These dates were finally decided to suit Lord Eglinton.[79]

The evidence is that Fairlie was indulging in his own enthusiasm for a professional tournament without much help or hindrance from the members and the prize was in the form of a belt, in the usual fashion of a prize-fighter's boxing trophy. Fairlie had, single-handed, set up a competition which was to prosper and grow into the world's greatest golf tournament.

The idea - a stroke-play championship open to professionals - seems obvious now, but it was not self-evident then. Professional *match-play* challenges were then the vogue and were exciting for the punters: stroke-play makes for dull wagering, especially with a strong favourite. Since there was no prize money for the first three years of this competition, we might suspect that the tournament was not quite what it seems in retrospect, and that the players had other reasons for attending. The clue is that the professionals' tournament was attached to the Prestwick club's own domestic competition that week. The attending professionals playing for the trophy would also earn a few days' work caddying for the gentlemen.

Associated Matches

There were even traditional-style challenge matches attached to the early Opens. Park won the first Open, and Prestwick's hopes for a local win by Morris were dashed. The day after the Open, this extra, now-forgotten money match was arranged, in which Morris played Park over 36 holes. Morris got his revenge by winning 7 and 6, and Prestwick's honour was satisfied. These extra challenge matches continued to be encouraged by the gentlemen golfers, and after the 1862 Open, Park (placed second) played Dow (who finished fourth). Only in 1863 was prize money offered for the first time for the stroke-play Open.[80]

Morris Senior won the second, third, fifth and eighth Opens, and this remarkable record was eclipsed by the wins of his son, 'Young' Tom Morris, who won the title in the years 1868, 1869 and 1870, and took possession of the Belt, as was the tradition at the time, for such a run of wins.

Without a trophy to play for, the Open Championship lapsed for a year. The Prestwick club seemed unwilling to buy another prize to replace the original championship belt, and instead Prestwick joined with the R&A and the Honourable Company to buy a handsome new silver trophy - the familiar claret jug - for the Open Championship. When the championship resumed, it was again won by Young Tom from a field of eight starters.

The format of the Open Championship was not a huge success: match-play was still regarded as the proper game. Nor was there much national interest in the tournament during its early days. When any newspaper report of the Open appeared, the tournament was mentioned only below the results of the host club's own meeting for its members. The Open in its early years was held in either April or November, the traditional golfing seasons, and close to the club's own Spring and Autumn Meetings.

'Old' Tom shown in a winter scene at the 17th Hole at St Andrews by the artist Thomas Hodge. Snow rarely lies on the east coast links.

By courtesy of PETER CRABTREE.

The Scene is Set

With these changes and events, the broad features of the modern game had evolved. The ancient woods-only game had changed and there was a new pluralism in equipment - woods for the longer shots but graded irons for closer precision play. The clubs were no longer carried loose under the arm, but in a bag. The feathery had gone and the new gutty ball was durable and inexpensive. Greenkeeping was no longer in the hands of nature and active management of the ancient courses was now routine. Match-play was still dominant but stroke-play was on the increase, with a primitive handicapping system emerging. The major amateur and professional stroke-play tournaments were in embryonic existence, and the newspapers were beginning to be interested in golf and sport in general.

But the Scottish game of the middle of the nineteenth century, though evolving, was not yet widely known, nor widely played. Though equipment was available for mass play from about 1850, and Scotland was being visited and the game studied, it was not until the 1880s that the game gained wider, British support. This boom, when it came, was remarkably sudden.

FURTHER READING

The numbered references are found at the end of the book.

General histories of sport in this period are poor, but the best contemporary accounts are in H. B. Farnie *The Golfers Manual* Cupar 1857, Peter Baxter *Golf in Perth and Perthshire* Perth 1890, Robert Clark *Golf: A Royal and Ancient Game* Edinburgh 1875, H. T. Peters *Reminiscences of Golf and Golfers* Edinburgh 1890, John Kerr *The Golf-Book of East Lothian* Edinburgh 1897, and J. L. Stewart *Golfiana Miscellanea* London 1887. Later, Henry Leach's *Great Golfers in the Making* London 1907 gives valuable insights into this period. Allan Robertson's life is described in Alistair Adamson *Allan Robertson, Golfer* Worcs 1985, and for 'Old' Tom Morris see Tulloch's classic *The Life of Tom Morris* London 1908. Recently Alastair and James Johnston's *The Chronicles of Golf: 1457 to 1857* Cleveland 1993, gives many of the documents from this formative period, as does Alastair Johnston's *The Clapcott Papers* Edinburgh 1985. Alistair Adamson's *Millions of Mischief: Rabbits, Golf and St Andrews* Worcs 1990 recounts the 'great rabbit controversy' at St Andrews.

Some recent books have excellent new material on this period, notably Stewart Hackney *Carnoustie Links and Players* Dundee 1989, and Stewart Hackney *Bygone Days on the Old Course* Dundee 1990; Wray Vamplew analyses early professional sport in *Pay Up and Play the Game* Cambridge 1988.

Some club histories give information on golf at this time. The best are
J. C. Roddie *The Chronicle of the Royal Burgess Golfing Society of Edinburgh 1735-1935* Edinburgh 1936 and this has had a limited update recently in Stewart
Cruden *Bruntsfield Links Golfing Society* Edinburgh 1992. For other clubs see
the R&A histories by Everard (1907), Salmond (1956) and Ward-Thomas
(1980). Other useful histories are Alistair Adamson *In the Wind's Eye* North
Berwick 1980, David C. Smail *Prestwick Golf Club* Prestwick 1989, James
Colville *The Glasgow Club 1787-1936* Glasgow 1907, James G. Dow *Crail Golfing
Society 1786-1936* Edinburgh 1936 (reprinted 1986) and R. C. Brownlee *Dunbar
Golf Club; a Short History* Dunbar 1980. The Honourable Company's historians
are George Pottinger *Muirfield and the Honourable Company* Edinburgh 1972
and Norman Mair *Muirfield - Home of the Honourable Company* Edinburgh 1994.

The early days of the (Old) Prestwick Club and the Open Championship are
well described in Smail's *Prestwick* (above). For golf in individual towns see
Horace Hutchinson *British Golf Links* London 1987, T. D. Miller *Famous Scottish
Links* Edinburgh 1911, and William Coull *Golf in Montrose* Montrose 1993; for
St Andrews see James Balfour *Reminiscences of Golf on St Andrews Links*
Edinburgh 1887, Andrew Bennett *The Book of St Andrews Links* Edinburgh
1890, and H. T. Peters *Reminiscences of Golf and Golfers* Edinburgh 1890; for
Musselburgh see George Colville *Five Open Champions and the Musselburgh
Story* Musselburgh 1980.

The first text with golf instruction was J. L. Stewart's *Golfiana Miscellanea*
Glasgow 1887. The early lives and careers of some of the professionals are
found in Leach's *Great Golfers* (above). For clubs and balls see David Stirk *Golf:
the Great Clubmakers* London 1991, and J. S. Martin *The Curious History of the
Golf Ball* New York 1968. For other sports see Roger Hutchinson *Camanachd!*
Edinburgh 1992, Hugh Dan MacLennan *Shinty!* Nairn 1993 and David B.
Smith *Curling: An Illustrated History* Edinburgh 1981. For sport in society at
this time, see J. A. Mangan *Athleticism in the Victorian and Edwardian Public
School* Cambridge University Press 1981.

CHAPTER SIX

THE NEW ENTHUSIASM

In 1898 a reviewer in the *Quarterly Journal* looked back at the century and marvelled at the new enthusiasm for sport. *The future chronicler of the Victorian era, when noticing social changes, will find himself compelled to devote much of his space to the enormous increase of sport and athletic games. Sixty years ago [i.e. circa 1840] boxing was dying, as duelling had perished shortly before, by a discreditable death. Golf was known only in Scotland, and like curling, the other favourite game of Scotchmen, showed no signs of sallying forth to conquer other lands. Cricket was just entering a more scientific stage, but no-one could have predicted the ascendancy it has since gained. The University boat race was not yet in its infancy... Football had not migrated from the boys' playground. In certain old towns, by ancient custom, at Eastertide, balls were unscientifically kicked about the streets to the danger of windows and the disgust of quiet people.*[1]

This view shows that sport had boomed from about 1840. But it also suggests that interest in sport was entirely new, grudgingly admitting to an earlier interest in some games in Scotland. The solution to this paradox is that sport had been popular in the 1700s, almost died out in the early 1800s, and then revived later. The new sportsmen and commentators at the end of the century were unaware of the earlier interest and could be forgiven for thinking that their sporting world was a novelty. The vitality of golf, noble and popular, in the 1700s had been forgotten, eclipsed by the crisis of the early 1800s.[2]

OPPOSITE: Organised women's golf started at St Andrews in 1867 with the foundation of the private St Andrews Ladies' Club - later called the Ladies' Putting Club. It used then, as now, the area known as the Himalayas. A major competition is in progress, with Old Tom in attendance.
By courtesy of the St ANDREWS UNIVERSITY LIBRARY, COWIE COLLECTION.

147

As we saw earlier, the revival of golf started about 1840. In 1850 the gutty ball appeared and the railway network was spreading rapidly. Some historians of golf describe an immediate increase in the popularity of the game of golf thereafter, and they point to the appearance of a number of new clubs - Westward Ho! in 1863, Wimbledon in 1865 and Pau in 1856. In the Empire, clubs at Calcutta (1829), Dum Dum, Bengal (1830) and Bombay (1842) already existed.

But this little burst of activity was not sustained, nor is it evidence of sharply rising enthusiasm. The rise and rise of golf came much later. Even in England, golf remained an oddity in the 1870s and was judged to be a dangerous game. Vardon recalled that, as late as 1877, when strangers came to play golf in Jersey they were made unwelcome by the locals. J. L. Low wrote that in his boyhood in England, at about the same time, even the word 'golf' was unknown. The boom was to come in the late 1880s. As late as 1888, Scotland still had more golf clubs than the rest of the United Kingdom combined.

The Role of Musselburgh

In this period 1850-1880, Scottish golf matured and slowly prospered internally. Musselburgh, the small town east of Edinburgh mentioned above, had a period of prominence and was leader both for standard of play and innovation in the making and marketing of golfing artifacts. In this later part of the century, Musselburgh continued to rival St Andrews both for its players and the quality of its golfing equipment.[3] Musselburgh had not been prominent in the earlier annals of golf, nor did it survive successfully into the great golf

Musselburgh's 'Pandy' (Pandemonium) bunker from Aikman's *A Round of the Links* 1893, a hazard later filled in.

boom later and the links today are neglected. The solid clubhouses of famous clubs now stand empty, as in a time warp; the crucial role of Musselburgh is easily forgotten.

The Rise

Musselburgh, as we saw earlier, had been a favourite venue for an occasional visit by Edinburgh golfers in the early 1800s and even earlier.[4] Thereafter, the increasing overcrowding of the golfing links at Leith and Bruntsfield led the Edinburgh players to look for space and peace. The new rail link from Edinburgh to Musselburgh quickly established the popularity and dominance of its links, which lasted until the end of the century. This slow translocation of play from Leith also brought Edinburgh club- and ball-makers, following the golfers, to work in Musselburgh.[5]

The Honourable Company of Edinburgh Golfers was first to make a new base at Musselburgh. In 1836 the inactive club revived following a meeting at an Edinburgh hotel. Though only six persons attended, they, and some older members, restarted match dinners, not at Leith as of old, but at Musselburgh. The finances of the new arrangements were simple in the extreme, and doubtless their earlier fiscal nightmare was still fresh in the memory. At Musselburgh, they had no burdens of upkeep of the course, and initially they had no clubhouse, keeping their golf clubs in the racecourse stand run by Gourlay the ball-maker. Dinners were held initially at McKendrick's pub, but the food seemed not to their liking, and dining reverted to Edinburgh.

There was also a mass of little clubs, with no clubhouse, playing at Musselburgh: at the height of its influence there were an estimated 60 or so of these smaller clubs, many of them Edinburgh societies, visiting and playing regularly for trophies and prizes. And there were many local and other golfers playing golf, outside the club system. Play on the links was free. At Musselburgh railway station, cabbies and caddies touted for work and raced to the first tee with their golfing patrons, eager to be first off.

The Honourable Company prospered at Musselburgh and in 1865 felt confident enough, when the membership had risen to 245, to open a new clubhouse, the second in their history. The local club, Royal Musselburgh, and the other Edinburgh clubs, Bruntsfield and Burgess, also followed in building their own clubhouses at Musselburgh in the next 20 years. At this, their new home, the Honourable Company once again took initiatives in links management. In 1871 they expended almost £100 at Musselburgh on sea defences against blown sand, and they fought for, or encouraged, independent legal actions to prevent any threat to golf on the links. The other local clubs also prospered, and a joint Links Management Committee appeared in 1877.

The Musselburgh golf links was not extensive. It had seven holes until 1833, eight until 1880 and only nine holes thereafter. There was no room for expansion of the town's compact links: it was enclosed on all sides and when expansion was necessary, it could not be arranged.

Clubs and Caddies

Though the great Edinburgh clubs had a powerful presence at the Musselburgh Links, few amateur golfers of distinction emerged there, unlike

Golfing dress in the late nineteenth century. Bonnet, cut-away jacket, breeches and spats. From Hutchinson's *Golf* 1890.

St Andrews which had a distinct group of gentlemen players. Instead, generations of professional golfers of great talent grew up in Musselburgh. As boys, they hung about the links seeking caddying work. Between rounds, while waiting for patronage, they sharpened their short game on a little course of four holes, about 30 yards each, found near the fifth hole of the ancient links. It is said that a baker came out with pies for the caddies' lunch, giving the short course the name 'Baker's Holes'. From the caddies' ranks came distinguished professionals, and they often obtained employment at local club- and ballmakers' shops. The first great player to emerge was 'Old' Willie Dunn, born in 1821 and apprenticed to Gourlay the ballmaker. Dunn was the first Scottish professional to venture over the Scottish border to a post in England, being engaged at Blackheath in 1851. He was a good enough golfer to be grouped with Morris and Robertson as the three top players at this time.[6]

Born four years after Dunn, Willie Park Senior was the next important figure at Musselburgh. Park also came up from the caddie ranks, and he is said to have held the record for the four Baker's Holes with a score of three under 2s. He burst into prominence at the age of 20 with an audacious challenge in 1845 to play any of the St Andrews players. This challenge marked the rise in confidence at Musselburgh and shows that there were enough local gentlemen sportsmen prepared to back the professionals in these challenges.

Park Senior and Morris Senior were to share six of the first seven Opens, but Park then faded from prominence, spending his time in his clubmaking business at Musselburgh, one greatly expanded later by his even more talented son. There were other Dunns and Parks. Old Willie Dunn's twin brother was a talented golfer and his sons also reached fame. Park Snr's brother, Mungo, won the first Open Championship to be held at Musselburgh. As well as these dynasties there were other players of golfing achievement. Bob Ferguson, a Musselburgh caddie, won three Opens in a row, 1880 to 1882, and narrowly missed a record fourth consecutive win in the following year. The second generation of Musselburgh golfers is considered later.

The Scottish Holiday

Musselburgh flourished through the patronage of the Edinburgh golfers: St Andrews was instead to flourish as a result of its visitors. Summer holidays were now part of the annual calendar, and fashion followed the royal habit in heading for Scotland, now seen as a land of romantic glens and stags rather than barbarous Highlanders. 'Of the different touring grounds of the United Kingdom, Scotland naturally attracts the greatest number', remarked a London newspaper without further explanation or curiosity.

The attractions of the coastal Scottish holiday towns were simple, cheap and municipal - free entertainment, a free beach and the free links. The Scottish seaside holiday had elaborate rituals and traditions. The hotels and houses had a pecking order of celebrity, and local newspapers were attentive to the arrival of families of note. The *Haddingtonshire Gazette* in 1862 was first to list visitors, starting with those staying at the Royal Hotel in North Berwick, later extending this listing to other visitors to the town,

A list from the St Andrews Citizen of 9th August 1890, shows the influx of summer visitors, particularly from England, staying at the fashionable St Andrews hotels. This was to spread the authority of St Andrews and the Royal and Ancient Golf Club and its rules, beyond Scotland.

Courtesy of ST ANDREWS UNIVERSITY LIBRARY, COWIE COLLECTION.

IMPERIAL HOTEL
Major-General Graham, from London; General and Mrs Dodgson, and Master Dodgson, from Islesworth; Dr and Mrs Ogilvie; Mr T. S. Christie, from Ballindean; Mrs Wylde, from Edinburgh; Major and Mrs Peploe and family, from Edinburgh; Mrs Thornton, from Eastbourne; Major Craigie, from Aberdeen; Dr Findlay, from Edinburgh; Mr Orr, from Edinburgh; Mr S. Couper, from Edinburgh; Mr Charles Innes, from Cambridge; Mr H. Rowland and Mrs Rowland, from Winchester; Misses Lamb (2), from Paisley; Miss Alice Gordon, from Glasgow; Mr J. Mitchell Innes, from Edinburgh; Mr Fred. Mitchell Innes, from Lockerbie; Mr D. J. Simson, from Edinburgh; Mr J. Thomson, from Perth; Mr D. W. Lambe, from Edinburgh; Mr J. L. Whiteley, from Glasgow; Mrs Pagan, from Edinburgh; Miss Howard, from Paris; Mrs Fraser, from London; Mrs Robertson and Miss Wilkinson, from Edinburgh; Mr J. K. Dobble; Mrs and Miss Gilroy; Miss Rankine, from Glasgow; Mr and Mrs and Master Murray, from Dollerie; Mr H. Willcox, from London; Rev. W. Wallace, from Peeblesshire; Mr Hillard, from Edinburgh; Mrs Hall and Miss Griggs, from Edinburgh

MARINE HOTEL
Mr and Mrs Lethbridge and family, from Blackheath; Mr and Mrs Charles Roundell and family, from Dorfold Hall, Nantwich; Dr and Mrs Wallace and family, from Harley Street, London; Miss Ada S. Ballin, from Tavistock Square, London; Mr Parkinson, from London; Dr Gordon Munn, from Edinburgh; Mr and Mrs Trail, from London; Mr and Mrs S. Hope Morley and family, from 43 Upper Grosvenor Street, London, W.; Mr D. M. M'Nab, from London; Mr and Mrs Gibson and family, from Dundee; Dr Saunders, from Crail; Mr O. C. Birch, The Admiralty, London; Mr and Mrs Amand Routh, from London; Mr G. H. Gibson Carmichael, from Castle Craig, Dolphinton; Mr W. F. Richmond, from London; Mrs Gairdner, from London; Mr and Mrs C. F. Combe and family, from Edinburgh; Mrs Ellvart and party, from London; Mr and Mrs Pirie Duff and party, from London; Mr Baker, from London; Mr and Mrs Glencay and party, from New York; Mr and Mrs J. Hamilton and party, from Barkston Gardens, London; Mrs Archer and family, from London; Mr and Mrs Longman, from London; Mr and Mrs Hart and Mr Hart, jun., from Glasgow; The Misses Eastwood (4), from Derby; Mr and Mrs Frederick Charlesworth and party, from East Hill, Bickley, Kent; Mr and Mrs Foulis and party, from Glasgow; Mr and Mrs Hately Waddell, from Whitekirk, Prestonkirk

and later including any worthy families staying at Dunbar, Prestonpans and Aberlady. Family holidays might be taken at a hotel or in a rented house, or father would send all the family to the coast for the two or three summer months, joining them for part of it. These summer arrangements meant that a group of women were left alone with family and staff and the ladies timidly began to consider playing sport. Towns like St Andrews and North Berwick had extra events for visitors - dances, balls, theatricals, outings and boating, and above all there were bathing and golf. The bitterly cold water of the North Sea (then known as the German Ocean) was promoted as health-giving.

Another type of holiday was developing on the west coast of Scotland. Workers from the heavy industries of the West of Scotland made a mass exodus at trade holiday time to the coast at Ayr, Troon, Girvan and Prestwick, and by steamer to Arran, Dunoon, and, above all, Rothesay. These west coast holiday-makers were traditionally sports spectators, rather than players, watchers of football rather than players at golf. But golf courses did emerge slowly round the Clyde coast in these holiday towns, and their income came largely in summer from these visitors. Many west coast players had their first taste of golf on holiday.

The Spas and Hydropathics

In the search for healthy holidays, it was not only the east coast towns with their allegedly therapeutic sea-bathing which prospered. The Victorians renewed their interest in water therapy, and started a hunt for new healing springs. Spa resorts began to flourish again in improbable places in Scotland, where there were wells with powerfully flavoured water of supposed medicinal powers. Success meant that sports facilities followed, including golf courses, to increase the facilities available to visitors. Doctors attached to the hydropathics wrote scientific works on the virtues of their establishment, the resort's remarkable climate and the virtues of the chemicals found in its disgusting water - as analysed by a learned professor. These puffs were distributed widely. As Dr Manson at Strathpeffer lucidly explained, his water

> *exerts the general retrogressive metamorphosis on tissue: it favours healthy progressive change, and in this way tends to prevent the formation of uric acid, the deadly enemy of the rich and luxurious.*[7]

Soon these unpleasant Highland springs were under suspicion, when the polluted water in the towns was found to be responsible for the cholera epidemics. Quickly, *pure* water spas emerged instead, notably at Crieff, Bridge of Allan, Rothesay and elsewhere. Even Strathpeffer managed to find an ordinary spring of clear water and the value of this pure Highland water was now extolled by the new resident doctor, the charismatic Dr Fortescue Fox. He wrote pamphlets lauding Strathpeffer's climate, its unique ambience, and its remarkably pure water, confirmed on analysis by a learned professor. Dr Fox wintered in Milan, where he wrote laudatory pamphlets on Milan's unique therapeutic ambience.

This revival of the spa was particularly strong in Scotland. Strathpeffer became highly successful and fashionable - in spite of its remote situation high in a Highland glen west of Inverness. In the season, a train came direct from London, Euston - 'The Strathy'. The Strathpeffer routine started at 7 a.m.

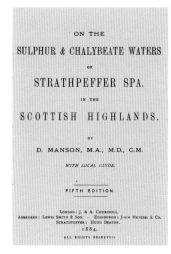

ON THE

SULPHUR & CHALYBEATE WATERS

OF

STRATHPEFFER SPA.

IN THE

SCOTTISH HIGHLANDS.

BY

D. MANSON, M.A., M.D., C.M.

WITH LOCAL GUIDE.

FIFTH EDITION.

LONDON: J. & A. CHURCHILL.
ABERDEEN: LEWIS SMITH & SON. - EDINBURGH: JOHN MENZIES & CO.
STRATHPEFFER: HUGH BEATON.
1884.
ALL RIGHTS RESERVED.

The ancient spa at Strathpeffer flourished early with mineral springs and later with a reputation for pure water in the late 1800s. The resort provided other recreational facilites including golf.

GLENBURN HOTEL HYDRO.

ROTHESAY, N.B.

Climate Mild and Equable

Sheltered from East Winds

SEA WATER, RUSSIAN, TURKISH AND OTHER BATHS
EIGHTEEN-HOLE GOLF COURSE

BEST CENTRE FOR STEAMER EXCURSIONS
ON THE CLYDE

Telephone No. 40 Rothesay   *Prospectus from Manageress*

The Glenburn Hydropathic in Bute - pure water and healthy living were offered in the 'Madeira of Scotland', plus a new golf course.

with a fine piece of Scottish kitsch - a piper woke the village. During morning and afternoon, bands played for the visitors' promenade.

And as these spas flourished they diversified and added extra facilities, notably a golf course, the result of the discovery that moorland could be turned into first-class golf courses with the help of the new grass-cutting machines; to the designer's surprise, when heather was cleared, and grass sown and mown, excellent inland courses evolved. The Strathpeffer golf course was founded in 1888 and was important in the spa's economy. It had distinguished members and hosted exhibition matches by the best professionals. The club had a full-time secretary until the 1920s, and the club still exists in the steep little valley. But the Strathpeffer spa is now neglected, the pump rooms decayed and its medicinal properties no longer as highly regarded as in its great days.

The Ladies

In the influx of golfing visitors to the Scottish coastal towns in summer, one group experimented for the first time with golf - the ladies. In mid-nineteenth-century Britain, women were involved in their first early attempts to escape from the assumptions which had limited their lives from earliest times. As we saw earlier, there are some scattered historical accounts of women at play, but for women in general at the start of the nineteenth century, indulgence in sport was not expected and there were powerful cultural taboos preventing such play. Early sport was tribal and often violent. Women were not expected to join in, and they kept clear. When play for pleasure came, it continued as part of man's domain. And the men were unenthusiastic about women joining them for such sport.

A short summary of the assumptions of the early 1800s, as applied to golf, is given in Carnegie's poem *Golfiana*:

The game is ancient, manly and employs
In its departments women, men and boys,
Men play the game, the boys the clubs convey,
And lovely women give the prize away.

The author's gallant division of labour had a role for everyone except little girls. Active opposition to women's sport appeared in Victorian times, when women showed their first interest in games. It was concluded by men that women were unfit for strenuous exercise, and even more pernicious doctrines appeared, helping to discourage any attempts to invade the men's world. The eminent specialist Dr Henry Maudsley of London intoned the doctrine of 'fixed energy', namely that, for women, energy expended in any direction used up finite, limited, reproductive power. If this fixed reserve of vitality was reduced by playing sport, announced the distinguished physician, it would reduce women's reproductive power and produce weakly, degenerate, sickly infants. Why risk good motherhood for poor sport, the doctor solemnly concluded.

Holiday Sports

But on holiday at the Scottish seaside, far from home, opportunities for sport presented themselves. Mother's traditional domestic tasks were light and were devolved on servants and nannies. The men might even be absent for much of the three-month summer break, and the uncluttered links and tennis courts were at hand. New thinking about women's role and women's sport was spreading, and challenged the vision of a downward spiral of infertility and degeneration of the race. To the new feminist leaders, sport was seen both as a demonstration of women's ability to play and enter into the male domain, and as an antidote to any alleged chronic physical defects. Though the women's activists were mostly preoccupied with winning the vote, they occasionally commented on sport and urged their sex, particularly the housebound swooners who were prone to little illnesses, the vapours and 'turns', to get out of the house, and take up sport. The *Women's Suffrage Journal* of 1871 reported the loss of a passenger ship in America; in spite of the usual gallant 'women and children first' order, it claimed that 400 men were rescued from the sea, but no women. The magazine saw this as a parable and an opportunity: it concluded that women had at least to learn to swim.

On holiday in Scotland, far from the town's constraints and warnings from Harley Street, and with even more time on their hands than usual, a growing band of ladies watched the game of golf with some interest. Male field sports had little attraction for middle-class women, nor did the evening play at cards or other gambling attract them. But the wave of new sports - croquet, tennis, hockey, lacrosse and golf - all looked possible.[8]

There were no organisational barriers to women's play on Scotland's golf links; golf in Scotland was played free on public links. Traditional male golf clubs existed but these private clubhouses at the edge of the Scottish municipal links had no jurisdiction beyond their own front doors. Nothing but society's assumptions prevented women's golf, and in Scotland women were not faced with fighting their way into private clubs, nor dealing with the deterrent of booking times for play nor the hurdle of paying daily fees. To play, one simply turned up. All the women had to do was walk onto the links and play. This they began to do, timidly.

Women's Dress

In addition to the traditional constraints on women's activities of all kinds, and active opposition by men, the sporting women had a major practical obstacle to their tentative moves onto the links and into sport of any kind. The assumptions about ladies' dress of the time prevented much normal movement of the body. It was beyond question that a hat was worn in public, and an extravagant hat, often with feathers, was placed on top of a vertically-organised hair arrangement, preventing a full golf swing, and keeping the ladies indoors in windy conditions. Fashion also dictated a stiff high collar, splinting the head and neck, and below the neck other contrivances were also in place to prevent much normal movement, and a full swing in particular. The upper part of the woman's body was laced into a stiff corset, splinted with vertical pieces of whalebone, a garment pulled tight when being dressed in the morning by the lady's maid. The sleeves were ballooned, and even if a pivot at the hips was feasible, which it was not, the sleeves alone might have obstructed a view of the ball. Below the waist the assumptions were that no part of the leg, not even an ankle, should be seen, and these taboos necessitated a wide-flowing skirt, descending to ground level and kept in shape by a complex infrastructure of petticoats and combinations. The skirt thus shaped might extend to conceal, or even cover, a golf ball in play, and when walking on damp grass these long garments immediately became wet and heavy.

These deeply held assumptions on clothing could not be confronted, and partly explain the tentativeness of the ladies' early ventures into golf. The first serious women golfers soon equipped themselves with an elasticated cummerbund, worn in reserve round the waist, and called the 'Miss Higgins', which was slipped down to below knee level, controlling the skirt, when playing in the wind.[9]

One of these two ladies shown in Lees's painting *The Golfers* of 1841 may be Mrs James Wolfe Murray, the first woman player to venture onto the Old Course, and play in the modern manner. She was the daughter of the enthusiastic player John Whyte Melville and both her husband and father are in the painting.

St Andrews Ladies

The first lady to flout the ancient conventions and play golf is said to have been a St Andrews resident, Mrs J. Wolfe Murray. She was the younger daughter of one of the notable St Andrews golfers, Mr Whyte Melville, and she married into the Wolfe Murray family, also a keen golfing dynasty; both her husband and father appear in Lees's picture, *The Golfers: A Grand Match*. Our pioneer may be one of a number of ladies seen in the left-hand side of the picture. In 1855 she was reported to have played regularly at St Andrews over the Old Course using two clubs. Little else is known about this important evolution, but it is said that her actions met with disapproval, but could not be prevented.[10]

The Ladies' Course

Soon there was support for a tentative start for organised women's golf. Ladies had started play using the caddies' putting course, where Rusacks Hotel now stands. In 1867 the St Andrews Ladies' Club was formed (later renamed the Ladies' Putting Club of St Andrews) which still plays over the area known as the Himalayas, and is now open to visitors. It is sometimes said that their play was merely on a putting green, but this part of the links was, and is, more than this. The holes are longer than for putting and there is a very varied terrain for the course. It may have been akin to the short golf courses noted earlier at a number of early golf courses. This ladies' course and club had a social function, allowing visits by gentlemen, the promenade, introductions and courtship.

Some other golf clubs soon made arrangements for women players. In 1868 a ladies' course was laid out at Westward Ho! and other clubs followed - Musselburgh in 1872, Carnoustie in 1873 and Pau in 1874.[12]

A Growth Period

By 1887, 20 years after its foundation, the membership of the St Andrews Ladies' Club had risen to the remarkable figure of 500, at a time when the nearby male-only R&A had 795 members. This interest in golf at St Andrews by the women was rewarded when the Jubilee course was opened in 1899, designed for the use of ladies and beginners. But the first ladies' club to have its own course and clubhouse was at Lundin Links, to the south of St Andrews, set up in 1890, with some hints at reverse discrimination against men.[13] But it should not be forgotten that the public links of Scotland were, as always, open to the ladies at all times, and there were increasing numbers of women golfers out on the links at St Andrews, Carnoustie, North Berwick, Montrose and elsewhere without formal club membership. Moreover, the large membership of the St Andrews Ladies' Club was mostly drawn from the summer visiting community. Local St Andrews women players were few, and none appeared in the early ladies' national tournaments. The first ladies' club and clubhouse at St Andrews - the St Rule Club - appeared therefore quite late, in 1898.

Cautiously, the women began their play on the full courses, as the rigours of dress declined, and their skill and confidence increased. The men conceded ground slowly. Lord Wellwood, in Hutchinson's Badminton volume on golf, patronisingly summed up the situation as late as 1890:

> We have always advocated a liberal extension of the right of golfing to women. Not many years ago their position was the most degraded. Bound to accompany their lords and masters to golfing resorts for the summer months, they had to submit to their fathers, husbands and brothers playing golf all day and talking golfing shop the whole of the evening, while they themselves were booted off the links with cries of 'fore', if they ventured to appear there. We therefore gladly welcome the establishment of ladies links - a kind of Jews' quarter - which have now been generously provided for them on most of the larger greens... We venture to suggest seventy or eighty yards as the average limit of a drive advisedly; not because we doubt a lady's power to make a longer drive, but because this cannot be done without raising the club above the shoulder. Now, we do not presume to dictate, but we must observe that the posture and gestures requisite for a full swing are not particularly graceful when the player is clad in female dress.[14]

In 1893 the Ladies' Golf Union was set up, with membership from 80 British clubs, and this organisation ran the first British Ladies' Amateur Championship. The first and second championships were won by the youthful Lady Margaret Scott, never beaten in any serious match. After her third win the presentation scene has been described thus:

> It would be unthinkable for her to make an acceptance speech. So her father Lord Eldon will make the speech for her. He will announce that his daughter will play no more championships. Three titles are quite enough for a young lady.[15]

Lady Scott hung up her clubs and made a fashionable marriage.

Scottish Input

But the Scottish ladies, notably the local St Andrews players, made no initial impact on ladies' golf at a national level. English women golfers took the game forward, and organised the first championships and took the prizes. Having learned the game in Scotland, they then forged ahead, and in the first three years, the national women's tournament was held in England. Scottish players were notably absent from these early tournaments. May Hezlet in her memoirs *Ladies Golf* of 1907 recalled that

> unfortunately the Scotch seem to have rooted objection to playing on links outside their own country and during recent years very few have entered their names to compete for championship honours...

Not until 1897 did the Ladies' Championship come to Scotland, in its fifth year. Curiously, the venue was Gullane, not St Andrews nor Lundin Links, home of the first women's club. Though the Scottish ladies had been absent from the early championships, they appeared on this occasion and dominated this Gullane tournament. Mabel Stringer recalled:

> We were all tremendously impressed by the play of the Scots ladies and we were sufficiently well versed in the game to realise that here we English golfers were quite outclassed. The natives were not very kind to us. They were most uncomplimentary about our beloved red coats. They made us pay the utmost farthing for everything...[16]

By the semi-finals the Scots were in command and the final was between two sisters, the Misses Orr of North Berwick and a third Orr sister had reached the quarter-finals. Lady Margaret Scott had retired and there is no way of comparing her with the Orrs, the best women golfers of the day. Having dominated the Gullane meeting, the Misses Orr did not travel to the English meetings in the following years, again preventing any further comparisons. It seems that Scottish women's golf at the time was not only afflicted by parsimony (and absence of red coats) but also by parochialism.

Horace Hutchinson went further:

> The sentiment of Scottish golf was too conservative... the tradition was that it was a man's game, and that women had no place on the links, was too ingrained in the mind of Scottish man and woman...

John Kerr said much the same:

> It is rather curious that in Scotland, the original home of the game, ladies' golf has not developed in anything like the same degree that it has in the south country... English ladies had, so to speak, a fair start. They took up the game at about the same time as their husbands and brothers, struck out on their own line, and discovered not a little ability in managing their own affairs. North of the Tweed the ladies were handicapped by a past...

This is clearly not the whole story, since the Scottish ladies were playing the game and there were very talented women golfers inside Scotland. It is likely that competitive sport, and 'pot-hunting' was considered indecorous in a lady in Scotland, and travelling to play in England may not have been contemplated. Scottish men may have been cool about any proposal that their wives and daughters had a world outside the home, such as travel to a distant tournament. Whatever the reason, the Scottish ladies, though talented, were simply not involved in early British women's competitive golf. Nor did they take a hand in its administration. Though the men's game was run from Scotland, and continued in this way, it was English women who ran national women's events.

This odd finding may explain the attitude of the famous St Andrews girls' school - St Leonard's - to golf. It was one of a small number of schools boldly breaking with the traditions of girls' education, or lack of it. It aimed 'to give girls a similar education to their brothers'. Like Cheltenham Ladies' College and Roedean, the St Andrews school encouraged sport, and St Leonard's is remembered as the pioneer of the game of lacrosse for girls. But golf was not favoured at this progressive school near the links: perhaps even at St Andrews there were limits. Team games were safe, but the girls may have been in moral danger in the freedom of the links.[17]

The Caddies

In the golf boom, the already high profile of the caddies became even higher. The neophyte golfer of the mid-nineteenth century knew that tradition demanded that he have a caddie as his companion on the links. Gentlemen did not carry parcels, nor did they carry golf clubs, and gentlemen certainly did not put away their clubs or clean them. The humble caddie was essential before, during and after play. But a good caddie was much more than a mere club-carrier. They had other skills and it was a boom time for caddies, young and old. Until now, they had been skilled assistants to the expert gentlemen players: now they could be teachers of the new players also. The relationship between the neophyte golfers and the experienced caddie was unique in amateur sport, exceeding the bond between angler and ghillie or climber and Alpine guide, those other indispensable supports for the Victorian gentlemen sportsmen. The caddies were servants, teachers, coaches and confidants to the new wave of golfers.

In a town like St Andrews, as the new wave started, numerous caddies were needed. Formerly the ballmakers and clubmakers had sufficed for these duties, but now an army of club-bearers was required. Fishermen and war pensioners found caddying an essential addition to their earnings, and boys were also keen for the considerable fees, as were their mothers. Caddying and teaching were seasonal and summer was becoming the peak of the season. But in winter, when the visitors had gone, the serious players still played and the best caddies now had work throughout the year. Much later, the successful caddies might do a summer season at an English or American club as a professional, and return to Scotland for serious winter employment, working as caddies for the experienced and respected club golfers.

Duties of the Caddie

Caddies carried the clubs, indicated the direction of play, recommended a club, knew the score, watched the opponent's progress, found lost balls, gave the line on the green, knew the rules and held the pin. If there was no pin to be seen, they knew where the hole was. They did not speak or move during shots, nor smoke during play. A capable caddie teed the ball skilfully at each new hole, and they now had to carry wet sand for this purpose, rather than use sand from the hole. To tee up, the player made a signal with his club where he wished the ball to be placed. The ideal tee had a sand pyramid below the ball which was not seen when looked at from above. At the short holes, a highly skilled caddie might also covertly coat his employer's ball with a little sand to make the ball hold on the green. The caddie stocked up with golf balls prior to play, ready for the round, anticipating any loss.

The magazine *Punch* regularly returned to the theme of the meeting between the well-off but hapless beginners and their bored caddies.
From E. V. Knox *Mr Punch on the Links* 1929.

NEW BREEKS
Golfer (after the fourth miss) : 'DEAR ME! WHATEVER CAN I BE THINKING ABOUT?'
Caddie : 'MEBBE YE'RE THENKIN' ABOOT YER NEW BREEKS.'

The ancient custom of having forecaddies as well as caddies was still in favour on important occasions in the mid-century, but was slowly dying out. The forecaddies positioned themselves ahead, near where the shot was expected to land. They sent back elaborate signals to indicate the position of the ball, including the thumbs-down sign. If the hole had no flag on the green they also sent back signals describing the position of the hole before the shot was played.[18]

After the round, the caddie cleaned the clubs. In this ritual he dried the shafts of the clubs, and polished the head, leaving, with the final strokes, a vertical burnish at the sweet point on the centre of the club face. The caddie then put the clubs away, or arranged for repairs, and brought them out again next day.

The Caddie and his Perks

Some curious traditions arose from the caddie's role earlier as part of the gentleman's household. At that time, as we saw above, some were given food and lodging in return for regular duties on the links and elsewhere. An element of this support was to persist into the boom times. If a caddie was employed for the day, he was given his lunch, and giving food tokens rather than money was encouraged, to discourage purchase of drink. If employed for a week, the caddie was entitled to other rewards, as if part of the house-hold. Breakfast, as well as the usual lunch, was supplied or paid for, and if the caddie visited the player's house to collect clubs - at the back door - he was expected to clean and polish the player's shoes. The caddie might also revert to an earlier role and collect and deliver the golfer's luggage to the railway station. Another odd practice was a relic of the caddie/servant era of the early 1800s. In this early period, the caddies were not only fed and watered; they were clothed. In the new era, after any long engagement, it was expected that the caddie would receive cast-off clothing from his patron. He might also get damaged clubs and could expect to retain the golf ball used during play.

Caddie fees in this middle part of the century were about 3/6 per day for two rounds and £1 for a week. The fee was doubled if the caddie carried two sets of clubs. An amateur employing a caddie/professional on a teaching round had to pay for a caddie for both players. These fees were quite high. It was judged not to be in anyone's interest to let the caddies be displaced by cheaper labour, and the skilled players prized the service given. To encourage the caddies and reward long service, benevolent funds for the older or infirm registered caddies, or their widows and children, were set up at the bigger courses, and part of each fee was deducted for this fund - generally 2d a round. St Andrews was a pioneer in this matter and their benevolent fund, set up in 1890, became so large as to require expert financial supervision. In addition to the usual levy on fees for each round, one tenth of all sweepstake money raised at the R&A meetings went to this fund, and the club might make an additional grant each year. The caddies at St Andrews could also obtain a primitive form of unemployment insurance from the benevolent fund. In return for additional contributions by them of up to 4d per week in the season, the caddie could claim benefits during temporary illness or inability to work.[19]

By the end of the century, caddying work was an important part of the holiday town economy. In the 1899 season, North Berwick recorded that 27,000 caddie fees were paid, suggesting about 90 rounds a day and that about 100 caddies were employed in summer. The *Haddingtonshire Courier* reported in 1903 that 'such a demand for caddies has arisen that very few are now found to do anything in the fishing line, for they can earn their board easier on the golf course'. To meet the demand at North Berwick, caddies would even walk the 16 miles from Musselburgh to North Berwick for work.

Caddie discipline was maintained in the bigger resorts by the simple strategy of licensing the caddies and giving them a badge with a number. This badge was owned by the caddie, and on arrival it was handed in to the caddie master. When work arrived, they were engaged and their number was announced. The players were told not to accept caddies outside this system, nor could a caddie refuse work with any client. The importance of the caddie as adviser was, and still is, enshrined in the rules, since the player is allowed advice from his caddie, but no-one else. Another local rule was controversial. Some clubs ruled that players without caddies could be passed, without request, by those playing with such help. Local humbler players at St Andrews disputed that this domestic club rule of the R&A could apply to general play on the links.

Within the list of caddies, the clubs often had a first-class group, who were expensive to hire, and second-class caddies, including boys, who were paid less, and of whom less was expected. At North Berwick the first-class caddies wore a red badge and the second-class had blue badges. Many youthful caddies absented themselves from school and also learned the game, and from their ranks came many successful professionals, notably the talented Musselburgh and St Andrews players noted above. Sandy Herd recalled gaining his first 5/- caddie fee, and that his mother, though joyful, wondered if he 'hadna better been at the schule'. An apprentice's weekly wage was then about 10/- a week.[20]

Other Caddies' Rules

Another rule seems rather severe. It was generally accepted that a penalty of 3d was exacted if the player lost his ball. The reason for this severity is that caddies were not averse to 'losing' a ball in order to return and find it later, having marked its position. A ball was worth 9d or so in mid-century, adding to the caddie fee. Moreover, if caddies were prepared to bet on a match, they might back their opponents, and the caddie might wish to assist their own player's downfall. To guard against the caddie losing a match, it was also customary to award 3d for a win. To help his player on the green, a caddie could shield the opponent's ball from a head wind, once past the hole, by shuffling near it.[21]

How many of the vignettes are true, and how many are embellishments is far from clear. Certainly, the caddies continued to be a law unto themselves. The *St Andrews Citizen* noted in 1897 that the brothers John and Andrew Kirkaldy, caddies in the town, were jailed for repeated incidents involving drunkenness and disorder - 'previous fines being ineffective'.[22]

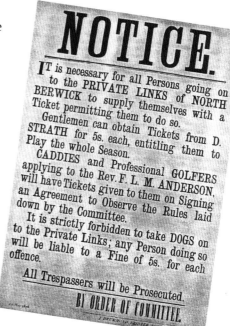

NOTICE.

IT is necessary for all Persons going on to the PRIVATE LINKS of NORTH BERWICK to supply themselves with a Ticket permitting them to do so.

Gentlemen can obtain Tickets from D. STRATH for 5s. each, entitling them to Play the whole Season.

CADDIES and Professional GOLFERS applying to the Rev. F. L. M. ANDERSON, will have Tickets given to them on Signing an Agreement to Observe the Rules laid down by the Committee.

It is strictly forbidden to take DOGS on to the Private Links; any Person doing so will be liable to a Fine of 5s. for each offence.

All Trespassers will be Prosecuted.

BY ORDER OF COMMITTEE.

The North Berwick Golf Club rules, including regulations for caddies.

By courtesy of the NORTH BERWICK GOLF CLUB.

Men and Boys

All the accounts of day-to-day play at this time mention the crowds of boys in attendance at the links, and they found their way into the earliest photographs of players on the links. Many could get formal caddying work, and many others hung about in hope of work, often playing truant to do so. At Musselburgh, they thronged the railway station touting for hire. Further east, when the coach to Muirfield from Longniddry station passed through Aberlady, boys ran from the houses, hoping for work. All the evidence is that they also enjoyed caddying, but many would become weary after half-way. If they gave up at this point, a modified fee was usually allowed.

Caddying by children was not without controversy. The caddie fee was quite large, and the work encouraged truancy and gambling. When the Inspection of Schools system was set up in 1840, truancy from school to caddie became less routine. Even so, at Gullane in the later 1800s the schools would bow to *force majeure*, and on big local golf match days, teaching stopped.[23] The golfers were not enthusiastic about the niceties of school attendance by the caddies. In 1886 the Ladybank club was asked to display a notice warning members not to employ school children during school hours. The club replied and suggested that the Board should bear the cost of a suitable notice-board to display the notice.

Another hazard for the new golfers of the mid-century were the non-caddying boys roaming on the links. They were not averse to lifting a ball in play, and in addition to outright theft, many variations on this theme existed. The best and most sophisticated scheme was that of the paddling boys at the Swilken Burn at St Andrews, who played about in the burn upstream of the 1st green. As the players came up playing the first hole, shots might go into the burn. The boys would then muddy the water upstream and prevent the submerged ball being seen. When the players proceeded to the second hole, after giving up the hunt, the boys allowed the waters to clear and then collected the ball. As a variant, they might follow a mishit ball into the water, apparently keen to help, but in reality tramping the ball into the mud, reclaiming it later, or offering to 'find' the ball for a fee. Such lads were also active at Carnoustie. In 1896 the club solemnly ruled:

> Nor shall anyone, excepting players and their caddies in search of their balls, do anything to discolour the water. No payment shall be made to boys taking balls out of the water.[24]

Another unstoppable prank was at North Berwick where boys hung about at a bunker at the short 'Gas Hole' green out of sight of the tee. After the tee shots, they would emerge unseen, put the ball in the bunker, and cover it in the bunker sand. If not found by the players, the boys removed the ball when safe to do so.

But at least the Scottish boys never colluded with the caddies to put the ball into the hole at blind short holes. At Europe's spas such arrangements were made: rich patrons, delighted at their success, rewarded their caddies.[25]

The Caddies and the Neophytes

The humble caddies viewed with ambivalence the new wave of Scottish holiday-makers. The older caddies were accustomed to a serious partnership in the skilled play of club members. The gentry knew the rules, and played quickly and purposefully. They understood the procedures and etiquette of golf and appreciated the work of their caddie and used his skills. The golfing boom now brought a mass of learners who were awkward, slow and ignorant about day-to-day play. This confrontation between the new, well-off, but hopelessly virginal golfers and the poor, humble, but knowledgeable caddies is one of the great moments in the history of sport, and caught the imagination of contemporary commentators and illustrators. The new golfers were in awe of the caddies' furtive behaviour, their arcane terminology, their authority on the rules, and their huffs and moods, and this inspired satirists, notably in numerous *Punch* cartoons. The caddies' revenge on this new wave of innocent employers has left many droll anecdotes and tales of impudence, bad temper and, above all, stinging repartee.[26] But the caddies' short fuse was generally tolerated, and it was generally agreed that the new caddies were entitled to alleviate the tedium of this boring work by such devices.

THE WORLD'S WORST

Golfer : 'HAVE YOU EVER SEEN A WORSE PLAYER ?' [*No answer.*] 'I SAID "HAVE YOU EVER SEEN A WORSE PLAYER ?"'

Aged Caddie : 'I HEERD YE VERRA WEEL THE FURRST TIME. I WAS JEST THENKIN' ABOOT IT.'

From E. V. Knox *Mr Punch on the Links* 1929.

Caddies Elsewhere

The Scottish-style caddies did not emerge quickly or completely elsewhere. In the new clubs in England, carriers of clubs could be obtained, and these slowly developed some of the ancient skills, but initially they lacked the traditional knowledge passed on through generations in Scotland. The new golfers in England often had to make do with a feckless club-carrier who irritated the now rapidly-improving Southern golfers. These players had learned the game in Scotland: their attempts to recreate the full Scottish ambience and mystique in England initially failed.[27] Only in Scotland could a visitor expect the luxury of a skilful and resourceful caddie, one who might be a skilled player himself. The list of St Andrews' first class caddies in 1870 included future Open Championship winners Fernie, Kidd and Martin. These men were probably sought after and they may have been allowed to be selective about their patrons.[28]

By this time the amateurs had stopped routine employment of their own personal caddie in the old style. But the new professionals now started regular employment of caddies of their own. Best known of these was 'Fiery', a caddie who constantly accompanied Willie Park, Jnr. and 'Big Crawford' was another, whose first duties were with Ben Sayers of North Berwick.[29]

Challenge Matches Continued

In the earlier part of the century, the gambling golfing sportsmen pitted their favourite caddie/professional against each other. These challenge matches increased in numbers into the middle of the century, though the huge stake involved in the Park/Morris match was never exceeded. These challenges continued to be popular for much longer than is supposed.
The Open Championship appears in retrospect to be the first professional tournament and the first chance for professionals to earn money in competition. Instead, in the period before and after the Open, (which had no prize money in the early stages), the challenge matches were more important, and though the professionals did not receive the money at stake, they were rewarded in other ways. 'These were the days of the matches', Ferguson recalled many years later. Ferguson also says that about this time he had a match against Strath for £50. The match was tied. Backers got their money back and the gentlemen 'did not forget him'. Dunn's backers failed to turn up on one occasion with the £50 stake and he had to raise it himself.[30] Ferguson says that when conventional prize money did appear, the professionals regularly shared out the winnings from tournaments among themselves, and mostly drank these winnings 'before pussyfoot put his paw in Scotland' - i.e. the Temperance Movement gained strength.

This golden time of professional challenges was but part of similar arrangements in professional sport, notably in boxing and athletics. Professional boxing matches re-emerged after crude pugilism declined in popularity. Other sports which caught the attention of gambling sportsmen were sprinting and running - pedestrianism - and the *Sporting Life* was the place for triage of challenges given and accepted. Routine local professional sprints were for a prize of £5 or £10 with agreed handicap, and the most favoured man was on the 'scratch' line, drawn on the ground. This word was adopted and incorporated into golf about 1860.

At St Andrews, Musselburgh and elsewhere, there were still enough wagering gentlemen willing to organise the necessary money for a challenge golf match. They arranged for the prize money to be raised, matched the players, and placed their bets, as did the crowds. The bets were arranged personally - bookies came later. The spreading railway network could now bring in the crowds for such an occasion.[31] Betting on match-play gave an element of chance and a well-matched foursome had endless possibilities, an uncertainty less inherent in stroke-play. The report of a Park vs Morris match reveals something of the betting at these matches. Though the winner was clear before the final round was finished, it was recorded that 'as numerous bets depended on the result of the day's play at St Andrews, without any reference to the principal match, the round was played out.' The players might gamble a bit on the side also, and might share any winnings. Willie Fernie recalled later that he put a bet on Andra' Kirkaldy in a challenge match in 1890 and the winnings 'paid his [Fernie's] rent for a year.' But golf seems to have been free from allegations of foul play, in spite of the money and the passions involved. Not a single allegation of nobbling, cheating or throwing a match can be found, in spite of the public interest and intensity of play.[32]

Unlike boxing and racing, early professional golf seems to have been above suspicion.

Smith's *Annual* of 1870 lists the celebrated challenge matches up to that date, and these are shown in the table.

What constitutes a challenge match 'of note' is arbitrary and many less celebrated challenges were played, but not recorded. But the table shows that major challenge matches were on the increase after mid-century, and that the Open Championship of 1860 was but one reflection of an increased tempo of professional play and interest in golf at this time.

Later, the rapid rise of interest in golf in the 1880s gave support to many local challenges which are not recorded, and these were a feature of the summer season at the golfing resorts. Slowly, towards the end of the century, stroke-play competitions also appeared and a more genteel form - the exhibition match - emerged, where a basic fee for both players was agreed in advance. By the First World War betting was increasingly discouraged, but continued in less obvious ways. The Park/Vardon matches in 1899 marked the beginning of the end of the old-style challenge match era.

One feature of golfing life at this time seems odd today. The best players did not practise their game off the course, nor did the professionals teach off the course. Instead, play was the only mode of practice and pedagogy. Playing was the thing: only foreigners, like the Germans, practised sport and used exercises in the gymnasium. Getting fit for golf is hardly mentioned, although 'Old' Tom Morris recalls that he did give up smoking prior to one of his great matches with Willie Park. Otherwise, German *Körperkultur* was unthinkable.

PROFESSIONAL CHALLENGE MATCHES OF NOTE TO 1870 FROM SMITH'S *Golfers Annual* 1870[33]	
1840	1
1843	1
1849	1
(Great match)	
1850	1
1852	1
1853	1
1856	1
(Great Match)	
1857	1
1858	1
1861	4
1862	5
1864	7
1865	10
1866	9
1867	about 20
1868	about 20
1869	about 20

The Audience

The golfing crowds witnessing a challenge match could be large and noisy. A challenge match was a good day out and the pubs were full. Crowd control was a problem since the moving crowds of the open links could not be contained. Ropes were used in attempts to limit crowd movement, but the players were close to spectators and minor harassment and crowd noise were common. Andra' Kirkaldy recalled later that booing of the opponent's play was routine, such were the town loyalties on the east coast of Scotland. There are even hints that in some of the golfing crowds there were paid hecklers.[33]

A little of the drama of these occasions can be seen in the game at Musselburgh between Tom Morris and Willie Park in 1870. It was a return match and Old Tom was one up. The match was umpired by Robert Chambers, the Edinburgh publisher and author. About 7,000 noisy, mostly local, spectators watched the match. Chambers repeatedly appealed for order, but the home crowd gave massive vocal support for the local man. Morris was increasingly ruffled by the crowd's attitude, and when he retired for refreshment at Mrs Forman's pub, he declined to return to the game, saying that the crowd's noise had made it impossible for him to continue. Park ostentatiously played out the remaining holes alone and

Robert Chambers, publisher, golfer and referee of the Morris/Park match. He encouraged the publication of the early books on golf.

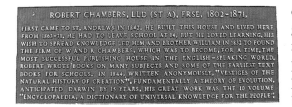

ROBERT CHAMBERS, LLD (ST A), FRSE, 1802-1871.

FIRST CAME TO ST. ANDREWS IN 1842. HE BUILT THIS HOUSE AND LIVED HERE FROM 1863-71. HE HAD TO LEAVE SCHOOL AT 14, BUT HE LOVED LEARNING. HIS WISH TO SPREAD KNOWLEDGE LED HIM AND BROTHER WILLIAM IN 1832 TO FOUND THE FIRM OF W AND R CHAMBERS, WHICH WAS TO BECOME, FOR A TIME, THE MOST SUCCESSFUL PUBLISHING HOUSE IN THE ENGLISH-SPEAKING WORLD. ROBERT WROTE BOOKS ON MANY SUBJECTS AND SOME OF THE EARLIEST TEXT BOOKS FOR SCHOOLS. IN 1844, WRITTEN ANONYMOUSLY, "VESTIGES OF THE NATURAL HISTORY OF CREATION", FUNDAMENTALLY A THEORY OF EVOLUTION, ANTICIPATED DARWIN BY 15 YEARS. HIS GREAT WORK WAS THE 10 VOLUME "ENCYCLOPAEDIA, A DICTIONARY OF UNIVERSAL KNOWLEDGE FOR THE PEOPLE".

Robert Chambers'
memorial at St Andrews.

claimed the match. Morris appeared next day to start the game, but Park refused to play. Morris in his turn then made a solitary but futile round of the links alone, a fine piece of sporting theatre. As late as 1890, when Kirkaldy played Park at St Andrews, the local man appealed to the crowd of 16,000 not to barrack the visitor.

The Later Challenges

The now-forgotten importance of the challenge matches is well illustrated by the later matches of Old Tom Morris. Old Tom was a draw to the crowds until the end of his life, and he continued to play in the Open Championship until the age of 77.

Less well known is his popularity, when quite senior, in challenge matches because he pulled in the crowds. In 1893, aged 73, he played Bob Dow at Montrose, for a 'considerable stake' and next day Tom plus Dow played a game, again at Montrose, against Dr Stone and the Honorary Secretary of the Montrose Royal Albert Club.[34] These matches, which had money prizes and considerable betting, involved amateurs who played unselfconsciously with the professionals, as was the Scottish tradition. The new anti-professional mood in England and the new tough laws on amateurism of about 1886, seem to have been ignored or initially resisted by senior amateurs in Scotland.

The Boom outside Scotland

An increasing number of travellers and visitors began taking the game back to England from the Scottish links from about 1860 onwards. But the rise in interest in the game came later. As late as 1875, even Murray's *Handbook for Travellers in Scotland* hardly mentions golf. Ten years later there was still little English enthusiasm for golf, and Horace Hutchinson could say that 'in 1885 golf was an eccentricity affected by a few'. In the same year L. Ayton, the St Andrews professional, was appointed to Yarmouth Golf Club but returned home, having been 'starved out'. He had seen no play for 3 months.

The origins of the English boom were in the new wealth and leisure spreading through the middle grades of society, as more people wished to join and imitate the earlier habits of the sporting gentlemen. Suburban life was prospering, and sport and sporting clubs thrived. Real wages had risen by 60% between 1870 and 1890, and this was accompanied by a fall in the value of agricultural land, caused mainly by cheap imports of corn from Russia and North America, together with some poor summer weather at home. This created a remarkable opportunity for land purchase or long leases for golf courses - a game hungry for space, but a sport not particular about the terrain used. The historical records of the number of clubs formed at this time confirms the *Golfer's Annual* verdict in 1891 that 'the year [1890] has been a remarkable one in the history of golf. The game has spread with surprising rapidity and to a wonderful extent not only in Britain but in many distant lands.' The Crail Golf Club minutes also mention 1890 as the *annus mirabilis* of golf. At a national and international level, this meant the rapid formation of new clubs, and at club level it showed as booming membership and income. On Scotland's municipal courses there were larger numbers than before, playing, as always, without fee on the public land. The new popularity made it possible for the Town Councils, for the first time, to charge for play on the links by visitors. These healthy municipal finances also opened the way to purchase and public ownership of the important Scottish golf links.

But in Scotland until about 1890 the golf courses were not sacred. At Elie in 1878 a serious dispute with the tenant farmer arose. He was displeased at the cutting of the fairways, since it affected the summer grazing allowed him. In the same year, golf at Inverallochy ceased temporarily. The *Golfer's Annual* recorded that

> *golf has been played for generations on the [Inverallachy] links and I am sorry to say has been put a stop to by the proprietor, owing to complaints by the farmers who individually share a part of the links. The fishermen [golfers] have not been able, from want of funds, to take the case before the Law Courts, where owing to the length of time the game has been played on the links, the verdict would assuredly have been in their favour.*

North Berwick and the Boom

In the golf boom, a number of Scottish towns rose in succession as fashionable resorts, drawing visitors from throughout Britain, and golf was prominent among the attractions of these newly popular resorts. Of these, North Berwick was to reach particular celebrity, and had a fashionable season at Easter and in summer. Joyce Wethered advised serious golfers to avoid these times 'when there is an inevitable overshadowing and loss of the genuine charm of North Berwick... the feeling becomes almost too pronounced that the latest creations of Chenil and Fortnum and Mason are occupying the centre of the stage'.[35] Like all seaside resorts, North Berwick had a plurality of attractions – concerts, bands, bandstands, excursions, balls, theatricals, and above all, titled visitors and polite company on the promenade, and the possibility of romance – with suitable people. Golf was important in these towns'

PREFACE.

————

To the making of Golf Clubs and Courses there would seem to be no finality. No fewer than 1750 Clubs are now included in the Directory, an increase of 283 from last year. Hence the exigencies of space have reluctantly compelled me to omit in all cases the names of Committees.

To Contributors and Club Secretaries alike I tender my sincere thanks for their valuable assistance.

DAVID SCOTT DUNCAN.

5, LOCKHARTON TERRACE, EDINBURGH,
May, 1898.

During the golf boom, the *Golfing Annual* of 1898 mentions the difficulty of keeping up with events.

North Berwick panorama showing the large villas, the prestigious Marine Hotel and the golf links beyond.

Ben Sayers, the diminutive North Berwick professional, had a central role as teacher, player and club-maker in the boom time for this fashionable town.

economy. At its peak, North Berwick had two main courses, a number of private clubhouses, eight teaching professionals and a host of caddies available. Davie Grant (Ben Sayers' brother-in-law) in that town took an interest in ladies' golf and soon had produced a champion – Miss E. C. Orr – and had creditable performances himself in major events.

Balfour and Golf

One man put North Berwick firmly in the lead in the list of fashionable resorts, and identified the town for ever with golf. Arthur James Balfour, Foreign Secretary and Prime Minister, a regular summer visitor at North Berwick, led fashion away from the grouse moor and towards the golfing links. Though he came from a golfing family, it was not until the age of 36 that he took up the game. He was part of a gifted group including Lord Curzon and the Tennant family, and Margot Tennant was to marry Asquith. Always quotable, he later regretted that he belonged to

that unhappy class of beings for ever pursued by remorse, who are conscious that they threw away in their youth the opportunity of beginning golf.

In his memoirs he recalled the choices of the sports available in summer:

...the ten-mile walk through the rain after missing a stag, a long ride home after a blank day, fielding while out while your opponent scores 400, cannot be described by the most enthusiastic deerstalker, foxhunter or cricketer as otherwise than wearisome episodes in delightful pursuits.[36]

He recalled his routine. Though close to his family home, he hid away alone in North Berwick.

I spent each September at North Berwick, at the Bass Rock Hotel, or in later years at Bradbury's, in rooms which looked down on the seventeenth green and the first tee, framed in a landscape embracing the little harbour, the Isle of May, and other islands which skirt the Firth of Forth, and the stately profile of the Bass Rock. When at North Berwick I lived a solitary and well-filled life, playing two rounds of golf or more a day, and in the evenings carrying on my official work, and such philosophical and literary undertakings as I happened to be engaged on. Each Friday after my morning's round I drove to Whittingehame [the family home] in the best substitute that could then be found for a modern motor-car, a brougham, with a pair of horses, and spent the week-end with my family and guests.

Behind the scenes there was more tension than this tranquil vignette suggests. Balfour's predecessor as Secretary for Ireland had been assassinated in Dublin, on common land occasionally used for golf. Detectives discreetly followed Balfour on the Scottish links.

About this time, in 1898, *The Times* reviewed Balfour's role in the newly popular national game:

Mr Balfour has insensibly attained to a sort of grandmastership of golf players in this country. It seems to be tacitly assumed that a new golf club can hardly be satisfactorily set on foot without his assistance. The correct thing to do is either to make him President or to enrol him as an honorary member and then induce him to play over the new course, or to make a little speech to the players or better still to do both.[37]

Distinguished players with Ben Sayers on the 18th tee at North Berwick c1900.

Other patrons of North Berwick ensured its social success. The *Haddingtonshire Courier* of 1903 claimed that out on the links that week were four MPs, the Speaker of the House of Commons, two bishops and the Prime Minister. Later, the group were joined by Lord Kitchener, and *HMS Dreadnought* on its way to Rosyth fired a ten-gun salute when passing the links. The wandering socialite Crown Prince Michael, exiled from Russia, discovered golf in Scotland, joined the R&A, and was also prominent at North Berwick. Also patronising the Marine Hotel, the centre of the North Berwick social scene, were Field Marshal Roberts and Prince Edward of Saxe-Weimar. The sociable King Edward VII appeared in the town in 1903, travelling by special train from Balmoral, preceded by a pilot train, and with all stations on the route cleared of the humble before the train passed through. At North Berwick an acceptable group of citizens was assembled in morning dress to greet the King.[38]

A. J. Balfour, the golfing Home Secretary and Prime Minister, made golf popular and fashionable by his enthusiasm for the game at North Berwick in the late 1800s.
He is shown here playing in as captain of the R&A in 1894.

Other Resorts

North Berwick's importance at this time is clear, but a number of other neighbouring towns, notably Gullane and Dunbar, also had a boom in holiday visitors and in golf. A contemporary epitome of Dunbar golf said:

The attractions of Dunbar as a golf resort are of a negative kind. The players to begin with on emerging from the railway station are not jostled by a lot of urchins with 'carry for you, sir' coming from all directions. The town is on an eminence above the links. This is its attitude toward golf. The game is kept at a respectable distance; you can live here and enjoy the strong sea-air and sea-bathing without being compelled to golf in self-protection. Dunbar was not made for golf, but golf was made for Dunbar. It is allowed as a favour and must keep its position, which is secondary... The air at Dunbar is not saturated with gutta-percha; the vocabulary of the people is not confined to golf and all that concerns it; the shop windows have the usual goods displayed in them, and clubs and balls are not to be seen. Boys can be had to act as caddies but you soon find that they, like the town, have not been made for golf...[40]

But there were areas where golf did not immediately revive. Aberdeen, in spite of the antiquity of play in the town, showed no early enthusiasm for the revived game. In 1876 the Aberdeen golf links still had a rifle range across the 2nd and 3rd holes, and the links were also the site of the annual Highland Show. Carnoustie had golf, but not mass golf, and the town was to rise later and cater for the middle-class holiday market, while Dornoch's national popularity came even later. Lossiemouth had a small, select, blue-blooded holiday clientele. But St Andrews was special, unaffected as a local said by the

social plague of other holiday haunts. German and other brazen bands know not the way hither, as we have no esplanade, no promenade, no theatre, nothing but golf.

And some revival in golf was occurring in the towns. In Glasgow in 1870 a group of keen citizens restored a golf club. These men were not survivors from the early club, nor holiday players used to east coast play. The innocence of these neophytes can be judged by the fact that they wrote for 'specimens of clubs' from St Andrews, Musselburgh and Prestwick prior to starting. A beginner at Glasgow tried to silence a noisy farmer in an adjacent field – 'plooin comes before hockey' was the farmer's retort. Golf had been extinguished and they were starting again from nothing. Their pioneer open stroke-play Tennant Cup dates from 1880.

Golf Literature

Until the end of the feathery era, the literature on golf was scanty. Apart from early poems of limited circulation like *The Goff* of 1743 and Carnegie's *Golfiana* (1833), virtually nothing else was published other than a few slim printed rules for domestic club use, like the *Rules of the Thistle Club* of 1821. Nor were the newspapers interested. Though London's *The Observer* was founded in 1792, no reports of sport are found in the first two months of publication of the paper.[41]

At the start of the gutty era, the new interest in golf encouraged the first books on golf for this small group of players.[42] H. B. Farnie, the erratic St Andrews student with many interests, published the first compendium on the game in 1857. Thirteen years passed until the first hesitant attempt at the year-book genre appeared, written by the Edinburgh golfer Charles MacArthur, and his *The Golfer's Annual for 1869-1870* was published in Ayr.[43] In the early 1870s nothing else appeared. Thereafter there was a quickening of literary interest in golf which was to be permanent. Printing costs were falling, distribution improving and sports readership rising, though the main market was still the gentlemen's library. In the decade 1875-86 three important and substantial books were published. First was Robert Clark's *Golf: A Royal and Ancient Game* of 1875, an elegantly produced history and anthology on the game by this Edinburgh printer and golfer. This was followed by Robert Forgan's *The Golfer's Handbook* of 1881, and then by Horace Hutchinson's first book *Hints on Golf* which was published by Blackwood, whose firm had produced Carnegie's *Golfiana* earlier. Sir Walter Simpson, a friend of R. L. Stevenson, died young, publishing only *The Art of Golf* in 1887, the first instructional book with photographs.

There is a hint of a St Andrews influence on these early Edinburgh publishers and publications. John Blackwood of *Blackwood's Magazine*, who played golf with Horace Hutchinson and was his publisher, rented Strathtyrum House near St Andrews, belonging to the Cheapes, and there in the 1860s he gathered an Edinburgh literary, publishing and printing clique, including Robert Clark, at week-ends for golf and gossip. Blackwood had Bob Kirk as his regular caddie, and Blackwood was eventually a captain of the R&A.[44] But thereafter the initiatives in writing, printing and golf publishing increasingly came from England.

As the golf boom started, a flood of publications from 1890 onwards met the growing interest in the game, first in Britain and then in America, and a wider readership appeared. Hutchinson's golf volume in the *Badminton Library* continued with huge success and ran to nine editions from 1890-1910. The magazine *Golf* also started in the boom year of 1890 and was the first in a distinguished line of periodicals. A. J. Robertson, a journalist originally with *The Scotsman*, was the first editor and John Kerr remarked after the first six years of the magazine that 'when he [Robertson] started *Golf* a good many shook their heads, thinking he would not find material to keep the venture going. His difficulty now is to find room for what is sent to him.' Other magazines also soon filled up their pages. *Golf* changed its name to *Golf Illustrated* in 1899 and *The Golfer* ran from 1897, *Golfing* from 1895, *The Golfer's Magazine* started in 1898, *Irish Golfer* ran from 1898, *Golfing and Cycling* from 1897 and *American Golfing* appeared in 1896. Among the numerous other 'firsts' in this decade 1890-1900 was the first biography of a golfer - F. G. Tait. The first book describing the more renowned British courses was Hutchinson's *British Golf Links* of 1896, the first book with engravings of views of golf courses was Aikman's *A Round of the Links* and the first golfing novel was Stobart's *Won at the Last Hole* (1893). There was also the first American book - Lee's *Golf in America* and the first book written for women's golf - Hecker's *Golf for Women*, and the first book written by a golf professional - Park's *Game of Golf* - published in 1896.[45] Scottish guide books, formerly preoccupied with the antiquities, now added accounts of the golf

Robert Clark the Edinburgh printer, golfer and author.

Clark's *Golf: A Royal and Ancient Game* 1875 was one of the first of the new wave of golf books for the sportsman's library.

Principal Tulloch of St Andrews University wrote this affectionate biography of 'Old' Tom Morris to add to his previous works on Queen Victoria and the Prince Consort.

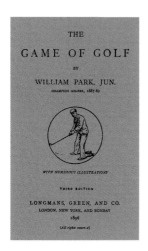

Willie Park Jnr's instructional book on golf was the first by a professional player.

links. Later, a remarkable series of autobiographies and biographies of the pioneer Scottish professionals appeared, notably Tulloch's *Life of Tom Morris*, Kirkaldy's *Memories* and Sandy Herd's *My Golfing Life*. The golfing yearbook was soon firmly established as a permanent feature with the *Golfer's Annual* starting in 1887/88 and the *Golfer's Handbook*, which continues to appear, was published in Scotland from 1899 until 1984.

But the literature of golf became increasingly written by Englishmen thereafter. The older Scottish communal golf on the links was written out of the story in the new enthusiasm for the suburban social game of the new private golf clubs.[46]

The New Clubs

As we saw above, golf had a brief and short-lived popularity outside Scotland in the eighteenth century. In London, Europe, Ireland, and North America these early cliques and clubs were only precariously in existence. It needed Scotsmen, enthusiastic Scotsmen, to sustain the game outside Scotland, and when the crisis in the domestic game in Scotland developed in the early 1800s, this loss of Scottish golf also caused these distant outposts of the game to wilt or die. When revival came later, the game beyond Scotland was often wrongly thought to be an entirely new one.

In the British revival, only Wales remained cool for a while towards golf. Traditional stick-and-ball games were less obvious in that country. It was some time before the game emerged in Wales.

Westward Ho!

Modern English golf could be said to have started when the new club and course were established at Westward Ho! in 1864. There had been clubs at Blackheath and Manchester, but Scotsmen had been the activists; Westward Ho! was the first club in which the initiative came from England. Its pioneer, the Rev I. H. Gossett, vicar of Northam, had developed an interest in the game and asked his brother-in-law, General Moncrieff, who lived in St Andrews, to comment on the suitability of the land for a new course in Devon. Following this, Tom Morris was asked to lay out the course. A local community leader, George Molesworth, was also active in floating a hotel and villa company to which he gave the name 'Westward Ho!' after the Charles Kingsley novel. They aimed to rival Torquay as a resort, and the golf course was part of the strategy.[47]

Liverpool

Of crucial importance to the development of the English game was the rising enthusiasm for the game at Liverpool.[48] Here were natural links, and Scots living in Liverpool started playing at Hoylake Warren, linksland with the usual adjacent racecourse: Robert Chambers the publisher and his faithful caddie George Morris laid out the links. Having established the club in 1869, the Liverpool golfers went further, and took the initiative in setting up a tournament for amateurs, later to be the national Amateur Championship. There had been an informal amateur tournament 'circuit' of the major domestic competitions of the main clubs, and the Liverpool activists sensed that their location half-way between the ancient Scottish links and the new clubs of southern England made them the geographical centre of British golf. Their open amateur tournament of 1885 was a great success. And from Liverpool came John Ball, who was to dominate the amateur sport.

The establishment of new clubs in England reached a peak in the late 1880s and '90s. In Yorkshire alone in the decade from 1890 the number of clubs rose from 2 to 50. English holiday resorts now wished to have golf clubs and first to act was Eastbourne. In 1887 the Duke of Devonshire leased some downland for a golf club and soon 500 members had joined and the fashionable club quickly gained a 'Royal' label. Other seaside towns soon opened golf clubs to keep their place as major resorts - Bournemouth in 1893, and Brighton in 1908.

These were private clubs with high subscriptions and they leased or owned their own golf courses, unlike the Scottish clubs who played over public land. In England municipal golf did not emerge naturally or early. Even if the town authorities attempted to reconstruct a St Andrews ambience, e.g. at Mitcham Common or on Brighton Links, other users of these open spaces, not sharing the ancient Scottish understanding of golf nor having any deference to the game, protested successfully at the hazards and danger to non-golfing citizens. This increased the pressure for English courses to be enclosed and exclusive. The crucial democratic and economical basis of Scottish golf could not be exported.

The Spread

The grass mower, invented in mid-century, was vital to the successful emergence of the game outside Scotland, and made the game possible in places where natural turf with short grass was not available. The revolution that this new technology caused cannot be exaggerated: golf now prospered in all seasons. In Scotland, inland parkland could now be used and golf on upland stretches of moor or heath emerged. Initially the mower was used only for the greens: sheep were still preferred for care of the fairways.[49] Alternatively the farmer might be asked to cut the fairways, and given payment for this in lieu of the grazing. A Scottish speciality was the flag pin with a spring segment incorporated in it just above the ground, which allowed sheep to rub against the pole, without levering the pole out of the ground and damaging the turf.

As the speed of the spread of golf increased, the planners for new clubs and courses throughout the world reflexly turned to Scottish professionals for help. Players like Old Tom Morris, Willie Park, Willie and Tom Dunn and other professional golfers now had a new career opening up for them as designers, particularly in their later years, and they had a variety of

Flag sticks with springs were required to protect the hole from the attentions of grazing animals.

The "Pattisson" Golf Patents

FIFTEEN YEARS HIGHEST REPUTATION.

As used on His Majesty's Golf Links and by the Principal Clubs at Home and Abroad.

The Best, Strongest and Most Durable.

Improved Steel "Bogey" Hole Tins — Galvanised. Improved Steel "Anti-Mud" Hole Tins — Galvanised. Steel "Bogey" Hole Cutter. Plain Hole Cutter — Steel. Steel Putting Green Renovators. Steel Starting Ball Troughs. Tee Sand Boxes — Galvanized Steel, various. Water Boxes — Galvanised Steel, various. Tee Boxes, Sand — Best Elm. Steel Flags — various. Flags, Bunting and Cotton — various. Tassels — Worsted. Flag Staffs — Tubular and Solid Wrought Iron; Bamboo; Steel Spring. Anti-Cattle. Rollers — Best Solid Elm, various; Hollow Wood and Water Ballast; Light Iron for Putting Greens. Horse Rollers — Iron and Wood. Roller Carts. Wide-Wheel Carts. Lawn Mowers — Best Makes at Special Prices. Horse Mowers — Best Makes at Special Prices. The "Pattisson" Roller and Sweeper. The "Bradford" Brush and Roller. Worm Cast Bamboos and Bamboo Brooms. The "Pattisson" Boot Scraper and Brush. Hand Mud Brushes with Scrapers, Tee Mats, the "Perfect Stance," etc. Monthly Medals, Caddie Badges, Notice Tablets, Tee Discs, Ball Scoops, Spades, Shovels, Barrows, &c.

Everything Required on a Golf Course.

RANSOMES' LAWN MOWERS
ARE USED ON

Possesing Important Improvements embodied in no other Maker's Machines.

New Designs, Patent Spring Handles, Double Angle Cutters, Single Screw Adjustment.

ALL THE PRINCIPAL GOLF LINKS,
INCLUDING

BRAY	FELIXSTOWE	ISLE OF WIGHT	PRESTWICK	ROYAL COUNTY, PORTRUSH
CROMER	GLAMORGANSHIRE	MACHRIHANISH	RANELAGH	ROYAL NORTH DEVON
CAMPBELTOWN	GREEN ISLAND	MORAY	ROYAL AND ANCIENT,	MALONE (BELFAST)
DULWICH AND SYDENHAM	HUDDERSFIELD	MID-SURREY	ST. ANDREWS	ST. GEORGE'S, SANDWICH
CO. DOWN	ORMEAU (BELFAST)	NORTH BEDS	ROYAL DUBLIN	WIMBLEDON
CARRICKMINES	KILLARNEY	LISBURN	ROYAL EPPING FOREST	ETC., ETC.

Hand-Power Machines made in all sizes to suit every requirement.

Illustrated Catalogues free on application to

RANSOMES, SIMS & JEFFERIES, LTD., IPSWICH.

Grass-mowing equipment evolved in the late 1800s and helped improve the quality of golf course upkeep.

'Old' Tom Morris was in demand as a course designer, and he often added the shrewd stipulation that he should also be sole supplier of golf clubs to the new club and its golfers.

By courtesy of CRIEFF GOLF CLUB.

projects. Some clubs needed only a 'staker' to mark out a rough course. Other clubs could afford a major project. Jamie Dunn laid out the new Blackheath course and Old Tom was much in demand as a designer. His agreeable habit of saying that 'surely Providence has intended this for a golf links' endeared him to anxious committee members. He stumped around Scotland, England and Ireland complimenting the locals on their choice of land, and laid out numerous courses and modernised others, notably the ancient links at Dornoch. One little extra was discreetly proposed by Morris and others, which added to their fees. Morris often obtained agreement with the committee that the local professional or golf supplier would stock only his clubs.[50]

The work of some of these designers has not been highly regarded by later commentators:

Between 1885 and 1900 may be described as the Dark Ages of golf architecture... The inefficiency displayed in designing them was so deplorable and misguided that, so far as golf architect and client were concerned, it was a case of the blind leading the blind... It was evident that someone had to be found to do the work, and the choice fell mainly on three professional golfers - Tom Morris, Willie and Tom Dunn... When we consider the wonderful advantages they enjoyed, it is amazing that they should have achieved such ineffectual results. They failed to reproduce any of the features of the courses on which they were bred and born, or to realise the principles on which they had been made. Willie Park, Jnr, it is true, was a redeeming example among professionals in showing any aptitude for the work...[51]

The Designs

This lofty verdict is unfair. Certainly, too many of the new courses had square greens, and rectangular bunkers symmetrically placed across fairways. Too many had the greens cut into hillsides - the 'gun platform' green. But it suggests that the Scots designers were only invited by prosperous clubs and always had generous budgets. This fails to take into account the constraints, and that most new clubs, particularly in Scotland, had only modest budgets, money which had to be raised in advance of the opening of the club. The new members, particularly in England, had low expectations and little knowledge of golf. Morris and others were only expected to visit briefly and be shown a field or two leased from a friendly farmer, and an instant plan was expected. Many of the new layouts were inevitably simple. On the one-day visit by the great man, he would only judge on the choice of sites, make a plan on the ground, and place marks for tees and pins on the selected ground. No earthworks were suggested nor could be contemplated, other than digging a few bunkers, and levelling some tiny tees. Many courses were to be untended other than by sheep and little further upkeep was proposed, even if it could have been afforded from the fragile finances of the new small clubs. At the smaller clubs later, many courses had to be redesigned once organisation and finances permitted. Of the 'remoulders' James Braid had some celebrity later in Scotland.

The best results came when natural links or sandy heathland was available and the new club was a wealthy one – as at Westward Ho!, Hoylake, St George's, Sandwich, Rye, Felixstowe and Machrihanish – where courses of championship standard immediately appeared. In the expansion of golf in the North of Scotland, Simpson from Carnoustie had success round the Moray Firth.

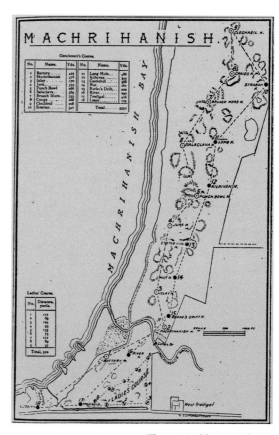

The original lay-out of the new course at Machrihanish, on a traditional shinty area. The first layout, by Tom Morris, measured 5,500 yards. From Dalrymple *The Golfers Guide* 1894.

The Scots Professionals

The new clubs often automatically turned to Scotland for their designer and then added a novelty. They employed a golfing factotum as a servant of the club – a professional. Few of the Scottish clubs had such a person, though at any major links there was always a group of caddies, who were often skilled players and clubmakers. The new English clubs employed one of this group to be their club professional. The stereotype of the dour, talented, taciturn Scottish professional as clubmaker, teacher, keeper of the links and the golfing mysteries is not always wrong. Gentlemen normally took instruction from other gentlemen when playing cricket or when riding or rowing. But in golf the new sportsmen deferred to the gruffest of Scottish professionals, and accepted them as the oracle on the rules, the swing, clubs and balls and agronomy. But English society did not share the collectivism of the Scottish links. The new clubs firmly excluded the professionals from the new club-houses. Many of the professionals were uncomfortable in their new situations far from the east coast of Scotland, and often found their way home.[52]

For many players, even the expanding game had uncertainties. Success in golf did not automatically reward the winners. Bob Ferguson, though Open champion 1880/81/82, never made a living from golf and reverted to caddy-ing. Jack Burns summarised the situation after his Open win in 1888: 'I am satisfied. Now all I want is a steady job, and I've got that on the railway.' Some personal entrepreneurial flair was required at that time to make money from golf, even for Open Champions. Andra' Kirkaldy won the Open in 1879 but joined the Army shortly afterwards for six years, returning to work on the railway and to be a caddie at St Andrews. The steady job of caddying was seasonal, and as the caddie grew older, his hiring became less. Drinking and caddying, it seems, went together, and the eventual toll was often taken.

But within the Scottish professional diaspora some others were not only gifted golfers but were also worldly and articulate. The talented player Willie Smith of Carnoustie left for America at the turn of the century. The magazine *Golfing* related that 'he had always been considered a suave fellow by the boys of the town' and that 'when arranging terms for his stay at the Midlothian Country Club in Chicago, Willie showed his good taste in specifying certain conditions relative to his own personal comfort. These conditions startled not a few of the members'.[53] Other contemporary comment shows that the new clubs of the USA were looking not only for a professional golfer but for a master of ceremonies as well. Americans welcomed Scotsmen in this role, and many émigrés flourished after escaping from the rigid social structure at home.

The Second Generation at Musselburgh: Willie Park Jnr

The sons of the first generation of Musselburgh players eclipsed even the reputations of their fathers. Willie Dunn Jnr emigrated and was runner-up in the first unofficial American Open, and his brother Tom had a playing and teaching career in Scotland and England, being sought as a designer for a dozen or so well-known courses in England, of which Woking is the best known. Abroad he was responsible for the pioneer courses at Biarritz, Dinard and Tenerife and he was also in demand for laying out private courses in Britain for the gentry.

Dunn would be better known if his considerable achievements had not been eclipsed by the remarkable career of his friend Willie Park Jnr, the dominant figure from this generation of gifted Musselburgh golfers. Brought up in a golfing family, and in the golf environment of Musselburgh, he started as usual as a caddie, and won the Open in 1887 and 1889. Park can be regarded as the first of the modern professional golfers, men who successfully capitalised on their golfing skills, and profited hugely. He used his name skilfully, obtained patents for his new clubs to increase the mystique of the products bearing his name, and used advertising, a novelty at the time, to bring in distant sales from strangers. 'Beware of imitations' was an inspired slogan. Others followed and the 1890s were a 'golden decade of golf patents'.

Park sensed that the future lay in the use of iron clubs for routine play. He also realised that sales of clubs existed beyond the professionals' shops and he successfully courted the big town stores, persuading them to stock his clubs for their sporting customers. His successful irons were the lofter of 1888, his driving cleek and, above all, his 'infallible' putting cleek of 1894. He watched for new technology and used it, notably for his compressed, moulded wooden-headed clubs.

Always perceptive of new opportunities, Park used the newspapers skilfully, and they were made aware of his movements and projects. He could be a showman and wore a light tropical suit instead of the dark heavy clothes of the traditional professional; he took taxis home for lunch during Musselburgh challenge matches. He prospered and owned a large house close to Musselburgh Links which gave him the right to stop the London train passing through his land, and in 1897 he also bought an expensive house in North Berwick, close to the first tee, for the remarkable sum of £3,000. He was the first professional to employ a regular professional caddie, the mysterious man called John Fiery or simply 'Fiery'. Park's book *The Game of Golf* of 1896 was the first written by a professional player; well-written and sensible, it sold steadily and went to a number of editions. By 1886 or so, Park was successful in his golf club and design work, and by 1891 he had branches and agents for his business in Edinburgh, Glasgow, London and Manchester, employing a total of 20 staff. In 1895 he again broke new ground by going to America, where he stayed with J. J. Astor and set up a branch of his business in New York at West 23rd Street.

Park as Designer

Park's interests had extended to course design, and he went well beyond the simple economical schemes favoured by others before him. Sunningdale was Park's first triumph. Park sought and obtained a large budget and suggested expensive major earthworks to create the desired layout. He was prepared to clear moorland and heather, and then sculpture the terrain, and plant or remove trees. He was breaking out of the Scottish assumptions that golf was to be played on the natural terrain available. *Golf Illustrated* concluded 'he was the first man to take on a contract for the laying out of a course on heathland which to the casual observer seemed to be peculiarly unadapted for the project in hand'.[54] Sunningdale was a huge success, but his next big project caused him difficulties. The plan for the Huntercombe club and course was based on the Sunningdale model but was even more ambitious, a plan greatly ahead of its time.[55] One golf course was to be built, followed by two others, plus a 100-bed hotel and a housing development. Park put up the huge sum of £30,000 from family money: he lost heavily when the project stalled badly.

In 1896 he attempted a return to competitive golf. Having been beaten in the Open by Vardon in 1898 in a close finish, he challenged Vardon to match-play, in the Scottish style. Park was aware of the decline in match-play, and part of his challenge was an attempt to reassert its old supremacy over stroke-play. The matches took place in 1899 and had the traditional home-and-away format. Park, trailing two down on the first leg at North Berwick, was soundly beaten by Vardon on the parkland course of Ganton, 11 and 10.

Exported Players

Musselburgh continued steadily to produce celebrated players. David Brown won the 1886 Open and, like Willie Dunn, then sought his fortune in America, winning the US Open in 1903 and teaching golf in Boston thereafter. Bobby Turnbull left Musselburgh to become a successful player and teacher, first in Copenhagen and then in Nice. Peter McEwan's six sons went respectively to be professionals at Huddersfield, Chicago, Ilkley, Formby, Birkdale and Hesketh.

The rapid movements and changes of post of some of these players does not necessarily mean restlessness or unhappy appointments. The mood of the

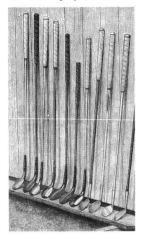

A set of clubs from the mid-gutty period, showing that iron clubs were becoming more popular for routine play.

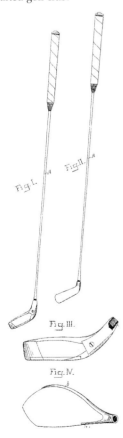

Horsburgh's forgotten patent in 1894 for a steel-shafted golf club.

time was to appoint a professional for one year only, or even just the summer. Many clubs wished to have this flexibility and hence obtain a variety of help and opinion in the early years of the club.

Further Innovation in Scotland

Until this time the development of the game had always been within Scotland. The long game played with the feathery ball and long-nosed woods had evolved in Scotland. The early artifacts of the new era – gutty balls and hickory clubs – were also developed in Scotland. But with the spread of the game to England and elsewhere came the appearance of the first non-Scottish innovations. In England the clubs were favouring stroke-play rather than match-play. English sports manufacturing companies started making golf clubs, in factories, far from the Scottish links. Moreover, inventions in Scotland were not pursued with the confidence of a former period. At Carnoustie in the 1880s, a Captain Duncan Stewart experimented with an early form of what was later to be called the rubber (Haskell) ball. Though he patented the ball in 1876, his experiments were not taken further, in a commercial sense, but he continued to make the ball and when he moved to Machrihanish, he presented these 'Stewart balls' as prizes during his period as captain in 1883.[56] When the Haskell ball appeared and swept the golfing world in 1902, the American makers tried to patent their discovery in Britain. The earlier attempt by Stewart was known and was described and explained in court. The patent was not granted.

On appeal, the matter went to the House of Lords and the decision was that the American ball could not be patented in Britain, because of the earlier experiments of Stewart, and others. The neglect of the Stewart/Carnoustie ball by Scottish golfers was commented upon by Mr Justice Buckley in his pithy judgement... He remarked dryly that the pioneer Stewart rubber-core ball

> had no click, and according to the sentiment of the day, golf without a click was not golf, but a waste of time.

Stewart had been ahead of his time, but failed to convince the golfing world. It was, however, a portent that pace-making in golfing matters would move from Scotland. Scottish patents for the first golf tees were taken out, but were never used. The first (mostly solid) steel shafts to be made were also developed in Scotland and patented, but similarly failed to be used or appreciated, notably by golfing legislators. The inventor, Thomas Horsburgh, a blacksmith of Baberton in Edinburgh, was not too disadvantaged: he had a good income from his patent on a new horseshoe.

The New Game

As the game was exported from Scotland it changed. Beyond Scotland golf projects usually involved a major financial undertaking and purchase of land for a course and clubhouse. This game beyond Scotland was inevitably exclusive, requiring an élite membership with money and social standing. The large membership of the new clubs encouraged stroke-play rather than match-play as the usual mode for the main club competitions. Principal Tulloch, of St Andrews University, said sternly of this evolution that 'the score card was an invention of the Englishry. The Scot is above strokes and only reckons holes.'

Having emphasised stroke-play, it meant that golf handicaps followed. The work-ethic and self-improvement were in vogue, and Victorian society was being urged, often from the pulpit, to do better next week; measurement of golf scores and grading of ability was easily accepted. The first Scottish club known to use handicaps was the Rose Club at Carnoustie.[57]

The new players were also different. The gentlemen golfers until now had been bred, not made. Now there was new money and education available for more citizens, the new upwardly mobile golfers made good imitations of gentlemen, and sought gentlemanly status in the new clubs, and their wives behaved convincingly like ladies. The 'amateur' was born: it was nothing to do with money, and everything to do with class.

The word was initially used to mean a gentleman sportsman, as distinct from one of the humble majority. The new English golf clubhouses were part of this suburban snobbery and membership was a badge of status. Their huge memberships included many non-golfers, and in the new clubs, undesirables were easily deterred by large entry fees, and if persistent, were excluded by the secret black-ball veto. In drawing the exclusion lines, the professionals were also notable among those excluded from the new clubs. Horace Hutchinson had a devious rationalisation of why professionals should not be brought into the clubhouse of a golf club:

> It should be observed, in dealing with the class of professional players, that their temptations to unsteadiness [i.e. drink] are very great. They live very much in the society of men who are better off than themselves - and they see these men when they are taking their pleasure and their whisky and soda... Since the soda water is unfamiliar to them [the professionals], whereas whisky is a friend of their childhood, they imbibe the latter gratefully, while declining the former... Bearing in mind then their special temptations, it behoves every member to be careful not to add to them. It has happened to the writer to see the resident professional brought into the clubhouse of a south country club and there given a drink by an amateur who he had been coaching... In Scotland of course it is scarcely possible that it should have occurred.[58]

Hutchinson's warning was not to invite the professional into the club because he did not dilute his whisky with soda. He was also untruthful about the status of the professionals in Scotland, hinting that all Scottish clubs excluded such players. Even at St Andrews, professionals were welcome inside most local clubs. The St Andrews Golf Club had Allan Robertson, Tom Morris, Sandy Herd and Jamie Anderson, all Open Champions, as members, Robertson being captain in 1854. Scottish golf, and its clubs, showed a plurality of players and background.

Noble Golf

Noble golfers had been out on the Scottish links from earliest times, mixing with the humbler players. In those stately days the noble golfers arrived on the links with caddies, forecaddies and servants, scattering the other users of the links, and putting on a show of wealth, power, and often skilled golf. As the Scottish links grew busier and club memberships rose, those with old

Noble golf beside Inverary Castle, home of the Duke of Argyll, with fences to protect the greens from cattle.

money and land were no longer inclined to join the new aspirants at play. The links were too crowded and the atmosphere less deferential. Moreover, there was now a group of well-off claimants to gentlemanly status and these *arrivistes* imitated the ancient habits of the landed gentry and sought their company.[59]

Instead, the ancient aristocracy now retreated to their own land. They increasingly laid out their own courses for personal play and for their guests, and these private courses were to be part of golf in the next 50 years or so.[60] A string of private courses appeared on Royal Deeside, notably those laid out by Farquharson of Invercauld, by the Duke of Fife at Mar Lodge and later by the Royal Family at Balmoral. Lord Rosebery laid out his own course near Edinburgh, adding golf to his private sporting facilities for tennis and cricket at Dalmeny House in 1904. Wemyss Castle continued its ancient connection with golf by adding a new private course, and Mr Penn the MP, set up his personal course at Archerfield beside Muirfield. In Glasgow, Lord Blythswood had a course at Renfrew, and near Banff, Lord Braco had his course at Duff House, retaining a private professional called Harris. In England, the all-conquering Lady Margaret Scott learned to play discreetly on the private course at Stowell Park, Gloucestershire, and Crown Prince Michael, exiled from Russia, had his own nine holes nearby. To these private courses the gentry brought in private professionals to teach for short spells when the big house had guests, and occasionally these professionals were offered longer contracts. Two Carnoustie players had noble appointments for a time: Peter Robertson spent the summer season at Haddo House in Aberdeenshire from 1900-1902 and later Eddie Martin became Lord Iveagh's private professional in 1906. British noble golf was played in the January pheasant-shooting period, before the aristocracy moved abroad to the European spas in March.

English Private Courses

In England, the best-known private links was the seven-hole course at Chatsworth laid out by the 8th Duke of Devonshire, who regularly brought Ben Sayers from North Berwick to play with and teach his house guests. A high point in aristocratic golf was the period 1903-1907. During this time Edward VII, familiar with the game from Biarritz, visited Chatsworth with his court for a week in winter. Balfour, the golfing politician, was among the guests at Chatsworth and the invited professionals included J. H. Taylor and Jack White. In 1903 Ben Sayers was summoned to Windsor to teach the Prince of Wales and Princess Victoria, and Jack Kirkaldy was commissioned to lay out a course for the King at Windsor.[61] King Edward also stayed with Earl Howe in 1902 at Gopsall, to which stately home Willie Park was invited to stay and play. Vardon was, for a while, greenkeeper and private professional at Lord Ripon's private course.

These interested aristocrats had withdrawn from the links and still regarded golf as a winter game, ignoring the new trend for summer play. The Duke of Devonshire and the King, plus Ben Sayers, played their game at Chatsworth in January, and the royal golf at Gopsall was in December. The European spas were visited in March, followed by a summer season crowded with their well-established sports - racing, hunting, and fishing. Other sports like tennis and rowing eventually found a niche in this packed summer season - Ascot in May, Goodwood in July and Cowes in August. In September the social circuit took them back to Scotland for hunting and fishing, but not for golf. Noble golf was on probation, and was experimented with cautiously, finding a temporary place in its ancient winter season, on the heavy winter grass of the inland estates usually after the January pheasant shooting. Such unpleasant arrangements for golf could not last.

Enthusiasm Declines

This widespread noble interest in golf declined quite rapidly in the early twentieth century. Even the enthusiasm for winter golf at the milder resorts of Pau and Biarritz was to decline; fashionable golf had been a passing phase with the English gentry. The private courses in Britain's estates remained primitive and particularly unattractive in winter. Only occasionally later did royal golfers play the game, like the Prince of Wales in the 1920s, but they played not in private but as members of established clubs. Few of these private courses now remain: some persist only as a perk for the estate staff.[62]

But the landowners still maintained a benign interest in golf through sale or lease of their land to the new golf clubs. Rough, barren land was easily released by landowners and this otherwise unremarkable terrain admirably suited the needs of golf courses. Throughout Scotland such arrangements were usually harmonious and relations between the landowners and golf clubs were generally good, though the factor (the estate manager) occasionally appears as a villain.[62] Considerable acreage of land was rented to the new golf clubs, and outright purchase later also generally went smoothly. Landowners like the Duke of Roxburghe, with estates at Dunbar, Machrihanish and Machrie, the Duke of Portland (owner of Gailes) Lord Dalhousie at Blairgowrie and Lord Bute in Rothesay, all supported the local golf clubs, granting long leases of low-grade land, with some reservations. At Glasgow Gailes the Duke retained the mineral rights, cattle and sheep grazing and rights to shooting and trapping of rabbits, and the links were also to be used for 21 days each year for military exercises. The landowners were often found as Honorary Life Presidents of these clubs formed on their land: their wives graciously gave away the prizes. The golf clubs in return made deferential presentations to the laird on the occasion of major life events.

The local gentry might also arrange for putting up the prize at local exhibition matches. In 1892, two tournaments at Machrihanish were arranged for £20, and at Machrie on Islay, local interest by the gentlemen meant that a remarkable pot of over £100 was raised for an annual tournament, exceeding the fund at the Open, and sufficient to attract the best golfers, including the great Triumvirate (Braid, Vardon and Taylor) to play on this Scottish island, in spite of a two-day journey after the Open. Doubtless there were associated

Scottish golf of the time still relied on natural layout and unmanicured bunkers. Machrie on Islay, was an aristocratic retreat in summer, and the venue for one of the notable professional tournaments of the golfing year at the turn of the century.

caddying and teaching arranged for the house guests, making an attractive package for the professionals.

Another development about this time was the rise of the Oxford vs Cambridge match in 1878, largely through Scottish student interest. The pioneer seems to have been a St Andrews student W. T. Linskill, who went to Cambridge in 1873, and founded their pioneer golf society in 1875, well ahead of the main English golf boom. From there, many student players spread the game in England.

Artisan Golf

At the new clubs in England a strategy was employed to allow those unacceptable for routine club membership to be able to play. This was the 'artisan' club.[63] Attached to the main private clubs, these clubs-within-a-club allowed restricted play by humble locals on the course but excluded any voting rights or use of the main clubhouse. They had restricted periods for play and, as tradesmen, were often expected to help with upkeep of the course and clubhouse. This help was to be given free. Some famous artisan players emerged, some having learned their play as caddies. The first formal artisan club arose at Royal North Devon in 1888, 24 years after the foundation of the main club. Included in the founders was J. H. Taylor and the club was called the 'Northam Working Men's Golf Club'. By the turn of the century there were about a dozen such clubs in England.

In Scotland there never had been any artisan clubs with these arrangements. Play on the major links was open to all, and there was a variety of private clubs playing over the course, and many golfers were in any case already artisans. A public links or suitable golf club was usually within reach of anyone wishing to play in the traditional golfing towns. But the new mood affected Scotland. At Carnoustie in 1862, the new stuffy Carnoustie Golf Club encouraged some of its humbler members to leave. Out they went, to form a new club, the Taymouth Club, taking with them most of the other members. The senior club was soon in difficulties, and eventually the two clubs reunited again, this time for ever. But as new golf development in Scotland appeared and as private courses and clubs appeared at new suburban sites, a modest demand for 'artisan' golf arose, and a few arrangements of the English type can be detected, though this name was often avoided. Machrihanish offered 'a reduced subscription to local tradesmen and farm workers' and at Rothesay 'special terms for working men' were allowed. 'Old' Prestwick initially allowed local 'mechanics' to play over their course for a reduced fee. At Elie the fashionable club was The Golf House Club and an artisan club called The Thistle Club was formed, one of the few such clubs with the English pattern, since the Thistle Club had its own clubhouse. The town of Elie and Earlsferry now had two clubs and the inhabitants solemnly agreed on the divisions in society appropriate to membership of each club. The bank manager was eligible for the superior club but the grocer was deemed an artisan. The senior club denied James Braid his play as a youth in this town and he went to Leven to play in the usual Scottish style. Another artisan from this area was Douglas Rolland who beat the unbeaten John Ball in challenge matches in 1885. The artisan arrangements eventually withered and have almost vanished in England.

The Amateurs

The new aspiring sportsmen who were now joining the older gentlemen players sought ways of ring-fencing their sports to reserve the prizes and the play for themselves and their select companions. There was still acceptance of the idea that intellectual, physical and sporting ability was hereditary, and the gentleman's domination of the sport of the time was thought to be natural

Douglas Rolland, the talented Elie stonemason, seen with J. H. Taylor, had remarkable triumphs in amateur play, notably against John Ball.

and inevitable. King James VI remarked to a supplicant 'I'll make your son a baronet, but the devil himself couldna' mak' him a gentleman.' Amateur sport was very successful. As late as 1883 the Corinthians, Old Etonians or other 'old boy' teams dominated the Football Association Cup in England and only in that year did Blackburn Rovers reach the final. In Scotland the amateur football team, Queen's Park, was regularly supreme. From 1867-74 they never conceded a goal to professional opposition teams, and the entire Scottish football team in 1872 came from this amateur club. This amateur supremacy was widely assumed to be the natural order in society.[64]

But steadily, as the working week shortened and leisure became available for the majority, new skilled play by the lower orders challenged this natural superiority of class. The gentlemen now shifted ground and sought to be admired for the style of play and their manners: participation, not winning, was important and was to be as much applauded in golf as it was to be desirable in the Olympics later. Some Corinthian rituals emerged, and the offence of 'ungentlemanly conduct' entered into the rules of all sports for ever. A habit of not discussing the score during match-play evolved as did a disdain for stroke-play and seeking to win open tournaments. Freddy Tait won praise from his biographer since.

he held himself entirely aloof from the pot-hunting fraternity. When quartered in York he could of course, being [Amateur] Champion, have easily mopped up all the pots and pans in Yorkshire. The Mess table of the Black Watch might have fairly groaned under the amount of plate or plated that he could have realised. He seemed always to prefer a quiet foursome.

The second tee at St Andrews in about 1890, showing the unsophisticated greenkeeping of the day.

Gentlemen and the Rest

Each sport devised ways of separating the gentlemen from the rest. The issue was not about prize money, at least not at first. It was about manners and class. The Amateur Athletic Association was set up in 1866

to afford as completely as possible to all classes of gentlemen amateurs, the means of practising and competing against one another without being compelled to mix with professional runners.

The AAA went on to define what it meant by an amateur, and money-winning was not prominent in the definition. In negative terms, an amateur was not 'a mechanic, artisan or labourer'. The sporting paper *Bell's Life* of 1846 had a clearer definition. Amateurs were 'men of property, and not journeymen or mechanics'. Horace Hutchinson wrestled fairly frankly with the problem of what was a golfing amateur:

...everyone knows in their own mind what we mean by professional and what we mean by amateur. The trouble is to find words to define the idea.

In the sport of rowing the words were found by the administrators. No-one who had 'worked with their hands' could enter for the prestigious Henley events. But other sports reacted differently, and in cricket all men of talent, amateur and professional, mixed in most sides, though they had their separate entrances to the field. The amateur W. G. Grace was covertly paid huge sums of money by the MCC to tour for England. But in athletics the exclusiveness was achieved successfully. The amateur athletes occupied centre stage, as if others did not exist or had inferior athletic skills.[65]

In golf, the gentlemen amateurs cast about for ways of maintaining their exclusiveness, and matters of money became a simple way of preserving their territory. If no prizes were offered, and a stiff entry fee was required and the tournament was a long one, held at a time other than the trades holidays, then the ordinary players, though amateur, would absent themselves.

The Separation

The mingling in Scotland of the gentlemen and professionals had been a fact of life for centuries. At St Andrews, Old Tom was made welcome at the nearby Ladybank Club playing off a special handicap, and he regularly played with amateur partners in challenges. Davie Strath and John Ball played a match for £100 over four rounds and the amateur A. M. Ross recalled playing the professional Davie Strath 'for a very great stake, much greater than I [Ross] would play for now [1898]'.[66] The gentlemen amateurs like Ross had regularly played for money, huge sums of money, and this continued into the late 1800s, and betting within the Honourable Company continued at a high level. The amateurs competing in the Open, including John Ball of Liverpool, had regularly accepted the prize money allocated to their place, at least until 1878.

The organisers of the first Amateur Championship, a group of Liverpool enthusiasts, also had to gather their thoughts in 1884 to plan for this first national amateur event. The tournament was evolving from the circuit of meetings at some clubs in the autumn of each year. The minutes of the planning meeting at Liverpool show the difficulty in keeping the competition open, yet closed to undesirables. The Liverpool captain stated that it was not in the interests of golf if 'a valuable prize [i.e. the Amateur Championship] was won by a fisherman or weaver from Scotland'.[67]

There is no evidence that the weavers and fishermen wished to join the gentlemen's play, but obstacles were erected. For English players, the solution was to stipulate that the entrant had to be an 'amateur member from a recognised golf club'. But Scotland had many humble members of long-established clubs at St Andrews, Leven, Carnoustie and elsewhere and the amateur tournament was arranged to have no prize money, and a high entry fee. The humbler golfers needed prize money for travel expenses, and as a subsidy for time lost from paid work - in the unlikely event that leave could be obtained. Lastly, the Amateur Championship format was made a week-long, match-play marathon, outside the usual holiday time, an event difficult to attend by ordinary wage-earning players.

A Definition

In the second year of the Amateur Championship, 'amateur' was defined as excluding those who had recently accepted prize money or had made money

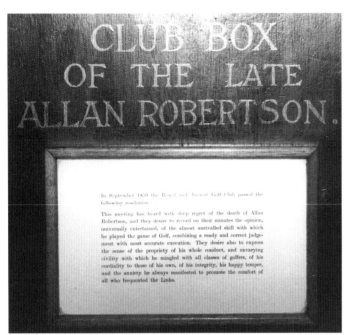

In September 1859 the Royal and Ancient Golf Club passed the following resolution :

This meeting has heard with sharp regret of the death of Allan Robertson, and they desire to record on their minutes the opinion, universally entertained, of the almost unrivalled skill with which he played the game of Golf, combining a ready and correct judgement with most accurate execution. They desire also to express the sense of the propriety of his whole conduct, and unvarying civility with which he mingled with all classes of golfers, of his cordiality to those of his own, of his integrity, his happy temper, and the anxiety he always manifested to promote the comfort of all who frequented the Links.

Allan Robertson was one of many professional members of the St Andrews Golf Club and his club box has been preserved.
By courtesy of ST ANDREWS GOLF CLUB.

from the humble golfing trades such as caddying or clubmaking. The list of entrants for the Amateur Championship shows that they came from the blue-blooded clubs only. In the 1886 Amateur Championship at St Andrews, there were 42 entrants of whom 25 were from St Andrews and all of these were R&A members, in spite of the presence of other flourishing clubs in the town. Two other entrants were disqualified having at one time 'carried clubs' and doubtless these were talented local St Andrews players.[68]

The amateur was increasingly judged by whether or not he had played for money. The new mood gave difficulties at some of the St Andrews clubs. In 1885, 24 years after the Open started, the St Andrews Golf Club still had members like Old Tom who played golf and caddied or taught or made clubs for a living. In 1885, a member, Jack Burns finished well in the Open and as usual accepted the cash prize for his place. Later in the year he won his own club medal at St Andrews. For the first time ever, a dispute arose about his 'status'. Eventually the club members ruled that he could not compete with the other members on equal terms, because of the Amateur Championship's new definition of an amateur. Other clubs also changed their rules in this way. The matter surfaced again when Douglas Rolland, the Elie stonemason, entered for the Leven tournament, having accepted money earlier for joint second place in the 1884 Open. His entry was refused.

Scotland held to traditional collective attitudes in small ways. Scottish professional footballers were accepted as amateur *golfers* while in Scotland. But when Robert Houston, golfing champion of Leven Thistle went to London to play for Tottenham Hotspur, he was regarded as a professional golfer in England, when playing in his leisure time.[69] Hints of separate Scottish thinking on these matters continued. Fred MacKenzie, a member of the New Club at St Andrews, left for America as a professional in 1904, but changed his mind and returned home in 1905. His amateur status was withdrawn, but he was given full membership at the New Club.

St Andrews and Musselburgh

Towards the end of the century, Musselburgh began to lose its importance in the world of golf. Though successful, Musselburgh's golfing mix lacked one essential ingredient, which, like its limited links, was to curtail its activities. The 'Honest Town' was not a major holiday resort. It had no grand hotels, and only a modest beach which did not attract summer visitors. Musselburgh's powerful amateur golfers were largely Edinburgh-based; they could, and eventually did, go elsewhere to play. St Andrews, in contrast, had spacious links on which to lay out more courses and had a large cadre of local golfers, and golfing university students and staff. Throughout the year, this group cherished, defended and extended the golfing facilities at the town, and in summer were joined by influential golfing visitors from England, and elsewhere. As the visitors returned home, particularly to England, after holiday or study, it was the fame of St Andrews that spread.

In all important matters, these visitors deferred to St Andrews, and the new golfers and new golf clubs naturally adopted 'St Andrews Rules' as their code: it was the only one they knew. Many activists in England and elsewhere were members of the Royal and Ancient Golf Club at St Andrews as a result of their summer visits, and the golfing world considered these rules were 'best practice'. For clarification of disputes on the rules, it seems that initially Tom Morris, not the R&A, was appealed to in these matters. Horace Hutchinson recorded that

from all parts of the country, communications reach him on recondite legal questions connected with the game; as an arbiter his authority is acknowledged beyond dispute.

The R&A club membership was rising, and rising fast. By 1869 the number of members had reached the remarkable total of 720, three times that of the membership of The Honourable Company, its rival in antiquity and authority.

REGULATIONS
FOR THE
GAME of GOLF,
ADOPTED BY THE
ST. ANDREW'S SOCIETY OF GOLFERS,
At their Meeting, Friday 1st May, 1812.

The R&A Rules of golf hardly changed from 1812 and were widely copied by the numerous new clubs throughout Britain and abroad, many of whose founder members had visited and played at St Andrews.

By courtesy of the ROYAL AND ANCIENT GOLF CLUB, ST ANDREWS.

Ginger Beer Hole used in commercial advertisement for a local soft drinks firm.

By courtesy of JOHN RIGG.

Refreshment at the Ginger Beer Hole, a stall run by Old Daw. Also seen on sale are new iron golf clubs and golf balls.

By courtesy of the ST ANDREWS UNIVERSITY LIBRARY, COWIE COLLECTION.

The R&A membership, not confined to Scotland, was heading towards being a national body, in the absence of any other organisation to take on this role. Horace Hutchinson was the first of many Englishmen to be captain. And the club has remained a national one, with only occasional tensions between the local and visiting members. Nor was the club deposed from its dominant position by an elected or representational body, and any likely moves in this direction were headed off, usually by prudent co-option to the club's major committees.[70]

Decline at Musselburgh

As St Andrews golf flourished, activity at Mussselburgh started to decline. The Musselburgh golfers on their cramped links increasingly caused irritation to other citizens. The main east coast road to England, the A1, passed on the edge of the first three holes, and travellers were at risk. The local rule had been to play the ball off the road, and it is said that the brassie club with its metal plate evolved at Musselburgh simply to avoid damage to the sole of the wooden clubs. Proposals to enlarge the links to nine holes (from six) had been considered from 1836 onwards, but were repeatedly put aside and delayed until 1870. The local Town Council never seemed to support the golfers, and instead backed the needs of the highly successful race meetings on the same site. This neglect and encroachment on the links caused one local resident to take legal action. In 1859 a Dr Sanderson went to court to prevent the Musselburgh Town Council's plans for extension of the racecourse buildings, which would have further restricted the golf links. He succeeded in preserving the golfing amenity and was rewarded with honorary membership of the Honourable Company.

But eventually a new racecourse and railings were constructed. These remain to this day, cutting through the ancient links and its golf holes. Golf at Musselburgh was increasingly uncomfortable. Long waits occurred at the first tee, and the small course, never long, and without room for expansion, was overplayed. Local rules were brought in to reduce over-use; for instance, only the better golfing pupils at Loretto, the famous local school, were allowed to use iron clubs on the links. Such rules, though well intended, were ineffectual in preserving satisfactory play on the links in the long term.

The exodus of golf clubs from Musselburgh, when it came, was rapid. The Honourable Company, first to arrive, were first to leave – in 1891. They had come down from Edinburgh and now migrated further along the railway line, to their new course at Muirfield, using Longniddry station first, and then Drem later, as their local station for travel. The lush Gullane turf had favoured horse racing and the famous winners Lanercost and Chanticler had been trained there. The East Lothian Race Meeting was held regularly at Gullane and in 1832 the important Musselburgh Race Meeting was transferred to there because of the cholera epidemic. At first, the Honourable Company leased their land at Muirfield, but soon felt secure enough to erect an English-style half-timbered clubhouse. The Burgess and Bruntsfield clubs at Musselburgh also moved out. With a largely Edinburgh membership, they pulled their golfing activities back into Edinburgh in 1893 and 1892 respectively, when the new technology allowed golf course construction on parkland sites in the Edinburgh suburbs. All three clubs left elegant clubhouses behind at Musselburgh as testimony to the wealth of these clubs in the golf boom.

The Musselburgh Opens

In its dominant days Musselburgh had a regular, undisputed slot in the Open Championship circuit. These routine returns to Musselburgh for the Open were disturbed when the Honourable Company decided to move their play away from Musselburgh to Muirfield. When the club moved out, there was confusion about who was to continue to run the Open, and on which course it was to be played. When the decision time came in 1892, to the distress of the Musselburgh players, the Honourable Company assumed that the Open would move from Musselburgh to Muirfield with them. Not unreasonably, the Musselburgh golfers organised another rival 'Open' competition prior to the Muirfield event, one with greater prize money. The new course at Muirfield had not won universal approval, and the devotees of the seaside game dubbed the new Muirfield course as an 'auld water meadow' so clearly did its green, springy turf contrast with the hard links familiar to the regular tournament players.

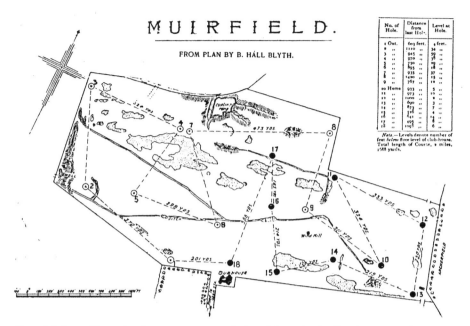

The original lay-out of the Honourable Company's new 5,108 yard course at Muirfield in 1894, after their move south from Musselburgh.

Local Musselburgh players assumed that historical allegiance and sentiment would bring the Championship back to the Honest Town, but it did not. Musselburgh finally dropped out as a tournament venue in 1906. Muirfield's 'meadow' increasingly became a firm and lasting favourite for the Open and other championships.[71]

The Puritans Return

As Scotland recovered from the social crisis and the unstable times of the early 1800s, there was a steady return to more fundamentalist attitudes and behaviour. The established Church in Scotland split in two over a matter of doctrine and religion now mattered again. A stern public morality appeared, or rather, reappeared. The two churches – the Church of Scotland and the Free Church – were both hostile to drinking and gambling and both churches were now cool towards sport. These churches, well supported, also moved to a restoration of Sunday observance, and in its Highland strongholds, the Free Church campaigned against sport in general and football and shinty in particular. The great Free Church preacher Roderick MacLeod of Bracadale and Snizort in the Isle of Skye, standing in the open with 'hailstones dancing on his forehead' preached a famous sermon against whisky, tobacco and shinty. Later, in 1857, he claimed partial victory, but against two of the three only. A Skye diarist later recalled the successes of the temperance campaign. In former days

on market day in Portree the farmers all joined in the ordinary at the village inn, where they sat eating and drinking till they were quite tipsy. No shame attached to the proceedings, and indeed they were quite 'en regle'. Nowadays [1905] things have changed for the better.[72]

The new mood led to hostility against betting. This led in turn to the Lotteries and Betting Houses Act of 1853 which prohibited the use of a 'house, office, room or other place' for betting and gambling. This restriction was not only a moral matter but was also directed at working-class betting as part of

Temperance hotels were part of the new sobriety of the late 1800s.

an attempt to improve industrial efficiency. The mood strengthened in the 1880s and peaked with the formation in 1894 of the National Anti-Gambling League. The aims, personae and activities of this organisation were remarkably similar to the Temperance Movement, and both these groups also encouraged a new mood of Sunday observance. Included within this movement were the Good Templars, who took a fourfold pledge to abstain from alcohol, tobacco, gambling and strong language. These attacks on gambling, drink and Sunday play all affected sport.

The new puritanical attitudes of the middle managerial class were not hypocritical. An example was set. In the new anti-gambling atmosphere, the gentlemen decided eventually to drop their own organised wagering, though on-course betting probably continued in a furtive way for a while into the twentieth century. Herd recalled that he was always told of the shifting odds during a challenge match. He says he was usually rewarded in cash immediately on leaving the last green. Joyce Wethered recalled that a small crowd followed her holiday matches at Dornoch in the early twentieth century with 'lively giving and taking of odds'.[73] Hilton's biography shows that he was betting heavily during the Open and the Amateur Championship at this time, and it seems that Ben Sayers was active in keeping 'a book' at major tournaments until 1904. But club bets were now frowned upon, and the extravagant money prizes involved in the older club events disappeared. Gone was the North Berwick club's 80 guineas prize money on medal days. Levels of betting at the Honourable Company continued to be high but discreet until the 1890s, but by 1900 it was accepted that 2/6 was the limit for a bet in a club golf match, the cost of a ball, as suggested by Walter Simpson.

The Scottish golf clubs took these moral matters seriously. With little debate, the clubs wound down what remained of their noisy dinners and drinking. Sunday golf was abandoned in the late 1800s. At the Prestwick Golf Club there was no Sunday golf from 1891 onwards and in many places Sunday golf was not to return for 50 or more years.

The Temperance Movement

The Temperance Movement also took root with particular energy in Scotland. The drive against the demon drink was a moral crusade at one level, but was also directed at efficiency in the new industrial society. In the 1700s, consumption of alcohol was a regular and conspicuous part of day-to-day life which attracted no censure. The heavy drinking at the golf club dinners was but part of a wider toleration of such consumption shown in earlier Scottish society. Drink, whether fermented or distilled, was regarded as a food and considered by medical men to be strength-giving - until the mid-1800s; these drinks were at least free of disease, unlike drinking water. And beer was cheaper than tea at this time. But in the new work ethic of the industrial nineteenth century, there was wide concern about the effects of alcohol on factory

THE

LIQUOR LAWS FOR SCOTLAND

INCLUDING THE

LICENSING AND EXCISE ENACTMENTS
PRESENTLY IN FORCE:

WITH

RULING DECISIONS OF THE SUPERIOR COURTS FROM 1854 to 1894,
EXPLANATORY NOTES, INDICES AND SCHEDULE
OF LICENCE DUTIES

BY

DAVID DEWAR,
CHIEF CONSTABLE AND PROCURATOR-FISCAL FOR THE CITY
OF DUNDEE

SECOND EDITION

EDINBURGH
WI   GREEN & SONS

THE
WHOLE DOCTRINE OF CALVIN
ABOUT
THE SABBATH AND THE LORD'S DAY:
EXTRACTED FROM HIS COMMENTARIES, CATECHISM, AND
INSTITUTES OF THE CHRISTIAN RELIGION.

BY
ROBERT COX, F.S.A. Scot.

WITH AN APPENDIX,
CONTAINING THE OPINIONS OF LUTHER, MELANCHTHON,
ZUINGLIUS, BEZA, CRANMER, AND KNOX

EDINBURGH:
MACLACHLAN AND STEWART.

The Scottish Liquor Laws increased in complexity in the new temperate society of the later 1800s. There was also powerful advocacy for restoration of Sunday observance.

output and safety. There was a new mood about, even in managerial circles. 'The reign of intoxication is coming to a close. We have no hosts who put the key of the dining room in their pockets, no sage philosophers who spend their happiest hours under the table,' announced a reformer.[74]

In 1879 at North Berwick the Secretary and Treasurer resigned from one of the local golf clubs in protest at its policy of meeting in a pub. Towards the end of the century some clubs became 'teetotal', i.e. not serving alcohol at any time, such was the success of the temperance drive. Even a blue-blooded, conservative club like Nairn, far from the industrial belt, voted to 'go dry' in 1903. In planning for the revival of the Thistle Club at St Andrews the activists met in Purdom's Temperance Hotel in 1865, and about the same time, the new Langholm Golf Club's steering meeting took place in the Eskdale Temperance Hotel, such was the mood of the times. The first relevant legislation in Scotland abolished the public sale of alcohol on Sundays, and pubs were shut on this day from 1853 onwards. A bizarre concession was to allow 'bona fide travellers' not to be disadvantaged in Scotland, and this ill-defined group were free to drink in hotels on Sundays. This, the Forbes-Mackenzie Act, was difficult to enforce and was later widely flouted.

The Puritan Cycle

These changes in opinion and attitudes to drinking, gambling and Sunday sport were but one phase in a long, slow cycle in Scottish affairs, a cycle revolving completely every 100 years or so. These shifts from liberal to puritanical mood and back again started when puritan leaders took charge at the Reformation and attacked the laxity of mediaeval life. In the 1700s the rigours of the Reformation were in turn abolished, and behaviour was less restricted, but by the late 1800s, the 100 year cycle had come round again and the Temperance Movement and the Sabbatarians were confidently back in charge. The cycle was to turn again and liberalisation of Sunday use and attitude to drink appeared again, 100 years later, in the 1960s.

Golf Again Spreads Abroad

The early temporary seedings of the Scottish game abroad, noted in earlier chapters, had appeared on Scottish and British trade routes, and in places reached by Scottish military or colonial men. A revival of enthusiasm for golf in places outside Scotland now occurred in the 1890s, and was to be permanent. Some clubs arose through the enthusiasm of emigrant Scots, and there was also a spread of golf to Europe, via the winter migrations of the wealthy British families, a development unconnected with empire or trade, and from Europe, golf spread to America, via Americans who visited these spas and wintered there, cultivating European society.

The first club and course to appear in Europe was at Pau, a spa town in the Pyrenees which had celebrated spring water with healing powers. Pau had gained a reputation in Britain when, after the Peninsular War, several British units were quartered there, and its climate and therapeutic ambience attracted favourable comment. It then evolved to become a tuberculosis sanatorium, and then to become a favourite resort in winter for the leisured rich from colder climes. As golf became popular in Britain, in 1856 Pau was first in

Europe to set up a golf club; the weather was suitable for play by the winter migrants. The Duke of Hamilton, from an ancient golfing family, was a founder member and Clark, the author of *Golf - a Royal and Ancient Game* played, and died in Pau.[75]

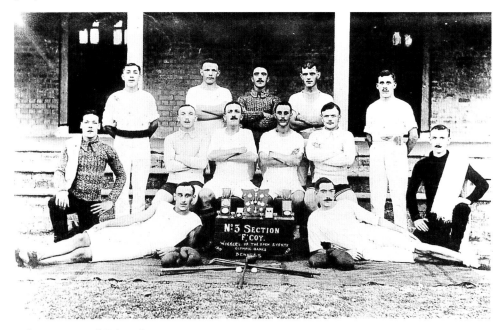

Military sport in the Empire included golf. The winners of the Benares 'Olympic Games' are shown with their trophies and golf clubs.

The Fame of Biarritz

A more fashionable, but more decadent, European resort was Biarritz: it was also to have its place in early European golf after the club was set up in 1888. At this Basque fishing village, the Emperor Napoleon III built a palace for his Empress Eugénie, and from 1854 onwards, Biarritz became the French summer court. It was a dazzling playground for European aristocracy. The winter season started on 1st October and ended in June, when the English sporting season started. Biarritz became a haunt of British aristocracy, and rich Americans, keen to acquire a veneer of European culture and polish, began to arrive. The town had a tradition of discretion, and the rich and famous could and did abandon their show of outward respectability while staying in the town. Later, during the season here, King Edward VII could be openly accompanied by his mistress Mrs Keppel, though the long-standing affair was not openly admitted in Britain. The King also patronised Mariánské Láznê in Czechoslavakia and a golf course opened there. When Prime Minister Campbell-Bannerman resigned in 1908, the King was in Biarritz and declined to return to London; Asquith, a golfer, had to travel instead to the spa to be invited to form a government.[76] Other resorts also had golf courses and North Berwick sent out David Grant to the Dinard Club in Ille-et-Villaine to be their first professional.

This early spread of golf to the French winter resorts also explains the inexplicable, namely that there was an early triumph in the Open Championship by a Frenchman. This winner of the Open in 1907 was Arnaud Massy. He came from the La Boulie Club, but he had begun to play professional golf by a very Scottish route, since he had been a caddie at Biarritz for British visitors, and had spent time at North Berwick in Ben Sayers' shop, during which time he married a local girl. Nor was his Open win unexpected: he had been close to taking the title in previous attempts.

Cannes and the Grand Duke

One important member of this élite European gentlemen's golfing world was the Grand Duke Michael, brother of Tsar Alexander III. Banished from Russia following his unsuitable but romantic marriage to a German princess, his fate was to roam Europe thereafter and in the social tango round Europe, his base seems to have been at Cannes. He departed from the usual fashionable circuit of resorts by visiting Scotland, and there he learned to play golf. At Cannes he was the dominant figure in an elegant era. He was founder and perpetual President of the golf club in 1892 and its golfing uniform was derived from the Romanoff colours. The Cannes club had an annual subscription of £5 and quickly enrolled 260 members. The Duke was in command and his natural authority and his Scottish training meant he was deferred to without question in matters golfing: nor did lunch start without him. Also frequenting Cannes and playing at the club were the Tennants, the volatile, aristocratic North Berwick family.

Though Europe played a crucial role in starting American golf, and had vitality, European golf seems to have entered a decline later. This loss of interest is easily explained. No enthusiasm for golf was evinced by the natives of France, except the caddies. The interest was only kept up by visitors, and as the British upper classes dropped golf and moved back to their traditional sports, so European golf declined. Golf appeared briefly at The Hague in 1893 – where colf had been popular in mediaeval times. But it was a British expatriate sport only: golf in the Low Countries took time to emerge again. And domestic French golf withered and died, though small tournaments attracted British players from time to time. Massy was the first and last French winner of the Open, thus far.

Prince Michael of Russia (centre), Life President of the club, with the Captain and Secretary of Cannes Golf Club. The members sported the club uniform based on their captain's Romanoff colours.

North American Beginnings

Canada had tentatively started golf prior to any interest in the game in the United States.[77] In Canada the activists were Scots sent out from Scotland, often businessmen, and these golfers included a remarkable number of bank employees. As in England, the new North American pioneers faced ridicule and complaint if they attempted to play as at home, and any play in the Scottish manner on public land was met with disbelief and hostility. At best, the balls were picked up and returned to the player; at worst there were complaints to the authorities about the danger of the game. The pioneer Scottish golfers of the Montreal club laid out their first course in a public park, but as their secretary explained later in the *Golfing Annual* of 1888-89:

> *Our green here is a public park, and therefore great care is required to be taken when playing, as there are so many people upon it, especially nursery maids and children, and should anyone be hurt I fear the city would step in and stop us.*
> *Our old country cry of 'fore' is no use here.*

In Scotland the cry of 'fore' gave an ancient, recognised warning to others on public land: the rest of the world was not ready for such subtleties in their parks.

But the first notice of golf in Canada came earlier, in 1854. A Scottish sailor aged 16 came ashore from a military vessel. He had played golf at Musselburgh and brought clubs with him on the voyage. He played a game by himself on the Plains of Abraham, and a newspaper reporter saw him hitting the ball, spoke to him and wrote up the story. The name of the man, as given by the reporter, was William Dibman. The Dibman legend grew and grew, but the man remained a mystery. However, the newspaper reporter had been inattentive: the player's name was in fact Doleman, a notable Scottish golfer and top amateur in the Open Championship on nine occasions between 1866 and 1884.[78]

Some native Canadians, led by Alexander Dennistoun, an Edinburgh timber merchant, founded the Royal Montreal Club in 1873, and the Royal Quebec Golf Club was set up shortly after, also with Scottish help, from James Hunter, a native of Prestwick, married to the only daughter of 'Old' Tom Morris. The Toronto Golf Club started in 1876 and employed George Cumming, a Scottish professional brought from Bridge of Weir in Renfrewshire. Cumming was to be known as the 'Father of Canadian Golf'. A charismatic teacher of golf and a skilled clubmaker, he taught both to many of the first generation of Canadian golfers, amateur and professional, and he designed many courses in Canada.

Many smaller courses and clubs appeared after the establishment of these now-famous early Canadian clubs. A typical vignette is from the town of Brantford, which then had a population of 10,000. A new Scottish employee had arrived at the Bank of British North America, and he laid out a four-hole course on the banks of the river. In 1879 the *Brantford Courier* announced thoughtfully that 'a golf club, whatever that is, has been formed in the city'.[79] It was Canada's fourth golf club: the links are now long gone, covered by the growth of the city, but the club thrives elsewhere.

TO SCOTSMEN.

A FEW TRUE SONS OF SCOTIA, eager to perpetuate the remembrance of her Customs, have fixed upon the 25th DECEMBER and the 1st JANUARY, for going to the Priests' Farm, to

PLAY AT GOLF.

Such of their Countrymen as choose to join them, will meet them before TEN o'Clock, A.M., at D. M'ARTHUR'S *INN*, Hay-Market. Steps have been taken to have CLUBS provided.

A *Montreal Herald* advertisement in 1826 proposing a new golf club. They used the traditional winter season to commence play.
By courtesy of JAMES BARCLAY, from his *Golf in Canada* 1992.

Canadian golf continued to be favoured, and several Canadian clubs and institutions obtained the 'Royal' title. In 1895, Lord Aberdeen, Governor-General, presented the nation with the Aberdeen Cup for a national amateur tournament, which was won in its inaugural year by a Scotsman, Tom Harley.

American Golf

The early phase of American golf can be seen as the work of a number of pioneers. No single player or advocate emerges from this time to be credited as the only founding father, and a number of independent innovations can be seen in the early days. Perhaps another view can be taken: golf was a sport whose time had come, and a number of people and places caught the mood. A number of towns have made claims to have been first in America to revive golf, and perhaps the priority of some well-established societies needs to be looked at again.[80]

In these important events, there was no significant re-emergence in America of any latent golf at its ancient sites in the Virginias and Carolinas. Instead, the game re-emerged and persisted in the New York area. In this new era, it was played not on common land, but at custom-built expensive clubs and courses. The major American input came from the American experience of golf at the European spas and thence to Long Island and New York, with only a modest Scottish input at the start.

The Dunfermline Link

John Reid had emigrated to New York from Dunfermline in Fife and, like Andrew Carnegie from the same town, had done well in iron. It seems that Reid was not a player, but was aware of golf from his childhood. In 1887 Reid, now leisured and wealthy but restless, induced his friend Robert Lockhart, also from Dunfermline, to purchase equipment for golf during Lockhart's trip to Scotland in 1887. It is said that Lockhart, a linen buyer, had previously attempted a solitary game in New York's Central Park, but, after complaints, had been warned off by the police. Six clubs were to be obtained from Tom Morris, plus two dozen balls. Lockhart made these purchases and shipped the clubs back to New York in the traditional golf box, filled with sawdust. On 22nd February 1888, on Reid's pasture land, Reid and some friends experimented with the clubs bought by Lockhart, whose interest had now faded.

Reid and his friends were smitten with the game and ordered more clubs from Scotland. As summer 1888 came, they moved from these three rough holes to a larger, 30-acre site nearby, owned by a butcher. On November 18th 1888, over dinner, Reid and his friends formed their informal club, unaware of its historic importance: their tiny, light-hearted 'St Andrews Golf Club', is certainly the oldest of the surviving American golf clubs. The regular players were Reid, Upham, Holbrook, Putnam and Tallmage, five in all.[81] They had no clubhouse and had to move their low-key activities a number of times, when the land was diverted to other use. The third of these moves was to an apple orchard of 34 acres, and they eventually reached their present location in 1897. Andrew Carnegie was a member later, keeping up the Dunfermline link. Carnegie was eventually to retire from business, as the richest man in the world, to

John Reid, from Dunfermline in Fife, was one of the founder members of the St Andrews Golf Club in New York.

194

The Apple Tree Gang - using an orchard in the early days of their New York St Andrews Golf Club.

return to Scotland and buy Skibo Castle near Dornoch in 1897, devoting himself to philanthropy, including support of golf at the local Dornoch club.

While these New York players were playing in primitive conditions, and without a clubhouse, golf started in Long Island. The Shinnecock Hills Golf Club, founded in 1891, was the result of local enthusiasm by a group of six Long Island summer residents, citizens who moved from New York to Southampton in summer. They had local linksland suitable for a course. But there is still controversy about the formative events at this club. One account has it that Willie Davis, the Scottish-born Toronto professional, laid out the new course. On the other hand, other accounts say that Willie Dunn, while at Biarritz in 1889, was visited by a group of three members of the proposed club – Vanderbilt, Mead and Cryder – and they invited Dunn to design their course on Long Island. There was a delay and Dunn did not arrive until March 1891, it is said. Up to 4,000 acres were available and, well financed from the start, the club built not only a course but a clubhouse, the first such building ever in America.

Newport, also on Long Island, also had early golf links with Europe, and soon formed a club. The local sugar baron, Theodore Havemeyer, had been in Pau in the winters of 1884 and 1885 and built himself nine holes in Newport. Eventually the golf club started in 1893, the third club to be formed in America, and was the first venue for both the US Open and the US Amateur.

The number of golf clubs in America rose from one in 1888 to 16 in 1893, and to 41 in 1895. By the start of the new century there were 1,040 clubs in the USA. It was a socially exclusive game from the start, but without some of the traditional attitudes of English golf. In particular, women members were admitted from the start, and the professional golfer had a high status within the club.

Associated American Trades

Scotland provided professionals, greenkeepers and designers to service this American golf boom, and from Scotland also came clubmakers, golf course architects and journalists, and as usual they were accorded natural authority

Theodore Havemeyer, founder of the Newport Golf Club.
By courtesy of the UNITED STATES GOLF ASSOCIATION.

195

James Dalgleish, the pioneer professional in Kansas, shown here as an apprentice clubmaker at the Glasgow Golf Club in 1885 before emigrating. He is second from the right in the back row.

By courtesy of EDITH DALGLEISH WUERTH.

in all matters golfing. In New York a store called, without embarrassment, 'The Greatest Golf Store in the World' opened at the corner of 42nd Street and 5th Avenue. It was run by John Duncan Dunn and in the clubmaking department there were three young Scotsmen, all called Macdonald. In New York there were other opportunities for clubmakers. Jack Jolly, a St Andrews seaman, suffering from malaria, was left behind in New York when his ship sailed, and instead he got a job with the Bridgewater Golf Manufacturing Company in 1898, later bought by the Glasgow St Mungo Golf Ball Company. He designed and marketed the successful liquid-centre Kempshall ball.

It seems that Jolly acted as an agent for the immigrant professionals, mostly from Scotland. He met them on arrival, and helped find employment for them at the new golf clubs. He stocked their professionals' shops from his warehouses, and to assist them gave extended credit until they were established.[82]

In this expanding market in America, Scottish clubs and balls sold well. Willie Park realised the potential and appointed agents and opened a shop in New York. In these pioneer days, the course designers had opportunities, and

Dunn, Park, Macdonald and later Donald Ross from Dornoch, had steady work available. At the growing edge of the expanding country there were opportunities for low-budget designs. New low-cost designers emerged, notably Tom Bendelow, an Aberdonian, who first took a job as a journalist in New York. He charged a modest flat fee of $25 for his visit and design of a course, marking it out and advising in one day, as did the pioneer Scottish 'stakers'. True to his origins, he pioneered low-cost municipal golf and only later turned to more ambitious projects at the upper end of the market, notably his layout at Merion.

Macdonald's Role

But the best golfer in America was not involved in the pioneering days of American golf in New York or on Long Island. Charles Blair Macdonald was born in Chicago in 1855.[83] He was sent to study at St Andrews University where his grandfather, an R&A member, started his play on the links and Macdonald turned into a golfer of skill. He was known to local golfers, including Tom Morris, in whose shop he had a locker, and soon the American was involved in some local challenge matches.

On his return to America in 1875 it is said that he tried to play golf in the New York public parks but, like others before him, he found it impossible. Whatever the reason, Macdonald spent ten years in Chicago without play, from 1875-85, though he returned to Britain three times and did play then. During this time, the pioneer American players became active near New York. Macdonald's chance came when he was asked to design a new course at Chicago and he laid out a seven-hole course at Belmont in 1892. Two novelties were required. He arranged for piped water to nourish the otherwise arid area, and it is said that the confines of his course meant that an out-of-bounds rule had to be introduced, one of the first of its kind.

Macdonald's greatest moment came when he moved to New York, and found that many others were interested in the game. He involved them in the construction of a new club, the National Links on Long Island, which opened in 1891. He set about the task with drive and enthusiasm, together with a hint of the brashness which was not unknown at the time in America. He wrote to Vardon, Braid, and Park asking them to name the best holes in the world of golf, and their replies included many Scottish holes, taken from St Andrews, Leven, Prestwick, North Berwick and Machrihanish. He took eight holes from this longer list - St Andrews 3rd, 11th, 14th, and 17th, Leven 7th and 9th, North Berwick 14th, and Prestwick 17th. He copied these holes at the new club, and took their essential features. His golf links, a montage of Scottish and English golf, remain to this day. Macdonald, though late on the scene, organised the first official amateur championships in America in 1895, being himself the first winner. He claimed special knowledge of the rules, favoured match-play and was deferred to in any dispute because of his time in Scotland.

Macdonald, a more than competent administrator, made another lasting

Jack Jolly, from St Andrews, was a pioneer of golf equipment manufacture in America, through his St Mungo Company.

By courtesy of St Andrews Golf Club.

Donald Ross from Dornoch, designer of Pinehurst and many other North American championship courses.

By courtesy of John G. Hemmer.

Charles B. Macdonald, a talented and determined player and administrator, was important in the early days of American golf. Retaining his R&A membership, from his student days at St Andrews, he established co-ordination of the rules of golf across the Atlantic.

contribution, helping set up the Amateur Golf Association of the United States, later to be the United States Golf Association. It was founded in 1894 from the first six clubs in America – St Andrews, The Country Club (Brookline), Newport Golf Club, Southampton, Shinnecock Hills and Chicago Golf Club. The new national body proposed to draw up their own rules for the game. But Macdonald was also on the R&A Rules of Golf Committee. His presence on both sides of the Atlantic meant a sensible accord on the rules in America and Britain, rather than an early split; this harmony persists to this day.

Elsewhere in America

The story of early pioneer golf courses in America has been told many times. Less well known is the piecemeal development of local club and municipal golf, and in this a recurring theme is the Scottish input to these less well-known courses and clubs. The activists were often Scots who demanded the presence of Scottish professionals and clubmakers. In Kansas there were events which were probably repeated numerous times in this expansionist age. The local activist was Dr John Binnie, a Scottish surgeon, who founded the Kansas City Country Club in 1894, and is otherwise remembered in America for his seminal five-volume text *Operative Surgery*.[84] Florida's early golf also showed a similar pattern. In the South, a prominent Scottish lawyer called Gillespie bought 60,000 acres unseen in Florida in 1884, and sent out his son, John Hamilton Gillespie, an Oxford graduate, to run it from the poor fishing town of Sarasota on the south-west Gulf Coast. Gillespie laid out a two-hole, then a nine-hole course in 1900, and a clubhouse followed in 1904.[85] The Scots golfers, amateur and professional, were everywhere. The highest club in the world, in Colorado at Cripple Creek (10,060 feet), was the work of R. W. Hadden, the son of a Haddington solicitor, who emigrated and became a gold miner and later a member of the Denver Stock Exchange.[86] New York clubs had the professionals Willie North from Prestwick and Robert White from St Andrews who later became President of the USPGA. Also from Prestwick came David Hunter, pro at Baltusrol and author of *Golf Simplified*, and Henry Whigham, who married Charles Blair Macdonald's daughter, and became editor of *Metropolitan*. Montrose also contributed to the Scottish-American input, with Harry Robb going out to be a player and designer in Kansas, coming from Winton's clubmaking shop. Charles Thom, pro at Shinnecock Hills for 55 years, was also from Montrose. If a club could not obtain a Scots professional golfer, then they might make do with a Scots professional footballer.

In the USA teaching by the professional was expected from dawn to dusk on practice areas rather than by teaching on a playing round. The professionals might only do the summer season with a North American club and then return home for traditional caddying and play in winter in Scotland. The contracts were usually for one year, giving a variety of teachers for the new clubs and this encouraged the mobility of professionals at this time. Until 1960, at the USPGA annual meeting dinner, those assembled sang the song *Loch Lomond*, a reminder of the ancient habit of groups of lonely wandering Scots in America to sing this song when in the bars and taverns as a signal to other wandering Scots to join them.

America had other advantages. The professional might be expected to be master of ceremonies and a good mixer and host. In the new democratic spirit of the frontier, the Scots were accepted on their merits and as equals. Harold Sanderson, the émigré professional recalled his early days in America:

> *I never was to feel like an employee or something less than a first class citizen. Why? we are an immigrant nation. I never considered golf a rich man's game in America, though I did in England...*[87]

Back in Scotland, Scottish golfers and their families became accustomed to expansive American tales from the expatriates. The magazine *Golfing* recorded in 1902 that James Foulis, a native of St Andrews, and formerly foreman in Tom Morris' shop, had returned home to tell of his success in American golf. Foulis had won the US Open in 1896 with a score of 78 and 74. He was employed as a professional at Chicago, at the suggestion of C. B. Macdonald, and to the astonishment of his St Andrews friends he explained that he had a greenkeeping staff of eight. By 1902, Foulis had laid out 27 of the 35 early golf courses in the Chicago area.[88]

Lastly, another Scottish export may have travelled with golf. Such was the deference to all things Scottish that, in addition to the necessary use of Scottish designers, Scottish clubmakers and Scottish golf professionals, the club members copied the traditions of the Scottish 19th hole and they increasingly drank Scotch whisky. Whisky and golf, it was noted at the time, went together.[89]

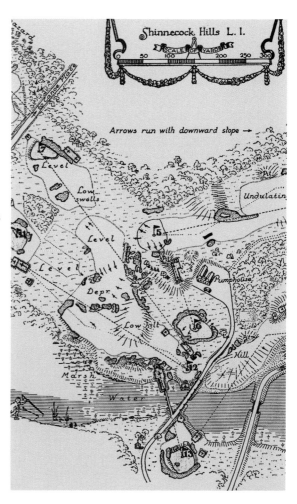

Charles Blair Macdonald copied many well-known British holes in his lay-out for the National Links at Shinnecock Hills in 1907. The seventh hole is based on challenge of the Road Hole, the 17th, at St Andrews.

Ladies in the USA

As golf emerged in America, women did not accept the traditional European female role. American women had been less conditioned against participating in sport and the American Civil War had shaken up traditional attitudes: in postbellum America, women had a new status. American women took to the game of golf, and many country clubs admitted women as equal members from the start. American women's golf can be traced to the European link again. Miss Florence Boit learned the game at Pau, like many men, and while visiting an uncle at Wellesley, Massachusetts, she enthused about the game. As a result, seven holes were built on his estate in 1892. Not surprisingly, the first instructional book on golf for women came from America, not Britain – Genevieve Hecker's *Golf for Women*, published in New York in 1904.

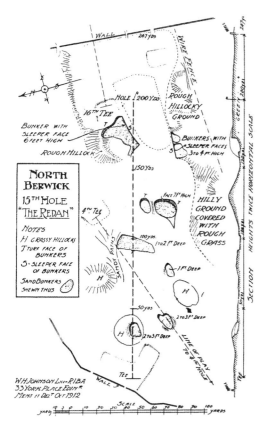

The natural hazards of the North Berwick 'Redan' hole were often copied in the golf boom.
From Aleck Bauer *Hazards* 1913.

Expansion Elsewhere

Irish golf restarted in the north at Belfast in 1881 and in the south at the Curragh in 1883. The Belfast enthusiast was a Scotsman, George Baillie.[90] The early history of Australian golf is still unclear, but the first known golf stroke played there was in 1874 by a Scotsman, the Honourable James Graham.[91] The Melbourne Golf Club was founded in 1874, but ceased a few years later, restarting in 1891, and in Sydney, John Dunsmore made the first local attempt at starting a golf club in 1881. In Australia, the great Sydney store Holdsworth and Macpherson hired Carnegie Clark from Carnoustie to head the golf department, and also from Carnoustie came D. G. Soutar who published the first journal, *The Australian Golfer,* from 1906. James Herd of St Andrews, an Auchterlonie apprentice, went to Tasmania via America as the first professional in the Island in 1905. In 1871 the first New Zealand club started when an émigré Scot, Charles Howden, set up the Dunedin Club.[93] In Malta, the energetic Governor Sir Henry Torrens organised golf in 1888. Golf appeared in the Empire in South Africa where Laurie Waters, a pupil of Tom Morris was the pioneer[94], and shortly afterwards at Calcutta[95], Hong Kong[96] and elsewhere. Study of the biographies of the colonial British governors from this period shows that golf was their commonest sport, exceeding even cricket or fishing. Lord Cromer noted that the first thing the governors did on a new appointment was to create a race-course and found a golf club.[97] In 1903, the Governor of Ceylon failed to attend the Coronation parade and was seen instead at the island's golf club, resulting in censure from London. In Japan in 1900, the first club, organised by a Scotsman called Arthur Groome, appeared at Mount Rokke.

The evolution in each country was similar and the Scots were usually the pace-setters. In Mexico, the first golf club opened in Mexico City, and was called the San Pedro Club – appointing David Honeyman from St Andrews as professional.[98] Nor did the smaller parts of the British Empire, like San Serriffe, lack golf. In Belize (British Honduras - Costa Rica) a medical practitioner called Cran, an Aberdeen graduate born in Fraserburgh, ran the golf club and was its perpetual champion.[99]

Continuing Scottish Expansion

As well as these important international developments, back in Scotland there was steady change and expansion of domestic golf. Municipal links expanded into any spare land available and at St Andrews new courses emerged beyond and beside the Old Course. Those ancient towns who did not own their links took steps to do so. Carnoustie Links were purchased for the town using the traditional way of raising money for public works, namely a grand bazaar, and a similar event occurred at Moniefieth where the links were purchased for the town for about £2,000. Newly popular seaside towns lacking a golf course, notably those on the west coast, made haste to add one to their public amenities, in view of the general benefit to tourism and to attract those wishing to retire to the area. The inland spa towns and hydropathic establishments also felt at a disadvantage and added a golf course if they had none. The Clyde Coast steamers, now linked to railways from Glasgow, carried visitors to the islands and the booming popularity of Arran, Millport and Bute meant a need for golf also.

Other towns, not always in holiday areas, like Aberdeen and Troon, added municipal golf to their amenities. Moorland when cleared made excellent golfing turf, and inland towns could now construct a course, particularly if they were on the railway lines. Each small village on the railway line

The Monifieth Bazaar of 1899 was typical of fundraising events to purchase land for municipal golf clubs late in the nineteenth century.

Courtesy of MITCHELL LIBRARY.

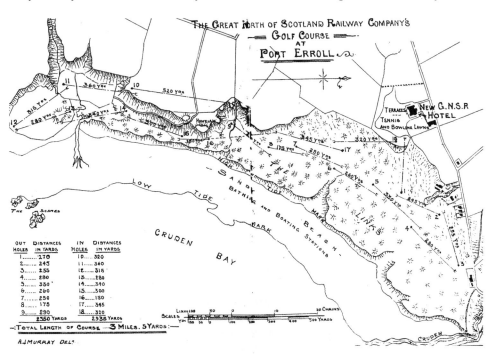

The Cruden Bay Golf Club started as a planned railway company complex involving a hotel, tennis courts, golf course and other recreational facilties.

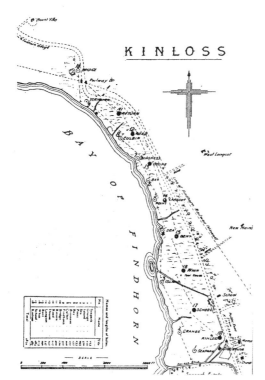

KINLOSS

Kinloss, one of the forgotten links courses in Scotland; the club moved inland to Forres later.

through the Spey Valley, for instance, now added a golf course, usually of nine holes. The railways might assist and could provide surplus equipment such as sleepers for protection of bunkers, tees and pathways. The rising popularity of the bicycle put such courses within reach of most railway stations and most holiday homes.

City Golf

But many of the older golfing areas were now under pressure, like Leith, Musselburgh and Glasgow Green earlier. Golf was restricted by statute at Leith in 1901, and the ground levelled. To protect the citizens an area at Craigentinny was offered instead. In other areas similar pressures made the golfers move. The *Golfers' Annual* for 1887-88 says of the land used for golf at Kingholm in particular, used by three Dumfries golf clubs, 'play is prohibited for two months in summer because of camping, parade and drill.' In 1894 a serious incident occurred on this parkland. A boy, playing on a football pitch adjacent to the golf course was hit by a golf ball and died some days later. The golfers moved shortly afterwards to their present private course.

Golf at Bruntsfield Links in the heart of Edinburgh finally ceased and the city provided municipal golf at the Braid Hills instead. The citizens of Edinburgh showed surprising enthusiasm for this, the ultimate in moorland golf. The revived private Glasgow Club also continued to move steadily outwards from the town centre, as each site in turn became impossible for golf. The Panmure Club was cramped in its activities on public land at Monifieth, and moved to their own links to the north. The narrow Montrose links were now entirely surrounded by houses and the town decided to move golf to the edge of the beach. This meant that the ancient

The ancient public links at Burntisland was still used by golfers *circa* 1910. Golf eventually proved impossible and and a new course was constructed inland.

Royal Albert Club clubhouse was stranded some distance from the new course, and a new clubhouse had to be built.

Suburban clubs appeared in the bigger towns, owning their own land, and an exclusive membership also appeared, with its customary prejudices. And the railway could now take city golfers to the coast. The Glasgow Club became unique in developing a second course of its own on the coast at Gailes, where excellent winter golf pertained.

But golf penetrated the Highlands only reluctantly. In the Celtic areas, in spite of the presence of many visitors, the locals were reluctant players. Oban and Fort Augustus obtained courses, and in the Outer Hebrides, Sir Reginald and Lady Cathcart invited Tom Morris to lay out a course on their wonderful ten miles of linksland on South Uist. Otherwise golf was hard to find in the shinty-playing areas.

But there was still some uncertainty about golf, arising out of the ownership of the land, even at St Andrews. Many towns did not own their links, having sold them in the crisis earlier in the century, and golf continued over land in private ownership, backed only by the vague legal right of 'servitude'. Now with finances improving, the towns wished to buy back the land. A fall in land values towards the end of the century allowed this, and the golf boom gave strength to those who saw the ancient common land as part of the town heritage and amenity. Since golf was part of the tourist attraction, it was desirable that the land should not be in private hands.

Use of railway sleepers in the repair of the North Berwick golf links.

By courtesy of DOREEN SAYERS.

A fund-raising publication for the Dalbeattie Golf Club in Dumfriesshire.

Parliament Acts

The main support came from the notable Burgh Police (Scotland) Act 1892. This important legislation (its intentions are not obvious from the title) gave burghs the power to enlarge their boundaries and make provision for sport.[101] St Andrews, North Berwick, and Carnoustie benefited, and the moving spirit was Provost Peter Brodie of North Berwick. He held office for 24 years as Provost, following another golfing leader – Provost Whitecross – and these towns and their leaders had powerful political friends among the summer visitors. Brodie's success was so important for the Scottish Burghs that he was given a civic dinner in Edinburgh, hosted by the other towns, and he was presented with a gold watch, a silver dish and an inscribed memorial recording this municipal triumph. At St Andrews much of the links was in the hands of the Cheape family, who sold first to the R&A, but compulsory purchase by the town followed.

But in other towns the land remained in private hands. At Prestwick, the linksland had been gifted by the King, not to the town but to the six burgesses, and the land was eventually deemed legally not to belong to the town, and could be sold; the Prestwick club bought it, making it private ground for their club.

Golf was now important in the economy of the holiday towns, and green-keeping was needed to reach higher standards. The visitors were well-off, and seemed happy to be charged for golf for the first time at St Andrews from 1891 onwards, though all local citizens still played for nothing. At Crail in the same year, visitors were 'invited to contribute 1 shilling a month', and a similar proposal was made at Montrose in 1903.

Elsewhere landowners were still keen to off-load land suitable for a golf course. In 1889 the Marchioness of Lansdowne, short of cash, took the advice of her son, the Viceroy of India, and rented out 42 acres for the new Blairgowrie club.

On the west coast the number of clubs rose. In 1892, the Provost of Rothesay, encouraged by the manager of the Hydropathic, stated that 'if Rothesay is to keep up with neighbouring watering places it is necessary that they provide a golf course.' But these holiday courses showed a curious pattern of member-ship. The majority of members of the clubs in holiday areas and even at a club like Kinghorn in Fife, were not local but came from the cities nearby. The Annual General Meetings of these clubs were often held in Edinburgh or Glasgow, rather than at the resort. This lavish provision for summer play gave the local town golfers a golfing paradise at other quiet times of the year, and their golf was heavily subsidised by the visitors.

All round the coast, in the small towns of Scotland, new clubs appeared. In the attractive coastal towns there was still a whiff of Empire in the affairs of the club. At Tain (founded 1890) the main trophy – the Oriental Vase – was presented to the club by Sir Abdul Ghany, Nawab of Dacca, Bengal. The same club added a Baden-Powell Shield in 1900 after the relief of Mafeking. Elsewhere Bombay, Rangoon and Calcutta featured in the prizes of other clubs, and some holes and bunkers allude to military matters - Kruger, Khyber, Spion Kop and Tel el-Kebir.

[57 & 58 VICT.] *St. Andrews Links Act,* 1894. [**Ch. lxxxiv.**]

CHAPTER lxxxiv.

An Act to empower the Commissioners of the city and royal burgh of St. Andrews to acquire the Links of St. Andrews for a public park and recreation ground and for other purposes. [20th July 18?

WHEREAS the inhabitants of the city and royal burgh of St. Andrews and others resorting thither have from time immemorial played golf and other games upon and used for recreation and other purposes the pasture and waste ground commonly called the Links of St. Andrews within and adjoining the said city and burgh (herein-after called " the burgh ") :

And whereas the whole of the said links prior to the year one thousand seven hundred and ninety-seven belonged to the burgh but were then or thereafter almost entirely alienated subject to certain reservations and servitudes and inter alia of the right of playing golf thereon :

And whereas the number of persons resorting to the said links for the playing of golf and for other purposes has in recent years largely increased and the present golf course is frequently over-crowded and it is expedient and would be for the advantage of the inhabitants of the burgh and the public generally that the said links should be acquired and held by the provost magistrates and council of the burgh as the Commissioners of the burgh under and for the purposes of the Burgh Police (Scotland) Act 1892 (herein-after called " the Commissioners ") as a public park and place of public resort and recreation and that facilities for the playing of golf and other games thereon should be improved and increased and provision made for laying out new golf courses and for the maintenance management regulation and control of the said links and of all golf courses thereon and that the Commissioners should be empowered to levy reasonable charges from persons or bodies using the golf courses :

55 & 56 Vict.
c. 55.

And whereas it is also expedient that the Commissioners should be authorised to borrow money for the purposes of this Act and to

[*Price* 1s.]   A   1

Many of the ancient Scottish golf links were returned to public owner-ship and public use when the Burgh Police (Scotland) Act 1892 allowed compulsory purchase of their former public land by the towns.

One little incident at the Blairgowrie Club gave notice of a new social change. In 1900 the entrance to the club from the road had to be widened to allow entry of a motor car belonging to a member.

The Eclipse ball, of secret composition, rivalled the gutty but only for a while.

The Golf Industry

This rapid expansion of golf brought work to many. At St Andrews the golf-related industry thrived. Forgan was the most successful businessman in the local group, and in the 1890s his firm was the world's biggest producer of golf clubs. Stewart of St Andrews had the reputation for the best iron clubs, and the town had a modest output of gutty balls, mostly from Willie Auchterlonie. At North Berwick, Ben Sayers also had clubmaking success, a firm which, like Nicoll of Leven, was to remain in the market when the older St Andrews firms had been eclipsed.

Carnoustie

The last golf town in Scotland to boom in this century was Carnoustie, beside Barry Links to the east of Dundee on the rail line to Aberdeen. It had ancient associations with golf.[102] Maule's play on Barry Links in the early 1500s is one of the most ancient references to golf available. There is some evidence of continuing interest in golf here in the early 1800s, and Allan Robertson remodelled the links in 1848. The links became much more popular when the railway ran from Dundee through Carnoustie to the north, and the Earl of Dalhousie brought in George Morris as greenkeeper about this time. Morris became tenant of the Golf Inn in Park Avenue and then became coachman and caddie to Robert Chambers from 1864 until his death in 1888.

Carnoustie's reputation reached its peak in the early 1900s. As at St Andrews and Montrose, a number of private clubhouses arose round the public links. Less austere and less academic than St Andrews, less fashionable

McEwan's business at Musselburgh continued to flourish.

By courtesy of DAVID STIRK and MRS I. T. HENDERSON

Forgan shop interior showing the founder Robert Forgan.

than North Berwick, Carnoustie was known as the 'Monaco of the North' and met middle-class needs for an economical seaside holiday. One hundred caddies were employed each day, and of all the towns, though peaking late, it had the biggest local playing population at this time, and led to a remarkable reputation for producing professional golfers, particularly for North America. From 1898-1930, it is thought that 150 club professional jobs in North America and elsewhere were filled by Carnoustie émigrés.

Carnoustie's influence abroad was considerable. In addition to professional players, others had other careers in golf. Kerr Petrie from Carnoustie went to the USA in 1908 and became a pioneer golf writer with the *New York Herald Tribune.* Carnoustie players and teachers influenced a generation of American golfers, and the town's main influence was through the Simpsons. Alex Simpson of the Dalhousie Club evolved a new swing, with the feet closer together and hitting the ball with a draw. This swing passed via the local players, notably the Smith brothers and Archie Simpson, to Stewart Maiden, who left Carnoustie for Atlanta in 1908, where at East Lake he taught and influenced Bobby Jones throughout his career. He also coached Alexa Stirling. Alex Smith went to the USA in 1898, and Will Smith also travelled in 1898 to be professional at Shinnecock Hills, winning the US Open in 1899 by eleven shots. Many reached other parts of the world from Carnoustie, including Germany, where Cuthbert Butchart won the German Open. The Carnoustie missionaries were unanimous on one point: the Germans would never make golfers.

Towns near Carnoustie like Monifieth and Montrose with ancient golfing traditions also contributed to the final period of staffing the great Scottish golfing diaspora. Monifieth sent out three professionals of note to the USA – Dave Livie,

Stages in making the gutty ball.

Marty Cromb and Reggie Myles. From Montrose to America came at least ten professionals. Alex Findlay, designer of over one hundred American courses, including Nebraska in 1885, finally settled at Boston's Woodland Golf Club and brought over Charlie Burgess from Montrose as professional, a post he held for 32 years. Burgess is remembered not only as coach to the Harvard soccer team, but also as the golf teacher who brought Francis Ouimet to fame.

This huge exodus of golfing talent from Scotland must have weakened the game at home. Had there been opportunities, sporting and social, for these men in Britain, the story of competitive golf in the twentieth century might have been different.

Envoi

Scotland had given a new sport to the rest of the world, and gave most of the support for the emerging game of golf in other lands. There is no point at which the Scottish dominance ended, but when Tom Morris died in 1908, the important role of Scotland's east coast towns seemed to pass away with him. His fatal injury followed a fall in the New Club at St Andrews, where he was a member, and there followed the biggest funeral ever seen in St Andrews.

Scottish golf was now reaching all parts of the world, but did so in new forms, and beyond Scotland the game was different, one based on private property and exclusive clubs. The traditional Scottish game could not be transplanted to new soil.

'Old' Tom Morris, patriarch of St Andrews golf, keeper of the Green, club-maker and course designer.

FURTHER READING

As always I. T. Henderson and D. I. Stirk *Golf in the Making* Crawley 1979 is full of information, as is David Stirk *The Great Clubmakers* London 1992. Much of the literature of the period is now relevant, beginning with H. B. Farnie *The Golfer's Handbook* Cupar 1857, through to Horace Hutchinson's works, notably his *Badminton Library: Golf* of 1890. For personal accounts of golf see James Balfour *Reminiscences of Golf on St Andrews Links* Edinburgh 1887, H. Thomas Peters *Reminiscences of Golf and Golfers* Edinburgh 1890, Rev J. G. McPherson *Golf and Golfers, Past and Present* Edinburgh 1891 and Alistair Adamson *Allan Robertson, Golfer* Worcs 1985. The historians of the Royal and Ancient Golf Club of St Andrews tell us much about this period - J. B. Salmond *The Story of the R and A* London 1956, H. S. C. Everard *A History of the Royal and Ancient Golf Club, St Andrews* Edinburgh 1907, J. B. Salmond *The Story of the R&A* and P. A. Ward-Thomas *The Royal and Ancient* Edinburgh 1980. There is much social history in Stewart Hackney *Bygone Days on the Old Course* Dundee 1990 and his *Carnoustie Links: Courses and Players* Dundee 1988; see also D. H. Fleming *Historical Notes and Extracts Concerning the Links of St Andrews 1552-1893* Cupar 1893. Other clubs have had careful study in this period, notably David Smail's *Prestwick Golf Club* Prestwick 1990. For Fife, see the Fife Golfing Association's *A History of Golf Clubs in Fife* Leven 1989, and Musselburgh has had attention in George M. Colville *Five Open Champions and the Musselburgh Story* Musselburgh 1980; see also John Adams *The Parks of Musselburgh* Worcs 1991 and Philip Knowles *A History of the Bruntsfield Allied Golf Club 1856-1996* Edinburgh 1997.

For discusson of amateur and professional sport see Peter Lewis *The Dawn of Professional Golf* Ballater 1995, Wray Vamplew *Pay Up and Play the Game* Cambridge University Press 1988, J. A. Mangan (ed) *The Cultural Bond: Sport, Empire and Society* London 1992 and Richard Holt *Sport and the British: a Modern History* Oxford 1989. Early professional British golf is described well in Henry Leach *Great Golfers in the Making* London 1907, and for the early American professional game see the account by Al Barkow *Gettin' to the Dance Floor* London 1986.

The best memoirs of players are W. W. Tulloch *The Life of Tom Morris* London 1908, 'Andra' Kirkaldy *Fifty Years of Golf: my Memories* London 1921 and Sandy Herd *My Golfing Life* London 1923. Corinthian golf is described in Horace G. Hutchinson *Fifty Years of Golf* London 1919 (reprinted USGA 1985), J. L. Low *Concerning Golf* London 1903 and J. L. Low *F. G. Tait: a Record* London 1900. There is much valuable material in John Kerr's *The Golf-Book of East Lothian* Edinburgh 1895, and this book is the last account of golf as viewed from Scotland. The curious story of early women's golf in Scotland has yet to be told, but there is some material in Mabel Stringer *Golfing Reminiscences* London 1924, May Hezlet *Ladies' Golf* London 1904, Elinor Nickerson *Golf: a Woman's History* North Carolina 1987 and Rosalynde Cossey *Golfing Ladies* London 1984.

Golf in North America is well dealt with by James A. Barclay *Golf in Canada: a History* Toronto 1992, Herbert Warren Wind *The Story of American Golf* New York 1956, Charles Blair Macdonald *Scotland's Gift - Golf* New York 1928, and for Europe see James Nolan *Of Golf and Dukes and Princes: Early Golf in France* Worcs 1982. For Ireland see the excellent William H. Gibson *Early Irish Golf* Naas 1988. There is a careful description of the Scottish contribution to international golf course design in Geoffrey Cornish and Ronald Whitten *The Golf Course* New York 1981.

For a professional bibliography of golf see R. E. Donovan and J. S. F. Murdoch's *The Game of Golf and the Printed Word 1566-1985* New York 1988, and also the thematic Don Kennington *The Sourcebook of Golf* The Library Association 1981.

For golf clubmakers in this period see the comprehensive work by Pete Georgiady *Compendium of British Club Makers* Greensboro 1994, and club professionals are listed in Alan Jackson *A Register of Professional Golfers 1887-1930* Worcs 1994. For the history of the caddie see David Stirk *Carry your Bag, Sir: the Story of Golf's Caddies* London 1989 and the language of golf is found in the scholarly work by Peter Davies *The Historical Dictionary of Golfing Terms* London 1993.

CHAPTER SEVEN

OUR TIMES

I n 1896 the Reverend John Kerr concluded his great 'Golf-Book of East Lothian' thus... *we have no sympathy with those fin de siecle alarmists who say that golf has been played out. Rather do we believe that as yet we see but the beginnings of its career as a game. Its history will become more difficult to write as the years go by, bringing with them new triumphs in new territories...*

John Kerr's reflection on the state of golf at the end of the nineteenth century suggests that he and others saw a fundamental change in the game coming, one which had caused dismay to the traditionalists. He and others had grown up when the game was firmly rooted in Scotland. All the serious players and all the major clubs were Scottish; the administrators, writers and historians of the game, mostly Scottish, were a small group known to each other. Kerr hints that some of this group had concluded that the golf boom was coming to an end, and that this meant the end of golf as they knew it.

Kerr was more optimistic: the game would survive and evolve, but would be different, and in this he was right. He anticipated the new international diversity of the game. The evolution of golf in his time had a certain simplicity since it had all happened in Scotland and Kerr knew that the new game would show pluralism, novelty and variety. But the transplanted game was not the original game. Outside Scotland, golf was necessarily a game based on private clubs and private courses, rather than the democratic game of the links. Kerr had noticed this and he concluded that the new 'club system is destroying the Scottish game'.[1]

This book has examined how the game evolved in Scotland and then spread elsewhere, and no further study of the game world-wide is made here. Many excellent accounts exist of the game's internal progress in those parts of the world which golf reached in the twentieth century, and this chapter looks instead at the surviving game in Scotland. Scotland retains its position as the historical home of golf, with a respectable showing in competitive golf, a presence in journalism, publishing and golf equipment manufacture, and a

OPPOSITE: Travel to distant courses was still by train in the early twentieth century, and numerous special golfing offers were available.

211

The Championships

Winners of Open Championship.

For Rules governing the Championship, see pages 108–109.

THE BELT.

Year.	Winner.	Score.	Venue.	Ents.
1860—W. Park, Musselburgh ..	.. ..	174 ..	Prestwick.	8
1861—Tom Morris, sen., Prestwick	.. ..	163	Prestwick.	8
1862—Tom Morris, sen., Prestwick	.. ..	163	Prestwick.	8
1863—W. Park, Musselburgh ..	.. ..	168	Prestwick.	14
1864—Tom Morris, sen., Prestwick	.. ..	167	Prestwick.	16
1865—A. Strath, St Andrews ..	.. ..	162	Prestwick.	10
1866—W. Park, Musselburgh ..	.. ..	169	Prestwick.	..
1867—Tom Morris, sen., St Andrews ..	..	170	Prestwick.	..
1868—Tom Morris, jun., St Andrews ..	..	157	Prestwick.	..
1869—Tom Morris, jun., St Andrews	.. ..	154	Prestwick.	14
1870—Tom Morris, jun., St Andrews	.. ..	149	Prestwick.	17

The belt having been won thrice in succession by young Tom Morris, it became his property, and the Championship remained in abeyance for one year, when the present cup was offered for yearly competition, to be held by the leading club in the district in which the winner resided.

THE CUP.

Year.	Winner.	Score.	Venue.	Ents.
1872—Tom Morris, jun., St Andrews	.. ..	166	Prestwick.	8
1873—Tom Kidd, St Andrews	.. ..	179	St Andrews.	26
1874—Mungo Park, Musselburgh	.. ..	159	Musselburgh.	32
1875—Willie Park, Musselburgh	.. ..	166	Prestwick.	18
1876—Bob Martin, St Andrews	.. ..	176	St Andrews.	34
(David Strath tied but refused to play off).				
1877—Jamie Anderson, St Andrews	.. ..	160	Musselburgh.	24
1878—Jamie Anderson, St Andrews ..	..	157	Prestwick.	26
1879—Jamie Anderson, St Andrews ..	..	170	St Andrews.	..
1880—Bob Ferguson, Musselburgh ..	..	162	Musselburgh.	..
1881—Bob Ferguson, Musselburgh ..	..	170	Prestwick.	..
1882—Bob Ferguson, Musselburgh ..	..	171	St Andrews.	40
1883—W. Fernie, Dumfries ..	.. ..	159	Musselburgh.	41
After a tie with Bob Ferguson, Musselburgh.				
1884—Jack Simpson, Carnoustie ..	..	160	Prestwick.	30
1885—Bob Martin, St Andrews ..	..	171	St Andrews.	51
1886—D. Brown, Musselburgh ..	..	157	Musselburgh.	46
1887—W. Park, jun., Musselburgh ..	..	161	Prestwick.	36
1888—Jack Burns, Warwick ..	.. ..	171	St Andrews.	53
1889—W. Park, jun., Musselburgh ..	..	155	Musselburgh.	42
After a tie with Andrew Kirkaldy.				
1890—Mr John Ball, Royal Liverpool	.. ..	164	Prestwick.	40
1891—Hugh Kirkaldy, St Andrews ..	..	166	St Andrews.	82
After 1891 the competition was extended to seventy-two holes and for the first time entry money was imposed				
1892—Mr H. H. Hilton, Royal Liverpool	.. ..	305	Muirfield.	66
1893—W. Auchterlonie, St Andrews ..	..	322	Prestwick.	72
1894—J. H. Taylor, Winchester ..	..	326	Sandwich.	94
1895—J. H. Taylor, Winchester ..	..	322	St Andrews.	73
1896—H. Vardon, Ganton ..	.. ..	316	Muirfield.	64
After a tie with J. H. Taylor. Replay scores for thirty-six holes : Vardon, 157 ; Taylor, 161.				
1897—Mr H. H. Hilton, Royal Liverpool	.. ..	314	Hoylake.	86
1898—H. Vardon, Ganton ..	.. ..	307	Prestwick.	78
1899—H. Vardon, Ganton ..	.. ..	310	Sandwich.	98
1900—J. H. Taylor, Mid-Surrey ..	..	309	St Andrews.	81
1901—James Braid, Romford ..	..	309	Muirfield.	101
1902—Alex. Herd, Huddersfield ..	..	307	Hoylake.	112
1903—H. Vardon, Totteridge ..	..	300	Prestwick.	127
1904—Jack White, Sunningdale ..	..	296	Sandwich.	144
1905—James Braid, Walton Heath ..	..	318	St Andrews.	152
1906—James Braid, Walton Heath ..	..	300	Muirfield.	183
1907—Arnaud Massy, La Boulie ..	..	312	Hoylake.	193
1908—James Braid, Walton Heath ..	..	291	Prestwick.	180
1909—J. H. Taylor, Mid-Surrey ..	..	295	Deal.	204

Scottish dominance of the Open Championship ended abruptly after Auchterlonie's win in 1893.

By courtesy of the GOLFERS HANDBOOK.

The extended St Andrews Auchterlonie family were an important influence in golf and club-making and Willie Auchterlonie was the last home-based winner of the Open Championship.

WILLIE AUCHTERLONIE, 1872–1963
LAURIE AUCHTERLONIE, 1904–1987
WILLIE AND LAURIE, FATHER AND SON, LIVED AND WORKED HERE FROM 1946. WILLIE WAS A FINE CLUBMAKER AND GOLFER, WHO WON THE OPEN CHAMPIONSHIP AT PRESTWICK IN 1893. FROM 1935 UNTIL HIS DEATH IN 1963 HE WAS HONORARY PROFESSIONAL AT THE ROYAL AND ANCIENT GOLF CLUB. THIS SPLENDID SERVICE AT THE R AND A WAS EXTENDED TO FIFTY-TWO YEARS BY LAURIE, WHO WAS HIMSELF A VERY FAMOUS CLUBMAKER, UNTIL HIS DEATH IN AUGUST 1987.

major role in golf administration. But the most robust surviving element of Scottish golf is the persisting tradition of economical golf on public courses. This not only enables mass participation by local players, but also makes Scottish golf attractive to visitors and a place of pilgrimage for the rest of the golfing world.

The Century

In this century of expansion, domestic Scottish golf was to show some cyclical changes in vitality. There were booms in the early part of the century, in the late 1930s and in the 1980s. The most obvious hesitations were during the First and Second World Wars, with their profound effects on British sport in general, and golf in particular. Between the wars, the century showed adverse economic cycles, notably the Depression of the 1930s and lesser ones in the 1950s, 1970s and early 1990s. These all affected golf, particularly private club golf; municipal golf was more resilient. At these times of decline, the clubs had to diversify and look for alternative sources of revenue. The stuffy men's clubs moved slowly towards a broader membership in times of crisis and looked with new interest on women's membership and even the presence of children. In difficult times, golf on Sundays and the serving of drink seemed less impossible, and in war time, opinion swung towards liberal attitudes.

Dominance Gone

At first sight, Scotland's ancient and dominant role in world golf appeared to diminish rapidly in the early part of the twentieth century. Scottish players no longer dominated the main golf events, and innovation in equipment design emerged outside of Scotland. Great St Andrews firms, like Forgan and Morris, and John Letters in Glasgow, were to survive but they steadily lost ground to the bigger southern English firms, and eventually to American manufacturers. In the early twentieth century there were some West of Scotland golf-club making firms which thrived and two new ballmaking companies flourished – the St Mungo Company and Hutchison Main. This second company successfully defeated claims by the American makers of the Haskell ball that they had a patent, and hence a monopoly on the rubber-cored ball.

In the late 1800s Scottish professionals quickly lost their dominance of tournament golf. In the Open Championship prior to 1893, only Jack Burns from England had beaten the Scottish professionals. Home-based Scots disappeared completely from the

The gutty ball was still the standard ball at the turn of the century, and its Scottish manufacturers still had importance.

winners list after Auchterlonie's win in 1893 and were never to reappear, though Scottish-born players like James Braid and Herd, working in English clubs, were consistent winners in this decade, as was Duncan later. To acknowledge the new mood, two English clubs were admitted to the Open Championship rota in 1893.[2]

In the Amateur Championship, the Scottish gentlemen golfers held their traditional place a little longer than the professionals. J. E. Laidlay, a pioneer of the overlapping grip and

Scotland's west coast golf was popularised by the railway to Ayrshire.

an advocate of physical fitness for all sport, was twice Amateur Champion, and leading amateur in the Open four times. He and Robert Maxwell, East Lothian players, were regular winners of the Amateur, but eventually they gave way to the new English wave of talent, notably Ball and Hilton. This English hold on tournament play then gave way in turn to challenges from abroad. An important moment came when Travis from America won the Amateur Championship in 1904 playing with a new controversial centre-shafted putter.

The Haskell ball appeared in 1902. Professional golfers did not like the ball, finding little benefit at first, but players of moderate skills felt the rubber-cored ball helped them, and the ball was quickly accepted by all. In the 1905 Open at St Andrews, new bunkers had to be added to compensate for the Haskell ball's better performance.

The early golf course designers had come from Scotland, but were quickly replaced by others, not brought up in Scotland. The Scottish designers, like

MACHRIHANISH GOLF LINKS.

THE ROYAL MAIL ROUTE.

GLASGOW to LOCHRANZA, PIRNMILL, CARRADALE,

CAMPBELTOWN and MACHRIHANISH BAY,

By the Steamers "DAVAAR," "KINLOCH," and "KINTYRE,"

SAILING TWICE DAILY DURING SUMMER SEASON, ONCE DAILY DURING WINTER SEASON.

TRAINS from GLASGOW (CENTRAL and ST. ENOCH STATIONS) in connection with the Steamers.

For full particulars see Advertisement in "Glasgow Herald," or apply to

R. M. DUNLOP, AGENT, 8 KINGSTON DOCK, GLASGOW,

OR

ROSS WALLACE, MANAGER, CAMPBELTOWN.

Machrihanish was probably closer to Glasgow in the early part of the century than now, being served by trains and fast boats in both summer and winter.

the professionals, had taught the rest of the world well – too well. Among the next generation of designers was Dr Alister Mackenzie, designer of Cypress Point and Augusta, who, like many of this new group, still felt it desirable to emphasise his Scottish links.

The Golf Resorts

There was still some confident expansion of golf in Scotland. The Glasgow and South Western Railway Company purchased the Turnberry course in 1906, built the large hotel and constructed a special line from Ayr through the Burns Country to Turnberry. Special golfers' express trains ran from Glasgow to the course, and there was a sleeper service from London to Turnberry, which lasted until 1942.

The last of the Scottish golf resorts to flourish was Dornoch.[3] The towns-people had an ancient right to graze their cattle, sheep and ponies on the links and this traditional use had survived surprisingly late – until the 1890s. A deliberate policy originated by Hector MacKay, the Town Clerk, and John Sutherland, the secretary of the golf club at that time, removed these ancient and embarrassing traditions, leaving the way open for an influx of visitors of taste, starting about 1910. Lord Rothermere was first to discover the town, and the head-master of Malvern School soon followed. A group of fashionable London doctors joined them and Andrew Carnegie, the richest Scotsman in the world, was at Skibo Castle nearby for part of the year, and laid out nine holes for himself in the grounds. The club became 'Royal' in 1906 and golfers and sportsmen appeared in summer at Dornoch in increasing numbers. J. H. Taylor often visited for two weeks and the town was eventually to attract the

Dornoch boomed as a golf resort at the turn of the century. The first lay-out of 5,285yds was mainly to the south of the present course.

214

Holderness family and the Wethereds, who took a house in summer close to the second hole from 1913 onwards. There Joyce Wethered described playing in a tough group of local women players such as 'the Misses Sutherlands, MacKays, Murrays and Grants that always came forward to claim battle'. The building of a branch railway line to the town was crucial and made possible a direct sleeper train from London to Dornoch in summer, such was the celebrity of the town. An American visitor, Prof Robert Wilson of Harvard, tempted Donald Ross, a local player to emigrate to the USA, where he gained his fame as a golf course architect.

John Sutherland, the Dornoch club secretary for decades, also organised a local cadre of young players who came up through the traditional route as caddies, and these players, reared on Dornoch's long, tough links, soon dominated the North of Scotland Championships and beyond. This group 'invaded' the Muirfield Amateur Championship in 1909, taking the world of golf by surprise. Sutherland himself beat Hilton, Henderson beat Jerry Travers and T. E. Grant the baker, drawing the ball unfashionably right to left, beat Ball. This remarkable series of wins drew attention to the town and its stern, beautiful links, and ensured the rise of Dornoch, the last of the towns to boom in Scotland, based on the need for fashionable, summer golf.

By 1900, the Highland Railway took golfers to the more northerly clubs and courses in Scotland.

Fashionable Strathpeffer Golf Club and Spa could still attract major exhibition golf matches. Lord Lovat is shown with Taylor, Aylmer, Sutherland and Herd. By courtesy of STRATHPEFFER GOLF CLUB.

Club Life

The expansion of golf in the Scottish cities continued in the early 1900s.
The golfers displaced from Edinburgh's Bruntsfield Links were instead given
the public Braid Hills courses, and the sentiment among the Edinburgh
players was still to play on public courses. But within two years, this public
venue was too busy and private clubs evolved, building new courses to meet
the demand. Of these, Mortonhall, founded in 1891, was the first private club
in the city.

In addition, a mass of clubs without courses enjoyed their outings to the
increasing number of clubs round the cities. This was a unique feature of golf
in Scotland and the clubs came from all kinds of institutions – banks, factories,
hospitals, churches and others. The railways were as helpful as ever in
making day outings possible.[4] Holiday resorts were reached by rail or
omnibus, and once there, bicycles were used to get to the local course. But
in many of the new holiday towns the local people were not interested in
playing. The club committee might be largely composed of visitors and only
later in the century did local interest rise to exceed the summer visitor
involvement and control.

In Scottish golf up to the First World War, club life continued much as before
and simplicity was the keynote. On Leven Links, the Leven club still played
from south to north on the links and back again, and the Lundin Club, at the
north end, played in the reverse manner. Golf was commonly free on the
municipal links, but this could not last. In 1912, visitors to St Andrews were
charged new fees for play, though local players were still exempt. Admission

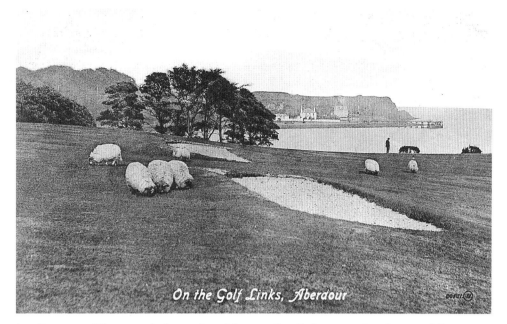

On the Golf Links, Aberdour

Sheep were an important part of the green-keeping of the Scottish links until the mid-1900s.

to all competitions and championships on the links was also free; public opinion was not ready for admission charges, nor could the organisers arrange for closure of the Scottish links. Restricting access, even for a few days, was illegal.

The clubhouses usually exhibited shabby gentility, and improvements came slowly: the Elie club installed a telephone and gas lighting in 1903. Greenkeeping at the start of the century continued to be elementary. When the Blairgowrie club opened in 1889, there was no provision for a greenkeeper, and any maintenance was by casual labour. At the Mortonhall club the course was tended by a flock of 250 sheep, grazing to the benefit of all. Daisies were a feature of the Scottish fairways and the horse-drawn mower was yet to come. Nor were the golf courses sacred. In 1895 the Enniskillin Dragoons galloped over the course at Mortonhall, and though this was permitted, an apology to the club later followed from the commanding officer.

The Royal and Ancient

At an administrative level, Scottish golf thrived in the twentieth century. Most of the world agreed to allow a Scottish club – the Royal and Ancient Golf Club of St Andrews – to run the rules of the game, to be the arbiter of permissible design of clubs and balls, and to run the major British tournaments.[5] The town was also involved when the Ladies' Golf Union moved its headquarters to St Andrews in 1977.

This role started in the late 1880s, when the Royal and Ancient Golf Club of St Andrews had a large membership throughout Britain and abroad, based on the summer visitors coming to the town, or studying at the university. The 'St Andrews Rules' had evolved to become an informal national and international code and the clubs wrote back to St Andrews for any judgement that was required.[6] The steady number of requests led naturally to the emergence of a Rules of Golf Committee of the R&A in 1897. Shortly afterwards, this committee sent out a core set of rules to each club, if only to pre-empt some of

DIE REËLS VAN GHOLF

PRYS 2/6

SANLAM Vir VERSEKERING

SANLAM

By the late nineteenth century, the Royal and Ancient Golf Club became dominant in matters related to the rules of golf throughout the world.

the common requests for guidance. Thus the domestic rules of the Fife club became the rules of golf world-wide.

But some clubs reacted against such standardisation. When the R&A ruled in 1902 that all competition scorecards should be signed and counter-signed by the players, all the members at Prestwick Golf Club ostentatiously declined to sign their cards at a medal competition, and their committee turned a blind eye to this protest.

The Championships and Matches

The ancient challenge match format now gave way to exhibition golf, and the first such event to have entry money was at Nairn in 1899. In the national competitions the R&A slowly took over responsibility for major champion-ships, one by one, starting with the Amateur, followed quickly by the Open Championship. These two events lapsed in the First World War, and when the competitions were to be restarted in 1919, a new structure was proposed. Formerly a consortium of leading clubs had run the Amateur Championship, and the Open Championship had been the responsibility each year of the host club. In 1919, just after the war had ended, Robert Maxwell proposed to the group of clubs involved that

the time has now arrived when there should be a supreme ruling authority for the management and control of the game. To further this end the Royal and Ancient Golf Club be asked to accept management of the Amateur Championship and the custody of the cup.

The responsibility for the Open was also quickly handed over to the R&A. This timidity on the part of the local clubs was understandable since these events could lose money. The R&A's acceptance of this risk and responsibility was rewarded later by the profits from the Open Championship, money which was returned by the R&A for support of the game. From the start, the Amateur and the Open, were run by a Championship Committee of the R&A, and in the first part of the century there was continuous concern about the finances of these events. There was no admission charge for the events, and the professional's prize money for the Open was only raised in part from the entry fees (higher for amateurs than professionals). An annual appeal to golf clubs was made to balance the books.

Thus the dominant position of the R&A in administrative matters evolved slowly and naturally. It survived a few half-hearted attempts to set up a national representative body, and some poorly organised rebellions arose from time to time, notably one encouraged by the magazine *Golfing* in 1902-1904. The club's national membership and one accident of history helped the R&A retain control: it had no course of its own and was not a private landowning club. Playing on the St Andrews municipal links gave the club some immu-nity from revolts against its position, in spite of the rise of other national bodies concerned with the amateur and professional game.

Clubs and Balls

The R&A Rules Committee was also increasingly consulted on other matters, notably on golf equipment and design. In 1902 the R&A Rules Committee debated, for the first time, the likely effect of the new Haskell ball.

Traditionalists felt that any change in the ball would alter the game, and that the new ball would shorten courses, remove challenging features and make many hazards inactive. In that year, S. Mure-Fergusson proposed to the R&A Rules Committee (seconded by John Low) that

the new rubber-filled balls are calculated to spoil the game of golf as now played over the links laid out for the gutta-percha ball and that it would be advisable to bring in a new rule for the regulation of balls and clubs to be used in the playing of the game.

This perceptive analysis was supported by a vote of seven votes to five by the committee. But Low and Mure-Fergusson lost the chance given to them of preserving the design of the established courses, action which was to be called for later in the century. Instead of defending the courses, they deplored the improvement in play by moderate players using the ball 'now the holes at St Andrews are within the compass of infirm old men', as Low said. He added that 'the vulgar... were only too ready to greet the advent of the rubber balls with satisfaction'. Low and other opponents of the rubber ball were seen not as defenders of the links, but as opponents of better play by senior players, humble golfers, and women and children.

The Rules Committee met again six months later and Mure-Fergusson came forward with the definitive proposal that the gutty ball, rather than the new ball, should be the standard ball for the Open and Amateur Competitions. There was other support for this action. The professional golfers had already voted late in 1902 to retain the gutty, and the golf clubs at Dornoch, Glasgow and elsewhere had banned the new ball in their domestic competitions.

However, the mood of the Rules of Golf Committee had changed. They now voted by ten to five to allow the use of *any* ball in major competitions. Perhaps they sensed that the R&A's position would be threatened by popular revolt if they ruled against a ball now increasingly used by the average player.

Mure-Fergusson, a vocal opponent of the Haskell ball at St Andrews was also a member of Blairgowrie Golf Club.

Non-standard clubs appeared in profusion in the early twentieth century, and were eventually banned by the Royal and Ancient Golf Club.

By courtesy of PHILLIPS, CHESTER.

The new ball was popular, helped new players gain skill quickly, and was particularly suited to women's golf at the time. A standard ball was eventually also required. In 1921 a 1.62 ounce, 1.62 inches diameter, version of the new ball was agreed.

But having declined to rule against the rubber-core ball in 1902, the Rules Committee had to act shortly afterwards on the question of club design and this time they banned a club sent to them for an opinion – a patent putter. This was one of a number of unusual clubs available for sale at the time, including centre-shafted and adjustable-head clubs. The R&A examined the club sent to them, and ruled against it, as a 'mechanical invention and as such could not be permitted'. As a result, in 1908, the Rules that year had an appendix termed

An Intimation on the Form and Make of Clubs, which stated simply that the Committee

> *would not sanction any substantial departure from the traditional and accepted form and make of golf clubs, which in its opinion consists of a plain shaft and a head which contains no mechanical contrivance such as springs.*[7]

In this choice of words there was a hint of nostalgia for the old days of the gutty. This declaration, vague though it was, opened up the debate on equipment again. Thereafter the R&A revealed that they also intended to ban the centre-shafted or mallet clubs, which they did finally at the full R&A club meeting in September 1910.

This was a bold move, since clubs of this type were already in the shops. In the United States the decision also caused surprise and a hostile reaction.

C. B. Macdonald's book on his career in golf acknowledged the Scottish influence.

There the game was developing rapidly and the centre-shafted Schenectady putter was widely used. The USGA came close to abandoning the entire R&A Rules and might have gone its own way, had not Charles Blair Macdonald intervened, and harmonisation was preserved by his diplomacy. A form of words kept the American code similar to the R&A rules, but allowed the centre-shafted clubs to be used in the USA. Informal contacts co-ordinated these rules on both sides of the Atlantic thereafter, and the first such meeting took place during the 1920 Amateur Championship.

In the later twentieth century, the R&A's role in the rules of golf extended increasingly to golf implements, ball velocity and performance, and they also ruled on the matter of amateur status. In 1938 a sensible rule limiting to 14 the clubs carried in the bag was brought in.

The R&A had a delicate role. Its committees were constitutionally only domestic committees of a private club. But by consulting and co-opting wisely, the membership of any committee could be national, and international when required. These committees reported to and advised the R&A members at the clubs' AGM, and any proposals required the meeting's approval. The members of the R&A could in theory turn down any decisions of its committees, but they prudently avoided precipitating such a crisis, though short-lived dissent occurred from time to time.[8]

Pre-war Hesitation

In national affairs the British economy had slowed before the First World War. 1907 was the peak year for golf course construction, and thereafter the rate of formation of new British private clubs decreased.[9] At St Andrews the New Club membership fell from 200 in 1907 to 149 members in 1914. The *Golfers' Handbook* peaked in size in 1911 at 1,119 pages, and it has never regained this bulk. The railway network expansion slowed and stopped at this time, never to recover. The most notable hesitation in Scotland was in the plan for an ambitious west coast rail route down the Kintyre peninsula with steamer connections to Ireland and the western islands. A major railway hotel north of Machrihanish was planned, but the increasing economic uncertainties prevented further progress on this idea, one never to be resurrected. This economic recession was the prelude to war.

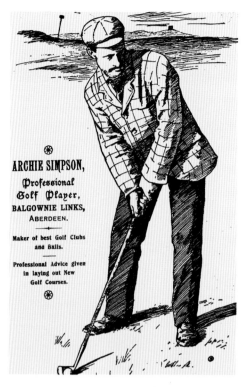

ARCHIE SIMPSON,
Professional
Golf Player,
BALGOWNIE LINKS,
ABERDEEN.

Maker of best Golf Clubs
and Balls.

Professional Advice given
in laying out New
Golf Courses.

Archie Simpson of Aberdeen designed courses throughout the north-east.

First World War

The war had a profound effect on sport in Britain.[10] Mass mobilisation took all able-bodied young men away to fight and it was not thought right to encourage professional sport at home. Full-time cricket and football ceased, and the Amateur Championship and the Open were cancelled. At North Berwick, the young clubmakers in Ben Sayers' shop were called up and left one by one.[11] Professional golfers enlisted, and those not enlisted, notably Vardon, Braid and Ray, were recruited by the War Relief Committee to play charitable exhibition matches. The Empire also sent young men to fight in Europe, and large numbers of young Canadian golfers were among those involved.[12] Some older men, like Willie Park, left for America, where they had golfing interests.

Wartime Golf

Members of the armed forces played golf while in camp. Many military camps and naval bases were in Scotland, and the local golf clubs often offered temporary membership - for the officers only. Men on active service were excused their subscriptions at their home clubs and competitions organised at the golf clubs raised funds for charities, notably the Prince of Wales Fund and Belgian Relief. Golf clubs helped with land for food production, and some of the golf courses were turned over to agriculture. At Aboyne, half the course was closed and the rest used for grazing sheep and cattle, and potatoes were grown in the rough. Even at Barnton in Edinburgh, the course was partly used for food production.

Some clubs' activities almost ceased during the war, and the Blairgowrie Golf Club could not obtain the turnout required for a formal AGM. At Kinghorn attempts were made to wind up the club formally, but not enough members attended to give a quorum, and the club remained as an empty shell throughout the war, with £27 in the bank. It revived later. Noble golf also contracted and two of the Earl of Home's 9-hole courses (at Coldstream and Castle Douglas) were dug up in order to grow crops. Golf course construction

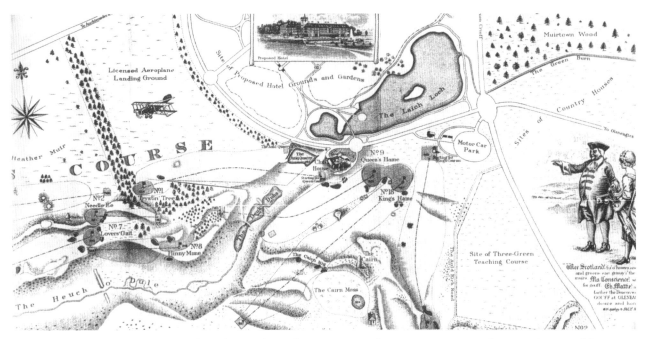

Gleneagles Hotel catered for the upper end of the golf market from 1920 onwards, even in the Depression. From R. J. Maclennan *Golf at Gleneagles* Glasgow 1921.

One of the many 'Braid's Brawest ' holes laid out in Scotland by the great player and designer.

• GLENEAGLES • KING'S COURSE •
• BRAID'S BRAWEST • 13TH HOLE • 435 YARDS •

ceased, industrial production turned to armaments and away from golf equipment, and golf magazines ceased publication. The use of caddies was abandoned; not only were there few about, but they were seen as a luxury in hard times.

After the War

After the war, much had changed, including the golfers. Old money had been eroded and inheritance tax took its toll on the traditional landed classes. Disposable income was less, and even the ubiquitous caddies were no more, since many golfers had managed without them in wartime and continued to do so. The National Insurance Act was the final blow. In 1923 it was ruled that golf clubs had to pay contributions for club-house staff, and caddies were deemed to be club employees. Formal arrangements by clubs for employing caddies therefore disappeared, and those who wished work made private hiring arrangements.

During this interwar period and shortly afterwards, a number of courses closed, chiefly the smaller courses along the holiday railway routes. Lost courses included Lochearnhead, Dirleton, Delvine, Dunbarnie, Taynuilt, Scone, Ballantrae, Laggan, Lairg, John o'Groats, Wormit, and many others.[13] These small clubs did not keep up with the rising standards of greenkeeping of other courses nearby, and after the war, family holiday golf was no longer limited to the radius of a bicycle ride from the holiday home. Wider use of the motor car extended choice into areas away from the local course. The most prominent railway closure was of the 'Golfers' Railway' - the scenic direct line from Alloway to Turnberry Hotel, which closed in 1930. Another sector to disappear after the war was that of noble golf. The

Turnberry's railway hotel continued to thrive through the century, and its courses joined the Open Championship circuit in 1977.

private courses of the nobility simply faded out, when the landed gentry lost interest or joined conventional private clubs and at the spas of Europe, the wintering gentry also dropped their interest in golf. But the upper end of the Scottish golf market survived: the major golfing hotel at Gleneagles emerged and thrived. There was *some* money about.

New Technology

The 1920s saw important changes in golf equipment. The ancient division of labour between wooden clubmakers and cleekmakers disappeared, and the new clubmakers now made both, notably Gibson of Kinghorn. At St Andrews, Forgan still flourished, as did Stewart's cleekmaking business. In Glasgow there was remarkable vitality in both club and ballmaking, and the city's 'Sportsman's Emporium' claimed to have the largest stock of golf equipment for sale in the world.

The new drop forge allowed mild rustless iron to be shaped easily and this made mass production of iron heads possible. 'Matched' sets began to appear. Prior to this time, players had accumulated favourite clubs, and it was Thomas Stewart, one of the most successful of the St Andrews clubmakers, one favoured by Bobby Jones, who is credited with producing the first graded sets. The distinguished amateur John Low was an enthusiast for such clubs, and may have had the first such matched set, the four irons being numbered 1,2,3 and 4. Stewart was first to associate his clubs with individual players and he stamped Braid, Vardon, and Herd's names on some special iron clubs.

Stewart of St Andrews was the best-known cleek-maker in Scotland, and his club-heads sold widely to club professionals, who then added their own shafts and motif.

Steel Shafts

Later, stainless-steel shafts appeared, as a result of a diminishing supply of good-quality hickory, and the new shaft was legalised first in the USA

in 1926.[14] The R&A Rules Committee considered the matter of the shafts and, perhaps still seeking to preserve the earlier traditional game, declined at first to support the steel shaft. This hesitation allowed the American companies to make a prompt start in the new market, and Bobby Jones let his name be used by Spalding in America.

But soon the change of shaft was inevitable in Britain. The ordinary players were beginning to use the new shaft, in spite of disapproval. In 1927 a tournament winner at Anstruther was disqualified for using steel shafts, by a decision of the R&A. The new shaft was eventually allowed in the areas served by the R&A in 1929, thus catching up with the USA, and by mid-1930, the majority of tournament players had changed to using steel shafts. This change meant some loss of income and status for the club professionals. Hickory shafts were often fitted to the player at his club, and they required some maintenance and repair. The steel shafts were standardised and much more robust, and were already fitted to the heads.

One familiar golfing device did not appear until the 1930s - the peg tee. Until this time, teeing-up was still on sand, and boxes of sand were a commonplace on the tees of all courses. Many experiments had been made to devise a reusable tee, using cork cups or paper platforms or rubber rings from bottle-tops. But not until 1925 was the simple wooden tee devised, and it was a permanent alternative to the pyramid of sand. A tee which penetrated the ground had been patented much earlier in the UK in 1899 by an American dentist George F. Grant, but did not find favour. But the 'reddy' tee of 1925 was the final modern solution and came from another American dentist William Lowell.[15]

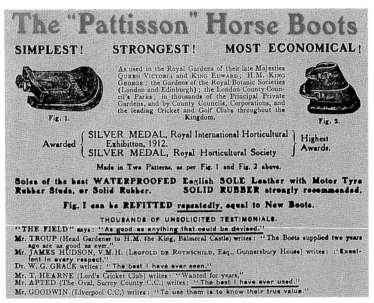

Horses were used to cut fairways until the 1930s, and to prevent damage to the turf, leather hoof covers were used.

Agronomy

Fairway mowers were drawn by horses. The Glasgow Golf Club bought their mower and horse in 1896 and Tain Golf Club obtained their horse in 1913 for £10. When the horses were used on the courses they wore special boots - flat, wooden platforms with leather uppers - to prevent damage to the turf. In the 1920s tractors started to appear in agricultural use, and this gave golf clubs a choice of a horse or the new tractor for golf course management.

Mechanisation proceeded steadily and the economics of using a tractor eventually became more favourable than keeping a horse. The choice by the mid-1920s was between a tractor at about £55 per annum for the five-year life of the early models, and a horse at £65 for each of its ten useful years. But soon the tractor's costs came down and the economic argument was reversed: 1927 was the year of the tractor and they appeared with success at Crieff, Mortonhall and elsewhere.[16]

Puritan Spirit

The puritan ethic was still on the increase in the 1920s. Sunday golf had become less and less common in Scotland, particularly in the north, and by 1910 only Aberdeen's Murcar club was open on Sundays.[17] A few clubs retained the ancient formula of allowing play in the afternoons, i.e. after the sermon time, and, in Aboyne and elsewhere in 1930, Sunday golf was still allowed after noon. In these clubs, it was strictly understood that the staff were not required to work on Sundays to serve players, and the clubhouse remained shut or if open was unstaffed. Sunday golf could cause divisions. The club at Bridge of Weir (Ranfurly Castle) split in two on this matter and those favouring Sunday golf formed a new club nearby - Old Ranfurly.

There was little open controversy about Sunday play; local sentiment usually sufficed to prevent golf on the Sabbath. After the British Ladies' Championship held at Troon in 1904 some competitors hired a boat on the Sunday intending to play the courses on the island of Arran across the Firth of Clyde. On arrival, the islanders refused to tie up the boat, having been alerted to the likely arrival of visitors and the purpose of the visit. In Edinburgh at this time, Bernard Darwin did get a game at Barnton on a Sunday, but had to drive through Edinburgh with his golf clubs concealed from view.

The Temperance Movement was still gaining in strength. Many golf clubs declined to sell alcohol, and the clubs which did sell drink had to adopt a curious strategy, enforced by the law. Sale of drink could not be at a bar, but instead had to be served through a tiny hatch to the lounge; some of these hatches can still be found, though the original reason is forgotten.

But not only the golf clubs were temperate. The Temperance Act of 1920 allowed for local veto on the sale of alcohol in any parish and Kilmacolm voted 672 to 500 to go 'dry' at this time, effectively closing all pubs and creating temperance hotels in the area. It was an echo of American prohibition. The temperance question caused divisions within some clubs. In 1925 some members of the 'dry' Kirkintilloch club left to form a new club at Hayston, for which a drinks licence was obtained.

The Extravagant 1930s

Beneath this puritan veneer, there was an unstable society. At a time of depression, some railway golfing hotels like Gleneagles prospered and attracted the rich and leisured to play golf in the atmosphere of a continental spa. The 1930s had vivid events and personalities. George Duncan, the Scottish professional, became personal professional to the Aga Khan. The British golfing scene was enlivened by the visits of the flamboyant Walter Hagen, not only for the Open Championship, which he won in 1922, but also for the Ryder Cup matches. Hagen also made high-profile visits to play exhibition matches on courses large and small, including some in Scotland, and

A local protest at golf on the Sabbath at Turnberry in 1908.

By courtesy of the BRITISH RAIL ARCHIVES.

225

George Duncan, from Aberdeen, receiving the Ryder Cup in 1929, as Captain, from Mr S. Ryder.
By courtesy of the GLASGOW HERALD.

CHURCHMAN'S CIGARETTES

T. D. ARMOUR

SPORTING CELEBRITIES
A SERIES OF 50

(Golf)
30

T. D. ARMOUR.

T. D. Armour, born in Edinburgh in 1895, is the present holder of the British Open Golf Championship. He won the French Amateur Champ. in 1920, represented Britain v. America in '21, and turned professional in '25. Recent victories are as follows: American Open Champ. and Long Beach 2,500 dollars tournament ('27), Canadian Open Champ. ('27 and '30), Western Open Champ. ('29), runner-up in Los Angeles Open Champ. ('29), American Professional Champ. ('30). Until he went to America Armour was one of our prominent amateurs; in the States he is now regarded as a leading exponent of golf.

W.A.&A.C.CHURCHMAN

ISSUED BY THE IMPERIAL TOBACCO CO. (OF GREAT BRITAIN & IRELAND), LTD.

Tommy Armour shown on a cigarette card. Born in Scotland, but living in America, he won the Open in 1931, and became one of America's best-known teachers of golf. Like all Scottish golf émigrés, he was not eligible for either side in the Ryder Cup matches.

his Highland jaunts, notably in 1937, were full of incident.[18] These tours were enlivened by the presence of Joe Kirkwood, a talented professional and trick-shot player. Hagen had links with the Kinghorn clubmaker Gibson, who ran a tournament with £200 prizes prior to any Open Championship in Scotland, which drew in the top players. Hagen made one other public contribution. His was the first public objection to the exclusion of professionals from the British golf clubhouses.

To these high-profile events were added new tensions in sport and society. During the General Strike some Scottish golfers were involved and supported it. At Ballingray Golf Club in Fife, all the members were miners and were on strike, and the committee cancelled the club subscription for the year. Thornton Golf Club in Fife nearby made all strikers welcome, and allowed them to play free of charge.

The Tensions

The First World War had further blurred the distinction between the gentlemen and the others. A host of military men – majors, captains and others – returned from the war with these badges of gentlemanly status. Local disputes about social standing and suitability for membership of the new clubs increased. At Nairn Golf Club the secretary of the local railway company was turned down as unsuitable for membership, and controversy followed.[19] The tensions between professional and amateur sportsmen increased. In golf, it was now thought unwise to play in a match with a professional, and a Scottish rugby team was forbidden to play against a Welsh team in which one player was found to have received payments. In English rugby, the top clubs were paying illicit fees to their talented humbler players.

Walter Hagen had a number of jaunts into Scotland. He is seen here surveying the steep first hole at Rothesay with fellow professional Joe Kirkwood and the Provost.
By courtesy of the GLASGOW HERALD.

The players wanted a more open system of payments, and when this was denied, a split emerged. Those who could afford to play for nothing stayed behind, on the high moral ground, and those who needed their expenses to participate, left to form the professional Rugby League.

Other incidents occurred. The best of the amateur golf tournament players were still men of private means, leisured, and playing sport as seriously as any professional, but this irony was seldom articulated or taken up by commentators. It was an American who did so, just before the war. Schmidt from America was beaten in the quarter-finals of the Amateur Championship by Hilton in 1913 and explained that he [Schmidt] did not play as much as Hilton 'as I work for a living. Hilton is fine sportsman and a good fellow'. About this time also the *New York Times* reported that 'Scottish artisan golfers say they are tired of seeing the Amateur Championship won by rich men who devote their whole time to golf'.[20] At the Open of 1921 at St Andrews, Roger Wethered, the favoured talented amateur, lost by a narrow margin to Jock Hutchison, a local St Andrean who turned professional in America, and at the presentation ceremony the organisers were less than gracious to the winner. Later, Bobby Jones' demeanour and success seemed to prove that a gentleman amateur still had claims to natural superiority in sport.

But not all the amateurs were from the Jones mould. Thomas Perkins, an English commercial traveller, rose to be top amateur in 1927 and 1928 and there were rumours that he might turn professional. He had to be interviewed by serious-minded Corinthian administrators before being picked reluctantly for the Walker Cup. He caused further offence by playing at Muirfield in an outfit described by a shocked *Golf Monthly* as 'a light cap, blue jersey, light plus fours, blue stockings and black and white shoes'. The journal added in astonishment that at lunch he changed from the blue jersey to put on 'one of cream colour or mauve'.

Lossiemouth was the birthplace of the socialist Prime Minister Ramsay MacDonald. He was expelled from the club for his pacifist views in the First World War.

In 1924 the Lossiemouth scandal re-emerged.[21] Ramsay MacDonald, now Prime Minister, had been expelled from the club during the war for his pacifist views. A special meeting was held to reconsider admitting him, but the vote went against him, and he played his golf at Spey Bay nearby thereafter. The club later reversed the decision, but MacDonald never went back.

The Walker Cup

But the traditional sportsmen were less dominant and the talent emerging elsewhere diluted their presence in the Amateur Championship. By the 1920s only one in ten entrants came from the older clubs, and eventually this small presence declined to zero. The Walker Cup team continued to be drawn largely from Oxford and Cambridge university teams. In 1923 there were muted criticisms about the failure of the team, and the narrow scope of its selection. Robert Browning, editor of *Golfing*, leapt to the teams' defence:

> ...*throwing open a few places to Scottish and Northern golfers would be a risky change, because the patriotic fervour of the Scots and the dogged courage of the Northern artisan have not the same match-winning values of the artless self-complacency which doth wrap the Varsity player.*[22]

But the artless, confident Oxbridge players kept losing, and by 1934 there was open mutiny even in conventional golfing circles. E. M. Wellings declared

> *There must be sweeping changes before the next match with America. If the navvy member of an artisan club has these qualities to win, then his social position should not be allowed to count against him.*

But the artisans had a long wait for recognition. And the professionals were still kept firmly in their place in the pecking order. No professional golfers or their representatives were placed on the Open Championship committee, in spite of patient requests from the Professional Golfers' Association. The Open Championship always finished on a Friday to allow the professionals to return to serve their club members at the week-end.

Women and Golf

The early women's movement had a minor involvement with golf. In taking action before the First World War to gain the women's vote, the suffragettes had sprayed acid on golf course greens in England as a protest against these male preserves. In Scotland, the greens seem to have escaped, possibly because women's play was more widespread, though in 1913 the R&A thought it wise to insure the St Andrews Links against any such attack. But other targets existed. The Westminster politicians were to be found on the Scottish links in summer, and could be attacked. Mrs Cruikshank, a suffragette living at Aboyne, verbally assaulted Mr Asquith while he was playing on the town course in August 1912. A little later, at Lossiemouth, Asquith was also attacked on the 17th green, and two ladies were detained by the police. But charges were not brought, to avoid giving the matter prominence.[23]

Suffragettes attacked the greens of English golf courses, but in Scotland instead attacked the politicians while on the links.

Women's Membership

In Scotland in the 1930s there was the usual pluralism in the matter of women's membership. Women were admitted from the start to membership at clubs like Aboyne and Selkirk, which like many other holiday towns saw no merit in excluding female members and players, not through greatness of mind, but simply because there were not enough men around. But in the cities, the matter of women members was never on the agenda. Some all-male clubs slowly opened up the membership, granting the women limited facilities as a club within a club, but without voting rights. This remained the usual arrangement. The New Club at St Andrews admitted women to limited membership from 1938, (but not into the dining room until 1962). Economic hard times were always good for the women's cause, and in the depressed 1930s the ladies gained more power and confidence. On the course their drives became longer, and their skirts shorter. Large hats gave way to small caps, but no-one was bold enough to dispense with a hat completely. Slowly, very slowly, other barriers came down. The first female caddie appeared – at the 1913 Amateur Championship held at St Andrews. Britain's first female assistant professional, Meg Farquhar, was appointed at Lossiemouth in 1929 and in 1933 she entered and played well in the previously all-male Scottish Professional Championship.[24]

At this time, middle-class women were leisured as never before, as a result of routine help from nannies and cooks. Golf became a favourite sport, and the ladies sections

Troon Ladies Club was one of the first women's clubs in the West of Scotland, founded in 1894.

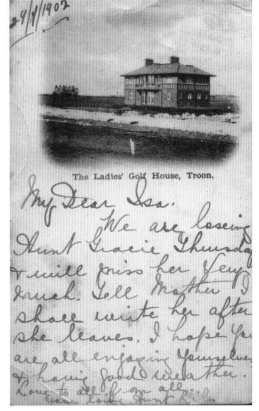

The Ladies' Golf House, Troon.

showed membership numbers as great as any before or since. Photographs of the leading women players show them to be composed, confident and tough. But the Second World War, particularly its economic consequences and the disappearance of domestic servants, meant loss of much of these earlier gains by the women.

Second World War

The war started with immediate fear of invasion. The First World War had involved a volunteer army at first, but total mobilisation was required early in the Second World War. The first war had been fought between armies far away. The second war was a mobile one and the threat of invasion in Scotland loomed. Such incursions would have been on the beaches and links on Scotland's east coast.

Sport survived in a small way. Professional cricket and football continued to manage along, as did golf. There were few competitions, and these were local ones only.[25] Charity exhibition matches were a bright spot, and Henry Cotton in particular tirelessly raised money in this way. Metal was in short supply and was used entirely for armaments. Many railings were cut down and taken away to use for making planes and tanks; no metal was available for the manufacture of golf clubs, and old iron clubs were handed in to be put in the melting pot.

War meant endless difficulties for golf clubs and courses. In the clubhouses, precautions against air raids had to be taken, and blinds and shades were required on all windows and sky-lights. Administratively, most golf clubs settled to a minimum of activities, and many had the same captain throughout the war. Clubhouse staff clothing was a problem, since clothing coupons were in short supply. No coal was allowed for the clubhouses, but log fires were permitted. Petrol rationing was universal, and little was spared for use by the tractor. At Rothesay Golf Club, ten gallons of petrol per month were allowed for the tractor, and fairways were cut once a month only. Another use of the clubhouse was found during emergencies: at Kilmacolm it housed refugees from the Blitz on neighbouring Greenock.

Club Property

Some clubhouses and golf courses were taken over for war purposes. Immediately after the war started, clubs were visited by local military personnel. In 1939 the Kinghorn Club clubhouse was requisitioned and their premises and property had to be cleared out abruptly. At the same time, the Royal Air Force took over Peterhead clubhouse and even their caddie hut was used by the local Territorial Army. The senior citizens of the Home Guard also requisitioned other clubhouses, even using them as a store of ammunition far from town centres. Other dangers existed. Crieff Golf Club's records were held in the tractor shed, and this was accidentally burned down by the soldiers billeted in it. The remaining traces of noble golf were also removed by the war: the private nine holes at Carnegie's Skibo Castle were dug up and used for food production.

In Fife, part of the Kinghorn links was ploughed and part grazed. Falkland Golf Club was entirely ploughed up, and the club never restarted again after the war. Markinch Golf Club also closed, revived for one year after the war, then shut down again until 1976. The Duff House Royal course at Banff was unique in being ploughed up for the second time, as it had been in the First World War.

Clubhouses large and small were looked on by the defence committees as buildings surplus to the immediate needs of the community. The larger clubhouses were considered with particular interest. At St Andrews the R&A clubhouse escaped conversion to war use but the adjacent New Club did not. The New Club did its best to stall, in the hope that the RAF would spare them, but to no avail, and the building, like four large hotels in St Andrews, including Rusacks, were used as bases for RAF training. Gleneagles Hotel – a symbol of conspicuous decadence in the 1930s – was taken over with glee by the socialist Scottish Secretary of State Tom Johnston, and turned into a hospital. This was possible because the hotel and golf courses, like Turnberry, were now public property after wartime nationalisation of the railways.

The golf clubs did their best to protect their land, within the limits of patriotism. Various strategies emerged to save the links from the plough, and Aboyne members offered their own personal land for war use to spare the golf course. Dunbar Golf Club innocently replied to the request from the local Agriculture Committee that the links be used for crops by saying the course was excellent for sheep, but the Burgess Club at Barnton had to turn over 26 acres to be ploughed up. Even the St Andrews Links were threatened, but were spared when the Town Council put 200 sheep out to graze. At Rothesay the Ministry of Food suggested that the golf course be dug up; the club replied that this was not necessary, as they had already increased the grazing on the course. The course was spared temporarily, and in 1942 cattle were put on to three holes, fairways narrowed and the blades of the cutters raised to allow longer grass for grazing. Golf courses were not only used for crops. Turnberry's championship links were turned into an airfield and used for a Torpedo Training Unit.

Greenkeeping during the war returned to a simple ancient regimen. Sheep were back on the links, much to the benefit of the turf. The return of the cattle also improved the soil, but they were more of a nuisance during play. The routine was that the cow pats were allowed to dry and then lifted every second day.

The Links

A Dunkirk spirit was about, and extended to golf. The coastal links were likely places for landings and various strategies were used to deter invasion or prevent progress of enemy troops from the beach. Wooden poles were sunk into the shallow waters of some beaches to prevent amphibian landings, and these can still seen on Bute and elsewhere. Concrete obstructions were placed in the dunes at other places to deter and obstruct tank landings, and some of these blocks are still visible at St Andrews and at Gullane, where large numbers of these 'Churchill Blocks' were destroyed or buried by East Lothian prisoners of war after the German defeat. Dunbar was thought particularly liable to invasion from sea or air, and old cars, buses, lorries and machinery were put on the fairways as obstructions. The links were often converted into

'Churchill blocks' placed on Scotland's east coast links to prevent tank landings during the Second World War.

minefields against such landings, and at Elie, Peterhead and Crail, mines were placed and defensive trenches dug.

The links were also eminently suitable for troop training and manoeuvres, as from earliest times in Scotland. On many courses, like Rothesay, Brora and North Berwick, observer stations were erected to watch for air raids, and the Aberdour links was restricted to ten holes by an anti-aircraft battery. Fortunately tank training was not thought suitable for the links.

Income and Attitudes

The recession in golf before the war meant that some clubs entered the war with serious financial problems which worsened during it. Little income came in, and even the reduced expenditure continued to drain reserves and resources. Those clubs which had been taken over by the military, like the New Club at St Andrews, faced a very uncertain future, nursing a chronic bank debt without any income. But as usual, municipal golf continued undisturbed, and survived: the links at St Andrews, Carnoustie, Aberdeen, Troon and elsewhere seemed eternal and unflustered by the short-term problems of war experienced by the private clubs.

The war helped the liberalisation of some of Britain's stuffier attitudes. Military golfers were again accepted into local golf clubs, and not a few opened their doors to all ranks. The US Navy Fleet used Rosyth Base, and after the war gratefully presented two trophies to the Dunfermline Golf Club. Women had another spurt in their slow golfing progress to equal status and gained their own sections in some clubs, mostly for the mundane reason that the club finances could not do without them. In wartime, older rules about dress, temperance and Sunday observance seemed less relevant, and were generally relaxed, heralding a new liberal mood in the post-war world.

Steel was still rationed in 1948 and the Auchterlonie firm had to work within their allocation when making golf clubs.
By courtesy of the NATIONAL LIBRARY OF SCOTLAND.

After the War

Though the war had been won, and Germany defeated, poverty and hard times continued in Britain and a further period of the Dunkirk spirit was required. Land was still badly needed for agriculture and the needs of industry still meant denying metal and other raw materials for golf club and ball manufacture. Golf balls were scarce and competitors in serious competitions were given certificates to enable them to buy the rationed golf balls at local shops. Eric Brown, winner of the Scottish Amateur in 1946, said that before the event he 'tramped the whole of Montrose and into every sports shop' looking for balls. Qualifiers for the Open Championship could obtain two balls via a certificate from the R&A. Not until 1947

Messrs. D.&.W. Auchterlonie.
4, Pilmour Links.
St. Andrews.
Fife.
Scotland.

BRITISH STEEL GOLF SHAFTS LTD.
TELEPHONE: WHITEHALL 3072
TELEGRAMS: GOFSHAFT. PHONE. LONDON
3 ST. JAMES'S SQUARE
In your reply refer to
LONDON, S.W.1
9th. June. Date

Your Order No. 342

Your Order as above was duly received and has been entered strictly in accordance with quoted prices, terms, and conditions, of which, if you have no trace, a copy shall be sent on request. Deliveries will be made subject to steel allocations.

was there the first national allocation of steel for golf club manufacture. At this time the older Scottish club manufacturing firms declined even further, under competition from bigger firms. Only Letters, Ben Sayers, and Nicoll of Leven remained.[26]

Food rationing continued until 1950, and this affected club life. No visitors or visiting teams could be entertained, since no food was available to permit such hospitality. As a result, inter-club competitions hardly existed. Even in 1947, rationing allowed the clubs to purchase only one bottle of gin and one of whisky per week, and this was cautiously sold on Thursdays and Saturdays.[27] Foreign travel for sportsmen was not contemplated and the Ryder Cup was played in Britain out of turn. Invitations to British golfers to attend the Augusta Masters could not be taken up.

But there was a bonus for the clubs whose clubhouse had been totally occupied in wartime: a cash sum was awarded to them for the use of, and wear and tear to, the building during the war. These sums were adequate and welcome, and those clubs who had been short of funds in the 1930s, such as Dunbar, did well out of such post-war compensation, which often cleared old debt. Many courses which had closed now opened, and even the runways at Turnberry and their robust four-foot-deep foundations were excavated and a new championship course laid out.

One ancient concession died after the war. Residents at St Andrews were no longer entitled to free golf: a small annual fee of £2 for local golfers was introduced in 1946. The R&A survived but had to tell the Town Council that it could no longer pay for the upkeep of the links. The Ladies' Putting Club at St Andrews also had financial concerns and profitably opened their adventurous Himalayas course to visitors. The routine use of caddies declined during the war and never revived. Lord Brabazon made the first, controversial use of a caddie cart on the Old Course.

Golf revived in the Far East after the war, and supplies of clubs from St Andrews to distant retailers re-started.
By courtesy of the NATIONAL LIBRARY OF SCOTLAND.

Lord Brabazon signalled the end of an era for regular use of caddies when he appeared at St Andrews with the first caddie cart.
By courtesy of St ANDREWS UNIVERSITY LIBRARY, COWIE COLLECTION

Playing the Game

The dominant Scottish amateur of the interwar period had been Jack McLean. Though he and other Scottish players regularly reached the final stages of the Amateur Championship, they always failed in the last two rounds – 'Black Friday', as it was known to the Scottish golfing journalists. Scotland did not have an amateur champion until Hector Thomson's win in 1936.

Peaceful and simpler times with unroped fairways at Turnberry during the PGA Match-play Championship of 1957, showing Peter Thomson playing Panton.
By courtesy of the GLASGOW HERALD.

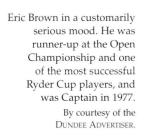

Eric Brown in a customarily serious mood. He was runner-up at the Open Championship and one of the most successful Ryder Cup players, and was Captain in 1977.
By courtesy of the DUNDEE ADVERTISER.

The important Scottish professionals in post-war golf were John Panton and Eric Brown. Radically different in temperament, they were dominant in Scotland for many years, particularly in the Scottish Professional Championship and the Northern Open, which started the British tournament year, and they later gained international respect and honours, particularly in team events.

John Panton, who with Eric Brown, were the dominant Scottish professionals of the 1950s and 60s.

By courtesy of the DUNDEE ADVERTISER.

Brown was a pioneer of touring in Europe and in 1950 he and Hector Thomson played in European tournaments, agreeing to split their winnings. Brown was also an early visitor to the American tour and was not only a highly successful Ryder Cup player, but narrowly failed to win the Open in 1958. Later Lyle, Torrance and Montgomerie were prominent Scottish golfers, and citizens of the new world of international tournament play. In the amateur game, Reid Jack was amateur champion in 1957 and Ronnie Shade had many wins and was best amateur in the 1966 Open: Charlie Green had prominence as an amateur and senior golfer demonstrating the Scottish tradition of extended golfing careers. In women's golf, Jessie Anderson (Mrs Valentine) started an extended series of wins in the British Ladies Championship in 1937, which did not end until 1958. Later Belle Robertson, the Curtis Cup captain, was the dominant amateur, also over an extended period. Jean Donald (Mrs Anderson) turned professional in 1953 and her sponsored clubs sold well.[28]

The Rules

After the war, the informal harmonisation of the rules across the Atlantic became formal. The United States Golf Association were approached by the R&A in 1951 and were dined at the House of Lords and then at St Andrews, and a joint set of rules emerged. These meetings were attended by observers from Australia and Canada. To achieve the concord, the R&A agreed to the use of the centre-shafted putter in Britain, a club long recognised in America.

Jessie Valentine, British Ladies champion, as sketched by George Houghton.

By courtesy of the HOUGHTON FAMILY.

Jean Donald who made a successful career as a professional in the post-war period.

By courtesy of THE GLASGOW HERALD.

After this, the next main joint change was in abolishing the stymie, not without low-key regrets by some. Later, the British 'small' golf ball was dropped in 1960. Agreement on the rules of golf was thereafter sustained by meetings every four years at the time of the Walker Cup match, and in addition, the R&A organises an international conference every four years with delegates from 333 affiliated golfing bodies, to discuss matters of interest. From 1984 onwards, the R&A, with the USGA, regularly issued *Decisions on the Rules*, a publication subscribed to by 3,300 organisations.

Booms and Recessions

Economic health slowly returned to Britain after the 1950s. Car ownership started to rise, and golfers were even less dependent on their local courses or those reached by rail. On holiday, distant courses could be reached by car, causing further loss of small courses in holiday areas. In Speyside, the courses at Rothiemurchus, Aviemore, Kincraig, and Carrbridge all disappeared, leaving the remaining three or four courses in the area to thrive.

But there were still to be variations in economic growth. There were crises in the late 1950s and 1960s and many clubs had to take firm action to balance the books. At the Brora Golf Club subscriptions were lowered to attract new members, and Peterhead Golf Club had a similar loss of income in this period.

In Edinburgh, Mortonhall's membership was not full, and even the R&A had low waiting lists at this time, as did Prestwick Golf Club. Other measures taken at this time of difficulty were to raise income from visitors including diversification of activities by the clubs. Caravan parks were developed on their surplus land and these successful innovations met the needs of the changing times. The first such scheme was at Dunbar in 1958, introduced when finances were tight. The rise of the caravan holiday filled a gap; the hotel holiday was no longer popular either with the well-off or with those of modest means.

The discovery of oil in the North Sea in the 1960s was unexpected and gave the towns of the north-east coast of Scotland an unusual boost to their economy and an influx of entrepreneurs who were not unused to playing golf. The oil men were delighted to have good cheap golf available and the clubs at Tain and Invergordon in particular gained many new members. The Chicago Bridge Oil Company offered to buy the Brora Golf Club outright – this offer was courteously declined.

Later there was a general financial boom in the 1980s. In the short term, the economy seemed to prosper and money was available for financing new schemes. Farmland was relatively cheap, and golf course construction boomed. But nemesis followed hubris and the early 1990s saw the end of expansion. The recession almost claimed the picturesque new Loch Lomond course and other clubs, designed for the business end of the golf market, also suffered.

Liberalisation

In this second half of the century, there was continuing relaxation in attitudes to alcohol, Sunday play and gambling. Even the amateur status laws became more flexible.[29] Tournament organisers could now present valuable prizes for play, and restoration of amateur status became easier. The liberalisation of the drinking laws continued.

But women remained firmly excluded from the remaining all-male clubs, and had only humble non-voting rights at many others. These exclusions attracted the attention of reformers, who investigated whether such exclusions infringed the conditions attached to the club's drinks licence, their local authority leases or grants from Sports Councils, which they did. The appearance of the first women as Lord Provosts in Scotland's major cities, automatically honorary members of the ancient male clubs, gave rise to delicate situations. As always, municipal golf remained above reproach. Women played as equals, and even the private clubs clustering round the course often had a sound record in their membership policies. Some older male clubs agreed that the world was changing, and the New Club at St Andrews considered giving full membership to women in 1997.

The railway in use behind the 17th hole at St Andrews in pre-Beeching times.
By courtesy of the ST ANDREWS UNIVERSITY LIBRARY, COWIE COLLECTION.

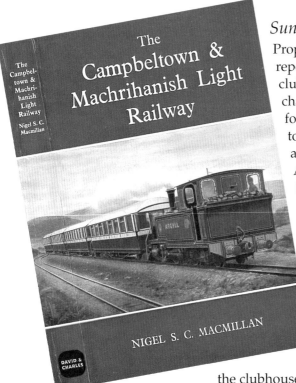

The Campbeltown & Machrihanish Light Railway

NIGEL S. C. MACMILLAN

DAVID & CHARLES

The small Scottish railway branch lines often completed the golfer's journey to the links

Sundays

Proposals for revival of Sunday afternoon golf were repeatedly made from mid-century onwards at many clubs, and the events at Rothesay give an index of the change in public opinion. Sunday golf was voted out by fourteen to two in 1931, but the vote against narrowed to eleven to six in 1936: Sunday play was eventually allowed in 1946. Elsewhere there was a similar pattern. At Cupar, the Ladybank club repeatedly discussed Sunday golf from 1934 onwards, but it was not allowed until 1955. There had been play at Crieff on Sunday during the Second World War, after pressure from temporary military members, and this continued after the war. At St Andrews, the Eden course was opened at 1p.m. on Sundays during the war, but it was agreed to consult local opinion after the war ended. When the vote came, it was two to one in favour of continuing golf on Sunday, but not on the Old Course. At Kinghorn, Sunday golf was allowed from 1947 onwards but the clubhouse remained closed on that day and did not open on Sunday until 1963. This general trend continued and in most of Scotland at present, Sunday play exists, except in the north of Scotland, notably in the areas adhering to the Free Church.

Traditionally, the Open Championship was not played on Sundays, and any 18-hole play-off would have been held on a Monday. The first Sunday play-off

Prime Minister Harold McMillan, seen at St Andrews, was the last premier to take regular Scottish golfing holidays.
By courtesy of the ST ANDREWS UNIVERSITY LIBRARY, COWIE COLLECTION.

was the famous Sanders/Nicklaus duel at St Andrews in 1970, when Nicklaus won the Sabbath rematch. In 1980 the first Sunday play at an Open Championship was permitted, the authorities having waited carefully until public opinion was ready for it, particularly in Scotland. The opening day of the Moscow Olympics on a Saturday looked likely to clash with the last day of the Open in that year, and the final round was moved to Sunday. Protests were minimal, and other tournaments thereafter also changed to a Sunday finish, the main complaint being from the distinguished golfing journalists of the Sunday papers. These Sunday tournament finishes also allowed the qualifying rounds to be fitted into the early part of the Open week. They also eliminated the exhibition matches, which traditionally followed on the Sunday.

Gambling

Gambling returned to golf in a small and different way in the post-war era, with the introduction of the first gaming or 'fruit' machines to the clubhouse in the 1960s. This introduction of low-key gambling into the clubhouses was not accompanied by the return of heavy betting during personal matches, or on-course betting at major competitions.[30] These gaming machines often rescued club finances in the mid-1960s at a time of difficulty, although a few clubs declined to install them. The New Club at St Andrews defeated a move to have a machine in 1965 but eventually installed one in 1967. Only a few clubs held out, such was the benefit to the balance sheets and the satisfaction given to the players' latent gambling instincts.

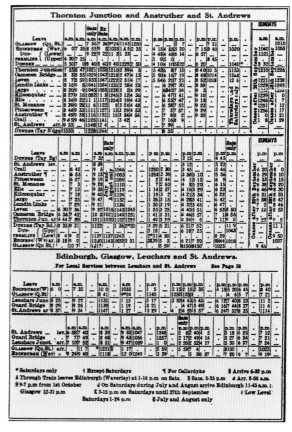

A pre-Beeching railway timetable from 1950s shows the frequent trains passing along the coastal route through the Fife golfing towns.

Agronomy

Greenkeeping remained simple for as long as possible in Scotland. The smaller holiday courses with their limited budgets could retain excellent turf, used by grazing sheep in winter and summer. At Gullane, sheep remained on the course until 1956, and the sheep were not removed at Aboyne and Dunbar until 1960. And in the remoter parts of Scotland the sheep still remain, maintaining the ancient springy turf.

The traditional Scottish links had survived, from ancient times, without artificial watering, but when the technology for regular watering became readily available, the advocates of additional watering for the older courses were successful. By 1959, one of a series of hot dry summers, the case for watering became irresistible. Slowly most clubs introduced piped water to the greens and later for the fairways, and Elie solved the problem of local supply by hiring a water diviner in 1974, with success.

But over-watering produced a new problem. The indigenous tough grasses were replaced by less hardy, shallow-rooted, but greener grass which initially pleased the eye. More and more water was required to sustain the new

The Open Championship started its rise in the late 1950s to be one of the world's premier sporting events.

Ben Hogan and his wife at Carnoustie prior to his win at the 1953 Open.
By courtesy of the DUNDEE ADVERTISER.

grasses, which were tender and liable to disease. One club after another reported difficulties throughout Britain. In Scotland, Lundin Links, Rosemount and Lossiemouth all lost fairways and greens. Prestwick endured a plague of leatherjacket pests. A return to traditional green-keeping methods with controlled watering and deep, hollow tining favoured the return of the old-style grass and old style greens suited to the Scottish soil and climate.[31]

The Open

The Open is always played on links courses, and its regular return to such Scottish courses, notably St Andrews, is a reminder of the ancient roots of the game.[32] The Open had, from its inception, a prestige which was out of proportion to the money involved. It was therefore not thought necessary earlier in the century to reward the winner with a large prize, nor were there funds to do so, there being no entry money in the early years. Not until 1926 were entry money and admission charged at the Open for the first time. At the next St Andrews Open, an Act of Parliament was required to allow the links to be closed for periods of up to 14 days.

The Open was suspended in wartime. After resumption in 1948, Henry Cotton had another win, but overseas players soon dominated, as they had done before the war. Ben Hogan visited Carnoustie to win in 1953, using the small ball, and Locke and Thomson were to take many Open medals. The first television screening of the Open was in 1955 at St Andrews, and a single camera covered 'The Loop'. As the coverage of the tournaments increased, television was to encourage the 'leaders out last' arrangement, and in general television favoured stroke-play.

But the Open had stagnated a little in the 1950s and the American players were not coming over regularly. The organisation was poor in comparison with North American events, as was upkeep of the courses, and even distinguished entrants had to pre-qualify for the Open. At Carnoustie in 1953 the same holes in the greens were used for all four rounds. The scoring and score boards showed play related to over or under fours, rather than par. The players did not go out in the last rounds in order of scores, and contenders could be well apart and unaware of rivals' scores. It was often far from clear who was winning.

Hogan's visit had been a single one, and was his last major win. In 1960 the entry of Arnold Palmer, already Masters and US Open champion, was important. The doubling of the gate receipts and profit in that year signalled the commercial revival and the beginning of a golden era for the Open. Palmer's charismatic personality, his exciting golf and his sportsmanship commended him to the public and to the organisers and sponsors. This personal success was not matched on the links at St Andrews, and this great attacking player suffered mightily at the Road Hole. Palmer used a personal caddie (James 'Tip' Anderson) and this signalled the general return of such regular partnerships in professional golf. The Open was now generally profitable and the 1975 Carnoustie event was the last to lose money. Prize money increased from £1,500 in 1950 to approach £1million in the 1990s. This financial success was

Peter Thomson, five times
Open champion between
1954 and 1965 at the
Swilken Burn, St Andrews.
By courtesy of the COWIE
COLLECTION, UNIVERSITY OF ST
ANDREWS.

Arnold Palmer helped
revive the fortunes of the
Open Championship by his
support. He is here shown
making a presentation to
the Royal and Ancient Golf
Club in 1960.

used by the R&A to aid loss-making amateur events and to put considerable
funds into deserving 'external' activities.

Palmer was followed by Nicklaus and a host of American aspirants.
Jacklin's Open win in 1969 boosted British confidence and Seve Ballesteros'
triumph in 1979, followed by Lyle's, in 1985, marked the start of a period of
European success. The Open evolved into a television spectacular, the BBC's
greatest regular outside broadcast. The attendance at St Andrews Opens is
usually the greatest and draws the largest number of overseas visitors, and
with no limit on entry tickets, the Open remains open to spectators as well as
to all players of skill.

Famous starts and finishes at St Andrews Open Championship:

RIGHT: A youthful Jack Nicklaus warming up for the St Andrews Open of 1964, won by Tony Lema.
By courtesy of the COWIE COLLECTION, UNIVERSITY OF ST ANDREWS LIBRARY.

BELOW: Sanders' tragic miss on 18th to lose the 1970 Open.
By courtesy of ASSOCIATED PRESS PHOTOGRAPHS.

Arnold Palmer's farewell at his last St Andrews Open Championship in 1995.

By courtesy of ASSOCIATED PRESS.

Arrangements for a modern Scottish links Open Championship: Turnberry 1994.

By courtesy of PHIL SHELDON.

Envoi

Present-day Scotland has a pluralist golf tradition. Scotland has not only famous Championship links, but also remote courses with fairways tended by sheep. It has some of the most deeply conservative clubs in the world, but also has a mass of municipal courses open to all.

But Scottish golf still has an importance beyond these pleasant arrangements for the inhabitants.[33] The nation's game still has a remarkable hold on the imagination of golfers world-wide. There comes to Scotland a stream of players, visitors and pilgrims in tribute to Scotland as the home of golf. The welcome they get is based on an assumption of shared property as well as an obligation of hospitality. This endearing and enduring vitality of Scottish golf is the result of its ancient origins as the democratic game of the town links.

In some ways, the real game of golf never left Scotland.

FURTHER READING

Numerous elegant, illustrated books on golf in the twentieth century are available, and perhaps the best is Malcolm Campbell *Encyclopedia of Golf* London 1991. The history of British golf in the twentieth century is rather anglicised – see Geoffrey Cousins *Golf in Britain* London 1975 and Bernard Darwin *A History of Golf in Britain* London 1952 but see Percy Huggins (ed) *This is Scottish Golf* Edinburgh 1990. A serious sociological work on British sport is Tony Mason *Sport in Britain: A Social History* Cambridge 1989. For some accounts of twentieth-century Scottish golf see Robert Price *Scotland's Golf Courses* Aberdeen 1989, David C. Smail *Prestwick Golf Club* Prestwick 1989, S. L. McKinlay *Scottish Golf and Golfers* 1992 and Robert Harris *Sixty Years of Golf* London 1953, which has east-coast interest.

Of the R&A histories, Pat Ward-Thomas *The Royal and Ancient* Edinburgh 1980 has the best account of the club's administrative role. Early Scottish women's golf organisation is described in the slim volume *History of the Scottish Ladies Golfing Association* London 1928, and one Scottish 'ladies' section' has its own history - Ruby Turberville's *The Aberdeen Ladies Golf Club* Aberdeen 1992.

The various yearbooks have essential data for historians - the early *Nisbet's Golf Year Book* from 1905 and the older *The Golfer's Handbook* and *Golfer's Annual*. Excellent historical articles are now appearing in the magazines *Through the Green*, published by the British Golf Collectors' Society from 1987; the American equivalents are the pioneer *Golf Collectors' Society Bulletin* from 1970, and the serious-minded journal *Golfiana* from 1987. For individual Scottish golfing memoirs see Eric Brown *Knave of Clubs* London 1961, his *Out of the Bag* London 1964 and also John Panton *My Way of Golf* Glasgow 1951. For Scottish clubmaking in the twentieth century see Henderson and Stirk and more recently Peter Georgiady *Compendium of British Golf Club Makers* Greensboro 1994. See also Leo M. Kelly *Antique Golf Ball Reference and Price Guide* Richton Park 1993, and Peter Georgiady and Leo Kelly *Quick Reference Guide to Antique Golf Club Names* Illinois 1993.

Professional golfers are listed in Alan F. Jackson *The British Professional Golfers 1887-1930: A Register* Worcester 1994, and their world described in Peter Lewis *The Dawn of Professional Golf* Ballater 1995. For the early professionals see Henry Leach *Great Golfers in the Making* London 1907 (facsimile edition USGA 1988) and for America see Al Barkow *Gettin' to the Dance Floor: the Early Days of American Pro-Golf* London 1986. Memoirs of Scottish women golfers exist: for Jessie Valentine see George Houghton *Better Golf* London 1967 and Belle Robertson *The Woman Golfer* Edinburgh 1988.

Among the best club histories are John McConachie *The Moray Golf Club at Lossiemouth* Lossiemouth 1988, Gray Laidlaw and David Mason *A Very Pleasant Golfing Place* Kilmacolm 1991, Archie Baird *Golf on Gullane Hill* Gullane 1982, W. G. P. Colledge *Mortonhall Golf Club 1892-1992* Mortonhall 1992, R. C. Brownlee *Dunbar Golf Club: A Short History 1794-1980* Dunbar 1980,

John MacDonald *The Crail Golfing Society* (2 vols) Crail 1986 (including a reprint of Dow's earlier history), Norman Mair *Muirfield: Home of the Honourable Company* Edinburgh 1994, Alistair Adamson *In the Wind's Eye* North Berwick 1980, Alan M. Thom *From Westlands to Eastlands: the History of Rothesay Golf Club* Rothesay 1992, *One Hundred Years of Strathpeffer Spa Golf Club* Strathpeffer 1988, John Freeman *Crieff Golf Club 1891-1991* Crieff 1991, Andrew Bennett *The St Andrews Golf Club Centenary 1843-1943*, Jim Stark and Douglas Lowe *Helensburgh Golf Club* Helensburgh 1993, Ian M. Mackintosh *Troon Golf Club* Troon 1974, *Brora Golf Club 1891-1991* Brora 1991, *Tain Golf Club 1890-1990* Tain 1990, J. G. Jarrett *A History of the New Club, St Andrews* St Andrews 1982, Graham Bateman *Selkirk Golf Club 1883-1983* Selkirk 1983, Anon *Aboyne Golf Club 1883-1983* Aboyne 1983, Dugald McIntyre *Beyond Mount Pisgah* Millport 1988, Stewart Cruden *Bruntsfield Links Golfing Society: a Short History* Bruntsfield 1992, Alex McIntosh *Blairgowrie Golf Club 1889-1989* Blairgowrie 1989, Robert Crampsey *Ranfurly Castle Golf Club* Bridge of Weir 1989, Alan Brandie *Peterhead Golf Club 1841-1991* Peterhead 1991, Donald Grant *Personal Memories of Royal Dornoch Golf Club 1900-1925* Dornoch 1978, G. S. Robertson *A History of Stromness Golf Courses* Stromness 1970, R. J. MacLennan *Golf at Gleneagles* Glasgow 1921 and Robert Crampsey *St Mungo's Golfers: the History of Glasgow Golf Club* Glasgow 1987.

For golf in particular areas see Angus MacVicar *Golf in My Gallowses* London 1983, which deals with Argyll, Stewart Hackney *Carnoustie Links: Courses and Players* Dundee 1989, William Coull *Golf in Montrose* Montrose 1993, Stewart Hackney *Bygone Days on the Old Course* Dundee 1990, Dawson Taylor *St Andrews: Cradle of Golf* London 1976, Masakuni Akiyama *Visiting the Home of Golf* California 1988 and for Fife in general see the excellent Fife Golfing Association *A History of Golf Clubs in Fife* Leven 1989. The St Andrews Links Trust produce a readable annual - *A Year at St Andrews*. For North Berwick see *100 Years of Golf at North Berwick, 1857 to 1962: the Doreen Sayers Scrapbook* North Berwick 1994.

The standard golf bibliography is R. E. Donovan and J. S. F. Murdoch *Golf and the Printed Word 1566-1985* New York 1988, and see also Don Kennington *The Sourcebook of Golf* The Library Association 1981. For golf definitions and derivations see the scholarly work by Peter Davies *The Historical Dictionary of Golfing Terms* London 1988 and 1993, and Percy Huggins *The Golfer's Book of Days* Whittingehame 1993.

Golfing ephemera are elegantly described and illustrated in Sarah Baddiel's books *Beyond the Links* London 1992 and *Golf: the Golden Years* London 1989, and in her *Miller's Golf Antique Guide* London 1994. See also Bruce Berdoch and Michael Baier *A Century of Golf Postcards* 1993, and John Olman and Morton Olman *The Encyclopaedia of Golf Collectibles* Alabama 1985.

For a listing of clubs see the *Golfer's Handbook* and Donald Steel's *Sunday Telegraph Golf Course Guide to Britain and Ireland*, the Scottish Tourist Board's annual *Scotland, Home of Golf* and Robert Price *Scotland's Golf Courses* Edinburgh 1992. For a technical guide see Sandy Lyle (with Bob Ferrier) *Sandy*

Lyle Takes You Round the Championship Courses of Scotland Tadworth 1982.
For golfer's travel guides see David Hamilton *Scotland's Golf Guide* Edinburgh 1995, Bob Kroeger *Complete Guide to Golf Courses of Scotland* Cincinnati 1992, Sam Morley *By Yon Bonny Links* Northaw 1990, George Houghton *Golf Addict Among the Scots* 1968 and Jerry Mosca *Experiencing Golf in Scotland* Mankato 1981.

The evolution of the Open Championship is described by Michael Hobbs *Great Opens: Historic British and American Championships 1913-1975* London 1976 and Geoffrey Cousins and Tom Scott *A Century of Opens* London 1971. A history of the Open is also given in Bobby Burnet *St Andrews Opens* Edinburgh 1990, the story of the St Andrews caddies is found in Richard Mackenzie *A Wee Nip at the 19th Hole* London 1998.

Scottish golf at its simplest
and most durable, at the Bute
Golf Club, Kingarth.

REFERENCES

CHAPTER ONE: THE LINKS

1. For this grass controversy see Eddie Park *Real Golf* Dovercourt 1990. Preparation of a modern links for a championship is described in *St Andrews Links Yearbook 1995*.

2. For the geology of Scotland's golf courses see Robert Price *Scotland's Golf Courses* Aberdeen 1989.

3. Stewart Hackney *Carnoustie Links: Course and Players* Dundee 1988, p2 describes the shift in lighthouses, and for links movements at Brora see Anon *Brora Golf Club 1890-1983*, p55. Hackney *Carnoustie* p31 describes the 1903 flood: a local paper recorded 'the bridge over the burn outlet was wrecked, while the sea invaded the Valley Hole to a considerable distance. Quite a change has come over the Sandy Hills at this point.' At Nairn small and large sand storms are common, each depositing more sand on the links. For contemporary erosion in Scotland see *The Scotsman* 8th October 1990, and for the loss of Pittenweem links see David Cook *Annals of Pittenweem* Anstruther 1867.

4. The change in Leith's high water mark is noted in James S. Marshall *The Life and Times of Leith* Leith 1986, p2.

5. Charles Smith *The Aberdeen Golfers: Records and Reminiscences* 1899, p2.

6. R. C. Brownlee *Dunbar Golf Club* Dunbar 1980.

7. Alistair Adamson *Millions of Mischief* Malvern 1990.

8. See Aleck Bauer *Hazards* Chicago 1913, reprinted and extended by Grant Books, Worcs 1993.

CHAPTER TWO: THE MYSTERIOUS YEARS

1. For the Kelso case, see Stair A.Gillon (ed) *Stair Society: Selected Justiciary Cases 1624-1650* Edinburgh 1953, vol 1, p204.

2. Recent scholarly work on the history of sport includes William J. Baker *Sports in the Western World* Totowa 1982, Norbert Elias and Eric Dunning *Quest for Excitement: Sport and Leisure in the Civilising Process* Oxford 1989, and Peter Moss *Sports and Pastimes Through the Ages* London 1962.

   The first modern golf history was Robert Clark *Golf: a Royal and Ancient Game* London 1893 (reprinted and facsimile editions 1975): though superseded, it has material from original sources which have now been lost. Modern authors rely on Robert Browning *A History of Golf* London 1955, though the scholarship is greater in the earlier works by Harold Hilton and Garden Smith *The Royal and Ancient Game of Golf* London 1912 and Bernard Darwin (and others) *A History of Golf in Britain* London 1952.

   For more recent histories of golf see Geoffrey Cousins *Golf in Britain; a Social History* London 1975, and the short article on golf in Tony Mason *Sport in Britain: a Social History* Cambridge University Press 1989. For the golfing geography of Scotland see Robert Price *Scotland's Golf Courses* Aberdeen University Press 1989, and Scottish sport in general is described in John Burnett *Sporting Scotland* Edinburgh 1995.

3. For sport in Egypt see Wolfgang Decker *Sports and Games of Ancient Egypt* Yale University Press 1992.

4. Forcellini's Latin *Dictionary* is quoted in Darwin *History* (ref 2) p43 and describes the various balls... 'pila paganica, quae et pila absolute,

erat pila lusoria pluma facta, major trigone et mollior, folle minor sed durior...' Martial VII, xxxii, p7, also describes a 'feather ball'.

5. Browning *History* (ref 2) p19 quoting Wace's *Roman de Brut*, generally thought to be an unreliable source: Bede's *Cuthbert* and Asser's *Alfred* are better.

6. Rymer's *Foedera* VI, p417, discussed in Darwin *History* (ref 2) p44.

7. Browning *History* (ref 2) p8 describes chole: see also Peter Dobereiner in Mark Wilson (ed) *Golfer's Handbook 1992*, p826. A scholarly account of chole is badly needed.

8. The 'long' version of jeu de mail is described in detail in George Robb ('Golfer') *Historical Gossip about Golf and Golfers* Edinburgh 1863.

9. See David Hamilton 'Yet another stick-and-ball game' *Through the Green*, March 1993, p14 - describing an illustration in *Les Très Riches Heures du Duc de Berry* Thames and Hudson 1989. For the early German stick-and-ball game see Heiner Gillmeister (1990) 'Wer erfand das Golfspiel...' *Schweizer Beiträge zur Sportgeschichte* vol 2, 20-29.

10. Van Hengel *Early Golf* (ref 53) p9 mentions the shepherds and their sticks and stones.

11. The quote from Duns Scotus was found by the late Father Howard Docherty. See also *Troubadour* vol 41, pp34-44: Duns Scotus was beatified in 1992.

12. Albert Hermann *The Taymouth Castle Manuscript of Sir Gilbert Hay's 'Buik of King Alexander the Conquerour'* Berlin 1898, as analysed in John Cartwright's 1974 PhD thesis for the University of Toronto Centre for Mediaeval Studies entitled 'Sir Gilbert Hay's *Buik of King Alexander the Conquerour.*' The relevant extract (beginning line 4326) is

Tharefore I send the here a playing ball,
And ane golf staff to driff the ball wt. all,
As barnis dois in cictcis for to play.

13. The recent discovery of an early stick-and-ball game in China comes from the research of Professor Ling Hongling of Lanzhou, Gansu Province, and was reported in the *Journal of the Northwest Normal University*, abstracted in *China Daily*, thence to the *Straits Times* and from there to *Golfiana* vol 1, no 1, p28, 1987. For an early stick-and-ball game in Chile see Henderson and Stirk p1.

14. For Samoa games see *Daily Telegraph* 14th October 1991, p32.

15. See Roger Hutchinson's excellent *Camanachd! The Story of Shinty* Edinburgh 1989, and Hugh Dan Maclennan *Shinty!* Nairn 1993.

16. Hutchinson *Camanachd!* (ref 15) p17.

17. Hutchinson *Camanachd!* (ref 15) p18.

18. Hutchinson *Camanachd!* (ref 15) p20.

19. Hutchinson *Camanachd!* (ref 15) p16. See also J. F. Campbell *Popular Tales of the West Highlands* Edinburgh 1860, vol ii, p463, and John Strachan *Stories from the Tain* Dublin 1944, p5.

20. Browning *History* (ref 2) p8, derived from Campbell *Popular Tales* (ref 19) vol ii, p449; see also Douglas Young *St Andrews: Town and Gown, Royal and Ancient* London 1969.

21. Ban on 'carrick' quoted in James Colville *The Glasgow Golf Club 1787-1907* Glasgow 1907, p1, based on the Glasgow Kirk Session Records of 1589. See also Anon *Amusements of Leisure Hours* Edinburgh 1809, which states 'At that period and from time immemorial it had been the practice in most of the country parishes in Aberdeenshire for parties of young men to assemble about the Christmas season to try their strength and agility at the athletic exercise of football. The contest usually took place in the kirk-yard.'

22. From David Murray *Memories of the Old College of Glasgow* Glasgow 1927, p425.

23. John Kerr *Golf-Book of East Lothian* Edinburgh 1898 (appendix) p1.

24. Martin Martin *A Voyage to St Kilda* London 4th Edition 1753, p62.

25. Traditional crafts and stick-making skills, now almost forgotten, are described in Edward Hart *Walking Sticks* The Crowood Press 1986, Jack Hill *Complete Practical Book of Country Crafts* Newton Abbot 1979, Herbert Edlin *Woodland Crafts of Great Britain* Newton Abbot 1949, and Jenny Carter and Janet Rae *Traditional Crafts of Scotland* Chambers 1988; see also Reader's Digest *Traditional Crafts in Britain* London 1982.

26. For Park's early play with wooden clubs see George M. Colville *Five Open Champions and the Musselburgh Story* Musselburgh 1980. A remarkable number of famous nineteenth-century golfers started play with simple sticks, and for the childhood clubs used by Auchterlonie, Ferguson and Vardon see Henry Leach *Great Golfers in the Making* London 1907, *passim*.

28. Childhood use of shinty sticks in Bell Street, St Andrews is described in Andra Kirkaldy *My Fifty Years of Golf: Memories* London 1921, p110 and confirmed in S. Herd *My Golfing Life* London 1923, p1.

29. Harry Vardon gives more details of his home-made tree clubs in his *My Golfing Life* London 1933, p20.

30. R. C. Maclagan *The Games of Argyllshire* Glasgow 1990, p14 onwards. In 1722 the game of 'cat and dog' was noted on the Moray Firth in north-east Scotland - see William Sievright *Historical Sketch of the Perth Cricket Club* Perth 1880, p5. A game called 'the knotty' is found in the *New Statistical Account* and is a simple form of shinty: see N. L. Tranter (1987) 'Popular sports and the Industrial Revolution in Scotland' *International Journal of the History of Sport* vol 4, 21-38.

31. See *A Dictionary of the Older Scottish Tongue* and *Scottish National Dictionary*. For 'golf' and 'golfand' see *The Tale of Cokelbie Sow* c.1450 in Bannatyne. The variant 'goff' was still in use in mid-nineteenth century golf literature, suggesting that the word was pronounced in this way until then: see James A. Barclay (1987) 'Golf, Goff or Gowf?' *Golfiana* vol 1, no 2, 35-39.

32. For the Church's encouragement of sport see John M. Carter (1984) 'Muscular Christianity and its makers: sporting monks and churchmen in Anglo-Norman society, 1000-1300' *British Journal of Sports History* vol 1, 109-124.

33. *Aberdeen Burgh Records* as quoted in John Stuart (ed) *Scottish Burgh Records Society: Extracts from the Council Register of the Burgh of Aberdeen* 1871.

34. 'Keich ball' is mentioned in the Bute Scottish Records Series *Kircudbright Town Council Records 1576-1604* Edinburgh 1939, p125.

35. For Brechin violence see *Registrum Secreti Sigilli Regum Scotorum* vol i, 1488-1529, entry for 16th September 1508. For Stirling golf injuries, see Robert Renwick (ed) *Extracts from the Records of the Royal Burgh of Stirling* Scottish Burgh Records Society 1887; see the year 1561, vol 1, p78, and also *Edinburgh Burgh Records* vol 6, p150. The serious assault with a golf club at Falkirk on 2nd February 1639 is found in D. M. Hunter (ed) *The Court Book of the Barony and Regality of Falkirk and Callander* The Stair Society, Edinburgh 1991 – noted by Olav Sutherland.

36. *Historical Manuscripts Commission: Report of Manuscripts in Various Collections* no 5, 43-44. For this and other violence attached to early football, see the excellent study by F. P. Magoun (1931) 'Scottish popular football 1424-1815' *American Historical Review* vol 37, 1-13.

37. Magoun (ref 36) p4, quoting *The Dictionary of National Biography* and *Pitcairne's Trials*. See also Margaret Sanderson 'Edinburgh merchants in society, 1510-1603' in Ian B. Cowan and Duncan Shaw (eds) *The Renaissance and Reformation in Scotland* Edinburgh 1983.

38. *Acts of the Scottish Parliament* ii p48, taken from Olive Geddes' transcription in her *A Swing Through Time* Edinburgh 1992 and for some background see Alastair Johnston and James F. Johnston *The Chronicles of Golf: 1457 to 1857* Cleveland 1993. When the Acts were reprinted in 1597 the references to Sunday and to drink were omitted: the censors did not wish to remind the population that intemperate Sunday sport had ever been encouraged. The original wording was not restored until 1814. The corresponding prohibitions in England are interesting and read 'every able-bodied man on feast days when he has had leisure, shall in his sports use bows and arrows, pellets and bolts, and shall learn the practice and art of shooting. Forbidding all and singular on pain of imprisonment to attend or meddle with hurling of stones, loggets or quoits, hand-ball, football, club-ball, cambuc, cock-fighting or other vain games.' See Darwin *History* (ref 2) p45. While this does not mention golf, it does talk of cambuca and club-ball. Another single English extract does use the word 'golf'. In a letter from Queen Katherine, wife of Henry VIII to Cardinal Wolsey in 1513, she says 'all his subjects be very glad, I thank God, to be busy with the golf, for they take it for pastime': quoted in Kerr *Golf-Book* (ref 23) p21. Golf was not listed in earlier English legislation of 1724, but the sport was not necessarily absent.

248

39. Louis T. Stanley *A History of Golf* London 1991.

40. John P. Paul (ed) *Accounts of the Lord High Treasurer of Scotland 1503-1504* Edinburgh 1900, vol ii, p341. Other entries for purchase of 'clubs' exist but may instead refer to the stick used in hawking.

41. *Lord High Treasurer* (ref 40) p418.

42. Reader's Digest *Traditional Crafts in Britain* 1982.

43. Gibson's estate is quoted in Craigie's *Dictionary of the Older Scottish Tongue* under 'golf-ball'. Iseabail Macleod of the Scottish National Dictionary Association kindly traced Gibson's occupation.
   The full text of the monopoly granted to Mayne is found in Clark *Golf* (ref 2) p20. See also Sanderson (ref 37) and the remarkable study of Charles E. Whitelaw *Scottish Arms Makers* London 1977, which lists the numerous early bowmakers, including the early club-making bow-makers Bayne and Deas (or Dais). Johnston and Johnston *Chronicles* (ref 38) p206 notes that there is a tradition in the Deas family of North Carolina that their forebears introduced golf to America. For the early methods of joining metal and wooden shafts, see David Caldwell *The Scottish Armoury* Edinburgh 1979.

44. John Stuart (ed) *Registrum de Panmure* Edinburgh 1974, vol 1, p xxxii.

45. *A Diurnall of Remarkable Occurants that have passed within the Country of Scotland, since the death of King James the Fourth until the Year 1575*, reprinted by the Bannatyne Club, vol 43 (1833), p285.

46. Douglas M. Ferguson *Dunfermline Golf Club* Dunfermline 1987.

47. The Sandilands escapade is given in *The Spottiswood Miscellany* Spottiswood Society (1845) vol ii, p428.

48. For the footballs made by the Glasgow cordiners see Magoun (ref 36) p3, and *Extracts from the Records of the Burgh of Glasgow 1573-1664*, p149: 'Johnne Neil, cordiner [to supply] yeirli during his lyftyme upoune Fastreinis-ewin of sax [six] guid and sufficient fut ballis.' The Town Council in Peebles warned footballers that there was to be no play in the High Gate and offenders would be fined with 'cutting of the ball', again suggesting that the ball was hair-filled, or perhaps was an air-filled bladder: see Magoun (ref 36) p3.

49. Johnston and Johnston *Chronicles* (ref 38) pp 38, 97 and 103.

50. Stirling merchants listed in the *Edinburgh Testaments* in *Scottish National Dictionary* (ref 31) under 'golf'.

51. Kerr *Golf-Book* (ref 23) p283 records this civil action in Haddington, in 1576, against a merchant failing to pay up for one dozen 'golf bais, a velvet hat and paintings'.

52. For mediaeval trade in golf balls see W. S. Unger *De Tol van Tersekeroord* The Hague 1939, quoted in van Hengel (ref 53). See also Scottish Record Office '*Scotland and the Netherlands*' SRO Exhibition Text no 20.

53. Colf is closely described in van Hengel *Early Golf* Bentveld, Holland 1982, a translation of his *Colf, Kolf, Golf* Zutphen 1982: the change of title to *Early Golf* for the English edition was unfortunate. Van Hengel dismisses earlier historians' accounts of Low Countries' colf and earlier terminology. Van Hengel blames lack of knowledge of the Dutch language as the reason for the misunderstandings, but when Browning's *History* says a Dutch game of 'het kolven' existed, he quoted 'J. A. Brongers the Dutch historian'; van Hengel also thanks Brongers as *his* mentor. See also Jaques Temmerman *Golf and Kolf: Seven Centuries of History* Belgium 1993. For a recent resurfacing of this old argument see *Golf Collectors' Bulletin* February 1985.

54. For Naarden see Browning *History* (ref 2) p16. For Halma's *Dictionary* I have trusted H. B. Wood *Golfing Curios and the Like* London 1911, p36.

55. The den Briel prohibitions are in van Hengel *Early Golf* (ref 53) p19.

56. Van Hengel *Early Golf* (ref 53) p22, and Browning *History* (ref 2) p16 for Dordrecht and Naarden.

57. Van Hengel *Golf* (ref 53) p52.

58. Wooden clubs exported from Scotland to Holland are described by van Hengel *Early Golf* (ref 53) pp 53 and 73: his source is J. Six van Chandelier *Poesij* Amsterdam 1657. For the Scots community in the Low Countries see Jean Morrison *Scots on the Dijk* 1981.

59. Van Hengel *Golf* (ref 53) p54.

60. Van Hengel *Golf* (ref 53) pp37 and 39.

61. The Kronenburg game is described in van Hengel *Golf* (ref 53) p17.

62. van Hengel *Early Golf* (ref 53) p31, and Johnston and Johnston *Chronicles* (ref 38) p103.

63. *The Scotsman* 27th September 1984 and *Golf Collectors' Society Bulletin* no 88, July 1986. For a full description, see C. T. C. Dobbs and R. A. Price (1991) 'The Kennermerland site' *International Journal of Nautical Archaeology* vol 20, 110-122 and for the 'Lastdrager' wreck see Johnston and Johnston *Chronicles* (ref 38) p102.

CHAPTER THREE: THE TURBULENT CENTURY

1. The complex interactions of politics and social life in seventeenth-century Scotland are described in T. C. Smout *History of the Scottish People 1560-1830* Glasgow 1969. For a good general account of local prohibitions see Agnes Keith *The Parish of Drainie and Lossiemouth* 1975, p107-118. For the role of the Kirk Session see Geoffrey Parker 'The Kirk by law established' in Leah Leneman (ed) *Perspectives in Scotttish Social History* Aberdeen 1988.

2. For general accounts of Leith see Alex Campbell *The History of Leith* 1827, James C. Irons *Leith and its Antiquities* Edinburgh 1897 and James S. Marshall *The Life and Times of Leith* John Donald 1986. For the laxity of Leith see the account in Ronald Selby Wright *The Kirk in the Canongate* Edinburgh 1986, p68.

3. Interestingly, the corresponding English regulations also ban a number of sports, but cambuca, golf and football are missing from the list: see Joachim K. Ruhl (1984) 'Religion and amusements in sixteenth- and seventeenth-century England' *British Journal of Sports History* vol 1, 125-165. See also R. D. Breckenridge (1969) 'The enforcement of Sunday observance in Post-revolution Scotland 1689-1733' *Records of the Scottish Church History Society* vol 17.

4. Scottish History Society *St Andrews Kirk Session Records 1559-1600,* 18th December 1583, Edinburgh 1890: see pp 515, 846 and 913.

5. Stirling Parish Records of 30th January 1621: quoted in W. L. Thomson *Old Stirling Sports and Pastimes* 1921. Another game mentioned in the church legal actions excites the golf historian briefly, namely occasional mention of play at 'nineholes'. This was a form of bowls, not golf: see A. I. Ritchie *The Church of St Baldred* 1880, p164, J. A. Gillespie *Dundonald: the Parish and its Setting* Glasgow 1939, p330, and R. C. Brownlee *Dunbar Golf Club 1794-1980* Dunbar 1980, p3. For the 1604 Aberdeen Ecclesiastical Records see *Selections from the Records of the Kirk Session, Presbytery and Synod of Aberdeen* Spalding Club vol 15, p38.

6. *The Autobiography and Diary of James Melvill* Wodrow Society Edinburgh 1842, p126.

7. *St Andrews Session* (ref 4) p515.

8. *St Andrews Session* (ref 4) p846.

9. David Robertson *South Leith Records* Edinburgh 1911, p8.

10. *St Andrews Session* (ref 4) p515.

11. L. A. Govet *The King's Book of Sports* London 1890 and S. R. Gardiner *Constitutional Documents of the Puritan Revolution* Oxford 1889; see also J. Tait 'The declaration of sports for Lancashire 1617' *English History Review* vol 32, p561.

12. Robert Baillie *Letters and Journals* Edinburgh 1775, and William Cramond *The Church and Churchyard of Cullen* p124.

13. Smout *History* (ref 1) p79.

14. Robert Wodrow *Analecta: Collections upon the Lives of the Reformers* Maitland Club, Glasgow 1845. For the Kelso minister's disgrace see R. C. Brownlee *Dunbar Golf Club* Dunbar 1980.

15. *Miscellany of the Maitland Club* vol i, 1834 and R. Clark *Golf - A Royal and Ancient Game* Edinburgh 1875, pxiii.

16. Alastair Johnston and James Johnston *The Chronicles of Golf* Cleveland 1993, p172.

17. See Chambers *Traditions of Edinburgh* Edinburgh 1824, p320.

18. The Tarbat fight and trial are found in *The Scots Peerage* vol iii, p74 and *Arnot's Criminal Trials,* p156.

19. New Spalding Club, Aberdeen 1890: William Cramond *Annals of Banff* vol i, p78.

20. Mark Napier *Memorials of Montrose* Maitland Club 1848, vol i, p103.

21. *Miscellany of the Scottish History Society* 1st Series, no. 15, 1893, pp xxviii and lxx. The King tried 'goulff' in Spital Fields in London in 1662 - see *The Diary of Alexander Brodie of Brodie 1652-80* Spalding Club, vol 33, Aberdeen 1841.

22. *Transactions of Society of Antiquaries of Scotland* 1812, p504.

23. John Row *The Historie of the Kirk in Scotland* Maitland Club Edinburgh 1842, pp 81 and 477. However, as late as 1674, an Edinburgh golfer visiting Haddington could write home to say 'send me out by the first carier my club and if ther be anie balls to the fore send them lykwayes.' *Scottish History Review* (1907) vol 4, 232-3.

24. Bernard Darwin *History of Golf in Britain* London 1952, p64: he did not give his source.

25. David Hamilton *Early Aberdeen Golf* Glasgow and Oxford 1985, p19.

26. *Seafield Correspondence from 1685 to 1780* Scottish History Society, 2nd Series (1912) vol 3, p64.

27. W. C. Dickinson *Two Students at St Andrews 1711-1716* Edinburgh 1952, p xxxix.

28. For Blair's sermons see Blair in Robert Chambers *Lives of Eminent Scotsmen* Edinburgh 1834, and Andrew Lang *Sir George Mackenzie, King's Advocate of Rosehaugh: his Life and Times 1636-1691,* London 1909.

29. Pett is mentioned in Napier's *Montrose* (ref 20), and Mill in *St Andrews* (ref 27). Charles E. Whitelaw *Scottish Arms Makers* London 1977 lists Baine (of Edinburgh) and Dais (at St Andrews).

30. *Edinburgh Testaments* are Mss volumes held in Register House Edinburgh. For commentary see Margaret Sanderson 'Edinburgh merchants in Society 1570-1603' in Ian B. Cowan and Duncan Shaw (eds) *The Renaissance and Reformation in Scotland* Edinburgh 1983.

31. Robert V. Agnew *Ayr and Galloway Natural History Society, No 14: Correspondence of Sir Patrick Waus of Barnbarroch 1540-97* vol 2, p341 describes the 'commoun' balls. 'Good' balls are noted in W. Ferrie (ed) *Letters and Correspondence of Rev John Carstairs* Edinburgh 1843, p110 and the Orkney analogy is in Johnston and Johnston *Chronicles* (ref 16) p66.

32. *Seafield Correspondence* (ref 26) p64. It is possible that a putting match was one of the choices.

33. These prices for the best balls in the later 1600s are an increase on earlier values. King James IV in 1505 paid 5d (Scots) for his ball, and a similar figure comes from a 1568 valuation of an estate noting 'three dozen of golf bawis, price thairof xxiijs (23 shillings)', making each ball about 7d. In 1610 a similar testament gives a figure of 1/6 per ball: see *Edinburgh Testaments* 52 and 44, quoted in William Craigie *A Dictionary of the Older Scottish Tongue* London 1937. Kincaid's ball price is found in David Hamilton *Early Golf at Edinburgh and Leith* Glasgow 1988, p25 and Napier *Montrose* (ref 20) p85. Napier gives these prices - golf ball 5s, chicken 8s, binding a book 8s, 1lb candles 7s, and a chopin of claret 7s. The Mackenzie prices are in Hamilton *St Andrews* (ref 51) p16. Nevertheless this wide range of prices is baffling and might need to be looked at closely again. Before the Union the Scots coinage had one twelfth of the value of the English equivalent, i.e. 4 shillings Scots = 4d sterling.

34. John Murray *Chronicles of the Families of Athol and Tullibardine* Ballantyne Press, Edinburgh 1908, vol i, pp 170,171 and 183.

35. This leather 'pock' was the property of General Thomas Dalyell of The Binns: see *Proceedings of the Society of Antiquaries* (New Series) vol 58, p356.

37. The Dickson family is analysed in I. T. Henderson and D. Stirk *Golf in the Making* Crawley 1979, p119.

38. Henderson and Stirk *Golf* (ref 37) p120.

39. Robert Clark *Golf: A Royal and Ancient Game* Edinburgh 1875, p xxi.

40. C. E. S. Chambers (1932) 'Early golf at Bruntsfield' *Book of the Old Edinburgh Club* vol 18, p1-10. See also Alastair J. Johnston *The Clapcott Papers* Edinburgh 1985.

41. For ball-makers at Leith see Henderson and Stirk *Golf* (ref 37) p119.

42. For Patersone as a player see Clark *Golf* (ref 39) p15.

43. Melville is described in Hume Brown (ed) *Register of the Privy Council of Scotland.*

45. James Gordon *A Description of Both Touns of Aberdeen 1670* Spalding Club 1842. If this is correct, it was unusual to number holes. As late as 1900, an area south of Leith Links, unconnected with golf, is named on Ordnance Survey maps as the 'Quarry Holes'.

46. David Wedderburn *Vocabula* Aberdeen 1636, and later editions, analysed in Hamilton *Aberdeen* (ref 25).

47. David Hamilton *Early Golf at Edinburgh and Leith* Glasgow 1988 and Olive M. Geddes *A Swing Through Time: Golf in Scotland 1457-1743* Edinburgh 1992.

48. Kincaid's Diary is National Library of Scotland Advocates Mss 32.7.7 and is examined in *Book of the Old Edinburgh Club* (1949) vol 27, 111-154.

49. James Maidment (ed) *The Autobiography of Sir Robert Sibbald* Edinburgh 1833.

50. The Bishop's demise is described in John Row (1842) *Historie of the Kirk in Scotland* Maitland Club pp 81, 477.

51. David Hamilton *Early Golf at St Andrews* Glasgow and Oban 1989, based on W. C. Dickinson *Two Students at St Andrews 1711-1716* Edinburgh 1952. For student archery see the remarkable article by A. J. S. Brook 'An account of the archery medals...' *Proceedings of the Society of Antiquaries of Scotland* vol 28, 343-468.

52. *Orkney and Shetland Papers* Register House 9/15/150. For Orkney golf see B. H. Hossak *Kirkwall in the Orkneys* Kirkwall 1900, and G. S. Robertson *A History of Stromness Golf Courses* Stromness 1970.

53. Sir Robert Gordon *Tutor Compt Book: 1616-1622.*

54. *A Selection of Extracts from the Ancient Minutes of the Kirk Session of Kinghorn* Kirkcaldy 1863.

55. Brownlee *Dunbar* (ref 5).

56. William Cramond *Records of Elgin 1234-1800* New Spalding Club 1903, vol ii, p46.

57. William Cramond *Annals of Banff* vol i, p77-79.

58. Johnston and Johnston *Chronicles* (ref 16) p66.

59. Brodie *Burgi* (ref 21) p333.

60. Even the village of Longforgan had golf on common land in 1693: see Scottish Record Office *Strathmore Papers* 0885 Box 198, Bundle 2.

61. But see Norman Macrae *Dingwall's Story of a Thousand Years* Wakefield 1974, which covers the period 1674-1733 and lists convictions for Sabbath-breaking by drinking, working and fishing, but there is no mention of golf or football. However, the choice of extracts for such volumes was in the hands of compilers, who may or may not have considered that sport was worthy of inclusion.

62. One fragment of information may help. In 1601 the King's Treasurer paid out for golf clubs and also to the same supplier for a 'pellettis'- a sheepskin - perhaps a covering for a bunch of clubs to keep the handles dry. See Treasurer's Accounts 1601 MS 68 quoted in *Scottish National Dictionary* under 'golf'.

63. For Smollett and the weather see *The Expedition of Humphrey Clinker* London 1771 and also Kirsty Duncan (1994) 'Climate and the decline of leprosy in Britain' *Proceedings of the Royal College of Physicians of Edinburgh* vol 24,114-120.

64. Early noble golf in Glasgow is found in Sir W. Fraser *The Annandale Book of the Johnstones, Earls and Marquises of Annandale* Edinburgh 1894, vol i, ccliii, quoting purchases of balls and clubs. At Glasgow it was decreed that 'schollars to be exercised in lawful games such as gouffe, archerie, and the lyk' *Munimenta Almae Universitatis Glasguensis: Records of the University of Glasgow from its Foundation until 1727* Maitland Club (1854) no 72, vol 2, p466, Glasgow 1854.

65. Excellent research, described in Johnston and Johnston *Chronicles* (ref 16) p55 and p170 has shown the antiquity of the game in Ayrshire. The Irvine link is found in Robert Blair *Memoires* (ref 28) p5 and the Marquis of Ailsa story is in Robert Browning *A History of Golf* London 1955, p32. Browning's source, the *Historie of the Kennedyis* was a manuscript, now lost, which formed the basis of Robert Pitcairn's *Historical and Genealogical Account of the Principal Families of the Name of Kennedys* 1830.

66. The Marquis of Argyll's *Instructions to a Son* London 1689 says of Scotland 'tennis is not used among us, but only in our capital city. But in lieu of that you have the excellent recreation of goff-ball.'

67. William H. Gibson *Early Irish Golf* Naas 1988.

68. Browning *History* (ref 65) p4 discusses the alleged delay by Charles in finishing his game.

CHAPTER FOUR: THE TRANQUIL CENTURY

1. T. C. Smout *A History of the Scottish People 1560-1830* Glasgow 1969. See also Grant G. Simpson *The Scots Soldier Abroad* Edinburgh 1992, T. M. Devine *The Tobacco Lords* Edinburgh 1975 and Linda Colley *Forging the Nation 1707-1837* Yale 1992.

2. Owen Silver *The Roads of Fife* John Donald 1987.

3. Carlyle *Autobiography* p293 and Dennis Brailsford 'Sporting days in eighteenth century England' *Journal of Sports History* vol 9, 41-54. Mondays were easily commonest day for sport, Saturday the least. Monday was the day of the week nearest the Saturday wages and farthest from the next pay: see W. B. Whitaker *The Eighteenth Century Sunday* London 1940.

4. Quoted in Roger Hutchinson *Camanachd!* Edinburgh 1989, p53.

5. For a discussion on the early links see Geoffrey S. Cornish and Ronald E. Whitten *The Golf Course* Leicester 1981.

6. John Sinclair *Statistical Account of Scotland, Drawn up from the Communications of the Ministers of the Different Parishes* 21 vols, Edinburgh 1793: see 'Fraserburgh Parish' for a mention of the mysterious stone holes.

7. For the unusual first hole at Leith see Alastair J. Johnston *The Clapcott Papers* Edinburgh 1985, p38, Leith Rotary Club *Leith and the Origins of Golf* Leith 1984, and David Hamilton 'A note on the holes at early Leith Links' *Through the Green* vol 2, June 1994. For St Andrews see J. B. Salmond *The Story of the Royal and Ancient* London 1956, p5.

8. Alistair B. Adamson *Millions of Mischiefs: Rabbits, Golf and St Andrews* Worcs 1990.

9. These march stones are described in J. B. Salmond *The Story of the Royal and Ancient* London 1956, p11.

10. J. C. Robbie *The Chronicle of the Royal Burgess Golfing Society of Edinburgh* Edinburgh 1936.

11. *Edinburgh Advertiser* May 29th 1770, noted by David White.

12. Alex Main *Fortrose and Rosemarkie Golf Club* Fortrose 1988, p6.

13. James Cant (ed) Henry Adamson *Muses Threnodie or Mirthful Mourning on the Death of Mr Gall* Perth 1774.

14. John Kerr *The Golf-Book of East Lothian* Edinburgh 1898, p41.

15. Minutes of the Glasgow Golf Club quoted in The Regality Club's *Articles on Old Glasgow 1889-1912*.

16. Michael Brander *The Life and Sport of the Inn* London 1973 and Leslie Gardiner *Stage Coach to John O'Groats* London 1961. For the pubs see Robert Kempt *Convivial Caledonia: Inns and Taverns of Scotland* Liverpool 1893 and Marie W. Stuart *Old Edinburgh Taverns* London 1952.

17. Leven golfing pubs were Cheen's, Marshall's and later the Caledonian Inn.

18. Early Bruntsfield golfers had met at Thomas Comb's, the clubmakers house cum premises. Later, the Burgess golfers had a rented room plus housekeeper's flat below, and then had their own tenement house: Stewart Cruden *Bruntsfield Links Golfing Society* Edinburgh 1992, pp 5 and 11. There was also a Golf 'Hotel' beside Bruntsfield Links. The present Golf Tavern was set up only in 1876 when the Bruntsfield golfers sold their rooms: see Marie Stuart *Old Edinburgh Taverns* London 1952.

19. For Glasgow pubs and inns see Robert Kempt *Convivial Caledonia* Liverpool 1893.

20. It is fashionable to view golf as a popular game only from 1850, and to state that prior to this, it was only played by a handful of aristocrats. Most historians obtained this view from Robert Browning's *History of Golf* London 1955 and share his view that the clubs were crucial: see John Lowerson in Tony Mason *Sport in Britain: A Social History* Cambridge 1989, p187-214, and Ian T. Henderson and David I. Stirk *Royal Blackheath* 1981.

21. Thomas Pennant *Tour in Scotland* Warrington 1774.

22. John Chamberlayne *Magnae Britanniae* 22nd English edition, 1st Scottish edition 1708, p524.

23. Tobias Smollett *The Expedition of Humphrey Clinker* London 1771.

24. Edward Topham *Letters from Edinburgh* 1774 and 1775 London 1776 and the *Statistical Account* 'Leith Parish' 1793; see also N. L. Tranter 'Popular sports and the Industrial Revolution in Scotland: the evidence of the Statistical Accounts '*Journal of History of Sport* 4, 21-38. One of the best-known eighteenth century golfers, 'The Cock o'the Green' in Kay's *A Series of Original Portraits* Edinburgh 1837, was not a club member.

25. This view that clubs alone counted is an understandable mistake prevalent in anglocentric golf histories. When golf spread to England, few players were outside the private club system. That a person could play golf in Scotland without being a member of a land- and property-owning club escaped the notice of historians, and this continues to elude and baffle contemporary writers and visitors.

26. Seafield Correspondence from 1685-1708 *Scottish History Society* New Series ii, vol 3, Edinburgh 1912.

27. Scottish Record Office: Maclaine Papers GD 174/1329.

28. For short courses see Johnston *Clapcott* (ref 7) p243, Colville *Musselburgh* p23, Tulloch *Morris* p30 and Alasdair M. Drysdale *The Golf House Club, Elie* Elie 1975. I doubt if these were merely putting greens.

29. Margaret Buchanan *Archery in Scotland: an Elegant and Manly Amusement* Glasgow Museums 1979.

30. Allan Ramsay *Works* vol iii.

31. *The Goff* has been reprinted many times: see Robert Clark *Golf: A Royal and Ancient Game* Edinburgh 1875 and *The Goff* United States Golf Association 1981. The poem is also reprinted in Alastair Johnston *The Clapcott Papers* Edinburgh 1985.

32. Kerr *Golf-Book* (ref 14) p51 gives the variations in the terminology of the Gentlemen Golfer's club. They were also called 'The Golfing Company' with or without 'of Edinburgh', and even 'The Edinburgh Golf Club' in the late 1700s. In 1800 a standard name was required for legal purposes and the cumbersome 'The Honourable the Edinburgh Company of Golfers' resulted; the present name simplified this awkward title later.

33. See for instance Peter Baxter *The Turf of Perth* Perth 1901.

34. The first silver club and the Town Guard are seen in the portrait of William Inglis, Captain of the Gentlemen Golfers in 1782-84. The Edinburgh Town Council nobly continued to provide new silver clubs until 1879. The players in *The Goff* played for a cup or quaich: until the 1950s it was customary after the Scottish Professional Championship to fill the trophy with whisky and pass it round. Curlers still have this ancient custom.

35. For these rules see Johnston *Clapcott* (ref 7) p44.

36. The rules are given verbatim in Johnston *Clapcott* (ref 7) p45

37. Salmond *R&A* (ref 9) p89.

38. The first entrants are described in Kerr *Golf-Book* (ref 14) p45 with some biographies given.

39. *The Fifeshire Journal* in 1855 listed 'The Gentlemen Golfers' and a club called 'The Leith Golf Club founded in 1744'.

40. For the change in rules regarding the Captain see Johnston *Clapcott* (ref 7) p48. From about 1806, though pre-elected, the captains played a token round. Now only a single stroke is required - the ceremonial driving in. The 'Champion as Captain' arrangement persisted elsewhere and Horace Hutchinson was champion and hence captain of Royal North Devon at the age of 16. This custom was last heard of at Minehead in 1930: see R. Browning *A History of Golf* London 1955, p54.

41. Browning *History* (ref 40) p6, doubtless from Alex Ewald *The Life and Times of Prince Charles Stuart* London 1883.

42. Robbie *Burgess* (ref 10) p10.

43. Salmond *R&A* (ref 7) p35.

44. Fortrose Parish in *Statistical Account* (ref 6).

45. Some hitherto unknown clubs keep turning up e.g. the Fraserburgh club, the Colinsburgh and Tweedside clubs of the early nineteenth century: see Johnston and Johnston *Chronicles* (ref 50) p413.

46. Stuart Lindsay *The Nairn Golf Club 1887-1987* Nairn 1987.

47. Andrew Cunningham *The Golf Clubs Round Largo Bay* Leven 1909, p2.

48. Archie Baird *Golf on Gullane Hill* Aberlady 1982, p7.

49. William McDowall *History of Dumfries* 4th edition, reprinted 1986: introduction p46.

50. Some of these golf sightings are new, and result from an energetic search by Alastair Johnston and James Johnston in *The Chronicles of Golf: 1457 to 1857* Cleveland 1993, pp 249, 279 and 291. For Cromarty see Hugh Miller *Memoir of William Forsyth* 1839.

51. David Hamilton *Early Golf in Glasgow 1558-1727* Oxford 1985, David Hamilton *Game at Golf* Glasgow 1987, James Colville *The Glasgow Golf Club* Glasgow 1907 and Gibson *The History of Glasgow* Glasgow 1775.

52. Kerr *Golf-Book* (ref 14) p42.

53. Foulis' rental is in David Hamilton *Early Golf at Edinburgh and Leith* Glasgow 1988, p79.

54. Johnston and Johnston *Chronicles* (ref 50) p481.

55. These rules have been discussed several times: see George Pottinger *Muirfield and the Honourable Company* Edinburgh 1972 and Johnston *Clapcott* (ref 7) p469. This period also saw the emergence of rules in other sports - cricket in 1727, racing in 1752 and even national rules for the game of bridge.

56. C. B. Clapcott *The Rules of the Oldest Golf Clubs from 1754-1848* Edinburgh 1935. Clapcott did not find the Honourable Company rules until 1945, after publishing this work: see Johnston *Clapcott* (ref 7) p469.

57. The relief from hazards rule changed in 1775 and gave the golfers a choice - almost a lottery. They could choose a short shot with an iron as before or take the chance of a much longer shot with a wood plus a penalty shot.

58. Robbie *Burgess* (ref 10) p34. The clarity of this passage may have resulted from the extensive help given to Robbie by Clapcott. For the rise of non-golfing clubs at this time see John Strang *Glasgow and Its Clubs* Glasgow 1857.

59. Johnston *Clapcott* (ref 7) p118.

60. Harry B. Wood *Golfing Curios and the Like* London 1911, p82.

61. See Johnston *Clapcott* (ref 7) and Salmond *R&A* (ref 9). The Aberdeen golfers a little later averaged three bottles of wine each per night before buying their own: see Browning *History* (ref 40) p46.

62. Clark *Golf* (ref 31) p63.

63. Johnston and Johnston *Chronicles* (ref 50) p350 gives a similar bill. See also Charles Smith *The Aberdeen Golfers: Records and Reminiscences* London 1909, facsimile edition by Ellesborough Press 1982, p46.

65. Dean Ramsey *Reminiscences of Scottish Life and Character* Glasgow 1872, p101. This return of puritan habits corresponded with a decline in Scotland's influence in Britain.

66. For early Scottish cuisine see Una Robertson *Scottish Records Association Conference Report* no 4, October 1985.

67. Johnston *Clapcott* (ref 7) p121.

68. Johnston *Clapcott* (ref 7) p122.

69. Browning *History* (ref 40) p49.

70. Smith *Aberdeen* (ref 63) p16. For first mention of 'tacket shoon' see Johnston and Johnston *Chronicles* (ref 50) p497.

71. David Stevenson *The First Freemasons: Scotland's Early Lodges and Their Members* Aberdeen University Press 1989. See also Margaret C. Jacob *Living the Enlightenment: Freemasonry and Politics In Eighteenth Century Europe* Oxford 1992. Freemasonry started in Scotland in the sixteenth century and the first English Lodge was set up in 1717.

72. Johnston *Clapcott* (ref 7) p72 has these postponements. Bill Gibson kindly found the R&A minutes which commented on the weather. A solitary Perth round in the rain is found in P. Baxter *Golf in Perth and Perthshire* p104.

73. For repairs to early clubs see David Hamilton *Early Golf at St Andrews* Glasgow and Oban 1986, p25 and W. Croft Dickinson *Two Students at St Andrews* Edinburgh 1935.

74. Personal communication from Bob Gowland.

75. C. B. Clapcott *Rules of the Ten Oldest Clubs from 1754-1848* Edinburgh 1935.

76. I. T. Henderson and David I. Stirk *Golf in the Making* Crawley 1979, *passim*.

77. Henderson and Stirk *Golf* (ref 76) p323.

78. Kincaid's *Diary* is found in the National Library of Scotland Advocates Manuscripts 32/7/7 and *Book of the Old Edinburgh Club* (1949) vol 27, 111-154.

79. These ball prices are noted in *Clerk of Penicuik Papers* Scottish Record Office GD 18/2178 and the *Annandale Papers* TD 86/65, Bundle 165. Prices for balls are given in Kincaid *Diary* (ref 78), Browning *History* (ref 40) p137 and Hamilton *St Andrews* (ref 73) p16.

80. Charles A. Malcolm *The British Linen Bank* Edinburgh 1950, p18.

81. The balls in the Samson's Bicentenary Catalogue were noticed by Dr John Strawhorn of Mauchline. An account for a cheap ball costing 3p in 1824 is found in Peter Lang *Duncan Dewar* Glasgow 1926.

82. W. MacGill *Old Ross-shire and Scotland* p71.

83. D. I. Stirk *Carry Your Bag, Sir: A History of Golf's Caddies* London 1989. Topham *Letters* (ref 24) quotes Tobias Smollett's book *Humphrey Clinker* and gives a vivid account of the activities of the caddies including a rather sinister evening of eating and drinking organised for the gentlemen by the caddies. The toastmaster was 'caddie Fraser' and he ran the proceedings, attended by a number of women of ill repute. At the end of the evening Fraser gave a toast to his masters. 'Here's a cup of thanks for the great and undeserved honour you have done your errand boys this day. Noo, we're your honour's masters, caddies again.' This strange gathering was held at lax Leith, not Edinburgh.

84. John G. Lockhart (ed) *Peter's Letters to his Kinfolk* Edinburgh 1817.

85. 'Disjeskit' balls are mentioned in Kerr *Golf-Book* (ref 14) p236. For forecaddies at North Berwick see Kerr *Golf-Book* (ref 14) p42.

86. *Statistical Account of Scotland XVIII*, p88-89.

87. See James Nolan *Of Golf and Dukes and Princes* Worcs 1982.

88. *Brora Golf Club 1891-1991* Brora 1991, p75.

89. Christopher Fyfe *Sierra Leone Inheritance* Oxford, 1964, p70.

90. Henderson and Stirk *Golf* (ref 76): supplement p4. Johnston and Johnston *Chronicles* (ref 50) have other Customs listings of exported golf equipment.

91. Charles Price and George C. Rogers *The Carolina Low Country: Birthplace of American Golf 1787* Charleston 1986, p54.

92. Benjamin Rush *Sermons to Gentlemen upon Temperance and Excercise* Philadelphia 1772.

93. James Barclay (1993) 'Early Golfers of Charleston and Savannah' *Golfiana* vol 5, no 1, 18-24. He points out that these early clubs' adverts mention the business meetings and dinner but make no mention of golf: he suggests they may simply have been social clubs, using the name of golf as a title only. This ignores the known shipments of clubs and balls to this area in this period.

94. William H. Gibson *Early Irish Golf* Naas 1988.

95. *Faulkner's Dublin Journal* 23rd October 1762, quoted in Gibson (ref 94) p9.

CHAPTER FIVE: THE INTERLUDE

1. For the crisis see T. C. Smout *A History of the Scottish People 1560-1830* Glasgow 1969, David Hamilton *The Healers: a History of Medicine in Scotland* Edinburgh 1981, and see also J. A. Mangan (ed) *Pleasure, Profit and Proselytism* London 1988, for sport at this time.

2. L. J. Saunders *Scottish Democracy 1815-1840* Edinburgh 1950, p315.

3. John Kerr *Golf-Book of East Lothian* Edinburgh 1896, p375 says 'more than once it has proved that the plough, in turning the sod, had only let loose a plague in the shape of a sandstorm, which had driven back agriculture by many a rood.'

4. Wray Vamplew *Pay Up and Play the Game: Professional Sport in Britain 1875-1914* Cambridge University Press 1988.

5. For the shinty malaise see Roger Hutchinson *Camanachd!* Edinburgh 1989, p55.

6. W. H. Murray *The Curling Companion* Glasgow 1981.

7. J. C. Robbie *The Chronicle of the Royal Burgess Golfing Society 1735-1935* Edinburgh 1936, p101.

8. Leith's golfing decline is noted in Alex Campbell *The History of Leith* Edinburgh 1827, p217 and Marshall *The Life and Times of Leith* Edinburgh 1986, p57.

9. Alastair J. Johnston *The Clapcott Papers* Edinburgh 1985, p184. For later decay at Leith see H. G. Hutchinson *British Golf Links* London 1896.

12. Johnston *Clapcott* (ref 9), p184.

13. Johnston *Clapcott* (ref 9) p185.

14. George Pottinger *Muirfield and the Honourable Company* Edinburgh 1972 describes the crisis circumspectly, and hints that the Secretary disappeared overseas with the club funds. See also Norman Mair *Muirfield - Home of the Honourable Company* Edinburgh 1994.

15. James Cundell *Rules of the Thistle Club* Edinburgh 1824.

16. For Carnegie's poem see Robert Clark *Golf: A Royal and Ancient Game* Edinburgh 1875, p157.

17. From a cheerful article in *St Andrews University Magazine* no 2, March 1863 – edited by H. B. Farnie.

18. Alistair B. Adamson *Millions of Mischief* Malvern 1990 and *Session Cases 1804-09*. For details of the litigation see Cleghorn vs Dempster, May 7th 1805, *Morison's Dictionary* 16141, 2 *Dows House of Lords Cases* 40, and J. B. Salmond *The Story of the R&A* London 1956.

19. H. Thomas Peter *Reminiscences of Golf and Golfers* Edinburgh 1890 (reprinted 1985) and *Chamber's Edinburgh Journal* 8th October, 1842.

20. Charles Roger *History of St Andrews* 1849.

21. From Henry Cockburn *Circuit Journeys* Edinburgh 1888 (reprinted 1975) p231.

22. David Stirk *The Great Clubmakers* London 1991, p59.

23. Robert Crampsey *St Mungo's Golfers: the History of Glasgow Golf Club 1787-1987* Glasgow 1990 and James Colville *The Glasgow Club 1787-1907* Glasgow 1907; the quotation is from *The Glasgow Herald* 13th April 1854.

24. James G. Dow *The Crail Golfing Society 1786-1936* Edinburgh 1936 (reprinted 1986) p31.

25. Dow *Crail* (ref 24) p50.

26. Kerr *Golf-Book* (ref 3) p70.

27. Archie Baird *Golf on Gullane Hill* Edinburgh 1982, p7.

28. The Fraserburgh and Montrose crises are described in H. Hutchinson *Golf Links* (ref 9).

29. For Kingsbarns see Harry B. Wood *Golfing Curios and the Like* London 1911, p74 and 75. The Bow of Fife trophy was auctioned at Phillips in 1993 and the Cruden Golf Club's box is described in *Scottish Memories* May 1994, p56.

30. For 'servitude' see David B. Smith 'The curlers of Lochwinnoch' *Journal of the Law Society of Scotland* January 1992, p33 and 34.

31. The moving spirit was a Mr George Fraser from Montrose. The club existed precariously and ceased in about 1882, when another group of golfers formed the modern club. See Jean M. Russell *Old Manchester Golf Club 1818-1988* Manchester 1988.

32. Carnegie's poem is reprinted in Clark *Golf* (ref 16) and Stewart *Golfiana* (ref 34). The updated *second* edition of the poem adds to the decadent mood. The men mentioned in the poem are Allan Robertson, Erskine Wemyss, Willie Park and Mr Hastie MP. For cross-membership of golfing societies at this time see Kerr *Golf-Book* (ref 3) p84. The Lees painting shows Sir David Baird and Sir Ralph Anstruther versus Campbell of Saddell and Major Playfair at the Ginger Beer Hole. Horses are seen on the links in some paintings from the times notably the St Andrews match by Lees, and the group at North Berwick painted by Sir Francis Grant in 1835. In mid-century, Sir John Low used a pony between shots at St Andrews, and James Wolfe-Murray is portrayed on his pony by the artist Thomas Hodge. 'Mounty' Melville also used such help – see Peters *Reminiscences* (ref 19) p2.

33. Cockburn *Circuit Journeys* (ref 21) p232.

34. The racing metaphor comes from J. L. Stewart *Golfiana Miscellanea* Glasgow 1887.

35. North Berwick's prizes are found in Kerr *Golf-Book* (ref 3) p87.

36. Kerr *Golf-Book* (ref 3) p84 describes the country-house gatherings.

38. Scottish Record Office GD 157/2414. For another description of the golfers' meeting and fully booked inns, see T. F. Dibden *A Bibliographical, Antiquarian and Picturesque Tour...* London 1838, p877, a book which contains the first illustration of the golf swing.

39. This hostile obituary of Carnegie is found in Clark *Golf* (ref 16) p155. This may be another example of how the next generation tried to dissociate themselves from the excesses, sporting and otherwise, of the earlier lax period.

40. See *Caledonian Mercury* 26th May, 1817. In the same newspaper, eggs sold for 7d per dozen, beef was 7d per pound, and a Waverley novel cost 5s. This match was reported in many of the Scottish newspapers. For an account of an earlier curling match for 1,000 guineas see James Taylor *The Ancient Scottish Game* Edinburgh 1884, p59.

41. 'Goufin Charlie' is mentioned in T. D. Miller *Famous Scottish Links and Other Golfing Papers* Edinburgh 1911, and he is one of the crowd in Lees's painting.

42. *First Statistical Account of Scotland:* Parish of Inveresk.

43. Even so, no clear description of the financing of these challenge matches has survived. Kerr *Golf-Book* (ref 3) mentions an awkwardness when Dunn's backers did not appear with the money, and Dunn had to put up his own: see Henry Leach *Great Golfers in the Making* London 1907, p112. Another match, Ferguson vs Strath for £50 a side, was tied: Ferguson says that in spite of this, his backers 'did not forget him'.

44. Bobby Burnett *The St Andrews Opens* Edinburgh 1990, p12.

45. See Baird *Gullane* (ref 27).

46. Saunders *Scottish Democracy* (ref 2) pp82 and 112.

47. Kerr *Golf-Book* (ref 3) p9.

48. For a history of swimming see Charles Sprawson *Haunts of the Black Masseur* Cape 1992 and Linda Colley *The Lure of the Sea* London 1994.

49. Scottish stage coaches are described in Leslie Gardiner *Stage Coach to John O'Groats* London 1961.

50. In spite of the considerable interest in railway history, a simple chronology of the spread of the network is hard to find. The time of arrival of the train service is blurred occasionally by previous indirect services, freight lines etc. But see P. J. G. Ransom *The Victorian Railway and how it Evolved*, C. J. A. Robertson *The Origins of the Scottish Railway System 1722-1844* Edinburgh 1983, John Thomas *Forgotten Railways: Scotland* Newton Abbot 1976, W. S. Bruce *The Railways of Fife*, Perth 1980, M. J. Worling *Early Railways of the Lothians* Edinburgh 1991, and Andrew Hajducki *Berwick and Gullane Branch Lines* Oxford 1992.

51. For black servants at Elie see Alastair Drysdale *The Golf-House Elie* Elie 1975; similar servants at Dunbar are noted in R. C. Brownlee *Dunbar Golf Club* Dunbar 1980. See also J. A. Mangan *The Cultural Bond: Sport, Empire and Society* London 1993.

52. David C. Smail *Prestwick Golf Club* Prestwick 1989.

53. A triumphal entry of the railway is described in Stephen Stoker *The Openin' o' St Andrews Railway: a Dream of Coming Glory* Cupar 1851.

54. The best early description of gutta percha is in the *Encyclopaedia Britannica* 9th Edition 1875, under 'Gutta Percha'. By 1875 at the height of its use, Sarawak had exported gutta from about 3 million mature trees which were not replaced. Gutta gave place eventually to vulcanised rubber. Gutta percha had one defect hardly apparent in Scotland: in very hot weather the ball softened a little. W. Park Jnr in his pioneering visits to America, carried gutty balls on the course in ice buckets.

55. For uses of this material see A. Goodman, H. Schilder and W. Aldrich (1974) 'The thermomechanical properties of gutta-percha' *Oral Surgery* vol 37, 954-61.

56. For the 'pioneer' controversy see Henderson and Stirk *Golf in the Making* Crawley 1979, pp48-54, and the close examination in Alastair Johnston and James Johnston *The Chronicles of Golf* Cincinnati 1993. For Paterson see J. G. McPherson *Golf Illustrated* 22nd February 1901, 1st March 1901 and 24th January 1902, and Kerr *Golf-Book* (ref 3) p82 gives the inventor in Edinburgh's Lawnmarket. See also John S. Martin *The Curious History of the Golf Ball* New York 1968.

57. Alistair Adamson *Allan Robertson* Worcs 1985, p51.

58. *Dundee Advertiser* 1859.

59. Hoyles *Games* 1744, p288 talks of 'the heavy iron... and the light iron.' H. B. Farnie's *The Golfer's Manual* of 1857 says 'the heavy iron must be used unavoidably in the manner of a pick-axe.' For a history of the cleek and details of hand-forging and other methods see Henderson and Stirk *Golf* (ref 56), supplement p173, and Peter Georgiady *A Compendium of British Club Makers* Greensboro 1994.

60. Henderson and Stirk *Golf* (ref 56) supplement, p8.

61. William Galbraith *Prestwick St Nicholas Golf Club* Prestwick 1950.

62. Dow's hickory is mentioned in J. S. F. Murdoch (ed) *The Best of the Bulletin 1970-1977* Golf Collectors' Society 1977.

63. Henderson and Stirk *Golf* (ref 56). For persimmon see Elmore Just *The Persimmon Story* Louisville 1984.

65. W. W. Tulloch *Life of Tom Morris* London 1908, reprinted Ellesborough Press 1982.

66. Hackney *Carnoustie* (ref 72) says a Carnoustie club invented the handicap system; this priority is also claimed for Madras College – the St Andrews school – see St Andrews Links Trust *A Year at St Andrews* 1994, p189.

67. Farnie *Manual* (ref 59) describes the long grass at Bruntsfield. As late as 1892, the Huntly Golf Club, playing on the Duke of Gordon's estate, were permitted play only from December to April.

69. Stewart Hackney *Bygone Days on the Old Course* Dundee 1990, p33. Various dates have been given for the decision to widen the Old Course, and the 1850s seem most likely, though plans in the R&A clubhouse still show a narrow course in 1870. There were two stages in this widening – twin pins in the existing greens first, then large double greens with course widening later. The huge double greens may have taken time to expand to the present size.

70. The Old Course 'backwards' route is discussed in the *Glasgow Herald* February 14th, 1989.

71. See *Dunbar* (ref 51) and Stewart Hackney *St Andrews* (ref 69).

72. For the Carnoustie complaint – see Stewart Hackney *Carnoustie Links: Courses and Players* Dundee 1989, p36.

73. See Hackney *St Andrews* (ref 69).

74. The Glasgow Club was also missing from Farnie's list. Early amateur tournaments are noted in John Behrend *John Ball of Hoylake* Droitwich 1989. Tony Mason's *Sport in Britain: a Social History* Cambridge 1989, p191 claims the Oxford/Cambridge match as the first club match, an irritating example of anglo-centric history.

75. Improved scores were noted at this time in A. Bennet *The Book of St Andrews Links* Cupar 1898. There was also an improvement in the links 'making the course five shots easier' - Hackney *St Andrews* (ref 69): see also James E. Shaw *Prestwick Golf Club* Glasgow 1938 and T. D. Miller *The History of the Royal Perth Golfing Society* Perth 1935.

76. See John Adams *The Parks of Musselburgh* Droitwich 1991 and George Colville *Five Open Champions and the Mussselburgh Golf Story* Musselburgh 1980. Harry Lauder was a caddie and golfer at Musselburgh: see his *Roamin' in the Gloamin'* London 1928.

77. Scottish Record Office Dept 375/36 Misc 1863.

78. An excellent account in Smail *Prestwick* (ref 52), and Burnett *Opens* (ref 44) p12 gives information on the Earl of Eglinton.

79. Smail *Prestwick* (ref 52) p52.

80. These forgotten match-play events are carefully recorded in Charles MacArthur *The Golfer's Annual for 1869-70*, Ayr 1870.

CHAPTER SIX: THE NEW ENTHUSIASM

1. *Quarterly Review,* 1898 p419. For the rise of sport in Victorian times see R. D. Anderson 'Sport in the Scottish Universities' *International Journal of History of Sport*, 4, 177-189, J. A. Mangan *The Games Ethic and Imperialism* London, 1986, and J. A. Mangan (ed) *The Cultural Bond: Sport, Empire and Society* London 1992. For the revival of the Highland Games see Michael Brander *The Essential Guide to the Highland Games* Edinburgh 1992.

2. David Hamilton (1993) 'The Golf Crisis' *Golfiana* vol 5, no 2, p3-8.

3. For Musselburgh see George M. Colville *Five Open Champions and the Musselburgh Story* Musselburgh 1980 and John Adams *The Parks of Musselburgh* Worcs 1991. For club- and ballmakers see I. T. Henderson and D. I. Stirk *Golf in the Making* Crawley 1979 and David Stirk *The Great Clubmakers* London 1992. See also Pete Georgiady (1987) 'The Park Family' *Golfiana* vol 1, no 2, 26-31 and also John Kerr *The Golf-Book of East Lothian* Edinburgh 1898, p40,who describes Musselburgh as the 'centre of east-coast golfing gravity.' See also William Maughan *Picturesque Musselburgh and Its Golf Links* Paisley 1906. The only well-known Leith gentleman golfer from this period at Musselburgh was Mr John Wood, mentioned in James Balfour *Reminiscences of Golf* Edinburgh 1887, p31.

4. For an outing to Musselburgh in 1672 see David Hamilton *Early Golf at Edinburgh and Leith* Glasgow 1988, p45.

5. Stewart Cruden *Bruntsfield Links Golfing Society* Edinburgh 1992. For details of the move to Musselburgh see Alastair Johnston *The Clapcott Papers* Edinburgh 1985.

6. For Dunn and Park see Colville (ref 3). Dunn's talents were overshadowed by Park's achievements, though Dunn laid out the courses at Felixstowe, Great Yarmouth, Mitcham, Woking, Stanmore, Chislehurst, Eltham, Richmond, Huddersfield, Worlington, Raynes Park, Ealing and a number of private courses. Abroad, he designed the courses at Dinard, Biarritz, and Tenerife for the English Grand Hotel Company.
    The neglect of Musselburgh's history is aided by the complexity of the relationships within the golfing families, notably the Dunns and the Parks, and the affection for William as a boy's name in this group.

7. For Strathpeffer see Fortescue Fox *Strathpeffer Spa* London 1889, D. Manson *Strathpeffer Spa in the Highlands* London 1869, Reid *Quick before the Memory Fades* Strathpeffer 1980, *One Hundred Years of Strathpeffer Spa Golf Club* Strathpeffer 1988, and W. A. R. Thomson *Spas That Heal* London 1978. See also Eric Simpson (1992) 'Dookin' and Gowf' *Scottish Local History* no 25, 5-8.

8. For women's sport in general see J. A. Mangan and Roberta J. Park *From 'Fair Sex' to Feminism* London 1987, Kathleen McCrone *Sport and the Emancipation of English Women 1870-1914*, London 1990 and Sheila Fletcher (1985) 'The making and breaking of a female tradition: women's physical education in England' *British Journal of Sports History* vol 2, 29-39.

9. Henderson and Stirk *Golf* (ref 3) p287.

10. May Hezlet *Ladies Golf* London 1904 is quoted in Rosalynde Cossey *Golfing Ladies* London 1984 as the source of the Wolfe-Murray story, but I cannot find the passage. For early Scottish women's organisation see *History of the Scottish Ladies Golfing Association 1903-28* London 1928. For ladies' dress see Muriel Monkhouse *Ancient History, some Reminiscences of the 'Eighties' and 'Nineties'* London 1938, which mentions the motor cap, veil and elastic waistband.
    One feature of St Andrews golf was rather diverting for the Victorian male golfer. At the Swilcan Burn at the first hole, local women washed clothes in tubs, trampling them with their feet and holding their skirts above the knee.

12. See Stewart Hackney *Carnoustie Links: Courses and Players* Dundee 1989, p80.

13. *Golf World* May 1991, p166.

14. Lord Wellwood in Horace Hutchinson (ed) *The Badminton Library: Golf* London 1890, p29. Hutchinson later showed some embarrassment at his 'Jews' quarters' phrase.

15. Charles Price (1987) *Golfiana* vol 1, no 2, 12-15.

16. Mabel A. Stringer *Golfing Reminiscences* London 1924. See the account in Pete Georgiady 'Early golf clubs for women and children' *Golfiana* vol 4, 25-26.

17. The girl's school is described in J. S. A. Macauley *St Leonard's School, St Andrews* St Andrews 1977 and Julia M. Grant *St Leonard's School 1877-1927* Oxford. The school later built a *private* golf course for their girls.

18. A good description of the life of a twentieth century forecaddy is found in Ernest Hargreaves *Caddie in the Golden Age* London 1993.

19. For caddie fees see Hutchinson *Badminton* (ref 14) p112 and 282. Further details are found in the early *Golfer's Handbook*, and Kerr's *Golf-Book* (ref 3) p237 describes sale of 'disjesit' balls.

20. Herd's mother's views are recorded in Sandy Herd *My Golfing Life* London 1923. For the 'Scholar's Holes' at St Andrews see Robert Browning *A History of Golf* London 1955, p171, and p153 for the Baker's Holes.

21. This 'shielding' probably had a detectable effect on the lighter gutty ball: see Horace Hutchinson *Fifty Years of Golf* London, 1919 p262. Other persistent stories were of caddies' shoes with false bottoms used to pick up opponents' balls. For the reverse 'finding' of a ball identical to the player's lost ball see Eric Brown *Knave of Clubs* London 1961, p121.

22. Stewart Hackney *Bygone Days on the Old Course* Dundee 1990, p26.

23. Kerr *Golf-Book* (ref 3) p424 describes the Aberlady boys.

24. For boys at the burn see Stewart Hackney *Carnoustie* (ref 12) and their equivalents at St Andrews are described in Stewart Hackney *Bygone Days on the Old Course* Dundee 1990 and Henry Leach *Great Golfers in the Making* London 1907 (facsimile edition USGA 1988) p212.

25. For boys at North Berwick see Kerr *Golf-Book* (ref 3) p386. For Italian boys 'losing' balls in the Tiber see *The Times* 4th June 1924. For a spate of holes in one on the Riviera see George Duncan *Golf at the Gallop* London 1951, p119. Recently the North Korean leader had a number of holes in one on his first visit to the links.

26. In a famous exchange at St Andrews, a caddie was asked if he knew the Prime Minister. The caddie replied that he did; 'Ah ken him weel; Ah'm wearing his breeks'. Hogan at Carnoustie was surprised when his caddie took his employer's golf shoes home at night and polished them, but was less pleased when the caddy ate Hogan's packed lunch, provided by the hotel, from the golf bag during a round. At the 1962 Open at St Andrews, one of Snead's caddies was jailed after a brawl in the town but returned to beg the winning ball from Snead 'to treasure all his days'; the caddie sold it immediately for £50: see S. L. McKinlay *Scottish Golf and Golfers* Classics of Golf 1992.

27. Hutchinson *Fifty Years* (ref 21) p292 shows irritation at the new English caddies.

28. The list of distinguished caddies is found in Bobby Burnett *The St Andrews Opens* Edinburgh 1990.

29. Fiery and Big Crawford are described in Adams *Musselburgh* (ref 3). For later use of a forecaddie see Hargreaves *Cotton* (ref 18) p119.

30. In 1866 a tournament for £25 total was arranged at Leith with £10 first prize. Ferguson says 'the newspapers made a great fuss...' See Leach *Great Golfers* (ref 24) p184 and Kerr *Golf-Book* (ref 3) p329.

31. John F. Burnett 'Pulling them in: assembling some large crowds in Scotland in the nineteenth century' *Scottish Records Association Conference Report* no 15, 9-11.

32. The only allegation, uncorroborated and withdrawn, is found in David C. Smail (ed) *Prestwick Golf Club: Birthplace of the Open* Prestwick 1990, p59. Sharing of winnings among young professionals is and was common: see Eric Brown *Knave of Clubs* London 1961.

33. Kirkaldy *Memories* in 1920 said 'it is much different nowadays when booing at golf would be like booing in the Kirk.' Paid hecklers are described in Alastair Johnston and James Johnston *The Chronicles of Golf: 1457 to 1857* Cleveland 1993, p562. In the 1950s there was strong disapproval of the noisy Ayrshire supporters of Hamilton McInally, the talented Scottish golfing miner.

34. Old Tom's matches are given in detail in W. W. Tulloch *The Life of Tom Morris* London 1908.

35. *Ben Sayers – One Hundred Years of Golf in North Berwick 1857-1962: the Doreen Sayers Scrapbook* North Berwick 1994. Wethered's caustic remarks are in her *Golfing Memories and Methods* London 1933, p277. Kerr's *Golf-Book* p71 gives an account of the early events in the town's growth.

36. Arthur J. Balfour *Chapters of Autobiography* London 1930, p229, and Blanche Dugdale *Arthur James Balfour* London 1939.

37. *The Times* July 23rd, 1894: John Kerr may have written this comment.

38. A flavour of the fashionable town is given in B. Jamieson *North Berwick: Biarritz of the North* Haddington 1995

40. Kerr *Golf-Book* (ref 3) p263.

41. Nor does appear much in the newspapers of the day. In 1872 *The Observer* did not report the first FA Cup Final, nor the First Test in Melbourne in 1877.

42. See Richard E. Donovan and Joseph S. F. Murdoch *The Game of Golf and the Printed Word* Castalio Press, New York 1988. For a readable personal commentary on the earlier literature see Joseph S. F. Murdoch *The Murdoch Library of Golf* Worcs 1991. The first history of this newly old subject is found in H. B. Farnie's *The Golfer's Manual* Cupar 1857. Farnie, then a student at St Andrews, was later an editor, controversialist, adulterer, bigamist, and librettist. Other early golf historians were Fittis, Millar, Low, Smart, and Charles and Garden Smith. See also H. Thomas Peter *Reminiscences of Golf and Golfers* Edinburgh 1890 and James Balfour *Reminiscences of Golf on St Andrews Links* Edinburgh 1887. For guide books to the golfing areas see Andrew Cunninghame *The Golf Courses Round Largo Bay* Leven 1909, and for St Andrews see *The Book of St Andrews Links* Edinburgh 1898. See also Peter Baxter *Golf in Perth and Perthshire* Perth 1899.

43. For details of these compendia see Richard E. Donovan and Joseph S. F. Murdoch (ref 42) which include the *Golfers' Handbook*, *Golfing Annual*, and *Spalding's Official Golf Guide* in America. Lesser known but readable handbooks and annuals are Dalrymple's *Golfer's Guide 1895-98* and John Low's *Nisbet's Golf Year Book* 1905-14.

44. This literary link with Strathtyrum House, which had its own reserved starting times on the Old Course until recently, is found in *The Lonsdale Library* vol 9 - *The Game of Golf* - p33, and further detail in Mrs Gerald Porter *William Blackwood and His Sons* Edinburgh 1898.

45. A summary based on Donovan and Murdoch (ref 42) p13.

46. Since English golf was based on private clubs, historians soon forgot that in Scotland much golf was played by non-club members. See Tony Mason *Sport in Britain* Cambridge, p191. For anglicisation in general see Eric Hobsbaum and Terence Ranger (eds) *The Invention of Tradition* Cambridge 1983.

47. Westward Ho! is described in E. J. Davies and G. W. Brown *The Royal North Devon Golf Club 1864-1986* Devon 1989.

48. John Behrend *Golf at Hoylake* Worcs 1989.

49. These pioneering experiments are found in *Lonsdale Library* (ref 44) p162 and Browning's *History* (ref 20) p167 says the land for Sunningdale was cleared and sown with seed, and succeeded against predictions. The introduction of grass-cutting equipment is credited to a Mr Budding of Stroud in 1852. Abroad, new tougher grass species were experimented with elsewhere and at Chicago, one of the first American courses, golf was only possible because regular watering was used. In Scotland there was a reluctance to interfere with nature, and watering of the greens was introduced cautiously. The animals were removed with little knowledge of the effects of this on the grass and some serious problems resulted later from this disruption to the ancient ecosystem.

50. Alan M. Thom *From Westlands to Eastlands: the History of Rothesay Golf Club* Rothesay 1992, and Dugald McIntyre *Beyond Mount Pisgah* Millport, 1988. See also Anon *Blairgowrie Golf Club 1889-1989* Blairgowrie 1989, p11.

51. These strictures on the pioneer designers are found in Tom Simpson's chapter in *Lonsdale* (ref 44) p162.

52. After their first visit south to the Open at Sandwich, Andra Kirkaldy and his friends had to spend the evening in London before catching the overnight train to Edinburgh. They found their way to the West End and, picking a fashionable restaurant, were overawed at the sophistication, the waiters and the prices. The image of the gruff Scots professional, beloved of P. G. Wodehouse, may have been based on Stewart Maiden, Jones' teacher, and the taciturn Maiden is described with affection in R. T. Jones and O. B. Keeler *Down the Fairway* London 1927.

53. For Smith see *Golfing* 23rd July, 1903.

54. Adams *Park* (ref 3) and for patent clubs in general see Peter Georgiady *Golfiana* vol 3, no 1, p15-20.

55. The Huntercombe venture is described in Adams *Park* (ref 3).

56. Stewart's exploits at Carnoustie and Machrihanish are found in Hackney *Carnoustie* (ref 12) p70 and D. J. McDermid *100 Years of Golf at Machrihanish 1876-1976* Machrihanish 1976, p7.

57. The first Scottish handicaps were given at the Rose Club, Carnoustie: see Stewart Hackney *Carnoustie* (ref 12) Dundee 1988, p15.

58. These Corinthian attitudes are found in Horace Hutchinson *Golfing* London 1893, p84.

59. For the gentlemen's attitudes in another sport see Chris Bonnington *The Climbers: A History of Mountaineering* London 1992. The first Alpine Club, formed in London, considered it improper to climb without a guide, and Whymper, who climbed the Matterhorn in 1865, was shunned by the Club for ungentlemanly use of artificial help – notably crampons etc.

60. Historicus 'Country club golf' *Golf Monthly* December 1987. 'Historicus' was Eddie Park (died 1989) and his interesting articles were gathered posthumously as Eddie Park *Real Golf* Dovercourt 1990. See also Geoffrey Cornish and Ronald Whitten *The Golf-Course* New York 1981, p32, and for Vardon at Ripon see Harry Vardon *My Golfing Life* London 1933.

61. The tenacious George Houghton penetrated to the private royal course at Balmoral: see his *Golf Addict Among the Scots* London 1967. Two private courses remain in the Edinburgh area, one of which belongs to Lord Rosebery, and is used largely by his estate workers.

62. For the Scottish 'factor' as villain – see W. G. P. Colledge *Mortonhall Golf Club 1892-1992* Edinburgh 1992.

63. For artisan golf see Mark Simpson *Golf World* February 1991, p64. Thom *Rothesay* (ref 50) describes the Rothesay artisan section: see also McDermid *Machrihanish* (ref 56).

64. Wray Vamplew *Pay Up and Play the Game* Cambridge 1988, p62. Amateur gentlemen 'caused no pain, were not rude to servants, did not wear ready-made suits, signet rings, nor club ties in public places.'

65. Madeleine Beard *English Landed Society in the Twentieth Century* London 1989, p2.

66. Kerr *Golf-Book* (ref 30), p331 describes the money match.

67. John Behrend *John Ball of Hoylake* 1993, p11 has this important quote.

The earliest use of the word 'amateur' is usually attributed to a clipping from 1853 in Allan Robertson's album: 'the captain...doing the whole round in 86, this number has rarely, if ever, been equalled by an amateur': see Peter Davies *The Historical Dictionary of Golfing Terms* London 1993, p12. However there was earlier use in reference to the great Montrose challenge match – see *The Scotsman* 9th November, 1825, which mentions the word.

The formal definition of an amateur came in the rules for the first Amateur Championships, and not as part of the rules of golf. An amateur golfer, the championship committee decided, 'shall be a golfer who has never made for sale any golf clubs, balls, or any other articles connected with the game, who has never carried clubs for hire after attaining the age of 15 years, and who has not carried clubs for hire at any time within 6 years of the date on which the competition begins each year; who has never received any consideration for playing in a match or for giving lessons in the game, and who, for a period of five years prior to the 1st of September, 1886, has never received a money prize in an open competition'. There are several nuances here. The exclusions are against manual golfing labour; golfing journalists and authors were not affected. Lastly, any humble player of talent from near any of the major links or clubs would always have been a caddie at some point, excluding him from the gentlemen's tournaments.

For recent remarkable professional sprinting results in Scotland see *Daily Telegraph* 2nd January, 1993. The great nineteenth-century runners were W. G. George and W. Cummings. The great Scottish professional sprint meeting at Powderhall is still held on New Year's Day. Professional running was under handicap and hence the times recorded were of lesser importance.

68. See Peter Ryde (ed) *Royal and Ancient Championship Records 1860-1980* St Andrews 1981, and the early *Golfer's Handbook*. Full-time amateurs like Hutchinson and Simpson had Corinthian ideals, but appear to have had considerable leisure to devote to play. Their means of support is far from clear: true gentlemen did not work for a living.

69. Vamplew *Pay Up* (ref 64): some suburban Scottish clubs still exclude professional footballers from golf club membership.

70. The rise of the R&A has not received close attention or explanation, but see H. S. C. Everard *A History of the Royal and Ancient Golf Club of St Andrews, from 1754-1900* Edinburgh 1907. The size of the membership and their home town have not been studied, but some of the early yearbooks have this basic information. For tensions between the local and distant memberships see Hackney *St Andrews* (ref 23), and more recently in *A Year at St Andrews*, published since 1994 by the St Andrews Links Trust.

71. The long queues at Musselburgh are described in Colville *Musselburgh* (ref 3) p22, and the legal case is *Sanderson vs Lees and Brown 1859, 21 Dunlop 1011* and *22 Dunlop 24*. For the move to Muirfield see Kerr *Golf-Book* (ref 3) p375. For similar pressure on Montrose links see *Golfing* 25th February, 1904.

72. J. A. MacCulloch *The Misty Isle of Skye* 1905.

73. For bets see Kerr *Golf-Book* (ref 3) p331. No account of the powerful Scottish Temperance Movement exists, but see W. R. Lambert *Drink and Sobriety in Victorian Wales* Cardiff 1983, and Mark Clapson *A Bit of a Flutter: Popular Gambling and English Society 1832-1961* Manchester 1992. For the punters following Wethered's summer matches see Wethered *Memoirs* (ref 35) p239.

74. Lambert *Drink* (ref 73) p5.

75. Fred Hawtree *Through the Green* June 1993, p11, and March 1994, p21-23. For Pau see Nolan *Cannes* (ref 76).

76. For Biarritz and Cannes see James Nolan *Of Golf and Dukes and Princes: Early Golf in France* Worcs 1982 and the *Daily Telegraph* 17th Aug,

1991. For general accounts of the British discovery of Europe in winter see John Premble *The European Passion* London 1987. The Czechoslovakian course closed under Communism, and golf was denounced as a capitalist sport, along with bowls and snooker.

77. Early Canadian golf is described in James Barclay *Golf in Canada: A History* Toronto 1992, p74.

78. James A. Barclay (1987) 'The legend of William Doleman' *Golf Collector's Society Bulletin* May 1987 and *Golfiana* vol 1, no 1, 1987, p37. See also L. V. Kavanagh *The History of Golf in Canada* Toronto 1973.

79. Lorne Rubenstein and J. Briggs *Brantford Golf and Country Club 1879-1979* Toronto 1979.

80. For the claims of White Sulphur Springs and its Oakhurst Links as pioneers in 1880, see *Golf Monthly* February 1995, p67. Other claimants for priority are Douglas Field (Chicago), Dorset (Vermont) and Foxburgh (Pennsylvania) – see Geoffrey Cornish and Ronald Whitten *The Golf Course* New York 1981. For the conventional story see Herbert W. Wind *The Story of American Golf* New York 1948, p78, who mentions the earlier attempts, notably by Horace Hutchinson, to introduce golf to America, as does Hutchinson in *Fifty Years of Golf* p216. See also Richard Tufts *The Scottish Invasion* Pinehurst 1962. The Dunfermline link is found in Douglas Ferguson *Dunfermline Golf Club* Dunfermline 1987, and the Shinnecock puzzle is examined in David Goddard (1987) 'A Shinnecock conundrum' *Golfiana* vol 1, no 2, p32. Some other, neglected, pioneer designers are listed in Cornish and Whitten *Golf Course* (ref 59).

81. Wind *American Golf* (ref 80) p78.

82. Jolly is mentioned in Barkow *Dance Floor* (ref 87) p59.

83. See his autobiography – Charles B. Macdonald *Scotland's Gift – Golf* New York 1928.

84. Kenneth Krakauer *When Golf Came to Kansas City* Kansas 1986, p6.

85. Bill Carey 'John Hamilton Gillespie 1852-1923: father of Florida golf' *Golfiana* vol 3, no 2, p13.

86. Cripple Creek is described in *Golfing* 17th October, 1901.

87. For acceptance of professional golfers in USA see Hackney *Carnoustie* (ref 12) p23, Al Barkow *Gettin' to the Dance Floor: the Early Days of American Pro-Golf* London 1986, and for a less tolerant US club (Myopia) see *Golfiana* (1994) vol 6, no 3, p9.

88. Foulis is mentioned in *Golfing* 6th Feb 1902, and in Herb Matter and James Knerr (1994) 'The Foulis legacy' *Golfiana* vol 6, no 2, 3-11.

89. For a possible link between the spread of golf and the widening popularity of Scotch whisky see *Golfing* 7th August, 1902.

90. The revival in Ireland is described in William H. Gibson *Early Irish Golf* Naas 1988.

91. Daniel G. Soutar *The Australian Golfer* Melbourne 1908 and Terry Smith *Complete Book of Australian Golf* 1967.

93. For New Zealand golf see G. M. Kelly *Golf in New Zealand: a Centennial History* Wellington 1971.

94. Early South African golf appears in C. F. Odell *History of the Pretoria Country Club 1909-1975* Pretoria 1977.

95. Pearson Surita *The Royal Calcutta Golf Club* Calcutta 1979.

96. For Hong Kong see T. F. R. Waters *History of Hong Kong Golf Club* Hong Kong 1930.

97. For the golf of the colonial governors see Mangan *Cultural Bond* (ref 1) p186. See also T. R. Clougher (ed) *Golf Clubs of the Empire* London 1927. The huge membership of golf clubs in the Empire, as given in the *Golfer's Handbook,* is probably a reflection of social membership, and facilities for other sports. The Country Club at Johannesburg had no less than 4027 members and the nearby Royal Golf Club had 1352. The Durban Club had 3500.

98. The Mexican connection is mentioned in *Golfing* 6th Feb, 1902.

99. Dr Cran of Belise is featured in *Golfing* 26th March, 1903.

100. Alan J. S. Paterson *The Victorian Summer of the Clyde Steamers* Newton Abbot 1972. For rail travel see *Dumbarton Golf Club* Dumbarton 1988, pp23,38 for railway concession tickets, and Fife Golfing Association *A History of Golf Clubs in Fife* Leven 1989, p71 gives some North British Railway golfing concessions.

101. House of Commons: Minutes of Evidence taken before the Select Committee of the House of Lords on the St Andrews Links Bill 1894, and the *Burgh Police Act 1892*: see Kerr (ref 3) p79.

102. Hackney's *Carnoustie* (ref 12).

CHAPTER SEVEN: OUR TIMES

1. This important quotation has been attributed to John Kerr. I cannot find it in his writings, but there is a hint of the sentiment in his article on Muirfield in *The Golfer's Annual* 1892, p117. Kerr was the last Scottish golf historian and his verdict is important.

2. Peter Lewis (1992) 'Prize money for pioneering pros.' *Golfiana* vol 4, no 1, 3-8.

3. Donald Grant *Personal Memories of Royal Dornoch Golf Club 1900-1925* Dornoch 1978. For Donald Ross see Donald Grant *Donald Ross of Pinehurst and Royal Dornoch* Dornoch 1973 and Richard S. Tufts *The Scottish Invasion* Pinehurst 1962. Dornoch summer golf is described by Joyce Wethered in her *Golfing Memories and Methods* London 1933, p238.

4. N. S. C. Macmillan *The Campbeltown and Machrihanish Light Railway* David and Charles 1970, Alan J. S. Paterson *The Victorian Summer of the Clyde Steamer* Newton Abbot 1972 and John Thomas *Forgotten Railways:*

Scotland David and Charles 1976. See also Colin Hogarth *The Killin Branch Railway* Stirling 1993 and David McConnel 'The golfer's railway' *Scots Magazine* March 1985, p616; for golfers' railway fares see *Dumbarton Golf Club* Dumbarton 1988, pp23 and 38 and Fife Golfing Association *A History of Golf Clubs in Fife* Leven 1989.

5. Pat Ward-Thomas *The Royal and Ancient* Edinburgh 1980 is sound on the R&A's 'external' activities; see also the earlier histories of the club by Salmond and Everard. The R&A obtained its 'Royal' title in 1834 and was previously known as the Society of St Andrews Golfers. The first 'Royal' golf club was the Perth society, and a Montrose club – the Royal Albert – obtained their title shortly after the R&A.
 The R&A opened the present clubhouse in 1854 and took charge of the Rules of Golf from 1897. It took over administration of the Amateur and Open Championships in 1919, the Boys Tournament in 1948, the Youths in 1963 and the Seniors in 1969.

6. Personal communication from Bob Kroeger, Cincinnati.

7. See Peter Lewis (1991) 'Mechanical contrivances and mallet heads' *Golfiana* vol 3, no 1, 3-10, Peter Lewis (1991) 'Bounding Billy bounces to Britain' *Golfiana* vol 3, no 4, 3-13, and Nicholas Parks' series of articles in *Golf Monthly* 1988. For the conservatives case, see John L. Low *Concerning Golf* London 1903, p10 and his additional views in Henry Leach *Great Golfers in the Making* London 1907, p2.

8. For anti-R&A grumbling see the journal *Golfing* 11th July, 1901. One other small revolt came from the male supporters of early women's golf: see James Barclay (1994) 'The Foxwell affair' *Golfiana* vol 6, no 3, 11-13.

9. Personal communications from Peter Lewis and John Adams. The Allied Club at Bruntsfield claims to be the oldest surviving club without its own course or clubhouse. Founded in 1856, they spiritedly abolished the stymie during domestic club play: see Stewart Cruden *Bruntsfield Links Golfing Society* Edinburgh 1992, p2. The oldest surviving itinerant club may be the Dundee Advertiser/Dundee Press Golf Club, established in 1870.

10. First World War sport is described in Tony McCarthy *War Games: the Story of Sport in World War Two* London 1989.

11. *100 Years of Golf in North Berwick, 1857 to 1962: the Doreen Sayers Scrapbook* North Berwick 1994.

12. Patrick Leahy (1992) 'Golf in the war years 1914-1918' *Golfiana* vol 4, no 3, 3-10.

13. Study of the increase in new golf courses by counting entries in reference books is misleading: the arithmetic is complicated by the *closures* which were occurring at the same time.

14. Even Jones' famous 'Calamity Jane' putter, of impeccable Scottish origin, was copied by Spalding.

15. Al Barkow (1993) 'Three refinements in golf equipment' *Golfiana* vol 5, no 1, 3-8, and Peter N. Lewis (1991) 'Mechanical contrivances and mallet heads' *Golfiana* vol 3, no 3, 3-10.

16. See the club histories above and David Patrick *For to Do the Country Good: the Working Horse in West-Central Scotland* Bishopbriggs 1987.

17. Sunday golf restrictions in Scotland in the twentieth century have not been studied closely yet, and the *Golfer's Handbook* has always mentioned any such prohibitions. For present-day controversy on Sunday swimming in the North of Scotland see *Sunday Times* 25th October 1992. In 1987, the Free Presbyterian Church in Inverness refused communion to a golfer because his *club* allowed Sunday play, in which he did not take part.

18. For Hagen's travels see Gray Laidlaw and David Mason *A Very Pleasant Golfing Place: a Centenary History of Kilmacolm Golf Club* Kilmacolm 1991 and Alan M. Thom *From Westlands to Eastlands* Rothesay 1992, p156. Hagen's failure to reach Machrie and other misunderstandings are recounted in S. L. Mackinlay *Scottish Golf and Golfers* 1992, p80. Some other details of his Highland jaunts are found in Walter Hagen *The Walter Hagen Story* New York 1956. For decadent interwar golf see R. J. Maclennan *Golf at Gleneagles* Glasgow 1921.

19. Hector Thomson's career is mentioned in *Golf World - Scotland* June 1988, p2. Some of these tensions are found in Stuart Lindsay *Nairn Golf Club 1887-1987* Nairn 1987. For a note on the passing of 'the gentleman' see *Daily Telegraph* 6th December 1993; see also Wray Vamplew *Pay Up and Play the Game* Cambridge 1988.
Until 1920, amateur status, when lost, was permanently lost. The situation that a member of the older clubs might turn professional was unthinkable, but happened when Frank Stranahan, an American

member of the R&A, turned professional in 1954. He was asked to resign and did so slowly – three years later – but remained a member of some USA clubs: see Ward-Thomas *R&A* (ref 5) p113. For loss of amateur status by appearing on stage with Henry Cotton at, among other places, Glasgow's Empire Theatre, see Ernest Hargreaves *A Caddie in the Golden Age: My Years with Walter Hagen and Henry Cotton* London 1993.

20. Dawson Taylor *St Andrews: Cradle of Golf* London 1976, p90 and John L. B. Garcia *Harold Hilton: His Life and Times* Worcs 1992. For the harassment of Perkins see *Golf Monthly* March 1979.

21. John McConachie *The Moray Golf Club at Lossiemouth 1889-1989* Lossiemouth 1988.

22. Fiona Grieve (1994) 'The early years of the Walker Cup' *Golfiana* vol 6, no 3, 35-40.

23. For the Suffragette activities see McConachie *Lossiemouth* (ref 21) p28 and (Anon) *Aboyne Golf Club 1883-1983* Aboyne 1983; for Suffragette activity in Scotland in general see Leah Leneman *A Guid Cause: the Women's Suffrage Movement in Scotland* Aberdeen University Press 1991.

24. Jessie Valentine's career is found in George Houghton *Golf Addict Among the Scots* 1968 and in his *Jessie Valentine: Better Golf – Definitely* London 1967. For later women's golf in Scotland see Belle Robertson *The Woman Golfer* Edinburgh 1988. For women's golf in general see Elinor Nickerson *Golf: A Woman's History* London 1987; see also *History of the Scottish Ladies Golfing Association 1903-1928* London 1928. Women were first allowed into the R&A clubhouse during the British Ladies Championship in 1970, and only two members resigned. In the private club sector, only one Scottish ladies club has its own course (Lundin Ladies) and a few others have a separate clubhouse (e.g. Troon and Aberdeen). 'Ladies sections' attached to male private clubs with little or no control of the club are the norm at present. There are also thriving ladies clubs playing over public courses with equal rights to the male clubs playing there.

25. McCarthy *War Games* (ref 10) p64.

26. The firm of Nicoll of Leven is described in *Golf Monthly* November 1981. Scotland's tiny golf publishing sector (*Golf Monthly* and *Golfer's Handbook*) survived for a while in Glasgow, before suffering the inevitable fate of moving to London.

27. These post-war events have been reconstructed from some of the many recent club histories listed above, notably those of Lossiemouth, Mortonhall, Kilmacolm, Dunbar, Brora, Selkirk, the Burgess (Edinburgh), Blairgowrie (Rosemount), Montrose, The Honourable Company, St Andrews (R&A, New Club and St Andrews Golf Club), Ranfurly Castle, Rothesay, Nairn, Millport, Glasgow Golf Club, Barassie, Prestwick, Strathpeffer, Dunbar, Dornoch and Crail.

28. Eric Brown *Knave of Clubs* London 1961, Eric Brown *Out of the Bag* London 1964, and John Panton *My Way of Golf* Glasgow 1951. Panton's career is described in *Golf World (Scotland)* May 1988, p2. For Jessie Valentine see *Glasgow Herald* 2nd Sept, 1995.

29. By 1992 attitudes on amateur status were relaxing, and the R&A allowed amateurs to attend the professional European Tour pre-qualifying schools without losing amateur status. There was even mutiny at the club level. In 1973 the (amateur) captain of Dunbar Golf Club won a car for a hole in one in a local competition. He took the car and was reported to the R&A: he was then deemed to be a professional. His own club ignored the ruling and allowed him to continue in their domestic competitions. Having 'turned pro' he was reinstated after the customary four-year wait.

30. For the return of on-course betting see *Golf World* May 1995, p22.

31. Malcolm Campbell quoted in Eddie Park *Real Golf* Dovercourt 1990, p33 says 'the courses were watered into submission for the benefit of top American players and colour-conscious TV producers. Colour was confused with condition.'

32. Geoffrey Cousins and Tom Scott *A Century of Opens* London 1971, R. Burnett *The St Andrews Opens* Edinburgh 1990, and Michael Hobbs *Great Opens* London 1976. The Open was unusual in Britain in not requiring local entrants to have membership of the British PGA.

33. Notable are David Hamilton *Golf Guide to Scotland* Edinburgh 1995, Bob Kroeger *Complete Guide to Golf Courses of Scotland* Cincinnati 1992, Sam Morley *By Yon Bonny Links* Northaw 1990, George Houghton *Golf Addict Among the Scots* 1968 and Jerry Mosca *Experiencing Golf in Scotland* Mankato 1981.

INDEX